FORGING THE SHIELD

Forging the Shield

Eisenhower and National Security for the 21st Century

Edited by

Dennis E. Showalter

Imprint Publications
Chicago
2005

First published 2005
For information on this book, visit www.imprint-chicago.com

Cover design by Elizabeth Callihan
Back Cover: The oval reproduction of Dwight D. Eisenhower's presidential portrait
is based on the presidential portrait by J. Anthony Wills in the White House
collection.

Library of Congress Control Number: 2005923336
ISBN 1-879176-44-0 (Paper)

Printed in the United States of America on acid-free paper

For

General Andrew Jackson Goodpaster

United States Army
(1915 – 2005)

Who served his country as
Soldier, Scholar, Statesman, and
Advisor to Presidents

Contents

Acknowledgments   ix
Carl W. Reddel

Preface   xi
Rocco C. Siciliano

Foreword   xiii
F. C. Wilson

Introduction   1
Dennis E. Showalter

Reflections on Eisenhower, the Cold War, and My Father   7
Sergei N. Khrushchev

The Grim Paraphernalia: Eisenhower and the Garrison State   13
Alex Roland

Eisenhower's Methodology for Intervention and Its Legacy in
Contemporary World Politics   23
Saki R. Dockrill

Eisenhower and the Korean War: Cautionary Tale and Hopeful
Precedent   41
Allan R. Millett

Crisis and Confrontation: Chinese-American Relations during the
Eisenhower Administration   59
Qiang Zhai

"Not Enough Bulldozers": Eisenhower and American Nuclear
Weapons Policy, 1953–1961   85
Gregg Herken

The Invisible Hand of the New Look: Eisenhower and the CIA   93
Clayton D. Laurie

Eisenhower and the NSA: An Introductory Survey   111
David A. Hatch

Clandestine Victory: Eisenhower and Overhead Reconnaissance in
the Cold War   119
R. Cargill Hall

Eisenhower and Space: Politics and Ideology in the Construction of
the U.S. Civil Space Program   151
Roger D. Launius

Eisenhower and Joint Professional Military Education   183
John W. Yaeger

Appendix A: Eisenhower and National Security for the 21st Century:
Roundtable and Discussion   205

Epilogue   219
Ernest R. May

Contributors   223

Index   227

Acknowledgments

An undertaking of this scope requires the diligent work of many talented individuals, all of whom deserve recognition.

The essays contained in this volume were developed for a special symposium on Dwight D. Eisenhower that was held during 26–28 January 2005 at Ft. McNair, Washington, D.C. This symposium, entitled "Eisenhower and National Security for the 21st Century," was co-sponsored by the Dwight D. Eisenhower Memorial Commission and the Industrial College of the Armed Forces at the National Defense University. The success of this symposium resulted from the work of a broad-based group of individuals, all of whom recognize the special and unique profundity of President Eisenhower's legacy in the fields of national and international security.

I would like to extend my particular thanks to the distinguished symposium speakers. We were very fortunate to hear from Richard Immerman, Eduard Mark, Allan Millett, and Saki Dockrill, all of whom spoke about the issue of "Eisenhower and the Changing National Security Environment"; from Philip Taubman, Roger Launius, Gregg Herken, and Peter Roman, who shared their views about "Eisenhower, Science and National Security"; from William Burrows, Clayton Laurie, Cargill Hall, and David Hatch, who explored the theme of "Eisenhower's Organization of the Intelligence Community"; from Raymond Garthoff, Sergei Khrushchev, Qiang Zhai, and Wolfgang Krieger, who spoke about various "International Perspectives of the 34th President and His Legacy as Commander in Chief"; and from Major General David Huntoon, Jr., USA and Alex Roland who gave stimulating presentations during two symposium luncheon sessions.

The symposium concluded with a memorable roundtable panel and discussion chaired by Brent Scowcroft with Andrew Goodpaster, Montgomery Meigs, and Louis Galambos participating.

This event took nearly two years to organize and it drew upon the talents and energies of many people. The idea for the symposium arose in a series of conversations between Cargill Hall, Herman Wolk, and me. A dedicated steering committee or working group was established. Over time, the members of this group came to include Bill Williams, Thomas Keaney, and Steve Rearden. All of them benefited greatly from the research and organizing talents of Justin Gilstrap. I am sure that their diligent work would make Eisenhower himself extremely proud.

With additional input from Peter Feaver and Richard Kohn at the Triangle Institute for Security Studies, the working group made inquiries with the Industrial College of the Armed Forces (ICAF) at the National Defense University. Under the direction of Commandant Major General F. C. Wilson, USMC and with special assistance from Walter Kreitler and John Yaeger, ICAF proved to be an indispensable partner in creating the symposium. Brian Scott, Larry Grubbs, and Frank Cooling each deserve individual thanks for their participation in the working group through their special contributions on conference planning and management. Robert Buchanan, Andrew Cook, Gerald Faber, Belinda Glass, Mike Harn, Edward Roman, Brad Simmons, May Kay Thompson, David Thomas, Roslyn Washington-Harper, Yuri Zhukov and the entire National Defense University multimedia department each deserve similar recognition.

The generous financial and material contributions of several organizations and corporations—notably the Boeing Corporation, Lockheed Martin, the ICAF Foundation, and the Military Officers Association of America—were essential to defraying the expense of such a large undertaking.

Over the course of its preparation, the project also received assistance from Joyce Jacobson, Richard Striner, JT Dykman, and Brian Krist from the Eisenhower Memorial Commission.

Since the successful conclusion of the symposium, I have become deeply indebted to Anthony Cheung of Imprint Publications for his efforts in preparing this book and to Dennis Showalter of Colorado College for his masterful editing. Elizabeth Callihan created a book cover appropriate to its remarkable content. Ernest R. May has honored us all with his contribution of an insightful epilogue.

To all those who have been a part of this effort, both named and unnamed, I extend my heartfelt thanks as well as my hearty congratulations for a job well done.

Carl W. Reddel
Executive Director, Eisenhower Memorial Commission

Preface

As Chairman of the Dwight D. Eisenhower Memorial Commission, it gave me great satisfaction to authorize the Commission's co-sponsorship of the important symposium on "Eisenhower and National Security for the 21st Century," hosted by the Industrial College of the Armed Forces on 26-28 January 2005. The results of the symposium—now published in this enlightening volume—represent another significant milestone in the ongoing interpretation of the legacy of this extraordinary twentieth-century leader.

Establishing and corroborating Ike's legacy has been central to the work of the Commission since its creation by Congress in 1999. As soon as our Commissioners began to deliberate, they reached the unanimous conclusion that the design of a suitable memorial to Eisenhower must begin with a comprehensive review of his role in history. To that end, the Commission engaged a distinguished Eisenhower Legacy Committee, composed of outstanding scholars and direct observers of President Eisenhower. In 2003, this Committee issued a report entitled *Eisenhower's Legacy: The General, the President, the Public Servant,* which can be easily downloaded from the Commission's website at <http://www.eisenhowermemorial.org>.

As a national and international public service, the Commission proposed and facilitated on-line access to a complete electronic reproduction of the eight printed volumes of *The Presidential Papers of Dwight David Eisenhower.* This achievement (an on-line "first") was made possible in partnership with Johns Hopkins University Press. To access the papers, researchers can click the "Presidential Papers" icon on the Commission's website.

In light of these preliminary projects, it was altogether fitting and a special opportunity for the Commission to co-sponsor—in partnership with the Industrial College of the Armed Forces—a major symposium on the theme of Ike's national security legacy and its relevance in the twenty-first century.

As an observer who actually worked for Eisenhower during his White House years, I am frequently struck by the fact that today, almost half a century later, the full dimensions of his remarkable leadership achievement are still unfolding. The quiet ways of this leader prevented numerous otherwise trenchant observers from appreciating, at least until very recently, his role as the planner and initiator of strategies that would serve this nation as a national security template for decades beyond his presidency. The full story may never emerge. But the accounts and analyses included in this volume are splendidly thought-provoking. I am proud that the Eisenhower Memorial Commission helped to make this symposium possible. I attended the proceedings, where I learned a great deal more about the man whom we seek to memorialize. On behalf of the Commission, I extend our heartfelt thanks to all the participants!

Rocco C. Siciliano
Chairman, Eisenhower Memorial Commission

Foreword

Dwight D. Eisenhower was always a very special friend to the Industrial College of the Armed Forces (ICAF). Early in the College's existence, Major Eisenhower supported its mission energetically. Indeed, he taught classes at the College (then called the "Army Industrial College") from 1931 to 1933.

His keen understanding of the nature of modern conflict, and its inherent demand for the strategic integration of forces—a principle General Eisenhower lived with daily as he planned the Normandy invasion—made him an early and strong advocate of joint professional military education. On an even higher strategic plane, he was an advocate of unified national endeavor. His career-long interest in domestic and social infrastructure (in its role as a necessary underpinning for advanced military effort) made Eisenhower an early supporter of our institution. For reasons that Eisenhower understood and supported early on, we were founded as America's *Industrial* College.

President Eisenhower's interest in developing America's strategic infrastructure expanded apace in his presidential years. His creation of the Interstate Highway System, proposed to Congress and the public in explicit terms as a project to strengthen our national defense, is an obvious example of this. His interest in ICAF expanded as well. Toward the end of his presidency, he visited the College for the formal dedication of the hall that is named in his honor. As late as the last six weeks of his life, he was still in correspondence with the College's leadership in regard to matters of curriculum.

It was fitting indeed that we hosted a symposium here at ICAF, in partnership with the Dwight D. Eisenhower Memorial Commission, for the purpose of exploring the strategic contributions of Eisenhower to long-term national defense—even to the point of applying the Eisenhower legacy to the new strategic challenges of the twenty-first century. The participants in this symposium were truly on the cutting edge of historical research and interpretation. And their findings may very well advance the urgent business of our nation in addressing the new strategic challenge of today—and tomorrow.

I can only think that if Eisenhower were alive, he would certainly be proud of this effort both to analyze and to extend his multifaceted legacy. We at the College are proud to have hosted this important event. We are deeply grateful to the authors and contributors for this book.

Major General F. C. Wilson, USMC
Commandant, Industrial College of the Armed Forces

Introduction

Dennis E. Showalter

The two-term presidency of Dwight David Eisenhower (1953–61) developed its dominant images almost from its beginnings. The "Eisenhower years" are regularly defined as an era of stagnation and conformity in domestic matters, and an age of unimaginative confrontation with the Soviet Union in foreign affairs. Eisenhower himself took on the aura of an amiable dolt, more concerned with polishing his golf swing than grasping the reins of government. The famous grin, pundits and cartoonists increasingly agreed, concealed a mind that, if not empty, was significantly limited relative to its responsibilities.

That image owed something to history. The last professional soldier to occupy the White House had been Ulysses S. Grant, and the textbook wisdom on his political career hardly suggested that even military greatness was a promising matrix for presidential success. And a strong, developing contemporary consensus, shared by soldiers and historians, contended that Eisenhower as Supreme Commander in the European Theater during World War II had functioned less as a dynamic strategic planner and battle captain than as a "chairman of the board," steering a diagonal course of unfortunate compromises among operational choices. Even in that role, Ike was increasingly described as overshadowed by such dynamic subordinates as Britain's Field Marshal Bernard Law Montgomery and America's General George Patton. A growing wave of German military memoirs at best dismissed Eisenhower's generalship with polite generalizations, characterizing his victories as consequences of overwhelming material superiority on one hand and the feckless interference of Adolf Hitler on the other.

When the critics' arguments were summarized, General Eisenhower stood accused not merely of failing to win the war with flair and elegance, but of prolonging the conflict by his operational shortcomings and making the Cold War inevitable by his strategic decisions—particularly his refusal to drive for the central European capitals of Berlin, Vienna, and Prague. It did not matter that the criticisms were often mutually contradictory. Growing national frustration with the outcome of World War II found a continuing target in Eisenhower the president.

President Eisenhower suffered as well from a subtle but significant shift in American political discourse. Historically, presidential elections had been about character and policy. In 1952, Democratic candidate Adlai Stevenson made self-conscious intellectuality a factor. Given his relative lack of practical experience compared to Eisenhower, it was hardly surprising that Princeton graduate Stevenson stressed his mental superiority, and argued that such superiority better fitted him to lead the United States in the unprecedented crisis of cold war between superpowers in a nuclear environment.

1

Eisenhower had never considered himself to be, nor cast himself as, an intellectual by any definition. Nor, even when he was trying, did Eisenhower's diction come close to Stevenson's polished cadences.

Eisenhower carried the 1952 election with the aid of as many as two million crossover Democratic votes. He won reelection even more handily in 1956. The Democratic Party and the national media nevertheless continued to agree on Eisenhower's cognitive shortcomings—in part because both institutions were themselves beginning a long-run process of development into self-defined elites with styles emphasizing mental quickness and verbal gymnastics. Eisenhower bore a corresponding burden among intellectuals and pundits as being in over his head even before he assumed office. He shared that distinction with predecessors and successors alike—Abraham Lincoln and George W. Bush come readily to mind. He never escaped it during his time in office. The two volumes about his administration that Eisenhower published after his retirement did little to change the images of his presidency. *Mandate for Change* and *Waging Peace* were detailed, but not especially exciting, not salted with new facts or fresh analysis. They read at best like staff papers. *At Ease: Stories I Tell to Friends,* which appeared in 1967, drew primarily on Eisenhower's military career, and its informal style gave it an air of casual reminiscence reinforcing its author's by-now firmly established image as a lightweight.

A decisive shift in evaluating the Eisenhower presidency began with the growing accessibility of relevant archives that started in the 1970s and reached critical mass in the years after the Cold War. Fred Greenstein defined its nature in *The Hidden-Hand Presidency: Eisenhower as Leader.* Published in 1982, Greenstein's work showed that far from being incoherent, Eisenhower was skilled in written expression—the result in good part of his years as a staff officer before World War II. His convoluted speaking style was to a degree cultivated, as a means of concealing his goals and procedures. Far from being dull-witted, Eisenhower possessed a formidable and incisive intellect, complemented by an ability to use his emotions for positive purposes: again a result of his military career. Far from being an amiable figurehead, Eisenhower was a decisive leader who applied a sophisticated, comprehensive technique to problem-solving and policy-making. His presidency was defined by direct involvement: a proactive, hands-on approach—but a "hidden hand." Eschewing public pronouncements and public impact for finely nuanced private negotiations, Eisenhower was consistently successful mobilizing support and isolating opposition in both domestic and foreign affairs.

Eisenhower's hidden hand rapidly became conventional academic wisdom among scholars of Eisenhower's presidency—a transformation facilitated by the increasingly obvious fact that none of his successors had achieved anything resembling Eisenhower's results in the field of foreign policy—except, perhaps, Ronald Reagan, and it would take another quarter-century for the latter's achievements to be recognized. It was clear that neither the obsessive secrecy of a Richard Nixon nor the compulsive openness of a Jimmy Carter, nor anything in between, matched Ike's record in international affairs. As the structural limitations of the overarching domestic ambitions of the 1960s became apparent, the stubbornly unspectacular achievements of the Eisenhower administration in fields from education to civil rights also attracted increasing attention—most of it positive.

When is a dolt not a dolt? When he can get his policies adopted in a complex system and carry them to success against sophisticated opposition. Such standard general-audience biographies as Stephen Ambrose's two-volume work and its young-adult spinoff, *Eisenhower: Soldier and President* (1990), and Geoffrey Perrett's seven-hundred-page account, *Eisenhower* (1999), structure their generally positive views of Eisenhower largely around his sophisticated use of the hidden hand. Carlo D'Este's equally detailed *Eisenhower: A Soldier's Life* ends in 1945, but establishes beyond question that the "hidden hand's" origins lay in Eisenhower's military career, and was as central to his role as a general as it was to his successes as commander in chief.

In January 2005, the Eisenhower Memorial Commission, in cooperation with the Industrial College of the Armed Forces and National Defense University, organized an international conference to investigate President Eisenhower's specific role in the field of national security. The papers and panel discussions incorporated scholars of Eisenhower's presidency and men who had participated directly in the events being discussed. The resulting dialogue highlights new opportunities for evaluating the Eisenhower presidency, generated by the increasing availability of archival sources, American and foreign; and by the increasing interaction of academic, military, and political communities since the end of the Cold War.

The sense of threat accompanying the Cold War tended to diminish with familiarity; even in its final years the conflict was increasingly taken for granted: a backdrop to international relations rather than their matrix. A steadily growing body of evidence from Eastern as well as Western sources is, however, establishing just how dangerous the Eisenhower years and their aftermath to 1963 really were. At several points World War III could have happened and almost did. As the first president to face nuclear weapons of mass destruction, Eisenhower confronted a threat different in kind than any of his successors. His intelligence on America's adversaries was far worse. He had to deal with a society unprepared for the kinds of long-term confrontation inherent to a Cold War between superpowers. Public opinion stampeding in any direction might trigger global thermonuclear destruction. Eisenhower's calm public demeanor, reflecting his experience of high-level military command, played no small role in helping the United States, and the world, develop a sense of perspective.

Even then, a single mistake or misunderstanding could have mortal consequences. Eisenhower's presidential decisions were correspondingly serious—deadly serious. The central principle informing them was nevertheless expressed in a homely phrase he repeatedly used: "Let's not make our mistakes in a hurry." In the contexts of this volume, the aphorism reflects three characteristics. First, Dwight Eisenhower understood to near-perfection his own limitations. He not only knew what he did not know; he was comfortable with it: unlikely to act from insecurity. Such self-perception is unusual enough to be almost unique among people in his kind of position. Second, Eisenhower trusted an intuition and an insight honed by a lifetime of public service.

His years of high-level experience in a wide variety of contexts shaped a confidence that he did not need to move first to achieve his ends. Third, Eisenhower was a master at orchestrating national resources on behalf of the country's security interests, securing support from a broad spectrum of individuals and constituencies in science, industry, education, business, and public service.

The material presented in the following pages reveals above all the fingertip sophistication of Dwight Eisenhower as commander in chief. He understood as well as any twentieth-century political leader the complex, comprehensive relationship between national security and the complex, vulnerable infrastructure of modern societies. At the same time he never lost his view of himself as a citizen who became a soldier—he entered West Point as a man of twenty—and he never lost his respect for the ordinary person, the individual American citizen. He was, in the best sense of both offices, a general who became president.

This volume directly enhances our understanding of Eisenhower's presidency—its shortcomings as well as its successes, for none of these contributions are whitewashes. Sergei Khrushchev, son of the Soviet premier, introduces the work with a discussion of Eisenhower as Nikita Khrushchev understood him—a crucial, perhaps decisive element of the Cold War's decisive years. Alex Roland shifts the focus to Eisenhower as policymaker in his general discussion of the president's approach to the developing "military-industrial complex." The essays of Saki Dockrill, Alan Millett, and Qiang Zhai then combine in a portrait of Eisenhower as an international statesman in an era of global crisis and confrontation. Gregg Herken's case study of Eisenhower and America's nuclear weapons policy and Clayton Laurie's analysis of Eisenhower and the CIA focus on two ongoing central issues of Eisenhower's presidency. David Hatch takes the subject of Eisenhower's behind-the-scenes activism further in his paper on the developing role of the National Security Agency. Cargill Hall describes one of its great successes: the "clandestine victory" won by aerial and space reconnaissance of the Soviet Union during Eisenhower's administration. Two contributions discuss aspects of Eisenhower's long-term vision. Roger Launius demonstrates the president's seminal contributions to America's space program. John Yaeger shows how Eisenhower nurtured a system of professional military education that gave the United States armed forces an intellectual as well as an operational framework that has endured well after the Cold War. And the transcript of the panel and audience discussion that concluded the conference (see Appendix A) synthesizes the experiences of participants and the insights of scholars on a presidency whose ramifications are still emerging.

In a wider context, this volume also contributes to the growing body of literature on comparative presidential leadership: the complex spectrum of ways a chief executive can be effective. Projected back into Eisenhower's military career, these presentations clarify Eisenhower's approach to exercising high command in a coalition war, and the ways he developed and tested the craft of generalship that contributed so much to his achievements as president. Finally, the essays in *Forging the Shield* combine to offer a unique insight into Dwight Eisenhower's character: a study of character at work. Most evaluations of presidential character are based on response to crises: Fort Sumter, Pearl Harbor, 9/11. An arguably better test is dealing with the everyday requirements of an office that has become the world's most comprehensively demanding. Across the spectrum of national security issues, Eisenhower combined consistent, perceptive awareness with a steady grip on particular situations. His decisions were not always optimal. They were not always wise. But they were made—and made by the responsible authority. Buck-passing had no place in the Eisenhower presidency. Dwight Eisenhower's life was not gentle. But the elements were indeed so mixed in him that nature might stand up and say to all the world: "This was a man." This assessment shows that in the 1950s, he was as president the right man in the right spot.

Reflections on Eisenhower, the Cold War, and My Father

Sergei N. Khrushchev

Now, when our eyes are open, we seem to know everything about the Cold War in the Eisenhower-Khrushchev era. But more than dates and facts were involved. I propose to talk about feelings and atmosphere during this time, perhaps the most important period in Cold War history. The leaders of both countries—Dwight D. Eisenhower who was elected president in 1952, and Nikita Khrushchev who came to power in July 1953—had to decide where the superpowers would go. Would they move toward war or peace?

This question involved more than discussion of specific Cold War issues. Beginning sometime after World War II, Joseph Stalin came to the conclusion that war with the United States was inevitable, and would begin sometime around the mid-1950s. Remembering the defeat of the Soviet Union in the first days of the war with Germany in 1941, he devoted the USSR to preparing for the next war. To offer a few examples from 1948 to 1953, the Soviet armed forces grew from 2.5 to 5.5 million. They built about 10,000 TU-4s, which were copies of the American Boeing B-29. They thought about building airfields on the ice of the Arctic Ocean. They sent 100,000 troops to the Chukotka peninsula, expecting an American invasion of Siberia from Alaska. Anti-aircraft batteries surrounded Moscow, awaiting American air attack every day. There were often no reasons for such decisions, but Stalin was aging. No one knew then, and we do not know now, what was reasonable and what was a product of Stalin's fears and his imagination. At that time, plans for a first nuclear strike against the USSR were being considered in the United States. Perhaps Stalin believed the United States would start a war before the USSR could counter America's existing atomic advantage and develop superiority. Whatever Stalin's reasoning, we did have in Russia a growing feeling that war was very close.

I remember what the freshman students of the technical students in Moscow felt when General Eisenhower was elected president. For us, at seventeen and eighteen years young, this was a clear signal that at last America decided to go to war with the Soviet Union. There was no other reason to elect a general as a president. When I asked my father, he said that he did not think so, but that had no impact on my feelings. But this very fearful image of President Eisenhower was balanced by an opposite image. In the hearts of all Soviets, including my father, General Eisenhower was an honest general with whom we fought together in World War II. It was very important to the Soviet people that he did not want to steal victory from General Georgi K. Zhukov. Everybody in the Soviet Union believed that when Hitler left open the gate to Berlin for him, Eisenhower decided not to take the city. They saw Eisenhower as very different from Field Marshal Bernard L. Montgomery, who wanted to steal Berlin although it was very important to Russians to capture the city as a sign of victory in a war that had cost them so much.

Then Stalin died, and the new leadership had to decide what to do. That leadership was not experienced in international affairs. My father and most of the others never even met foreigners. It was very dangerous at that time to meet foreigners. You would be accused of being a spy if you were an ordinary person. If you were in power, it was even more dangerous. So the new leaders first of all had to choose. As my father told them, we have to prepare for war in a country that suffered so badly through World War II. Or we can deal with the other side. Here we must consider the nature of the Cold War. In the West, it is usually now regarded as the struggle of democracy versus tyranny, or capitalism versus communism: two opposing ideologies. But we can also look at the struggle in a different way—as a dispute over the control of the world by two emerging superpowers, a dispute having really nothing to do with ideology. I have concluded that U.S.-Soviet relations were 80 percent about power and only 20 percent about ideology. I think it is very important to have this in mind, because power issues can ultimately be negotiated.

The new Soviet government tried to test the water. It published President Eisenhower's speech in April 1953 to the National Press Club, from beginning to end—the first time in postwar history when the Soviets published a president's actual words, as opposed to commentary. The successor leadership took steps that discussed the end of the Korean War. It resumed the Austrian peace treaty negotiations. Above all, there was the first summit meeting in Geneva. The key people on both sides met and looked into each others' eyes. And my father concluded that "we can deal with these people. We can find the answer to our differences by dealing with an American President, but we have to be strong. If we are not strong, they will push us and they will take control over us. So we have to increase our strength in order to secure peace."

Much more important, however, was Khrushchev's concern for concealing Soviet weakness. That was the one thing he wished above all to hide from the Americans. He thought that if they knew how badly off Russia was, it could encourage the United States to attack while the balance of forces was in its favor. And that led to an immediate misunderstanding. When the president offered the "Open Skies" idea to Khrushchev, he just answered "No." As we know, America was driven by the Pearl Harbor syndrome to prevent surprise attack. But the Soviets were driven by the same concern: the attack by Germany in June 1941. Before this attack, the Germans regularly overflew the Soviet territory, explaining it as a failure of navigation systems, pilot error, and similar alibis. Accepting the same kind of risk again was impossible. The new minister of defense, Marshal Georgi Zhukov, in July 1955 at a meeting of the Central Committee, reported to the people that if America started war against us, we will lose. This was an open statement that is now declassified. Khrushchev said that "you cannot balance our military forces with the United States, because the American economy is three or four times bigger than ours. If we do it then we'll lose everything. We have to concentrate our resources on the production of food" because there was not enough food. There were huge lines even at the bakeries, for the basic need of bread.

Soviet economic priorities shaped Khrushchev's first clash with Admiral Nikolai Gerasimovich Kuznetsov about the surface navy. He said, "You must not build this surface navy, first because we have no intention to invade the United States, and secondly we will never balance our navy with theirs. We will just lose these resources." Khrushchev made the decision to stop building the surface navy, focusing only on the submarines and on shore defenses.

But at the same time, Khrushchev, along with the Soviet policy he shaped, wanted to be recognized as an equal player. Because America was much stronger, it did not want to accept Soviet parity. And if you are not recognized as an equal, you start to challenge the leader. It is a law of nature, the same as bulls fighting with each other in the autumn over who will control the herds. That was the beginning of the pattern of crisis without intention of starting a war, but at the same time insisting the USSR must be recognized. The first case was the Suez crisis. By the way, Khrushchev claimed that it was not President Eisenhower but it was he who sent the ultimatum to the British and French to stop this fighting. Maybe he was right, maybe he was wrong, but Suez has a very different history in Russia than in the United States. In the Russian version, Khrushchev told the British ambassador that "you have to remind Mr. Anthony Eden about our conversation near the fireplace." He had visited Britain along with Premier Nikolai Alexandrovich Bulganin several months before this, in April 1956. Khrushchev, who exploited his image as an unpredictable person at that time, started to play missile diplomacy. He asked Mrs. Eden, "Do you know how many missiles are needed to destroy your island?" And she looked at him in surprise: "you can't talk about this at the five o'clock tea." Khrushchev persisted: "you don't know?! We will tell you: eight, and we have them; and we can do it."

It is funny in retrospect. The Soviet Union had no missiles deployed. It had only tested a single R-5 missile with a nuclear warhead in February 1956. Of course, Khrushchev had no intention of starting a war. He wanted to threaten the West that the Soviets were strong enough to do so—and that strength must be taken into account. That was one of the very important parts of his diplomacy in any crisis— Middle East, Far East, Berlin. He wanted to be recognized as an equal.

Khrushchev's visit to the United States was a very important part of that recognition. Leaders now meet routinely, just to sign some papers for a negotiation. At that time, a state visit was more of a general education, looking at how these people are living, looking at how many people in uniform are on the streets, how many officers there are, and how they live. My father was in World War II from the beginning to the end; he was at the defeat of Kiev and then at the victory of Stalingrad. He told me all the time that everything you hear and see about war is not true. War is much dirtier, much more dangerous, and much more destructive than its images and its legends. So he had no desire to have the USSR casually start a war. He did not want to sacrifice our country, our people. Instead, he believed the Soviet system would eventually present a better life to the Soviet people that America would join us peacefully.

It was the same with President Eisenhower. When I talked with David Eisenhower, his grandson, he told me "my granddad never watched a movie about the war because he could not sleep afterwards." Khrushchev and Eisenhower were the last civilian leaders who thought that they could say to the military, "we have to reduce spending on the armed forces." President Eisenhower tried to do this and then Khrushchev did it drastically; he reduced the armed forces to 2.5 million at the end of his reign.

When we are talking about the Soviet system under Khrushchev, we have to understand that it was no different than the revolutionary system; there was no democracy, there were first steps toward democracy. Khrushchev tried to introduce some democratic changes, but in Russian society the goodwill of the leaders was more important than a constitution. Once Khrushchev started to tease the president: "Why don't you want to run for a third term?" The president replied, "Because it is against the constitution." Khrushchev replied, "you can change the constitution; it's very easy and the Americans will support you." Underneath, he was trying to understand why so popular a president cannot run a third time. And in 1961, Khrushchev offered to the Soviets to put two-term limits on the highest posts of Soviet leadership.

So it was important, this mutual understanding, to give us some hope, but at the same time it was no resolution of real problems. U-2s still flew over Soviet territory; there was no recognition of East Germany; there was no stopping of nuclear tests. When Khrushchev told about the end of the Camp David meeting, he said the American president had big expectations, but it was not a wedding. And it was not a funeral. The "spirit of Camp David" was expected to inspire the later meeting in Paris, and after that the official visit of the American president to Russia. Khrushchev thought that they could find some common ground. The Soviet Union built a golf course near Moscow without any understanding of what playing golf meant! Nobody played there but they knew that the president liked it. They built a mansion on Lake Baikal because Khrushchev said, "the president invited me to Camp David I will invite him here for a discussion."

Where could the premier and the president find common ground? By themselves they could not resolve the German problem. They could not end the arms race as long as the Soviet Union believed it needed enough ICBMs to balance America's power. But they could, I think, agree on the nuclear test ban. My father had strong feelings that this madness, which was a position also strongly held in the Soviet military and military-industrial complex, had to be stopped. He declared in 1958 a unilateral moratorium on Soviet nuclear tests. I worked with missiles at that time and told my father, "we have a new warhead for our missile, twice the original 250 kilotons. We must test it." He replied "it's an endless process. You can design better and better until we can destroy the earth." And I think that maybe, emotionally, President Eisenhower could accept a preliminary agreement with Khrushchev, and maybe at the end of his term sign the thing.

The U-2 flights in April and May 1960 were a mystery. Khrushchev described after the first flight on 4 July 1956, "how they are laughing at me at the State Department," not the White House but the State Department who was laughing because the Soviet Union could not shoot them down. We started to design new surface-to-air missiles and interceptor aircraft. But why were the U-2 planes being sent in 1960? It was no time to spy with so many crucial meetings being held. The first U-2s flew over in April. But why they sent Gary Powers on 1 May, I cannot understand. His route was one major strategic objective after another: Baikonur, Sverdlovsk, then Kirov and Plesetsk, then Arkhangelsk, and then Murmansk. Soviet air defenses were on alert after the April flights. There could have been no doubt on the part of the CIA that even these stupid Russians would shoot down the plane in one of these places.

I have a theory that someone in the U.S. power structure wanted to prevent any possible agreement over nuclear testing. After the U-2 scandal grew, it was said in America that the Central Committee pressured Khrushchev to take a conciliatory approach during the Paris summit of May 1960. In reality, Khrushchev controlled the Central Committee from A to Z; there was no opposition. On 9 May, five days before the summit, Khrushchev sent a signal through U.S. Ambassador Llewellyn E. Thompson to the president that he wanted to resolve this scandal and that he wanted to have a serious discussion in Paris. The next day, the State Department replied, "We will continue flying over Soviet territory."

My father was strongly influenced by his belief that in foreign relations, President Eisenhower was fully dependent on the secretary of state. He repeated this all the time. During the first Geneva summit in July 1955, when it was time for the president to make his talk, Secretary John Foster Dulles gave him a sheet of paper. He then read it like a school boy from beginning to the end. The head of Soviet negotiations, Deputy Premier Nikolai Bulganin, did the same, only it was not the foreign minister but Khrushchev who gave him the paper that he had to read! Now in May 1960, for the second time Khrushchev had a signal that it was the State Department in charge— not the president. After that, when Khrushchev offered to meet before the official summit, he did not insist upon an apology from President Eisenhower. He understood that it was impossible to ask an American president to apologize openly in front of the press. He expected that in this preliminary official summit, with both of them behind closed doors, once the furor had died down, the issue could be resolved and the two leaders could go together in May to the Four Power discussion in Paris.

That never happened. The U.S. State Department replied that Eisenhower would not meet privately with Khrushchev. Khrushchev was humiliated and he refused to attend the official meeting. He blew up the summit, and that was the beginning of the decline of relations between the two countries. Khrushchev decided: "You Americans want to overfly our territory? I will invite the world's heads of state to the United Nations in October, to discuss colonization. And you will host them, and you have to do this even against your will." And he banged his shoe on the table at the United Nations. And he refused to return the pilots from the RB-47 that was shot down over Russia on 1 July. And relations kept getting worse for the rest of Eisenhower's administration.

So what were really the results of the relations between President Eisenhower and Khrushchev? Despite the unfortunate ending, I consider them extremely positive. They built the foundation for future relations, for eventual peaceful existence. Things would have been different with less balanced leaders, especially on the American side. Instead, the balanced president of the United States who really understood all the atrocities of war wanted to find some common ground while at the same time defending his own interests. President Eisenhower, together with my father, built that foundation in the 1950s. And on that foundation, later presidents, President Kennedy and then all the others, based the future negotiations with the Soviet Union over the next three decades. For this, I am a great admirer of President Eisenhower, and I believe that he is one of America's greatest presidents.

The Grim Paraphernalia:
Eisenhower and the Garrison State*

Alex Roland

At the risk of preaching to an increasingly large choir, I would like to portray Dwight D. Eisenhower as a visionary. I take as my text his famous farewell address, especially the warning about a military-industrial complex and a scientific-technological elite.[1] These passages presented a negative vision, but one nonetheless powerful for that. Throughout his presidency he preached about what America must *not* become. His culminating, farewell warnings attracted little attention when first pronounced. But later, they gained great currency, entering the permanent American lexicon of political speech. The meaning they acquired during and after the Vietnam War differed from what Eisenhower had intended. As Michael Sherry has argued, the term "military-industrial complex" came to mean "the entrenched machinery of racism, imperialism, militarism, and corporate capitalism."[2] That is a far cry from the idea that Eisenhower was trying to convey. My goal is to recapture his meaning, explore the sources of his insight, and discuss the implications of his warning. I hope in the process to show that his vision of America and the Cold War was both powerful and prescient.

Such an exegesis offers a window on the Cold War and how it took shape in the 1950s. The United States found itself adjusting then to the unprecedented experience of maintaining a large, standing military establishment in peacetime. With that establishment came what critic Seymour Melman and others called a "permanent war economy." Never before had American military spending in peacetime risen much above 3 percent of gross domestic product. In the Cold War, it averaged 7–8 percent, peaking at 10 percent in the Kennedy administration. Much of that spending was being driven by an imperative for more and better weapons, thus, Eisenhower's related warning about a scientific-technological elite. This second caution illuminated another Cold War dilemma, which had been identified by wartime science advisor Vannevar Bush, in the immediate aftermath of World War II. The growing importance of science and technology in national life, said Bush, posed a problem for policymakers: the scientists and engineers with sufficient expertise to understand the complex technical issues facing the nation were likely to be co-opted by the communities within which they operated. Informed and independent advice would be hard to come by.[3] Eisenhower was president during that part of the Cold War when the impact of research and development on defense spending became manifest.

President Eisenhower's warnings also open a window on Ike himself. They reveal in part who he was, what he had experienced, and how he came to see the world on the occasion of leaving public life in 1961. A case can be made that he saw the world more clearly and presciently than most of his contemporaries, or at least that he understood the Cold War more fully. He believed that the enemy was totalitarianism in general, not communism in particular. The Great Depression had spawned a challenge to democratic, free-enterprise capitalism in the form of authoritarian command economies prepared to use force to organize the world to their satisfaction. The Cold War was, as President Eisenhower's successor put it, "a long twilight struggle" of this contest, and it would be won not on the battle field but in the marketplace of both goods and ideas.[4]

To open these windows on the Cold War and on Ike, it is best to start with the text. "We have been compelled," Eisenhower said in his address to the nation, "to create a permanent armaments industry of vast proportions." When combined with "an immense military establishment," the complex's "total influence—economic, political, even spiritual—is felt in every city, every Statehouse, every office of the Federal government." While recognizing the need for this development, Eisenhower worried about its "grave implications." In the most quoted passage of his address, he warned:

> In the councils of government, we must guard against the acquisition of unwarranted influence, whether sought or unsought, by the military-industrial complex. The potential for the disastrous rise of misplaced power exists and will persist. . . . Only an alert and knowledgeable citizenry can compel the proper meshing of this huge industrial and military machinery of defense with our peaceful methods and goals.[5]

The term "military-industrial complex" was not one that Eisenhower had used before in public. It was coined for the occasion by his speech writers, though it described a phenomenon that Eisenhower had long contemplated. In private, he referred to a "delta of power," combining Congress with the military services and the defense industry.[6] Neither term, however, was as clear as it might have been. What was the "unwarranted influence" and on whom was it exerted? What power was misplaced and why was its rise disastrous? What disaster did Eisenhower fear? And what did all of this have to do with a scientific and technological elite? The fact that his warnings were largely ignored, save by a handful of pundits and policy wonks, to be revived in the Vietnam era with a meaning he did not intend, suggests that this trope of American politics warrants reexamination.

Eisenhower clarified his meaning in a classified speech he gave at the Naval War College in 1969. As reported in the *New York Times,* the former president spoke of

> the Congressman who sees a new defense establishment in his district; the company in Los Angeles, Denver, or Baltimore that wants an order for more airplanes; the services which want them; the armies of scientists who want so terribly to test out their newest view. . . . "Put all these together," he continued, "and you have a lobby."[7]

So it was a lobby he was talking about. Furthermore, the lobby was not a binary, as implied by the "military-industrial complex," nor even a triangle as implied by his "delta of power." It was four-sided, one corner manned by armies of scientists. As he had said in his address, "a technological revolution during recent decades" was "akin to, and largely responsible for the sweeping changes in our military-industrial posture." In other words, research and development drove a qualitative arms race that was just as dangerous as the quantitative race for more aircraft carriers, more bombers, more tanks, more missiles. In short, the quest for more and better weapons was driving the country, in his view, to dangerous and unwise policies.

Research and development deserved special mention because they posed a double threat. First, the scientific enterprise itself was threatened. Big science was displacing the "lone inventor" and the "free university."[8] "The prospect of domination of the nation's scholars by Federal employment, project allocations, and the power of money is ever present," he warned, "and is gravely to be regarded." This was Vannevar Bush's worry. To it, Ike added his own concerns about the power of science and technology. "In holding scientific research and discovery in respect," he said, "we must also be alert to the equal and opposite danger that public policy itself become the captive of a scientific-technological elite." Vannevar Bush, of course, had been less concerned on this account because he was himself a scientific-technological elite. But it worried Eisenhower.

The concept is simple. To Ike, the military-industrial complex was a lobby. The scientists made common cause with the congressmen, the businessmen, and the officers of the military services to drive up defense spending. This lobby frustrated Eisenhower's efforts to balance the budget, a goal he achieved only in 1956 and 1957. So was this famous passage in his farewell address really just a fit of pique over lobbying, the perennial game of Washington politics?

Ike's famous warning was more than that. Dwight Eisenhower had a sophisticated, fully developed political philosophy and a strong conviction about the Cold War. His views combined his own experience as an army officer and a president with intellectual currents that circulated in the United States at mid-century. Eisenhower appears to have internalized those currents, mixed them with his own views, and formulated a clear vision for American policy in the Cold War. The vision appears to have taken shape before he entered the presidency and to have been reinforced by his experience in office. His warning about the lobby flowed from that vision.

Most of the experience that shaped Ike's understanding of the Cold War will be well known to some readers. As a staff officer and perennial major between the world wars, he watched the Depression breed totalitarian states in Germany, Italy, and Spain, while a militarized state arose in Japan. He also knew that the United States was far from immune; he worked in the 1930s on a congressional commission to study war profiteering in World War I, the notorious investigation of the merchants of death, and he reluctantly helped Douglas MacArthur disperse the bonus marchers in Washington in 1932. He surely understood American idealization of World War II as the good war, a "Crusade in Europe," as his called his part of it. But, like all commanders, he knew the darker side of war: the mistakes at Normandy, the Battle of the Bulge, the execution of Private Slovik, the dropping of the atomic bombs. If Germany set history's standard for barbarism with the Holocaust, the United States still had its own concentration camps to account for. American conduct of strategic bombing, as Curtis LeMay admitted, would have made senior American commanders guilty of war crimes had the United States lost the war.[9] When he first became president, Eisenhower had to face the demagoguery of Joseph McCarthy and the recommendation of Adm. William Radford that the United States use nuclear weapons to save the French at Dien Bien Phu.

The real Ike hated war. Equally as much, he hated what it did to states. Deeply patriotic himself, he had seen the United States compromise its ideals and undermine its principles in the face of economic and military threat. He sought for the country a military security that would deflate the McCarthys and the Radfords, and an economic security that would empower the United States to remain the city on the hill. He preferred Atoms for Peace and Open Skies to the policies of containment and peacetime mobilization that he inherited from Harry Truman. He was mindful of the threat posed by the Soviet Union, chastened and informed by the lesson of Munich. But unlike many in his generation, he worried as much about the perils of militarization as about the menace of godless communism.

The tension he experienced was between guns and butter. He certainly recognized the need for guns. Indeed, he first favored roll back of Soviet expansionism before settling for the more realistic containment. And he was aware that the United States needed an industrial policy that would provide the military arms and technology to balance Soviet superiority in personnel. In a 1928 paper at the Army War College and again in a 1932 paper at the Army Industrial College, Eisenhower had called for closer cooperation in peacetime between industry and the military, so that when war came they would be prepared to work in harmony.[10] Again in 1946, then General Eisenhower, Chief of Staff of the Army, called for even more "cooperation with science and industry" than the country had achieved in World War II. But how was the country to achieve this without falling into a permanent war economy? Ike's answer, never entirely satisfactory, was the New Look and then the New, New Look, defense policies that offered adequate deterrence and at least two balanced budgets.

But Eisenhower drew on more than his own experience and observations in formulating his farewell address. He also incorporated ideas that were coursing through intellectual circles in the decade and half following World War II. In addition to Vannevar Bush's concerns about the co-opting of science advice, five of these ideas seem particularly salient: aping the enemy, the power elite, militarism, the permanent war economy, and the garrison state. Four of them warrant brief mention. One begs closer scrutiny, for it seems to have exerted the greatest hold on his imagination.

First was the age-old dilemma of being drawn down to the level of your enemy. Diplomat George Kennan described the challenge facing the United States after World War II and formulated the policy that the country would pursue to the end of the Cold War. In his famous "long telegram" from Moscow of 22 February 1946, later revised for anonymous publication by Comrade X in *Foreign Policy,* Kennan portrayed the Soviets as patient, determined, brutal, paranoid, isolated expansionists bent on spreading their system of government around the world. Diplomacy and politics carried less weight with them than brute force. If the United States wanted to block their ambitions, it would have to contain their interventions in other countries with force or the threat of force. President Truman lent his name and his support to this policy of containment. So too did President Eisenhower, once he realized that his preference for rollback was unattainable, at least in the short term.

And Eisenhower embraced another principle advanced by Kennan. The long telegram from Moscow had ended with the caution: "The *greatest danger* that can befall us in coping with this problem of Soviet communism, is that we shall allow ourselves to become like those with whom we are coping."[11] Eisenhower echoed this sentiment early in his administration. In a radio address in May 1953, he said that "there is no such thing as maximum military security short of total mobilization of all our national resources. Such security would compel us to imitate the methods of the dictator."[12] The statement is significant on at least two counts. First, it dismisses the absolutist argument for total security, opening the way to the balance of terror and even mutual assured destruction. He understood early on that to achieve security in the nuclear age the United States would have to accept a certain degree of vulnerability. Furthermore, he characterized the enemy not as Communists but as dictators. For him, the constant enemy was always totalitarianism.

President Eisenhower's policies and ideas, especially his aversion to lobbies, also appeared to resonate with C. Wright Mills's influential book, *The Power Elite,* which appeared in 1956.[13] Mills, a sociologist, argued that power in the United States was concentrated in the hands of a few hundred government officials, corporate executives, and military officers. Eisenhower invoked the rhetoric of an elite to describe the scientists and engineers who were part of the military-industrial lobby. In practice, however, Eisenhower's public statements and policies display less influence by Mills than appears at first glimpse. Eisenhower was, after all, a member of the power elite. One of only nine five-star flag officers in United States history, a university president, and finally president of the United States, he moved among the power elite for the last twenty-five years of his life. He played poker and golf with captains of industry. In spite of his public image as an avuncular old soldier slightly out of touch with the demands of the presidency, he was an astute and accomplished government executive and politician. He was not only plugged into the power elite, he was an influential player. Far from worrying about the impact that the power elite had on national policy, he welcomed its contributions and agreed with most of them. His farewell address may have warned about a scientific and technical elite, but not about Mills's power elite.

His speech did, however, reveal some concerns about militarism. By the time Eisenhower bade farewell, political scientist Samuel P. Huntington had formulated his influential theory of the ideal relationship between *The Soldier and the State.*[14] Huntington's goal had been to identify workable civil-military relations for the United States. The American military, in Huntington's view, was a necessarily conservative institution within a liberal state. The country needed a military strong enough to meet the security threat but not so strong as to threaten democratic institutions. Was this not Eisenhower's complaint? Did he not warn of "an immense military establishment" reaching with the arms industry into "every city, every Statehouse, every office of the Federal government"? Was he not concerned about the circumvention of his authority as an elected official? Could it not be said that the military-industrial complex was really just a special form of militarism?

Indeed it could. As historian Arthur Schlesinger, Jr., put it, "the military-industrial complex was more a consequence than a cause of the problem," which "lay in the feebleness of civilian control of the military establishment."[15] In a very real sense, the warning about the military-industrial complex euphemized the more troubling issue of militarization or militarism. Throughout his presidency, Ike worried about civilian control of the military. His repeated attempts to reorganize the Department of Defense and his search for an authoritative secretary of defense were just the most public manifestations of these concerns.

Closer still to Eisenhower's vision and his policies was a set of conflicting notions that animated the phrase "permanent war economy." Like "military-industrial complex," this term gained salience during the Vietnam War, when Seymour Melman invoked it both as the title of a book and as an organizing theme of his most influential work, *Pentagon Capitalism.* Ironically, it was first voiced by Charles E. (Electric Charlie) Wilson, president of General Electric, vice chair of the War Production Board during World War II, and head of the Office of Defense Mobilization in the Truman administration. Noting in 1944 that the New Deal had failed to achieve the economic recovery finally spawned by World War II, Wilson urged a national economic policy built around military spending.[16] His counterpart and namesake at General Motors, Charles E. (Engine Charlie) Wilson, one of Eisenhower's secretaries of defense, attracted even greater outrage by asserting that "what is good for General Motors is good for America." But "Electric Charlie" Wilson's breezy encomium about the salubrious effects of defense spending had a greater impact on the debate over America's role in the Cold War. C. Wright Mills, for example, used it in *The Power Elite.*[17]

This permanent war economy was the natural result of what Melman later called "state management," what scholars in the 1980s would come to call a "command economy." In the 1990s, Aaron Friedberg called it "statism," a term invoked by Eisenhower himself in 1949. But in the 1950s, Eisenhower more likely would have thought of it as a "planned" or "administered" economy.[18] It denoted nothing more than the attempt by government to shape economic development for national purposes. It was best understood as the opposite of a free market economy, which may or may not be capitalist. Eisenhower's clear preference was for free market capitalism, with minimum state planning. He understood, of course, that the state necessarily played some role in shaping the economy, but he wanted that role to be minimal. State planning for him was a tool of dictators. The real problem with socialism and communism, as he saw it, was not their theoretical principles of government but their practical disposition to decay into totalitarianism.

However much Eisenhower's farewell warning might appear to have arisen from Mills's power elite or Huntington's militarism or Electric Charlie Wilson's permanent war economy, the president preferred the metaphor of a "garrison state," which he associated with dictatorship, not communism. In 1941, political scientist Harold Lasswell had warned about "the garrison state, . . . a world in which the specialists on violence are the most powerful group in society."[19] This possibility had suggested itself to Lasswell when he learned of the Japanese bombing of China in 1937. He wondered if the subjection of civilians to military attack, what he called the "socialization of danger," would not empower the military to permanently organize society for war. The "specialist on violence," he suggested, might displace the businessman, the bureaucrat, and the politician atop "the power pyramid." C. Wright Mills's "power elite" might be militarized, paradoxically, by "specialists on violence [who] are more preoccupied with the skills and attitudes judged characteristic of nonviolence. We anticipate the merging of skills, starting from the traditional accouterments of the professional soldier, moving toward the manager and promoter of large-scale civilian enterprise."[20]

Two trends converged in Lasswell's garrison state. On the one hand, a conventional militarization of society allowed uniformed officers and military considerations to gain purchase in the formulation of national policy. Those given to such fears might see the appointment of Gen. George C. Marshall as secretary of state in the Truman administration as evidence of this trend, to say nothing of the election of General Eisenhower. On the other hand, civilian leaders elected and appointed to oversee the military were themselves imbued with many of the values Lasswell dreaded. Secretary of State John Foster Dulles envisioned a moral crusade against godless communism and was prepared to take the United States to the brink of Armageddon in defense of "security."[21]

Before he introduced the term "military-industrial complex," Eisenhower spoke of the garrison state as a shorthand for the related problems of the arms race, escalating defense costs, and economic crisis. "If we let defense spending run wild," he said, "you get inflation . . . then controls . . . then a garrison state . . . and *then* we've lost the very values we were trying to defend."[22] The futile quest for "maximum military security," he said in a 1953 radio address, "would compel us to imitate the methods of the dictator, . . . to devote our whole nation to the grim purposes of the garrison state."[23] Throughout his presidency, in private discussions and correspondence, in closed meetings, and in public fora, Ike invoked the garrison state as the real peril posed by the Cold War. While he did not always use the term exactly as Lasswell had, he always envisioned an external threat driving the United States away from democratic, free-enterprise capitalism toward a dictatorial state running a command economy.

At a certain level, Ike's position simply reflected Republican philosophy on social spending, a defense of free enterprise against the encroachment of government statism.[24] He linked liberals to ideas that represented "one more step toward total socialism, just beyond which lies total dictatorship."[25] This veiled critique of New Deal liberalism did not lead him to recommend more guns and less butter. He was equally concerned with excesses in military spending. Always he preached "balance," by which he meant enough security to protect the country but not so much as to bankrupt it. For bankruptcy by either social or military spending led to the same garrison state.

More often, however, Eisenhower focused on military imperatives, on the constant pressure from the military-industrial complex or the delta of power to increase defense spending. It was a paradox, he told his National Security Council (NSC) in 1953, that the spending necessary to meet the Soviet threat could transform the United States into a state that looked like the Soviet Union.[26] "New formations in the defense forces," he told a press conference in 1959, "meant steadily increasing budgets. Everybody with any sense knows that we are finally going to a garrison state."[27] If guided missiles were introduced without other weapons being phased out, he told another press conference, "we better go into a garrison state, because there is no other way to meet the expenses."[28]

In one meeting of the NSC, presidential special assistant for national security affairs, Robert Cutler, presented a preliminary report by the NSC Planning Board outlining two alternative models of defense spending. While one, in column A, called for "whatever measures were necessary," the other, in column B, recommended "all practical measures." Predictably, Ike chose column B. He said that column A was predicated on "the erroneous premise that you could have an absolute defense. . . . The President . . . said that if the Council came to believe what was set forth in the left-hand column we might just as well stop any further talk about preserving a sound U.S. economy and proceed to transform ourselves into a garrison state."[29]

Eisenhower's garrison state incorporated some of Lasswell's concerns, blending them with Republican fears of big government, socialism, and collectivism. It also took up Kennan's concerns about aping the enemy, Huntington's worries about militarism, and Eisenhower's own worries about a permanent war economy. When he came to his farewell address, he warned that all of these forces had been strengthened by a lobby that threatened to move defense spending from the practical to the absolute. Contributing to the lobby was a scientific and technical elite that combined Mills's power elite with Vannevar Bush's worries about the biases inherent in technical advice. Ike combined all these currents in the catch-phrase "garrison state," which, in his farewell address, he converted to military-industrial complex. This was his vision. Imperfect though it might be, American democratic, free-enterprise capitalism had produced, to paraphrase Winston Churchill, the worst form of government except all those other forms that have been tried from time to time. That political/economic system could triumph over communism just as it had triumphed over the earlier totalitarian challenges of the twentieth century. The country had only to believe in its own principles and resist the temptation to impose a command economy or a garrison state.

Nowhere did his passion and conviction come across more powerfully or poignantly than in his 1953 address to the American Society of Newspaper Editors. The arms race, he told the editors, promised

> a life of perpetual fear and tension; a burden of arms draining the wealth and labor of all peoples. . . . Every gun that is made, every warship launched, every rocket fired signifies, in the final sense, a theft from those who hunger and are not fed, those who are cold and not clothed. This world in arms is not spending money alone. It is spending the sweat of its laborers, the genius of its scientists, the hopes of its

children. . . . This is not a way of life at all, in any true sense. Under the cloud of threatening war, it is humanity hanging from a cross of iron.[30]

Eisenhower's keenest insight, his vision, and his constant sermon was that the arms race with the Soviet Union was as dangerous as the Soviets themselves. He believed that the Cold War would not become a shooting war, that the real contest was not between arsenals but between economic and political systems. We would win the war against a garrison state if we did not become a garrison state ourselves. His vision, I believe, was right on all counts.

Notes

*"Maximum military security . . . would mean . . . all the grim paraphernalia of the garrison state." Dwight D. Eisenhower, address at the annual convention of the National Junior Chamber of Commerce, Minneapolis, Minn., 10 June 1953, <http://www.presidency.ucsb.edu/ws/index.php?pid=9871&st=&st1=>, accessed 30 May 2005.

1. The material presented here is drawn in part from Alex Roland, "The Military-Industrial Complex," in Andrew J. Bacevich, ed., *The Columbia History of U.S. National Security since World War II* (forthcoming).

2. Michael Sherry, *The Rise of American Air Power: The Creation of Armageddon* (New Haven, Conn.: Yale University Press, 1987), 273.

3. The Joint Research and Development Board and the Research and Development Board, both of which Bush chaired in the years immediately following World War II, were attempts to provide such unbiased technical advice to the military services. See G. Paschal Zachary, *Endless Frontier: Vannevar Bush, Engineer of the American Century* (Cambridge, Mass.: MIT Press, 1999), 318–32, *et passim*.

4. John F. Kennedy, "Inaugural Address," Washington, D.C., 21 Jan. 1961, <http://www.jfklibrary.org/j012061.htm>, accessed 14 Mar. 2005.

5. Dwight D. Eisenhower, "Farewell Address," <http://www.americanrhetoric.com/speeches/dwighteisenhowerfarewell.html>, accessed 25 May 2004.

6. In the published literature, this is most often represented as the "iron triangle." See, for example, Gordon Adams, *The Politics of Defense Contracting: The Iron Triangle* (New Brunswick, N.J.: Transaction Books, 1982).

7. Dana Adams Schmidt, "Eisenhower Talk Scored Moon Race," *New York Times,* 13 June 1971, 67, quoted in Reita Priest, "The Military-Industrial Complex: A Content and Usage Analysis from 1961 to 1990" (undergraduate research paper, Department of History, Duke University, 21 April 2004), 3.

8. The term "big science," which Eisenhower did not use, appears to have been introduced by Alvin Weinberg, "Impact of Large-Scale Science on the United States," *Science* 134 (21 July 1961):161–64.

9. Robert S. McNamara, "We Need Rules for War," *Los Angeles Times,* 3 Aug. 2003, <http://www.wagingpeace.org/articles/2003/08/03_mcnamara_rules-for-war.htm>, accessed 24 Apr. 2005.

10. Stephen J. Zempolich, "Dwight David Eisenhower and the Military-Industrial Complex: Advocacy to Opposition, 1928–1961" (Senior Honors Thesis, Duke University, 1985).

11. Kennan to Secretary of State, 22 Feb. 1946, <http://www.gwu.edu/~nsarchiv/coldwar/documents/episode-1/kennan.htm>, accessed 15 Aug. 2004; emphasis added.

12. Dwight D. Eisenhower, "Radio Address to the American People on the National Security and Its Costs," <http://www.presidency.ucsb.edu/site/docs/pppus.php?admin=034&year=1953&id=82>, accessed 10 Aug. 2004; emphasis added.

13. C. Wright Mills, *The Power Elite* (New York: Oxford University Press, 1956).

14. Samuel P. Huntington, *The Soldier and the State: The Theory and Politics of Civil-Military Relations* (Cambridge, Mass.: Harvard University Press, 1957).

15. Arthur Schlesinger, Jr., *A Thousand Days: John F. Kennedy in the White House* (Greenwich, Conn.: Fawcett, 1965), 292.

16. Richard J. Barnet, *The Economy of Death* (New York: Atheneum, 1969), 116.

17. Mills, *Power Elite,* 215, 275–76.

18. As Max Weber had pointed out as early as 1922, "planned" was not synonymous with either "socialist" or "Communist." Max Weber, *Economy and Society,* ed. Guenther Roth and Claus Wittich, 2 vols. (1922; Berkeley: University of California Press, 1978), 1:109–13.

19. Harold Lasswell, "The Garrison State," *American Journal of Sociology* 46 ((January 1941):455.

20. Ibid., 458.

21. These were the conditions of subjective control of the military warned about by Huntington in *Soldier and the State,* 80–83, *et passim.*

22. Emmet John Hughes, *The Ordeal of Power: A Political Memoir of the Eisenhower Years* (New York: Antheneum, 1963), 250.

23. "Radio Address to the American People on the National Security and Its Costs," 9 May 1953, <http://www.presidency.ucsb.edu/ws/index/php?pid=9854&st=&st1=>, accessed 22 Jan. 2005.

24. Dwight D. Eisenhower, "The Middle Road: A Statement of Faith in America," *American Bar Association Journal* 35 (October 1949):810–12, 879–80.

25. Eisenhower to Amon Giles Carter, 27 June 1949, *The Papers of Dwight David Eisenhower; Columbia University,* ed. Louis Galambos (Baltimore, Md.: Johns Hopkins University Press, 1984), 10:665–69, quotation on 666.

26. "Memorandum of Discussion at the 163d Meeting of the National Security Council, Thursday, September 24, 1953," *Foreign Relations of the United States, 1952–1954,* vol. 2, *National Security Affairs* (Washington, D.C.: Government Printing Office, 1984), 469.

27. "The President's News Conference, March 11, 1959," <http://www.presidency.ucsb.edu/ws/index.php?pid=11678&st=&st1=>, accessed 6 Aug. 2004.

28. "The President's News Conference, November 5, 1958," ibid.

29. "Memorandum of Discussion at the 204th Meeting of the National Security Council, Thursday, June 24, 1954," *Foreign Relations of the United States, 1952–1954,* 687, 689.

30. Dwight D. Eisenhower, "The Chance for Peace," delivered before the American Society of Newspaper Editors, 16 Apr. 1953, <http://www.presidency.ucsb.edu/ws/index.php?pid=9819&st=newspaper&st1=editors>, accessed 30 May 2005.

Eisenhower's Methodology for Intervention and Its Legacy in Contemporary World Politics

Saki R. Dockrill

At the beginning of his presidency, Dwight D. Eisenhower was taken, as part of a civil defense drill, to a secret bunker in the Carolina mountains. The place would become an emergency White House in the case of a Soviet nuclear attack. The president went through many gates, and finally reached the "very bowels of the mountain." At that moment he told his national security adviser, Dillon Anderson, "Good God; I did not realize we were this scared."[1]

Eisenhower assumed office in January 1953. By then, the world had lived for several years with a frosty and confrontational U.S. relationship with the Communist bloc headed by the Soviet Union. The new Republican administration regarded the Cold War as a long-term, tenacious, and unpredictable threat to American security. It hoped that the Soviet system would eventually decay from its own internal weakness, as it did in 1991. Until then the world was, in the words of Eisenhower, "living in the age of danger," and it was impossible to predict the "year of the maximum danger." American intelligence experts believed that there would be no "general war" until Moscow acquired the ability to "cripple U.S. war-making capacity" in a first strike. War could nevertheless be triggered by many accidental or unpredictable factors.[2] Yet the Eisenhower period is remembered as a period of "prosperity and peace."[3] During the presidency of Eisenhower, the United States did not suffer from any political, economic, or military upheavals, such as the war in Vietnam in the 1960s, hostages in Iran in the 1970s, or the Iran-Contra affair in the 1980s. This did not mean that the United States was free from international challenges in the 1950s. On the contrary, President Eisenhower confronted numerous international crises from Indochina to Berlin during his eight years in office. How did Eisenhower manage to keep the peace, keep Communists at bay, and keep the Western alliance together?

This paper will discuss Eisenhower's methodology for intervention and its outcome. It will examine as well the ideas behind Eisenhower's grand strategy for the Cold War, especially the relationship between the perceived threat and the nation's security, and how these helped him to deal with international crises.

Eisenhower's Grand Strategy for the Cold War

Like the current war on terror, the Cold War was fought very much on the assumption that "if you are not with us, you are against us." That assumption figured more prominently in American society than in its Western European counterparts. The American president, Ronald Reagan in the early 1980s, called the Soviet Union an "evil empire," while the current U.S. president, George W. Bush, has defined all terrorism as "evil."[4] At the core of the Cold War polarization, however, was mutually perceived fear of a possible attack, a fear fed by mutual misperceptions and mutual lack of understanding. Each side had a tendency to depict the other in the worst possible light. That in turn created a situation whereby both sides misread each other's intentions and overestimated each other's capabilities. The East-West ideological competition added to the dynamic to expand, and intensify, the Cold War worldwide. The possession of nuclear weapons by both superpowers made the confrontation deadly.

The Cold War was not symmetrical. The image of bipolarity masked the differences between the blocs. The Soviet Union had never been co-equal with the United States. Aside from the obvious disparities of economic and military power between the two, their different ideologies and different historical backgrounds created totally different states. One led a bloc consisting of mostly liberal democratic capitalist societies; the other's system was based on totalitarian state socialist regimes. The Eisenhower administration had a clear view of America's primary enemy. In the address of 1953, Eisenhower said, "the enemies of this faith know no god but force, no devotion but its use. They tutor men in treason. They feed upon the hunger of others. Whatever defied them, they torture, especially the truth. . . . Freedom is pitted against slavery; lightness against the dark." However, Eisenhower continued, "We know, beyond this, that we are linked to all free peoples not merely by a noble idea but by a simple need."[5] Eisenhower's belief, shared by other Western leaders, was that there was no mutual ground to be found between the East and the West during the Cold War. If the Soviet Union wanted reconciliation, it was the Soviets who must change their ways unconditionally. In fact this was how the Cold War ended in 1989–91. While Mikhail Gorbachev took the initiative by accepting that Moscow's interests could be met more effectively by taking on the West's values and systems, and by reducing East-West tensions, the terms of the end of the Cold War in Europe, the Third World and over nuclear and conventional arms were shaped by the West.[6]

The Cold War turned out to be a lengthy and extraordinary affair. Although it avoided an apocalyptic military showdown, for nearly half a century it was waged by other means in an effort to counter and contract the expansion of the adversaries' strategic zones. These means included the competition of ideas and ideology, intelligence gathering, covert operations, and proxy battles in the Third World. In retrospect, these methods of fighting the Cold War were laid down during the 1950s under Eisenhower's New Look doctrine, which combined the unity, not the conformity, of the Western alliance with limited mobilization, emphasis on American nuclear deterrence, the utilization of allied ground forces, and "all feasible diplomatic, political, economic and covert measures" to deal with the Soviet Communist challenge.[7] In doing so, the Republican administration sought to "discover a reasonable and respectable posture of defense . . . without bankrupting the nation." These ideas were based on the Republicans' appreciation at the time that the existing method of Cold War fighting, based on the improvisations of the previous Truman administration, was becoming "too costly, too erratic too inconclusive" for the United States and its allies to follow.[8]

Eisenhower understood that the Cold War was a literal hell of a waiting game. He stated publicly in November 1957 that "Eternal vigilant and increased free world military power, backed by our combined economic and spiritual strength, provide the only answer to this threat until the Soviet leaders themselves cease to consume their resources in warlike and expansionist purposes and turn them to the well-being of their own peoples."[9] This explains why the Eisenhower administration took a long-haul approach to combating communism, as he wrote to his military friend, Gen. Alfred Gruenthur in May 1953: "our organized, effective resistance must be maintained over a long period of years and that this is possible only with a healthy American economy."[10]

Thus, the New Look doctrine, launched in the fall of 1953, was designed to achieve a long-term American grand strategy for the Cold War. It is important to note that the Eisenhower administration did not equate national security with national interest, but the president endeavored to broaden the concept of national security so that it came closer to the British idea of "grand strategy." The word "strategy" is often used parallel with "tactics." According to Carl von Clausewitz, tactics are the "art of using troops in battle"; strategy is the "art of using battles to win the war." With the passage of time, both words have tended to be used in much wider contexts than the purely military, such as "economic strategy," or "a strategy for peace." Grand strategy is correspondingly more than just strategy in that it embraces both wider goals and long-term objectives: the art of managing and controlling national resources to ensure that national interests of all kinds—economic, military, political, and cultural (values and beliefs) are maintained at a minimum cost.[11] In Eisenhower's view, U.S. national security policy should not be seen to be inhabiting a different realm than the nation's domestic concerns. He thought that this distinction had in the past resulted in national security being controlled by budgetary considerations or that such considerations had been ignored entirely during the Korean War. Instead, the president insisted that economic factors were to become the main elements in the formulation of the nation's security policy. As a step toward achieving this, Eisenhower included the secretary of treasury and the director of budget as permanent participants at National Security Council (NSC) meetings.[12]

Eisenhower and his trusted secretary of state, John Foster Dulles, both tended to downplay the military dimension of the Cold War. Neither of them believed that the Soviet threat could be regarded solely in the military and nuclear terms which the Truman administration had seen as the main danger after the outbreak of the Korean War. The Eisenhower administration saw the Communist threat as a combination both of Soviet military power and of a gradual Soviet political, psychological, and economic encroachment into the West. Overall, Eisenhower imposed a degree of restraint on the use of American conventional forces in small wars which might provoke the Soviet Union into retaliation, or might entail the danger of enlarging what was intended to be a small military conflict into a large one by involving the Soviet Union and/or China in such a conflict. The view was reinforced by the White House's perception at the time that the Soviets would not be deterred by "the fear of general war" from "taking the measures they considered necessary to counter Western actions that they viewed as serious threats to their security."[13]

Three Features: Initiative, Balance, and a Case-by-Case Approach

Initiative

If the above can be defined as Eisenhower's "bottom line" security policy, the following three principles guided this policy. First was an attempt to gain the initiative which, he believed, was lost under Truman by adopting more selective and flexible responses to Communist challenges. The United States was no longer prepared to try to meet every Communist threat or every security requirement of the United States or of its allies. Such an endeavor would necessitate massive defense expenditures, and also, given the fact that the threat would remain for several decades, it would exhaust the United States politically, economically, and spiritually, ending up with the nation becoming a garrison state, which was totally against its national security interests and its traditions. Thus, the United States must not remain on the "defensive" in fighting the Cold War, because "there is one factor, always important in a military struggle. . . . This is the selectivity and flexibility that always belongs to the offensive. The defensive must normally try to secure an entire area, the offensive can concentrate on any point of its own selection."[14] The notion of initiative also led to the idea of choice. The United States could *choose* to respond to international conflict if this was judged to be in the interest of the nation and of its allies. The gist of Eisenhower's crisis management boiled down to Dulles's famous but misunderstood passage in his speech on 12 January 1954 that the United States "would respond . . . at places and with means of its own choosing."[15]

Balance

Eisenhower's second principle was balance. He stressed this notion repeatedly during his years as president, and he also raised it in his farewell address on 17 January 1961. In this address, he first emphasized the importance of having a strong and effective military establishment as a way of keeping peace, but, "each proposal must be weighted in light of a broader consideration, and the need to maintain the *balance* in among national programs, such as the balance between the cost and hoped for advantages, balance between the clearly necessary and the comfortably desirable."[16] Eisenhower was keen to strike the right balance between the means of attaining security and the outcome of security itself. It became a divisive issue for the NSC members: as the Treasury often stressed the need for a "sound, strong and growing U.S. economy" in order to support "over the long pull a satisfactory posture of defence," while the overseas agencies put national security first, and was not prepared to balance the "budget at whatever cost to national security."[17] Eisenhower's efforts to place the American economy on a sound footing cannot be explained solely in terms of his fiscal conservatism. His interest in defense economy was also based on his belief that the fundamental national interest of the United States was to safeguard the nation's economic strength, and that national security "could not be measured in terms of military strength alone." Other factors of long gestation—economic, spiritual, intellectual, and institutional—had also to be taken into account. In a letter to Gruenther in May 1953, the president explained that "we have a free economy; its health and strength depends upon the incentives that induce people to produce. Experience indicates that failure in this regard usually results in regimentation."[18] Thus the notion of balance was the core of Eisenhower's New Look, which sought to "equate national security with the defense of permanent interests" rather than to attempt to accommodate U.S. national security policy to the fluctuating scale and nature of external threats.[19]

The notion of "balance" came close to what Stephen Ambrose termed the "common sense" which Eisenhower displayed in formulating the nation's security strategy. He made it clear to his subordinates that the United States should seek a "respectable" if not "perfect posture of defense" related to the "long pull." As long as the United States could show that a Soviet military and/or nuclear attack would not pay in the face of American massive retaliatory power, and show as well that "the free world can prosper despite Soviet pressure," Eisenhower estimated that the main requirements of America's security would be met.[20] During his second term (1956–61), with Moscow's launching of the first earth satellite in October 1957, Congress and the media began to voice concerns about Eisenhower's apparent lack of determination to increase America's efforts to counter the Soviet Union's growing nuclear capability. Eisenhower continued to believe that a sufficient deterrence, and not nuclear superiority, should be enough to deal with Moscow's ballistic missile threats. He lamented the world's tendency to see a ballistic missile as the "ultimate" weapon and "have a picture of guided missiles raining out of the skies in almost uncounted numbers."[21] It was impossible even for Ike to figure out what would be the shape of future nuclear warfare, but he thought it absurd to get into the numbers game. He once asked "how many times do we need to kill each Russian?"[22]

A Case-by-Case Approach

These considerations—initiative, choice, balance, and common sense—when applied to crisis management, necessitated the prioritization of U.S. national security requirements, and the elimination of undesirable options for the United States. For instance, the president was clear that if America ever became involved in a military conflict with the Soviet Union, its response would be nuclear. He was also clear that any military conflict in the NATO area was "bound to become an all-out war," hence the importance of diffusing any crisis such as that over Berlin in 1958–59. He was very "reluctant" to involve the United States in another Korean War, because during that conflict, the America had been compelled to fight "with handcuffs on," and as a result, the United States had been unable to defeat its Communist adversaries outright and was forced to end the war on less than satisfactory terms.[23]

From this example, he concluded that the United States should not become involved in "small wars" or "peripheral wars," wars which were likely to prolong America's involvement in a particular regional conflict.[24] Instead he preferred giving support and advice to indigenous troops in small wars. His anti-imperial stance also indicated that the United States would not follow in the footsteps of Britain and France in trying to occupy foreign territories over a long period of time.

The third point was Eisenhower's effort to deal with crises in a variety of ways, and on a case-by-case basis. While the NSC and the Pentagon wished to be clear about whether or not the United States was likely to become involved in local aggressions or small wars, defined by Eisenhower as "conflicts occurring in less developed areas of the world"; and if so with what weapons, Eisenhower remained unwilling to commit American troops to the less developed areas of the world unless "U.S. interests are involved."[25] The NSC also agreed in July 1957 that the United States would reserve the right to decide whether or not to fight in other more controversial regions, such as in the NATO area, in the Middle East, in the Far East and in Southeast Asia, and where conflicts might or might not be kept "local" in character. Finally, if the United States was compelled to fight in areas where Soviet and/or Chinese forces became involved, the Americans would be more likely to use nuclear weapons, but their use would be "determined by the President."[26] Thus, the major decisions during international crisis were the prerogative of the president.

The Case for Non-intervention?: The Dien Bien Phu Crisis (1954), the Suez Crisis (1956), and the Hungarian Uprising (1956)

With these criteria in mind, we will first consider the crises in which the Eisenhower administration chose not to intervene militarily. The Dien Bien Phu crisis of 1954 is often remembered as one where the president skillfully avoided U.S. military intervention, despite the fact that the Joint Chiefs of Staff and the State Department recommended it.[27] The United States had been providing the French with financial assistance for their struggle with the Vietminh in Indo-China since 1950, and by 1953, the Americans were covering two-thirds of the entire costs incurred by the French in the Indo-China War.

In mid-March 1954, a major Vietminh offensive threatened to annihilate the French garrison at Dien Bien Phu in northern Vietnam. The Eisenhower administration feared that a French defeat in Indo-China would seriously undermine resistance to communism throughout Southeast Asia. However, there were three obstacles. Congress was opposed to any hasty American intervention so soon after the end of the Korean War. Eisenhower was also aware that American involvement in Indo-China without any regard to the wishes of the peoples of Indo-China would expose the United States to the charge of imperialism and colonialism. Since France refused to grant independence to Indo-China, and would not agree to defend Indo-China against communism in cooperation with its allies under American leadership, Eisenhower judged that there were no justifiable grounds for the Americans to intervene to support the French troops in Dien Bien Phu. Thus, Eisenhower's famous domino theory was not as rigid as it was made out to be, as he was not prepared to use military means unilaterally unless he secured legitimacy, that is, allied agreement on "United Action" during the crisis.[28]

The Suez Crisis of 1956 fell into a category similar to Dien Bien Phu. The United States sought legitimacy before resorting to the use of military force, but this was lacking in the case of the Suez crisis. The French and the British went ahead with their intervention despite Washington urging them not to do so. This was also the case where the allies disagreed about the nature of threats which might warrant the use of force. The American president gave a higher priority to the defense of Southeast Asia than the British did during the Dien Bien Phu crisis. Britain was, in Eisenhower's words, demonstrating a "'woeful unawareness' of the risks" the United States took in the region.[29] When it come to the Middle East, the reverse was the case during the Suez crisis.

Britain staked its credibility and prestige in the Middle East, but the United States was not prepared to give London all-out support for this purpose. While Britain's imperial pretensions were declining after 1945, the pressure to keep the Soviets at bay was growing and so was the growth of oil consumption in postwar Western Europe (80 percent of the oil consumed in Western Europe came from the Middle East).[30] Anthony Eden, the foreign secretary in the Churchill government (1951–55), regarded Britain's world role as more useful and important than a deep commitment to Europe, and it was Iran where Eden first cooperated with the American president, Eisenhower, who also saw Iran as a serious Cold War issue. The subsequent Anglo-American covert operation successfully ousted the ultra nationalist and anti-British Iranian prime minister, Mohammed Mussadeq.[31]

Mussadeq's firm stand against Britain encouraged Arab nationalism and anti-British sentiments in Egypt where, under the 1936 Anglo-Egyptian treaty of friendship and alliance, Britain was committed to defend Egypt against aggression and had the right to garrison the Suez Canal, Britain's largest base in the Middle East. In 1954, the British agreed to sign a treaty with Egypt whereby Britain would withdraw its troops from the Suez Canal base by June 1956, and thereafter the base could only be reactivated by the British in the event of aggression (except by Israel) against an Arab state or Turkey. However, the new Egyptian leader, Col. Gamal Abdel Nasser, had a more radical approach to Arab nationalist aspirations in the Middle East. The timing coincided with Moscow's growing interest in the Third World under Nikita Khrushchev, and he supported publicly the "yearnings of the peoples of the Arab countries who are fighting for their full liberation from foreign dependence."[32]

Colonel Nasser began to take advantage of the Cold War by purchasing arms from the USSR in the fall of 1955, although Nasser was advised by the Central Intelligence Agency's local operatives in Cairo to say that they were coming from Czechoslovakia and not from the Soviet Union. This was done in an effort to minimize the shock in the White House, increasingly concerned with Egypt's military challenge to Israel. Nasser also recognized Communist China in May 1956, thereby minimizing the chance of securing generous economic assistance from the U.S. Congress. By that time, Eden (now prime minister) was furious about Nasser's behavior, comparing him to Hitler or Mussolini,[33] while the French were angered by Nasser's support for the anti-French rebellion in their colony of Algeria. In retaliation for the collapse of negotiations with the Americans for a loan to build the Aswan High Dam in the summer of 1956, Nasser nationalized the Suez Canal, which was owned by both the British and the French. The United States' efforts to strengthen the more pro-Western Middle Eastern countries as a counterpoise to Nasser had failed, while Nasser's nationalization of the Suez Canal, was "celebrated throughout the Arab world."[34] Eden had already seriously been considering a plot to eliminate Nasser: he told Anthony Nutting, minister of state in the Foreign office, "I want Nasser murdered, don't you understand?" After the nationalization, while the French and British began to prepare for military action to oust Nasser, Eden encouraged Eisenhower to "take a stand," as otherwise, Eden cabled Eisenhower at the end of July 1956, "the influence of Britain and the United States throughout the Middle East would be 'irretrievably undermined.'" The U.S. Joint of Chiefs of Staff also urged the president to consider urgently measures to place the Suez Canal "under a friendly and responsible authority."[35]

This is where Eisenhower's judgment became important—unlike the British and French, who thought firm action was essential if the downfall of Nasser was to be achieved, the president and John Foster Dulles rejected military action out of hand, explaining to Eden that "American public opinion flatly rejects the thought of using force," while Eisenhower was also doubtful whether "we could here secure Congressional authority even for the lesser support measures for which you might have to look to us."[36] Eden was predictably frustrated by the inability of the United States to cooperate with him, which made him more amenable to the French idea of securing Israeli assistance against Egypt. Thus, the French and British forces began to bomb Egypt at the end of October under the pretext of intervening to end the Egyptian-Israeli war. Eisenhower and Dulles were furious, and publicly condemned the British and the French.[37]

Eisenhower's actions did not mean that he had not contemplated a possible critical situation over the Suez in Cold War terms. If the Soviet Union had attacked Britain and France on the side of Egypt—Khrushchev had warned the West that this might happen—Eisenhower knew that "we would be in war, and we would be justified in taking military action even if Congress were not in session." On the presidential election day, 6 November 1956, the president was informed that the latest reconnaissance plane, the U-2, had not detected any Soviet planes in Syria and no movement of the Soviet troops to Egypt either. This was obviously good news, and Eisenhower only resorted to a minor form of mobilization, by recalling military personnel on leave, which he thought would give the Soviets "pause."[38] To make the situation even better, on the same day Eden announced that Britain was prepared to accept a ceasefire in the Middle East. The crisis was now over. Indeed, the Suez crisis came the worst moment for Eisenhower, who was in the middle of the presidential elections, while Dulles had become critically ill and required an emergency operation three days before election day. Moreover, the Hungarian crisis also necessitated the White House's urgent attention.

The Hungarian uprising challenged the Republican policy of liberation, but the 1956 crisis boiled down once again to the justification of the use of force. True, the liberation of captive nations had been an integral part of the Republican Party election platform in 1952. The Eisenhower administration revamped propaganda and psychological warfare, and considered ways in which the Americans could reduce Soviet influence in Eastern Europe by covert and peaceful means. The trouble was the Soviet Union and the Eastern European rulers were quite capable of penetrating the Eastern European resistance groups, for the stability of the Eastern bloc depended on the elimination of actual or potential anti-establishment elements. This did not change after the death of Stalin in March 1953.

The new Kremlin leadership successfully created a mood of détente, which helped to end the Korean War in July 1953, but Moscow's approach to its Eastern European satellite countries remained the same. The USSR suppressed the East German uprising in 1953 by military force, and increased its control over East Germany.[39] Khrushchev's speech denouncing Stalinism at the 20th party congress on 25 February 1956 created further confusion in Communist parties outside the Soviet Union. This led to the outbreak of a riot in Poznan, Poland, in June 1956 and by October, its neighbor, Hungary. On 23 October, workers in Budapest joined a student demonstration and fighting broke out at about 10:00 p.m. local time between the Hungarian demonstrators and the Hungarian army. The Hungarian demonstrators demanded the removal of the existing Communist government and the withdrawal of Soviet troops from Hungary, and called for the return of Imre Nagy, a moderate Communist, who had been prime minister between 1953 and 1955. Stalin's statue was pulled down and the Red Star was torn off the trade union building.[40]

The Eisenhower administration recognized that it could do little to exploit the situation in Hungary beyond offering sympathy and humanitarian aid and by referring the issue to the United Nations. On 1 November, Soviet troops began to reoccupy Budapest. In response, Nagy proclaimed Hungary's withdrawal from the Warsaw pact and appealed to the UN secretary general for UN help in defense of Hungarian neutrality. On 2 November, the president authorized the provision of $20 million's worth of food and relief for the Hungarian people. The Western alliance was disrupted, with Britain and France accusing the United States of using delaying tactics in the Security Council over Hungary, and the Americans attacking Britain and France for using Hungary to divert world attention from the Suez crisis.[41]

While the Suez crisis was reaching a climax with French and British expeditionary forces approaching Port Said, the Hungarian tragedy reached its dénouement. On 4 November, the Soviet Union invaded Budapest with 200,000 troops and 4,000 tanks and Janos Kadar, who had briefly served as interior minister in the Nagy government, was appointed prime minister. Nagy was "kidnapped" by the Russians and executed later in 1958. Khrushchev recalled that "it was all over in three days," while Andrei Gromyko, his foreign minister, in his *Memories,* too, believed that "the help given to Hungary was absolutely justified."[42] Eisenhower recalled in his memoirs that the new Hungarian government would be as "inaccessible to us as Tibet."[43]

A number of specific factors explained the low-key and confused American response to the Hungarian crisis. First, American liberation policy had always excluded the direct use of military force. Eisenhower sought only peaceful liberation. Some 400,000 Soviet troops were stationed in East Germany, Poland, Hungary, and Rumania. Given this harsh reality, the concept of peaceful liberation was bound to fail. In any case, Hungary, a land-locked country, presented a difficult military problem for the West. Allied troops, in order to reach Hungary, would have to move across "neutral Austria, Titoist Yugoslavia, or Communist Czechoslovakia," which was, in Eisenhower's view, "out of the question." The president knew that "sending United States troops alone into Hungary through hostile or neutral territory would have involved us in general war."[44] The West's attention was diverted to the Suez crisis, which helped to reduce condemnation of the Kremlin for its military suppression of Hungary, and for Hungarian freedom fighters, the Suez crisis had stolen the limelight from Budapest.

In these three crises, Eisenhower was probably closer to intervention in Dien Bien Phu than he was during the Suez crisis. The Hungarian uprising was regarded as occurring almost within enemy territory, and the United States and its European allies were reluctant to meddle in the Soviet sphere of influence, with a minor exception in the case of the Western response to the Polish crisis in 1980–81. The president was more concerned not to provoke the Soviet Union unduly over Hungary than with upsetting the Hungarian anti-Communist demonstrators—he thought that the Suez crisis has increased the East-West antagonism in the Middle East, which enhanced the need to deal with the Soviet Union carefully. Hungary fell into the black hole of the politics of the great powers.

The Case for Intervention?: Lebanon (1958), the Taiwan Offshore Crisis (1954–1955, 1958), and the Berlin Crisis (1958–1959)

There was one case where the United States did resort to a decisive use of military force: its intervention in Lebanon in the summer of 1958. In response to an appeal to Washington by a Lebanese government facing an internal uprising promoted by Nasserite Syria and Egypt, Eisenhower sent nearly 120,000 troops. No nuclear weapons were taken. Nor was the American intervention solely an American undertaking, since it was a collaborative project with the British in Jordan. The American landing was nevertheless to be seen to be "as much as of a garrison move as possible," with troops confined to the capital and its adjacent airfields.[45] No external power had invaded the country. The United States instead successfully displayed traditional gunboat diplomacy, with an intervention that fell into the grey area of an

Eisenhower Doctrine launched in the aftermath of the Suez crisis. This was the time when Eisenhower's continued emphasis on massive retaliation by nuclear weapons was being subjected to rising criticism from Congress, the media, and intellectuals. The Lebanon intervention served to demonstrate the fact that the United States had an effective military capability to counter small wars if it judged that this would not provoke the Soviet Union or that the conflict would not drag the nation into any long-term commitment.

Perhaps the two Taiwan offshore crises (the first between 1954 and 1955, and the second in 1958) were more difficult and delicate for Eisenhower to deal with, especially as Washington could expect little or no support from America's European allies if the United States intervened. Washington was not clear what were the motives behind China's bombardment of Quemoy, and was concerned that it was a prelude to Beijing's invasion of Taiwan. Moreover, Jiang Jieshi's (Chiang Kai-shek) Nationalist China regarded its retention of these offshore islands as "their main hope of returning to the mainland," while the United States hoped to avoid a major war with China over the offshore islands. Eisenhower was clear that if "we get our prestige involved anywhere then we can't get out." On the other hand, if China became involved in a war with the United States, the Soviet Union would certainly "help China without getting involved itself," as it had during the Korean War.[46]

Chinese Party Chairman Mao Zedong's objectives during these two crises fluctuated from time to time. It is clear that he did not mind creating a degree of international crisis in order to increase the revolutionary mood at home (which was necessary in view of his Great Leap Forward campaign in 1958) and abroad, but he was certainly not prepared to fight the United States militarily over Taiwan.[47] Mao's familiar description of nuclear weapons as a "paper tiger" is now seen by scholars as more of a rhetoric. He feared America's massive retaliation strategy during the 1954–55 crisis. By 1958, the United States moved to the debate over the use of tactical nuclear weapons or clean weapons, and Beijing interpreted this to mean that the United States might choose to use these weapons in a local conflict, and to counter this threat, China itself decided to become a nuclear power. Thus, Eisenhower's massive retaliation strategy did work to a degree by scaring the Chinese, but this did not prevent them from probing the Americans over the Taiwan question.[48]

In the end, the United States resorted to a spectrum of political and military measures to discourage Communist China from taking an aggressive stance against the Nationalist Chinese: a UN resolution, the conclusion of the U.S.–Nationalist Chinese mutual security treaty (signed on 2 December 1954), and the so-called "Formosa" (Taiwan) resolution. This gave the president congressional authority to use armed force to protect Taiwan and the Pescadores against armed attack and included the protection of "such related positions and territories of that area now in the friendly hands" for as long as they were regarded as essential to the security of Taiwan and the Pescadores. The president assured Congress, however, that the United States would not "enlarge its defensive obligations beyond Taiwan and the Pescadores."[49]

The Eisenhower administration also issued veiled threats to use nuclear weapons against mainland China, while trying to persuade Jiang to evacuate Quemoy and Matsu or to downgrade the islands to the status of outposts. In the second crisis in 1958, the administration seriously suspected that Mao intended to re-take Taiwan, possibly "with Soviet backing"; although Mao had not discussed his plan for the shelling of the islands with Khrushchev during their August meeting, and the subsequent Communist Chinese action took Moscow by surprise. To the particular horror of its European allies, the crisis also brought the United States close to a general war against China. The United States resorted to gunboat diplomacy, with limited support designed to protect the passage of Nationalist China's supplies to the offshore islands, and the president authorized the despatch of tactical fighters, tactical bombers, reconnaissance and transport planes to Taiwan as a "precautionary" measure.[50] Although he did not make any definite response to pressure by the Nationalist Chinese leader, Jiang Jieshi, for American military intervention, Eisenhower did try to convince Beijing that the United States would "actively intervene . . . perhaps using nuclear weapons."[51] The ominous tensions thus created in the Taiwan area were, however, greater than either Chinese or American security interests warranted. Within two weeks after the crisis began, Beijing decided (as Khrushchev had been urging them to do behind the scenes) to climb down, and the crisis was defused.

Finally, the Berlin crisis (1958–59) probed America's determination to stand firm against Soviet threats in Europe. For Eisenhower, the confrontation over Berlin had far more significant implications for the United States than the crisis in the Far East. In November 1958, Khrushchev sent the West an ultimatum, demanding the withdrawal of the Western occupation troops from West Berlin, calling on the Western powers to acknowledge the legitimacy of East Germany. This threatened a clash with the Soviet Union in the NATO area, where the president had rejected any possibility of relying on conventional warfare. The threat of an all-out nuclear exchange implicit in the crisis suggested that the United States should not resort to any action which might be considered as provocative by the Kremlin. There was no possibility of waging ground warfare in Europe. In Berlin a garrison of only 12,000 security police and troops, including 4,000 Americans, faced the Red Army of 315,000 stationed in East Germany, plus 75,000 East Germans. From the beginning, the question was how to find a solution through diplomatic means.

Khrushchev apparently hoped that the West might be persuaded to abandon their position in Berlin or decide to deal with East Germany as "an independent state" to get access to Berlin in the future. It is now clear, however, that the Soviet leader wanted negotiations and not military conflict with the West over Berlin. The Eisenhower administration was initially flexible about the West's position. Dulles even contemplated dealing with the East Germans as Moscow's agents, but it was unlikely that Bonn could accept such a proposition, given that the Federal Republic of Germany under Konrad Adeanuer had laid down the so-called Hallstein doctrine in December 1955, whereby Bonn would refuse to have diplomatic contacts with those countries who recognized East Germany, except for the Soviet Union.[52]

In the face of Khrushchev's efforts to test America's determination, Eisenhower did not want to "move an inch from our rights" in Berlin. Nor would he allow the United States to be threatened into handing over West Berlin to the East German government, a regime which the Americans refused to recognize. Washington coordinated its responses with France and Britain, and the three powers showed a resolute determination not to abandon the city.[53]

To demonstrate to the Soviets that the United States was serious in its resolve not to be forced out of West Berlin, Eisenhower ordered the Pentagon, in January 1959, to embark on a "sufficient replacement" of American units stationed in Europe. Although this move was in fact merely a routine rotation of American troops, Eisenhower hoped that the Soviets would interpret it as a "sign of our determination." Eisenhower's top officials were also assembled at the White House on 29 January 1959 to discuss possible Western military options if the Soviet Union turned over control of the access routes to Berlin to the East Germans on 27 May as it threatened. The Joint Chiefs of Staff suggested that the United States should send an armored division to Berlin, but Eisenhower did not think that this was desirable in "a non resistance situation." Nor would one division be sufficient if the West was forced to try to occupy the "entire [East] German zone." Secretary Dullles agreed that the United States would be "risking defeat and humiliation by the use of one division." In any case, Eisenhower had no intention of waging ground warfare in Europe. Instead, parallel with military preparations of "a kind that would be detectable by Soviet intelligence," the United States tried to encourage Moscow to agree to a meeting of the foreign ministers (as suggested by the British) of the Western allies and the Soviet Union.[54]

Since the West had made it clear that the Soviet proposal on Berlin was unacceptable, Khrushchev realized that the pressure he could exert on the West to force a compromise over Berlin was extremely limited, and he began to look for a graceful exit. In March, the Soviet leader invited Eisenhower to visit the Soviet Union, and also agreed to the resumption of the four-power conference of foreign ministers. Khrushchev also told the British prime minister, Harold Macmillan, who visited Moscow between 21 February and 3 March, that the deadline (27 May) was not meant to be an "ultimatum."[55]

In September 1959, when Eisenhower met Khrushchev at Camp David (Dulles had died by then), the four-power Geneva conference had reached a stalemate over Berlin and Germany, while the Soviets had extended the deadline or the resolution of the Berlin crisis to 27 November 1959. Eisenhower realized that there could be no early solution to the German question, including Berlin, and this was the only aspect of the subject on which he and Khrushchev agreed at Camp David.[56]

Conclusion

The differences between the Cold War and the September 11 terrorist attacks are immense, but the fundamental similarity is also stunning. 9/11 was a wake up call for pushing "national security" back to the forefront of the national political agenda as it had been during the Cold War. 9/11 led the United States to prepare for a surprise attack wherever and whenever this might occur. When the world entered the nuclear missile age in the 1950s, America's initial reaction was somber. Eisenhower reminded his close advisers in 1960 that "For the first time in its history the United States is now fearful, the reason being, of course, the existence of a surprise attack capability on the part of the Russians."[57] The West knew then who was its enemy. What the United States did not know was how difficult, despite America's superiority in technology, it would prove to eliminate the deadly Soviet ICBM threat to the nation. The United States received virtually no advanced warning of the timing or the place of the next Communist territorial advance from which a surprise attack could easily have been made against the nation. Communism came as close to America as Cuba, Guatemala, Nicaragua, and El Salvador.

What Eisenhower did not do then was merely to equate U.S. national interests with national military security. Eisenhower sought to make good use of American military power, but knew its limits. The Cold War, though a mortal threat to the American way of life and Western democratic values, was ultimately for him a lengthy hearts and minds campaign.[58] Its end would come, he believed, correctly as it turned out, when Western values prevailed over those of the East. Waging this type of war, Eisenhower believed, required cooperation with America's allies who shared the same values and beliefs as the United States. It was a war for freedom, and that was how he understood the Cold War. Throughout these international crises, Eisenhower kept a vigilant eye on Moscow's possible reactions, and dealt with each crisis in a calm and pragmatic manner. The president never resolved any of the crises mentioned in this paper. Instead, what he tried to do was to defuse them at a reasonable cost and within a reasonable time.

Eisenhower did not formulate a doctrine for his intervention methodology as Casper Weinberger (defense secretary during the Reagan years) did in the Weinberger doctrine in the aftermath of the Lebanon intervention of 1982–83, or the similar Powell Doctrine announced in 1992 by Colin Powell in connection with U.S. humanitarian intervention in Somalia. The use of force, asserted Weinberger, should be considered "only as a last resort" when "truly vital interests are at stake," and when the government had secured the "support of the American people and Congress." If a decision to intervene with combat forces was made, they must be deployed in "sufficient numbers to win" and given "clearly defined political and military objectives," which in the case of the Lebanon intervention and in the Vietnam War had been clearly lacking.[59]

In contrast, Eisenhower wanted to keep his hands free when he faced a crisis, rather than being bound by a cut-and-dried formula for intervention. Eisenhower considered the use of military force in the traditional and conventional sense and the introduction of nuclear weapons undermined the notion of a decisive victory by force. Commenting on the Vietnam War in the 1960s, he stated: "if you go in, go in to win as soon as possible with all available means. The object of the war . . . was to destroy the enemy's will to resist further. . . . Of course, . . . the kind of heavy blows that can be dealt today cost many lives; that is the nature of war. But in the long run, a quick resolution of the struggle can save many more lives." Neither did he relish the idea of fighting limited war again in Asia after the experience of the Korean War.[60] His priorities remained nuclear deterrence, waging the Cold War by non-military means, and limited war.

Eisenhower, however, possessed a number of basic ideas when he dealt with crises. He avoided incurring new security commitments by hastily intervening in a country. Despite what he said about the Vietnam War, Eisenhower generally avoided the use of military force unless it was absolutely necessary. He hated war—he once stated that war was "terrible." He had to write many letters of condolences to "bereaved mothers and wives," which was in his words, "a sobering experience."[61] Even when Eisenhower felt the use of force might be justifiable, he wanted to be convinced that this was indeed the case by seeking support from the administration, the public, Congress, and American allies. In other words, Eisenhower sought legitimacy. He often spent considerable time talking to his subordinates, looking for alternatives to the use of force, and provoking or airing many different ideas at NSC meetings before he made a decision.

These basic ideas were guided by Eisenhower's notions of balance, common sense, initiative, and his familiar case-by-case approach. Even during the height of the Cold War when Eisenhower was seriously concerned about the danger of nuclear war, he knew the United States had the luxury of choice: the choice to engage or not with a crisis far away from his country, and the luxury of time: the time to think about what was "the best for America?"[62] In the final analysis, these came from the considerable degree of confidence the president had in his power of judgment, in his loyal advisers and trustworthy allies (with whom he had occasional disagreements) and in his belief that the enemy would eventually weaken and decay within. Dwight Eisenhower thus adopted a pragmatic, clear-headed, and ultimately successful approach to the problems the United States confronted in the 1950s.

Notes

1. Dillon Anderson, "Recollection of Eisenhower," 11, box 1, Dillon Anderson Papers, Hoover Institution Archives, Stanford University.

2. Stephen E. Ambrose, *Eisenhower: The President, 1953–1969* (London: Allen & Unwin, 1984), 2:89; "Probable Long Term Development of the Soviet bloc and Western Power Position," 8 July 1953, *Foreign Relations of the United States, 1952–1954* (Washington, D.C.: Government Printing Office, 1988), 8:1196–205 (hereafter cited as *FRUS* with years and volume).

3. Stephen E. Ambrose, "Epilogue: Eisenhower's Legacy," in Günter Bischof and Stephen E. Ambrose, eds., *Eisenhower: A Centenary Assessment* (Baton Rouge: Louisiana State University Press, 1995), 248.

4. Jeffrey Record, "Threat Confusion and Its Penalties," *Survival* 46 (Summer 2004):52–53.

5. Dwight D. Eisenhower, "First Inaugural Address," 20 Jan. 1953, <http://www.barleby.com/124/pres54.html>.

6. Saki R. Dockrill, *The End of the Cold War Era: The Transformation of the Global Security Order* (London: Hodder Arnold, 2005), chap. 9.

7. For Eisenhower's New Look, see Saki R. Dockrill, *Eisenhower's New Look National Security Policy, 1953–1961* (London: Macmillan, 1994), 19–47; Dwight D. Eisenhower, "Second Inaugural Address," 21 Jan. 1957, <http://www.bareleby.com/124/pres55.html>.

8. See NSC 162/2, *FRUS, 1952–1954*, 2:577–97; Eisenhower Diary, 6 Jan. 1953, box 9, DDE Diary Series, Ann Whitman File (AWF), Dwight D. Eisenhower Library (DDEL), Abilene, Kans.; John Foster Dulles, "A Policy of Boldness," *Life*, 19 May 1952, 146.

9. *Public Papers of the Presidents of the United States, 1960* (Washington D.C.: Government Printing Office, 1961), 168–69.

10. Eisenhower to Gruenther, in *The Diaries of Dwight D. Eisenhower, 1953–1961* (Maryland: A Microfilm Project of University Publications of America, 1986) (hereafter cited as *DDE Diaries*), Liddell Hart Centre for Military Archives (LHCMA), King's College, London.

11. Paul Kennedy, "Grand Strategy in War and Peace: Towards a Broader Definition," in idem, ed., *Grand Strategies in War and Peace* (New Haven, Conn.: Yale University Press, 1991), 1–5ff.

12. Cutler to Eisenhower, 16 Mar. 1953, *FRUS, 1952–1954*, 2:248–51; Fred I. Greenstein, *The Hidden-Hand Presidency: Eisenhower as Leader* (New York: Basic Books, 1982), 124–26.

13. NSC 162/2, *FRUS, 1952–1954*, 2:580–81; see also Robert R. Bowie and Richard H. Immerman, *Waging Peace: How Eisenhower Shaped an Enduring Cold War Strategy* (Oxford: Oxford University Press, 1998), 154.

14. Michael Howard and Peter Paret, eds. and trans., *Carl von Clausewitz: On War* (Princeton, N.J.: Princeton University Press, 1976), 358: Eisenhower to Dulles, 5 Dec. 1955, *FRUS, 1955–1957*, 9:11.

15. "The Evolution of Foreign Policy," *Department of State Bulletin*, 25 Jan. 1954, 107–10.

16. Dwight D. Eisenhower, "Eisenhower's Farewell Address to the Nation," 17 Jan. 1961, <http://mcadams.posc.mu.edu/ike.htm>.

17. NSC 165th meeting, 7 Oct. 1953, *FRUS, 1952–1954*, 2:515–23ff.

18. Dwight D. Eisenhower, *Mandate for Change: The White House Years, 1953–1956* (New York: Doubleday, 1963), 446; Eisenhower to Gruenther, 4 May 1953, *DDE Diaries*, LHCMA.

19. John Lewis Gaddis, *The Strategies of Containment: A Critical Appraisal of Post-war American National Security Policy* (New York: Oxford University Press, 1982), 136.

20. Ambrose, "Epilogue," 253.

21. Eisenhower's minute on conservation with Bernard Baruch, 28 Mar. 1956, *DDE Diaries*, LHCMA.

22. Ambrose, "Epilogue," 254.

23. Andrew J. Goodpaster, interview by Maclyn Burg, 26 June 1975, Washington, D.C.. Oral History, DDEL; NSC 325th meeting, 27 May 1957, *FRUS, 1955–1957*, 19:503.

24. Eisenhower's meeting with Goodpaster and Admiral Radford, 14 May 1956, *FRUS, 1955–1957*, 19:302.

25. NSC 325th meeting, 27 May 1957, ibid., 502–3; para.15, NSC 5707/8, 3 June 1957, ibid., 512.

26. Para.11, NSC 5707/8; see also Dockrill, *Eisenhower's New Look*, 200–202.

27. Ambrose, "Epilogue," 252; George C. Herring and Richard H. Immerman, "Eisenhower, Dulles, and Dien Bien Phu: 'The Day We Didn't Go to War' Revisited," in Lawrence S. Kaplan, Denise Artaud, and Mark R. Rubin, *Dien Bien Phu and the Crisis of Franco-American Relations, 1954–1955* (Wilmington, Del.: Scholarly Resources, 1990), 82.

28. Dockrill, *Eisenhower's New Look*, 94–96.

29. Herring and Immerman, "Eisenhower, Dulles, and Dien Bien Phu," 94.

30. Percy Cradock, *Know Your Enemy: How the Joint Intelligence Committee Saw the World* (London: John Murray, 2002), 109.

31. Saki R. Dockrill, *Britain's Retreat from East of Suez: The Choice between Europe and the World?* (Basingstoke: Palgrave Macmillan, 2002), 17–18.

32. Cradock, *Know Your Enemy,* 112.

33. Richard J. Aldrich, *The Hidden Hand: Britain, America and Cold War Secret Intelligence* (London: John Murray, 2001), 477–79.

34. Chester J. Pach, Jr. and Elmo Richardson, *The Presidency of Dwight D. Eisenhower* (Lawrence: Kansas University Press, 1991), 126–27; Cradock, *Know Your Enemy,* 118.

35. Dwight D. Eisenhower, *Waging Peace, 1956–1961* (New York: Doubleday, 1965), 36; Robert J. Watson, *History of the Office of the Secretary of Defense,* vol. 4, *Into the Missile Age, 1956–1960* (Washington, D.C.: Historical Office, Office of the Secretary of Defense, 1997), 53.

36. Cradock, *Know Your Enemy,* 122.

37. Diane B. Kunz, *The Economic Diplomacy of the Suez Crisis* (Chapel Hill: University of North Carolina Press, 1991), 116.

38. Ambrose, *Eisenhower: The President,* 368–69; John Ranelagh, *The Agency: The Rise and Decline of the CIA* (London: Widenfeld & Nicolson, 1986), 300.

39. Christian F. Ostermann, "The United States, the East German Uprising of 1953, and the Limits of Rollback" working paper, no. 11 (1994), Cold War International History Project (CWIHP), Woodrow Wilson International Center for Scholars, Washington, D.C.

40. Legation in Hungary to Department of State, 23 Oct. 1956, *FRUS, 1955–1957,* 25:263–65. See also Csaba Békés, "The 1956 Hungarian Revolution and World Politics" working paper, no. 16 (1996), CWIHP.

41. 42d meeting of the Special Committee on Soviet and Related Problems, Washington D.C., 1 Nov. 1956, *FRUS, 1955–1957,* 25:359–63; Dulles to Lodge, 2 Nov. 1956, ibid., 365.

42. Jerrold L. Schecter, ed. and trans., with Vyacheslav Luchkov, *Khrushchev Remembers: The Glasnost Tapes* (Boston: Little, Brown, 1990), 124, and for the fate of Nagy, see 126n36; Andrei Gromyko, *Memories* (London: Hutchinson, 1989), 23; Bennett Kovrig, *Of Walls and Bridges: The United States and Eastern Europe* (New York: New York University Press, 1991), 85–89.

43. Eisenhower, *Waging Peace,* 95.

44. Ibid., 88–89; Stephen Ambrose with Richard Immerman, *Ike's Spies: Eisenhower and the Espionage Establishment* (New York: Doubleday, 1981), 238.

45. Eisenhower, *Waging Peace,* 275; Nathan Twining, *Neither Liberty nor Safety : A Hard Look at U.S. Military Policy and Strategy* (New York: Holt, Rinehart & Winston), 64–65.

46. NSC 214th meeting, 12 Sept. 1954, *FRUS, 1952–1955,* 14/pt.1:615–17.

47. Chen Jian, *Mao's China and the Cold War* (Chapel Hill: University of North Carolina Press, 2001), 168–83.

48. Shu Guang Zhang, "Between 'Paper' and 'Real Tigers': Mao's View of Nuclear Weapons," in John Lewis Gaddis, Philip H. Gordon, Ernest R. May, and Jonathan Rosenberg, *Cold War Statesmen Confront the Bomb* (Oxford: Oxford University Press, 1999), 200–203.

49. NSC 233rd meeting, 21 Jan. 1955, *FRUS, 1955–1957,* 2:90–96; Eisenhower's message to Congress, 24 Jan. 1955, and congressional resolution, 29 Jan. 1955, both in ibid., 115–19, 162–63.

50. Dockrill, *Eisenhower's New Look,* 242–45.

51. Memo on "Taiwan Situation," 4 Sept. 1954, *DDE Diaries,* LHCMA; Conference with Eisenhower, 25 Aug. 1958, ibid.

52. John Lewis Gaddis, *We Now Know: Rethinking Cold War History* (Oxford: Clarendon, 1997), 140.

53. Eisenhower-Dulles telephone conversation, 24 Nov. 1958, *FRUS, 1958–1960: Berlin Crisis,* 8:118; Conference with Eisenhower, 11 Dec. 1958, ibid., 172–77; Eisenhower, *Waging Peace,* 337.

54. Eisenhower, *Waging Peace,* 330; White House meeting, 29 Jan. 1959, *FRUS, 1958–1960,* 8:299–305. See also Kori Schake, "A Broader Range of Choice? U.S. Policy in the 1958 and 1961 Berlin Crises," in John Gearson and Kori Schake, eds., *The Berlin Wall Crisis: Perspectives on Cold War Alliances* (Basingstoke: Palgrave Macmillan, 2002), 22–29; Mark Trachtenberg,

A Constructive Peace: The Making of the European Settlement, 1945–1963 (Princeton, N.J.: Princeton University Press, 1999), 256–63.

55. Dockrill, *Eisenhower's New Look,* 250–51.

56. Thomas A. Schwartz, "Eisenhower and the Germans," in Bischof and Ambrose, eds., *Eisenhower,* 220.

57. Eisenhower's meeting with Herter, Dillon et al., 22 Apr. 1960, *DDE Diaries,* LHCMA.

58. Richard H. Immerman, *John Foster Dulles: Piety, Pragmatism, and Power in U.S. Foreign Policy* (Wilmington, Del.: Scholarly Resources, 1999), 61–62.

59. Casper Weinberger, "U.S. Defense Strategy," *Foreign Affairs* (Spring 1986), 686–87.

60. Dillon Anderson Papers, box 1, Hoover Institution Archives, Stanford University.

61. Ambrose, "Epilogue," 247.

62. Andrew J. Goodpaster, "Foreword," in Bischof and Ambrose, eds., *Eisenhower,* xix.

Eisenhower and the Korean War: Cautionary Tale and Hopeful Precedent

Allan R. Millett

Like most real history, the Korean War left ambiguous, selective, and complex lessons for the policymakers of the Eisenhower administration. The president himself, to borrow Dean Acheson's phrase, had been "present at the creation" of the war in 1950. He had then distanced himself from it as Supreme Allied Commander Europe (SACEUR) and as a presidential candidate. He inherited the conflict—a war to be ended—as president. Yet the war never became a defining experience for Dwight D. Eisenhower, nor did it play an inordinate role in his foreign and defense policies. His geo-strategic views had developed well before 1950, most obviously during World War II. The Korean conflict, a post-colonial civil war that became an internationalized regional conflict, was not even unique enough in its own time to dominate the national security conceptualization that became "the New Look" or "the Great Equation." It might have encouraged a "Great Evasion," an unwillingness to deal with instability in the Middle East and Asia, but instead the Eisenhower administration coped, more or less successfully, with comparable turmoil in the Philippines, Thailand, Iran, and Lebanon. It is true that the next land war in Asia—to be avoided at all costs according to the Korean "never again" strategic gurus—awaited a change of presidents, but President Eisenhower committed an Army-Marine Corps expeditionary force to Lebanon in 1958. So much for avoiding the use of American ground forces in local wars.[1]

The Korean War fit into Eisenhower's vision of a proper national security policy for an era of Cold War competition with the Soviet Union. It did so as an example of the strengths and weaknesses of a security system based on forward, collective conventional defense, reinforced by the deterrent influence of nuclear weapons of varied destructive capabilities and delivery systems. The war liberated national security policy from the unrealistic economic shackles imposed by the Truman administration, but its presumed effect on future defense budgets, fiscal policy, and national economic growth made it a war of diminishing utility. The Korean War had also reshaped the politics of north Asia before Eisenhower took office. Although it strengthened the alliance between the Soviet Union and People's Republic of China, the war also had an important, positive impact on the growing alliance of free market economies and stable governments in non-Communist Asia. Japan signed a peace treaty in 1952 and moved toward a mutual security agreement with the United States (1960). The Republic of China returned from the dead on Taiwan with a security agreement and economic and military aid from the United States. Anathema to the State Department as late as 1952, President Syngman Rhee sold his acceptance of the Armistice

Agreement (July 1953) for a bilateral mutual security treaty, almost $1 billion in aid, American soldiers guarding the Demilitarized Zone, and a chance to address a joint session of Congress. Rhee's demands had been constant since 1948 but Eisenhower did complete the negotiations, begrudgingly, accepting most of Rhee's terms in 1953.[2]

One might argue that Eisenhower received useful lessons for dealing with erstwhile Third World security partners from Syngman Rhee. However, the president had survived almost forty years of Army service, a career in which he dealt face-to-face with Douglas MacArthur, George C. Marshall, Franklin D. Roosevelt, Winston Churchill, Bernard Law Montgomery, and Charles de Gaulle. He would hardly find Rhee more than an occasional aggravation. However antique some of Eisenhower's social and economic views now seem, no twentieth-century president took office with more direct foreign policy experience, before or since. The core lesson of the Korean War was how little personal influence Eisenhower had on the war's causes, conduct, and consequences, a telling lesson about the limitations of the modern American presidency.[3]

Eisenhower and Korea, 1945–1950

Eisenhower's legendary "hidden hand" is plainly visible in one of the decisive American actions that caused the Korean War: the final withdrawal of U.S. Army troops from Korea in July 1949. Acts, not words, turned Joseph Stalin's conditional *nyet* of March 1949 to Kim Il-sung's invasion plans into an affirmative *da* a year later. One of these acts was the withdrawal of American tactical units—the 7th Infantry Division and U.S. XXIV Corps troops—from South Korea. Stalin himself made such a withdrawal one of several preconditions to a "war of national unification." As Army Chief-of-Staff and de facto Joint Chiefs of Staff (JCS) Chairman until 1949, Eisenhower played a key role in pulling American troops out of Korea. The fate of XXIV Corps and U.S. Army Forces in Korea became a matter of JCS attention in 1947 when the State Department despaired of direct negotiations with the Soviet Union over unifying Korea and turned to the United Nations for help. The JCS read the runes correctly: Korea would be divided into two hostile regimes, both bent on military unification. Korea became an official potential trouble spot, so identified by the JCS in drafting the FY 1949 defense budget in February 1948. Two months later, however, the Joint Strategic Plans Committee identified Korea as irrelevant to the execution of HALFMOON/FLEETWOOD or Joint Emergency War Plan No. 1, a global conflict with the Soviet Union waged primarily by bombers with nuclear weapons. The American troops in Korea (about 45,000 officers and men) should be withdrawn and transferred to the U.S. Eighth Army in Japan. Predictably, General Douglas MacArthur as Supreme Commander Allied Powers, the occupation authority, supported the withdrawal plan, assuming correctly that he would get the 7th Infantry Division.

Although he retired to become president of Columbia University in June 1947, Eisenhower, officially a special advisor to the president and the secretary of defense, remained active in defense affairs until August 1949 when Eisenhower's friend and collaborator, General Omar N. Bradley, became Chairman, Joint Chiefs of Staff. After an abortive attempt to supplement the FY 1949 and FY 1950 defense budgets, the JCS faced a president and Secretary of Defense Louis A. Johnson determined to set a ceiling on defense spending at $15 billion for FY 1951. Truman summoned Eisenhower back to Washington in January 1949 to set force levels for the services if the JCS could not do it within the budget ceiling. Eisenhower did not yet have JEWP-1 for guidance, but he knew what contingency plan assumptions were operative. He imposed four different budget ceilings on each service department and forced the JCS to prepare force structures for each ceiling (designated "Ike I-IV"). Almost as soon as the JCS finally produced an acceptable force structure and budgets, Truman dropped the ceiling to $13 billion. Eisenhower was as surprised as the JCS. The general did not like Truman's budget cutting, but a good soldier—as he testified to Congress—he followed orders, even if it gutted the U.S. Army's active divisions.[4]

Eisenhower's position on the value of American troops in Korea shifted with the Army's mandated force reductions. As Army Chief-of-Staff, he testified in 1947 that a hasty troop withdrawal might have unpleasant consequences. He later recalled that the American units might have been an effective deterrent: "If we had left a division or two in Korea, there would never been a Korean War." This bit of insight, however, came after 1950 and would have had no more impact than State's warnings from 1948 into 1949. Eisenhower later admitted: "I didn't foresee that the trouble spot would be Korea." In any event, the JCS, not Congress, made deployment plans. Eisenhower consistently supported the withdrawal of American troops from Korea in both contingency planning and budget-drafting as the defense budgets and force structure shrank in 1948–50.

No influential member of the armed forces senior leadership wanted to keep American combat troops in Korea. That argument came from senior Asian foreign service officers of the State Department, who convinced Secretary of State Dean C. Acheson that withdrawal was a clear signal of abandonment to the Communists. Although supported by alarmist—and accurate—analysis from the Central Intelligence Agency (CIA) that a troop withdrawal could be the cause of a wider war in Korea, Acheson negotiated only a one-year reprieve, the conversion of the U.S. 31st Infantry Regiment and reinforcing units into the 5th Regimental Combat Team, stationed across the Kaesong-Munsan-Uijongbu invasion corridors north of Seoul. The 5th RCT, however, shipped out for Schofield Barracks, Hawaii, in June–July 1949, where it virtually disbanded.[5]

The JCS position on Korea's fate may be followed in the original drafting and subsequent revision of National Security Council Memorandum 8 (NSC 8), "The Position of the United States with Respect to Korea," 2 April 1948. The military planners argued that Korea's future did not depend on the presence of American troops, but upon South Korea's economic development, political maturation, and military effectiveness. The United States should *not* provide a clear "guarantee [of] the political independence and political independence and territorial integrity of South Korea, by force of arms if necessary" against "external aggression or internal subversion." Truman approved NSC 8 the same day, although he did not attend the Council meeting or study the supporting analysis. General Eisenhower was not on the record about NSC 8, but he presumably agreed to the troop withdrawal as a budgetary and war planning action. The same day—3 April in Korea—Communist rebels began a guerrilla war on Cheju-do Island, a war that spread to the mainland in October and still plagued rural southern Korea in June 1950. The insurgency did not convince the Army to do more than maintain a 500-man military mission in Korea, the Korean Military Advisory Group (KMAG), whose task was to create an eight-division, 60,000-man South Korean army while fighting 5,000 partisans at the same time.[6]

The irony of Eisenhower's muted role in influencing Korean policy is that he filled the institutional role of a senior military advisor whose advice should be closely bounded by worst-case contingency planning, force structuring, and defense funding—not the diplomacy of deterrence. As president, Eisenhower cautioned his own Joint Chiefs that he wanted them to take a far broader view of national security planning than just preparing budgets and championing weapons systems.

Eisenhower and Korea, 1950–1952

As surprised by the North Korean invasion as any serving member of the JCS or Army senior staff officer, General Eisenhower went to Washington on 28 June, three days after the first attacks, to be briefed on the Korean situation. Just back from a conference with MacArthur, Omar Bradley had been felled by the flu, but Eisenhower met with the Army's key leaders: J. Lawton Collins, Wade Haislip, Charles L. Bolte, Alfred M. Gruenther, and Matthew B. Ridgway. Eisenhower found his friends awaiting more presidential guidance on the depth of America's commitment. He himself felt uncomfortable with Truman's reluctance to use the word "war" in discussing the Korean crisis. He felt he had "no business" talking about Truman's decision to intervene, but he also thought "we'll have a dozen Koreas soon if we don't take a firm stand," but he feared Truman would not prosecute the war with vigor. Like MacArthur, Eisenhower believed "an appeal to force cannot, by its nature, be a partial one."[7]

Eisenhower, however, had some very precise recommendations for the Army's leaders. The crisis provided a new political context that should allow mobilization and rearmament. The highest priority should be sending two divisions to Europe. As for waging war in Korea, no part of Korea should be off limits to American strikes. Even nuclear weapons should be considered. The general believed he and Truman shared the same views on these matters. The challenge would be to supervise MacArthur, who would run his own war his way and keep Truman poorly informed. In his turn, Collins told Eisenhower that the entire Army staff agreed with his assessments.[8] Reassured, Eisenhower met with reporters and told them he believed the president had no choice but to intervene: "The best check for sustaining world peace was to take a firm stand, and when our Government guaranteed the Government of South Korea, there was no course but to do what President Truman did."[9]

Eisenhower and his mentor, George C. Marshall, accepted Truman's invitation to discuss Korea over lunch at the White House on 6 July. Both generals assured the president they supported his Korean commitment. Truman called them back to the colors, Marshall as secretary of defense and Eisenhower to be Supreme Allied Commander Europe: NATO's field general. At the time of the Chinese intervention, Eisenhower saw Truman trapped by his decision to unify Korea by force. "And poor HST, a fine man who, in the middle of a stormy lake, known nothing of swimming." By 5 December 1950, Eisenhower now characterized the Korean situation as "tragic."[10]

In his eighteen months as SACEUR, Eisenhower followed the Korean War through limited OSD/JCS reports and correspondence with Robert A. Lovett, Marshall's deputy and later successor as defense secretary and from W. Averell Harriman, director of mutual security programs. The Pentagon did not share all its classified assessments because the JCS feared security violations by European officers. Eisenhower had his own concerns in building a coalition army and tactical air force to defend West Germany. He did not respond strongly to MacArthur's relief or the appointment of Ridgway and Lt. Gen. James Van Fleet to command United Nations Command (UNC) and U.S. Eighth Army. He sympathized with MacArthur's disgrace but urged his old commander to back coalition defense in the hearings on Asian strategy. His own pressing problem was extracting British and French divisions from their imperial deployments. He worried that the stalemated war of late 1951 and 1952 would fuel public discontent and congressional fiscal stinginess and kill the emergency rearmament program begun in late 1950 and designed to checkmate a predicted Soviet readiness for war in 1954. The more he studied the Korean "sorry mess," he wrote his friend Swede Hazlett, the less he thought he understood it. He saw no obvious way out of the war that preserved America's reputation as an ally and convinced the Communists that conventional aggression would be met with force. "I guess the most we can hope out of the thing is that soon the Communists will quit pushing the conflict (terminating it somewhat as they did the attacks on Greece), and that we succeed in developing a sufficient strength among the South Koreans to withdraw the vast bulk of our forces."[11]

As he weighed his decision to run for the presidency as the candidate of the internationalist wing of the Republican party, Eisenhower reviewed his own thinking on Korea. He still believed the commitment of 1950 had been unavoidable: "it is my own opinion that, had we allowed the South Korean Republic, which was sponsored by the free nations, to go under, we would have by this time been kicked out of Southeast Asia completely, and it would have been touch and go, as to whether India would still be outside the Iron Curtain." The economic future of the United States and Western Europe depended upon access to the raw materials of post-colonial Asia, but Eisenhower saw the Korean intervention principally as an example of America's moral commitment to oppose Communist military adventurism in regions important to American security: "I am one of those who believes we did the right thing in defying and opposing the Communist advance into Southern Korea."[12]

As Eisenhower moved more clearly into an active campaign for the Republican nomination in the first five months of 1952, he opened an extensive correspondence with John Foster Dulles, who had already begun campaigning to become the next secretary of state. Although he shared Eisenhower's primary emphasis on European security, Dulles stressed the importance of China, Taiwan, Japan, and Korea to global peace. Dulles had been an active participant in the Korean intervention decision. As a State Department special representative, he had visited South Korea and Japan in June 1950 to reassure Syngman Rhee that the United States was committed to the survival of the Republic of Korea (ROK), and to begin discussions on a Japanese peace treaty. Even more rapidly than MacArthur, Dulles now urged American military action to save South Korea, whose security he linked to Japanese-American relations and the defense of Formosa. As their personal relationship developed, Eisenhower and Dulles discovered a like-mindedness on America's security challenges. Their vision included ending the Korean War but doing so only at a time and in a way that did not endanger the future of South Korea or weaken the developing Asian coalition that opposed Soviet-Chinese socialist, revolutionary imperialism.[13]

Safely nominated by the Republican Convention, 7–12 July 1952, Eisenhower campaigned on a foreign policy plank that stressed economic and psychological challenges but did not ignore the defense requirements of continuous and stable containment through nuclear deterrence and forward, collective defense. He avoided any stress on ending the Korean War, although he criticized Truman for failing to defend Formosa before June 1950. He accepted his responsibility for removing American troops in 1948–49, but he stressed that the 1950 commitment had changed the Asian strategic calculus. In fact, the Truman administration put the first pressure on Eisenhower to make his Korean views more public and precise. The most generous interpretation of the Truman-Acheson political entrapment of August 1952 is that the administration did not want the Panmunjom negotiations poisoned by American electoral politics. A less sympathetic interpretation is that Truman wanted Eisenhower to endorse the negotiations or, refusing to do so, expose himself as an irresponsible critic and partisan but planless candidate.[14]

On 12 August, at Truman's invitation, Democratic candidate Adlai Stevenson met with General Bradley and CIA director Walter Bedell Smith to discuss the status of Korea negotiations and Asian security issues. Eisenhower objected to this favoritism, but Truman apologized for an administrative error that had prevented Eisenhower from receiving the same invitation. Bradley reassured his old friend that there had been a misunderstanding, but Eisenhower was unconvinced by a "repeated" invitation and Truman's apology. He did not accept the invitation nor the offer of weekly foreign policy briefings. As Eisenhower later wrote his running mate, Richard Nixon, the only real alternative in Korea was to "stay the course" as the South Korean armed forces increased and improved and the Korean economy grew. In the meantime, they should build other alliances that would deter the Chinese-Soviet alliance. Eisenhower's campaign advisory team and speechwriters, especially C. D. Jackson, believed that Eisenhower needed to be more aggressive in criticizing Truman's handling of the

Korean crisis. Eisenhower should hint that as president he would end the Korean War on his terms without expanding the war.[15]

In a series of speeches begun in Champaign, Illinois on 2 October and culminating with a major address in New York City on 17 October, Eisenhower launched an attack on the Truman administration's handling of the Korean situation since 1945, especially "inviting" the invasion of June 1950. In a speech in San Francisco on 8 October, Eisenhower made a commitment: "Without weakening the security of the free world, I pledge full dedication to the job of finding an intelligent and honorable way to end the tragic toll of America's casualties in Korea. No one can pledge you more." Gauging media reaction to Eisenhower's first Korea speeches, C. D. Jackson, who as an Army lieutenant colonel had served as a media and psychological warfare expert on Eisenhower's wartime staff, thought the candidate needed a more forceful, positive message. Eisenhower wisely resisted specific war-ending proposals, but he agreed on one bit of campaign dramatics. In a speech on 14 October in Detroit, Eisenhower promised that if elected, "I shall go to Korea." The press impact was exactly what Jackson hoped, a strong general impression that America's most active and revered World War II senior field general had some personal insight on how to bring the war to a close without widening it.[16]

Eisenhower, President-Elect, 1952–1953

Empowered by a decisive electoral mandate in November 1952, Dwight D. Eisenhower understood that the Detroit pledge needed rapid redemption, and he immediately set his staff working on the trip to Korea. Since the trip was a Pentagon responsibility—and Robert Lovett and Omar Bradley took the mission seriously—Eisenhower had complete confidence that the trip presented an unparalleled opportunity to closet his advisors and cabinet and cabinet-level appointees-designate in military planes and ships. He would use the trip to lay his administration's fundamental plans for foreign and defense policy. The Korean War slid into a secondary issue behind "security with solvency," the long-term plans for rationale force-structuring, stable-state budgeting below current levels, and a NSC-centered decision-making architecture. Eisenhower wanted to see all the relevant studies and hear a wide range of expert opinion on security issues. Korea may have served as a negative example of how the government should *not* do business, but it did not emerge as a single powerful influence on the series of consultations that eventually produced NSC 162/2 "Basic National Security Policy," 30 October 1953.[17]

Eisenhower had no expectation that he would discover some magic formula for a Korean peace, and within his close circle of associates he admitted as much. He reassured Secretary of Defense Lovett that his real interest in Korea was learning about the plans to strengthen the South Korean armed forces and bolster the Korean economy. He would do nothing to compromise the continuing negotiations or follow some independent path in dealing with Syngman Rhee: "I am quite sure that you and my old friends there [the Pentagon] know that I am not pretending that I will find answers that they have overlooked."[18] Nevertheless, Eisenhower felt obligated to attend a pre-trip briefing at the White House on 18 November. His transition team, led by Henry Cabot Lodge and Joseph M. Dodge, was already at work in Washington, but he had remained in New York City, planning his trip and recruiting the key figures of his administration. He suspected Truman wanted something, and he was right.[19]

Eisenhower's White House visit satisfied none of the parties despite Truman's sincere effort to be cooperative. Neither man held the other in much esteem. The twenty-minute conversation between the president and president-elect became a monologue by Truman, who urged Eisenhower to do everything he could not to damage the sensitive negotiations at Panmunjom. Truman stressed that until 20 January 1953 he would be president, and he would exercise all those powers as he thought best. After Truman left the room, Dean Acheson, masking his irritation about the Republicans' vicious attacks on his personality and diplomacy, reviewed the state of the negotiations. The prisoners of war (POW) repatriation issue remained unsolved, and the Russians were attempting to use a coalition of neutral nations to stop a General Assembly Draft Resolution endorsing the principle of voluntary repatriation. Acheson asked Eisenhower to consider a public statement drafted by his staff and given to Lodge that gave Eisenhower's endorsement of the United Nations' role in solving the Korean War. Eisenhower acknowledged the seriousness of the issue, but made no commitment. He knew that State had refused to deal with Dulles, and he was in no mood to appease Truman. He did not issue the statement.[20]

Eisenhower turned to the JCS for information and advice that he found useful. Acheson told him that America's allies found the general's election worrisome; Eisenhower believed he could mend any fences he felt inclined to mend. He was more pleased to learn that the Chinese believed that his election, coupled with General Mark W. Clark's assignment to replace Ridgway as head of United Nations Command, meant they faced the threat of an intensified air war and amphibious landings in North Korea. The Communist armies broke off their October–November offensives and thickened their reserve divisions on both coasts, a nice demonstration of the Communists' sensitivity to their own misperceptions. Eisenhower had not yet publicly taken a position on the utility of nuclear weapons except as an ultimate deterrent, although he and Dulles had discussed whether the threat of nuclear weapons could deter or compel the end of conventional warfare, as in Korea. In early November, a representative of the Atomic Energy Commission briefed the president-elect on the results of the "MIKE Shot," the first test of a thermonuclear device (ten megatons) at Eniwetok. The day after his trip to the White House, Eisenhower received a two-hour tutorial at the Commission's headquarters on the state of America's nuclear programs. Eisenhower believed that he should adopt a declaratory policy of treating nuclear weapons as just another usable bomb, but he could not escape a sense of dread that nuclear weapons had given mankind the ultimate tool for human extinction.[21]

Eisenhower knew what he really wanted to know: the status of the South Korean army. He requested—and received—a complete report on the expansion of the army to twenty divisions, its artillery procurement program, its logistical system, its officer education and training program, and its creation of a complete training command. The answers were not reassuring. The reform of the ROK army was under-funded by $2 billion and could not be accomplished under the current military assistance program. The South Koreans, for example, had only half the ammunition they required. Military weapons, munitions, and vehicles that should have been sent to Korea had instead gone to French Indochina.[22]

Traveling to Korea by air, Eisenhower and his official party reached Seoul on 2 December, but returned to New York City on 14 December on the cruiser *Helena,* boarded at Guam on 6 December. The initial party included Dulles, Attorney General–designate Herbert Brownell, Secretary of Defense–designate Charles E. ("General Motors") Wilson, JCS Chairman Omar Bradley, CINCPAC Admiral Arthur W. Radford, Press Secretary James C. Hagerty, and Maj. Gen. Wilton B. Persons, USA, an Eisenhower aide and staff officer extraordinary. In Seoul they met Gens. Mark W. Clark and James Van Fleet. The visit, much to Syngman Rhee's dismay, was primarily military theater: pro forma situation briefings, receptions, and inspections of nine UNC units of differing nationalities. Eisenhower did enjoy a reunion with his son John, a major on the 7th Infantry Division's staff. Eisenhower already knew from Bradley the details of a Clark-Van Fleet plan to strike behind the Communist frontline armies, Operations Plan 8-52 (October 1952). Eisenhower did not find a plan that required seven more divisions and thirty-two artillery battalions very attractive, especially since the air plan contained a nuclear strike option on enemy air fields in Manchuria. The on-site discussions of the armistice negotiations with Lt. Gen. William K. Harrison, USA, another trusted Army contemporary, revealed no special insights. Even Syngman Rhee's demands were predictable and foolish: $1 billion in aid, freeing all non-repatriate Koreans immediately, more military assistance, the withdrawal of Chinese troops, and a bilateral defense treaty with the United States, and no armistice. Eisenhower listened politely and non-committedly. If he had something special in mind for Korea, his companions could not identify it. He did not. Instead, Eisenhower wanted to move ahead with far broader policy discussions on the *Helena,* where he was joined by more members of his prospective cabinet and White House staff. As he planned, Eisenhower wanted to focus on a strategic blueprint for America's security, not the tactical problems presented by Syngman Rhee and the Panmunjom negotiations.[23]

With members coming and going from Wake Island and Pearl Harbor, the participants in the *Helena* talks all recognized that Eisenhower intended to create an executive branch structure around the National Security Council that would deal with policy issues in a measured, comprehensive, politically inclusive, and rational manner. The discussions continued at the Commodore Hotel, New York City, and went on in Project Solarium after the inauguration. To the degree that the discussions varied from the organizational challenges of budget preparation and policy formulation and execution, the discussants wrestled with the issue of dealing with the Soviet Union, building regional coalitions opposed to Communist imperialism and subversion, and living in a world with nuclear weapons. The Korean War and the armistice that could not be made were not central to Eisenhower's concerns for at least his first four months as president, at least in public. The war went on, and so did the president's thinking about it. The problems of a Korean peace also provided some specific examples of the difficulties in making the "New Look" work.[24]

President Eisenhower and Korea, 1953

As president, Eisenhower first thought most about waging the war differently, not just ending it. In fact, he hoped he could find a way to conduct operations that would increase the Communists' incentives to accept an agreement that would include voluntary repatriation. He first wanted to increase the number of South Korean and UN troops on the frontlines and to get the sponsoring nations to pay for their troops, which they were not, with the United States' acceptance. Eisenhower also thought about OpPlan 8-52, which required at least three more American divisions as reinforcements, a twenty-division ROK army, and an expanded air war. He thought about the use of nuclear weapons, whose use "should depend on military judgment as to their advantage of their use on military targets." Should he authorize strikes into Manchuria? How could one do maximum damage to the Chinese? What were the likely losses to the U.S. armed forces? Eisenhower hoped to have the NSC reexamine the Korean commitment and provide actionable answers in April.[25]

At a special NSC meeting on 31 March to consider national strategy and the defense budget, a meeting attended by Eisenhower's inner circle of advisors and General Bradley, "the President then spoke his mind on the Korean problem." He had considered OpPlan 8-52, the drive back to the Pyongyang-Wonsan line, abandoned in December 1950. The president had not yet ruled out an offensive, even the use of nuclear weapons, but all he could see were risks of a larger war with China and Russia. Any use of nuclear weapons would shatter the UNC alliance. Eisenhower accepted his popular opinion/political consultants' assessment: Americans would support him whether he ordered an offensive or negotiated an armistice. General Bradley and Secretary of State Dulles agreed with the president's assessment. Dulles went further and predicted an agreement soon on the existing terms. The secretary may have already divined a change in the Communist position, prematurely, occasioned by the death of Joseph Stalin on 5 March. Mao Zedong and Kim Il-sung remained very much alive. When Dulles asked for more analysis by his own area experts, who leaned slightly toward an offensive, they soon shared the reluctance of the JCS to endorse a course of action that threatened Japan and might lead to a nuclear exchange.[26]

Eisenhower decided to test the global atmospherics with a major speech, "The Chance for Peace," a general statement of his sense that Stalin's death might bring a moderation of the Kremlin's hostility. Never have so many helped with a speech directed at so many, a global audience far beyond the American Society of Newspaper Editors. Among Eisenhower's challenges to the Soviet Union was to use its influence to end the Korean War. Although veiled in imprecise language, Eisenhower's proposal reflected his judgment that only a negotiated armistice would do, probably on terms already approved by Truman, however unpalatable: "it would be impossible to call off the armistice now and to go to war again in Korea. The American people would never stand for such a move."[27] The administration did not expect any rapid, meaningful response from Moscow, and it got none that it recognized. What the Eisenhower administration did not know—or did not believe—was that the Soviet Council of Ministers on 19 March had directed Mao Zedong and Kim Il-sung to work toward an armistice or risk the reduction of Soviet support. Instead, Dulles advocated an Austrian peace treaty as an experiment in détente and an increase of military pressure in Korea as a demonstration of America's patience. The JCS position, however, was still stark with risk. General Bradley saw only two military options that would compel the Communists to make peace immediately: the destruction of the Sino-Soviet air forces in Manchuria; and driving the Chinese from their caves and tunnels with mustard gas so they could be shelled and bombed with tactical nuclear weapons. This offensive, however, could not be mounted until 1954. Eisenhower, citing his concern for defenseless Japanese cities, let the matter ride.[28]

As the Eisenhower administration continued to work on an authoritative statement of defense policy for "the long haul" that would provide "security with solvency," the negotiations at Panmunjom continued, but Eisenhower, through Dulles, opened another negotiating front with Syngman Rhee. The Korean president fundamentally wanted the United States to reunify Korea by force, and he droned on about the United Nations resolution of 7 October 1950, for everyone else rendered null and void by the Chinese intervention. Rhee saw himself as the embodiment of Korean betrayal and victimization. Eisenhower and Dulles attempted to persuade Rhee that the United States would not abandon the Republic of Korea. They did not, however, respond to Rhee's specific alliance proposals. At Panmunjom, the plenary negotiations resumed with "an era of good feeling," fueled by the agreement of 11 April to exchange sick and wounded POWs. Rhee, however, became furious when he learned that the United States accepted a Communist–United Nations proposal that all non-repatriate POWs be reprocessed under neutral nation supervision, including the introduction of "neutral" troops (Indian) on Korean soil. Such a policy would require the rescreening of 35,000 North Korean POWs who had renounced any loyalty to North Korea and who had been rescued from the violent Koje-do POW camp and placed in mainland compounds. Dulles reminded Rhee that he had in principle been offered a larger army with modern arms, economic aid, bilateral security agreement, and continued negotiations to unify Korea.[29]

Although the course of negotiations at Panmunjom, focused on the process of repatriating or not repatriating POWs, continued without interruption, the Chinese People's Volunteers Force had mounted a sustained offensive to drive back United Nations Command to less desirable defensive terrain and to inflict last-minute casualties on its enemies, especially South Korean divisions. The new Eighth Army commander, Lt. Gen. Maxwell D. Taylor, shifted American divisions to support the Koreans, but used air support and artillery to slow and eventually stop the Chinese. Eighth Army casualties, however, soared to their highest levels since October 1952; after suffering around 3,500 casualties a month from January to May 1953, the Eighth Army took more than 10,000 casualties in the war's last two months. The South Korean army's losses for the same period were 15,000. The developments on the South Korean political front were equally depressing. In June, the Korean National Assembly rejected the prospect of an armistice, 149-0; an American economic mission reported that the South Korean economy was "appalling" and would need $553 million to survive; and on 18 June 18, at Syngman Rhee's orders, South Korean military police released 27,000 non-repatriate POWs, leaving only about 7,000 Koreans to be questioned about their choice to stay in South Korea. Although close to accepting the armistice agreement, the Chinese refused to come to terms, and the war continued.

For several days in mid-June, President Eisenhower, furious with Rhee, mused about coups, offensives, nuclear weapons, and economic retaliation, but the JCS could not promise acceptable results, and Dulles thought Rhee now might accept American terms. He and Eisenhower dispatched Assistant Secretary of State Walter Robertson to Seoul to seal the assistance agreements with Rhee in return for his tacit acceptance of an armistice. Rhee agreed to tone down his "march North" rhetoric and to keep his army under UNC operational control. Whether Rhee received the full message or not, Eisenhower had decided to deploy nuclear weapons to the theater (Guam) to deter an attack on Japan and threaten the Communists if they broke the armistice. Eisenhower and Dulles—and their champions and critics—remembered this decision as a nuclear threat that persuaded the Chinese and North Koreans to sign the armistice. The objects of the American nuclear compellance did not appear impressed, but the UNC allies and neutral nations bloc in the United Nations fretted again over American nuclear diplomacy. In any event, the Chinese, North Koreans, and American military leaders signed an armistice on 25 July 1953, and the conventional phase of the Korean War ended with a mix of bangs and whimpers.[30]

Not communicated to Rhee was the National Security Council's alternative vision for Korea, the adoption of an "Austrian solution." On 7 July 1953, Eisenhower approved NSC 157/1, "U.S. Objective with Respect to Korea Following an Armistice," which was guidance for the international conference included in the armistice terms. Although the odds for negotiated unification were long, the United States preferred a neutralized, demilitarized, unified Korea protected by international guarantees and its own small army. Such a Korea would be Western-oriented ("with U.S. political orientation") but it would have no foreign bases of any kind, thus ensuring the security of China and Japan.[31]

The lessons of the war suggested that Syngman Rhee and Dwight D. Eisenhower had attended different schools of conflict resolution. Rhee, who had surrendered almost all his preconditions for accepting the armistice, believed that the agreement started Korea's course toward permanent division and threat of more warfare. He wrote to Dulles, "For Korea itself, the indecisive ending of this war is our ultimate disaster . . . our nation long cannot survive such a truce."[32] For Dulles, the end of the war meant more negotiations. He thought the Communists would never surrender their goal of a unified socialist Korea, but the United States would strengthen the Republic of Korea enough to survive. If it could not be neutralized, it could be integrated into an Asian alliance system. Eisenhower went further: the Korean armed forces could spearhead Korean economic development, coached by Americans. Eisenhower also believed that the armistice would not soon be abrogated by the war-fatigued Asians.[33]

The day before the armistice, Eisenhower evaluated the effect of the war on American security. The war's primary benefit was its proof that the United States would fight for its allies. The United States had made Japan safer and more prosperous with its military commitment. The use of the United Nations could cut two ways, to legitimize or to discredit American security efforts. Rhee, an "unsatisfactory ally," showed how a weaker but aggressive ally could shape the American effort to its own ends. The commitment had allowed Eisenhower to marginalize the isolationist Republicans and give him more freedom from congressional oversight. He feared, however, that all the benefits were perishable and the war's ill effects lasting. His challenge was to make the war forgotten, a fading memory that would not endanger "the New Look."[34]

The Effect of the Korean War on "The New Look"

The resolution of the Korean War and the development of the Eisenhower administration's national security policy ran in parallel courses in 1953. The final collapse of non-repatriated POW screenings at Panmunjom came in January 1954, and the Geneva conference three months later switched negotiations from the Korean crisis to the Indochina crisis. On 30 October 1953, President Eisenhower approved NSC 162/2, "Basic National Security Policy," further refined in continuing interdepartmental negotiations on the interpretation and implementation of the policy into December. It is difficult not to infer some direct influence of the war upon NSC 162/2 even if all the parties to the document did not cite the Korean War as the prime mover of their political-strategic thinking. On the other hand, the founders of "The New Look" had ample experience since the 1930s upon which to form a world view of America's interests and international politics.

There is, however, a striking similarity between the Eisenhower administration's actions not just to end the war, but to ensure that the armistice held. The U.S.-ROK Mutual Security Treaty (September 1953), according to Secretary of State Dulles, cemented the American commitment to "deter aggression" in the Pacific in partnership with Japan, Korea, the Philippines, New Zealand, and Australia. Although the United States did not rule further negotiations on Korean unification, regional defense cooperation would reduce the threat of Communist strategic opportunism. Dulles's signing statement did not mention nuclear retaliation. The alliance reassurance package negotiated with Syngman Rhee and developed in the 1950s was impressive enough: the U.S. Eighth Army and Fifth Air Force remained in South Korea; the United States pledged to develop a twenty-division ROK army with a supporting navy and air force, granted almost $1 billion in economic assistance, sponsored the ROK for United Nations membership; and used its good offices to improve Korean and Japanese relations. The resultant entanglement of U.S.-ROK affairs also ensured that Syngman Rhee could not "march north." It did not ensure that Rhee, much to his dismay in 1960, could continue to keep himself in office, by any means fair or foul.[35]

One clear impact of the Korean War on "the New Look" was the change in political context for European rearmament, including the resurrection of the German armed forces. The Eisenhower administration, however, inherited policies and plans for NATO developed by the Truman administration, including Eisenhower as SACEUR. The major developments linked the two administrations: German rearmament in principle (1950), the Lisbon Agreement on force structure (1952), NATO Military Committee-48 (1954), the collapse of French resistance to the creation of the Bundeswehr (1954), and the commitment to the use of tactical nuclear weapons in the case of a NATO-Warsaw Pact war in Military Committee-14/2 (1957). The Asian war (as Koreans constantly assert) created an alarmism about the Soviet military threat that galvanized the apathetic European political elites to face their security problems.[36]

The Korean War era also allowed (or forced) the Truman administration to negotiate security arrangements with two Moslem nations it considered important additions to containing the Soviet Union: Turkey and Pakistan. The Eisenhower administration completed the process of integrating Turkey into NATO and cementing the relationship with Pakistan with a mutual defense assistance agreement (1954). Pakistan then became a key member of the Southeast Asia Treaty Organization (1954) and the Baghdad Pact (1955). Whatever the interaction of international and domestic politics, the Eisenhower administration also revealed a considerable reluctance to be drawn into regional conflicts in the Middle East and Asia, even when non-intervention discomfited allies like Great Britain, France, Israel, and Nationalist China. The analogies with the Korean crisis of 1950 are imperfect, but Eisenhower certainly had an aversion to interventions that might draw the American armed forces into battle. Interventions held at the level of covert operations and proxy forces—as in Guatemala (1956) and Iran (1954)—were acceptable. The legacy of Korea then combined active policies like mutual security agreements and military assistance with negative lessons on the costs of putting the American armed forces into combat in regions of national interest, but not national survival.[37]

Notes

1. The definitive study of the Eisenhower administration's national security policy is Robert R. Bowie and Richard H. Immerman, *Waging Peace: How Eisenhower Shaped an Enduring Cold War Strategy* (New York: Oxford University Press, 1998). The equivalent book for the Truman administration is Melvyn P. Leffler, *A Preponderance of Power: National Security, the Truman Administration, and the Cold War* (Stanford, Calif.: Stanford University Press, 1992). A book that bridges the two administrations is Walter Isaacson and Evan Thomas, *The Wise Men: Six Friends and the World They Made* (New York: Simon & Schuster, 1986). See also Douglas Kinnard, *President Eisenhower and Strategy Management: A Study in Defense Politics* (Lexington: University Press of Kentucky, 1977).

2. For the Korean War in its international context, see especially William Stueck, *The Korean War: An International History* (Princeton, N.J.: Princeton University Press, 1995).

3. For Eisenhower's military career, Carlo D'Este, *Eisenhower: A Soldier's Life* (New York: Henry Holt, 2002) now supersedes Stephen E. Ambrose, *Eisenhower: Soldier, General of the Army, President-Elect, 1890–1952* (New York: Simon & Schuster, 1988) through World War II, but not the postwar period. Eisenhower's informal autobiography, *At Ease: Stories I Tell to Friends* (Garden City, N.Y.: Doubleday, 1967) is rich with humor and insight.

4. The JCS/DOD perspectives may be found in Kenneth W. Condit, *The History of the Joint Chiefs of Staff: The Joint Chiefs of Staff and National Policy*, vol. 2, *1947–1949* (Wilmington, Del.: Michael Glazier, 1979), 257–81, 283–309.

5. Dwight D. Eisenhower, oral memoir (1967), 9–10, Dwight D. Eisenhower Presidential Papers, Eisenhower Library, Abilene, Kans. The Department of State's position on Korea may be found in NSC 8/2, "The Position of the United States with Respect to Korea," 22 Mar. 1949, National Security Archive, Washington, D.C.; Director, Northeast Asian Affairs Division to Director, Office of Far Eastern Affairs, 17 Dec. 1948, *Foreign Relations of the United States 1948*, 9 vols. (Washington, D.C.: Government Printing Office, 1972–76), 6:1337–40 (hereafter cited as *FRUS*). The CIA assessments are ORE 32-48, "Communist Capabilities in South Korea," 21 Feb. 1949; ORE 44-48, "Prospects for Survival of the Republic of Korea," 28 Oct. 1948; ORE 3-49, "Consequences of US Troop Withdrawal from Korea in Spring, 1949," February 1949 with dissent, Department of the Army.

6. Although an edited version of NSC 8 appears in *FRUS 1948*, 6:1163–69, I have used the original with annexes and transmittal letters filed with the records of 9th Meeting, NSC, 2 Apr. 1948, NSC Records, 1948, President's Secretary's Files, Presidential Files, Harry S. Truman Papers, Harry S. Truman Library, Independence, Mo. The Army position, developed by Gen. J. Lawton Collins, USA, Chief of Staff and Gen. Douglas MacArthur, CINC Far East and SCAP, is in memoranda, January, 1949, JCS File 091 (Korea) 1953, RG 218, Records of the Chairman Joint Chiefs of Staff, National Archives and Records Administration (NARA). The experience of KMAG appears in detail in Chief, KMAG, *Semi-Annual Report Period Ending 31 December 1949*, AC/S G-3 Army Staff, File P&O 091 (Korea), 1949–1950, RG 319, Records of the Army Staff, NARA, and Chief, KMAG, *Semi-Annual Report,* January 1–June 15, 1950, File 52-40 (MDAP, 1949–1951), RG 59, General Records of the Department of State, NARA. Syngman Rhee's position in his own words may be found in Robert Oliver, *Syngman Rhee and American Involvement in Korea* (Seoul: Panmun Books, 1978), 238–65.

7. Entries, 30 June 1950, in Robert H. Ferrell, ed., *The Eisenhower Diaries* (New York: Norton, 1981), 175.

8. Diary notes, 28 June 1950, Matthew B. Ridgway Papers, U.S. Army Military History Institute, Carlisle Barracks, Carlisle, Penn.

9. Eisenhower interview, *New York Times,* 29 June 1950.

10. Entries, 6 July, 6 Nov., and 5 Dec. 1950, in Ferrell, ed., *Eisenhower Diaries*, 176, 181–82.

11. The quotes are all from Eisenhower to Edward E. Hazlett, Jr., 21 June 1951, in Louis Galambos, ed. et al., *The Papers of Dwight D. Eisenhower,* 17 vols. (Baltimore, Md.: Johns Hopkins University Press, 1989), 12:270. Eisenhower's 1951 views on Korea are contained in a letter to A. H. Sulzberger, 7 May 1951, a letter to Douglas MacArthur, 15 May 1951, and diary entries, 9 Apr., 15 and 30 May 1951, ibid., 17:200–201, 266, 303. American defense concerns reached Eisenhower from Secretary of Defense R. Lovett (21 Oct. 1951); Chief of Staff J. Lawton Collins (11 Feb. 1952), and W. Averell Harriman (9 and 26 April 1951), Personal Papers Files, 1916–1952, Eisenhower Papers.

12. Diary entry, 22 Jan. 1952, in Galambos, ed., *Eisenhower Papers,* 17:901.

13. Dulles's role in the Korean decision is reviewed in memo of conversation, Dulles and Secretary of State, 1 July 1950, John Foster Dulles Papers, Seely Mudd Library, Princeton University. For my assessment of the Eisenhower-Dulles relationship, I have relied upon Louis L. Gerson, *John Foster Dulles*, vol. 17 in Robert H. Ferrell, ed., *The American Secretaries of State and Their Diplomacy* (New York: Cooper Square, 1967); Richard H. Immerman, *John Foster Dulles: Piety, Pragmatism, and Power in U.S. Foreign Policy* (Wilmington, Del.: SR Books,

1999); and Frederick W. Marks III, *Power and Peace: The Diplomacy of John Foster Dulles* (Westport, Conn.: Praeger, 1993). On Eisenhower's transition from general to candidate, see William B. Pickett, *Eisenhower Decides to Run: Presidential Politics and Cold War Strategy* (Chicago: Ivan R. Dee, 2000).

14. Bowie and Immerman, *Waging Peace,* 70–95.

15. The August 1952 Korea incident is described by Eisenhower in his dairy entries, 16–19 August 1952, and his correspondence with Truman and Bradley in the same period, printed in Galambos, ed., *Eisenhower Papers,* 17:911–13. The Eisenhower to Nixon letter, 1 Oct. 1952 is in ibid., 1366–69. Eisenhower's first focused criticism appears in W. H. Lawrence, "Eisenhower for Korean War but Says Blunders Led to It," *New York Times,* 22 Aug. 1952.

16. The Eisenhower speeches are in the Speech Files, 1952, Eisenhower Presidential Papers (the Ann Whitman File). The episode is explained in Stephen E. Ambrose, *Eisenhower,* vol. 2, *The President* (New York: Simon & Schuster, 1984), 13–29, and Dwight D. Eisenhower, *The White House Years,* vol. 1, *Mandate for Change, 1953–1956* (New York: Doubleday, 1963), 72–73. Charles Douglas Jackson (1902–1964) left a successful family quarry business in 1931 to become a senior editor and vice president of Time, Inc., publisher of *Fortune,* founder of Radio Free Europe, and confidant and spokesman for Henry and Claire Booth Luce of the *Time-Life* empire.

17. Bowie and Immerman, *Waging Peace,* 83–241.

18. Eisenhower to R. A. Lovett, 8 Nov. 1952, Ann Whitman Administrative Correspondence Series, 1952, Eisenhower Presidential Papers.

19. This episode is recounted by Ambrose, *Eisenhower,* 2:21–22, and by the principals: Eisenhower, *Mandate for Change,* 74–92; Harry S. Truman, *Memoirs: Years of Trial and Hope, 1946–1952* (New York: Doubleday, 1956), 579–87; and Dean Acheson, *The Korean War* (New York: Norton, 1971), 137–48.

20. I have, however, used memo of conversation, Truman and Eisenhower, 18 Nov. 1952, Acheson's Memorandum of Conversations File, Dean C. Acheson Papers, Truman Library. The departmental position is explained in Policy, Planning Staff, Department of State, "Outline for Secretary's Use in Briefing General Eisenhower, November 18, 1952," in Office of the Historian, Bureau of Public Affairs, *FRUS, 1952–1954,* 15 vols. (Washington, D.C.: Government Printing Office, 1979–84), vol. 1, *General: Economic and Political Matters,* pt. 1, 6–13.

21. JS, JCS, briefing for General Eisenhower, 3 Dec. 1952, CJCS File 091 (Korea), 1952, RG 218. For Chinese reaction to Eisenhower's election, see Shu Guang Zhang, *Mao's Military Romanticism: China and the Korean War, 1950–1953* (Lawrence: University Press of Kansas, 1995), 232–39. The nuclear briefings are described in Office of the Historian [Dr. Joseph P. Harahan], Defense Threat Reduction Agency, DOD, *Defense's Nuclear Agency, 1947–1997* (Washington, D.C.: Defense Threat Reduction Agency, 2002), 98–99.

22. CJCS, memo to C/S USA, 19 Nov. 1952, and C/S USA to CJCS, 26 Nov. 1952, Miscellaneous File, 1952, CJCS Files, RG 218.

23. The Korea trip is summarized and assessed in Eisenhower, *Mandate for Change,* 93–97; Gen. Mark W. Clark, *From the Danube to the Yalu* (New York: Harper & Row, 1954), 230–39; Eisenhower to S. Rhee, 5 Dec. 1952, in Galambos, ed., *Eisenhower Papers,* 13:1443–44; Adm. Arthur W. Radford and Stephen Jurika, Jr., *From Pearl Harbor to Vietnam: The Memoirs of Admiral Arthur W. Radford* (Stanford, Calif.: Hoover Institution Press, 1980), 303–9; Robert A. Divine, "Eisenhower's Trip to Korea," in James I. Matray, ed., *Dictionary of the Korean War* (Westport, Conn.: Greenwood, 1991), 154.

24. Bowie and Immerman, *Waging Peace,* 84–138. The best general accounts of Eisenhower and the Korean War, January–July 1953, are Eisenhower, *Mandate for Change,* 93–97, 171–91, and Ambrose, *Eisenhower,* 2:97–107.

25. U.S. Rep. to the UN H. C. Lodge to Secretary of State, 24 Feb. 1953, and memo, Admin. Assistant to the President for National Security Affairs (Robert Cutler), 21 Mar. 1953, *FRUS 1952–1954,* 17/pt. 1:795–97, 815.

26. Memo of record, special meeting, NSC, 31 Mar. 1953, NSC Series, Ann Whitman Files, Eisenhower Presidential Papers, with an edited version in ibid., 15:825–27. State's assessment is memo, Deputy Assist. SecState for Far East Affairs (U. Alexis Johnson) to SecState, 6 Apr. 1953, ibid., 880–82.

27. Quoted from memo of discussion, 139th meeting, NSC, 8 Apr. 1953, ibid., 894.

28. The "Chance for Peace" is reprinted in National Archives and Records Service, *Public Papers of Presidents of the United States: Dwight D. Eisenhower, 1953* (Washington, D.C.: Government Printing Office, 1957–61), 179–88. The post-speech discussions are in memoranda of discussions, 141st meeting, NSC, 25 Apr. 1953, and 145th meeting, NSC, 20 May 1953, both in the declassified versions, NSC Files, Ann Whitman Files, Eisenhower Presidential Papers.

29. Assist. SecState Walter S. Robertson to Acting SecState, 22 Apr. 1953, Secretariat File 1953, RG 59, NARA. Eisenhower to Rhee, 23 Apr. 1953, *FRUS 1952–1954*, 15:929–30. Rhee to Eisenhower, 30 May 1953, ibid., 1124–26; CINC UNC to JCS, 7 June 1953, ibid., 1149–51; Dulles to Rhee, 11 June 1953, ibid., 1165–66. See also Rhee to Gen. J. Van Fleet, 25 May 1953, James Van Fleet Papers, and Oliver, *Syngman Rhee*, 400–410. The complete Rhee-Dulles-Eisenhower correspondence for June 1953 is in File "Korea 1953," Ann Whitman File, International Series, Eisenhower Presidential Papers.

30. Memo of conversation, Dulles and Nehru, 21 May 1953, *FRUS 1952–1954*, 15:1068–69; memo of discussion, 150th meeting, NSC, 18 June 1953, ibid., 1200–1205; memo of discussion, 156th meeting, NSC, 23 June 1953, ibid., 1420–28, with originals in the NSC File, Ann Whitman Files, Eisenhower Presidential Papers. The assessment of the ROK economy comes from the mission of Dr. Henry J. Tasca, "Strengthening the Korean Economy," 15 June 1953, special report to the president, NSC Staff Papers, Eisenhower Presidential Papers. The political negotiations with Rhee are reported in aide memoir, "Rhee-Robertson Understandings," Seoul, ROK, 2 June 1953, Rhee File, Van Fleet papers. The assessment of the June–July operations is from Hqs. Eighth U.S. Army, "Lessons Learned . . . Communist Offensives of June and July, 1953," 1954, File 220.509, 8th Army Historical Files, Dean Center, U.S. Army Base, Yongsan, Seoul, ROK, and Korea Institute of Military History, MOD, ROK, *The Korean War*, 3 vols. (Seoul: Ministry of National Defense, 1999), vol. 3, chap. 5, "Final Military Operations," 574–681. The most recent document-based accounts of the MacArthur-Dulles nuclear threat may be found in Conrad C. Crane, *American Airpower Strategy in Korea, 1950–1953* (Lawrence: University Press of Kansas, 2000), 164–219.

31. PPB, NSC, draft memo, "To Determine the Basic U.S. Objective with Respect to Korea," 15 June 1953, *FRUS 1952–1954*, 15:1180–83; memo of discussion, State-JCS meeting, 16 June 1953, ibid., 1183–88; NSC 157/1, "U.S. Objective with Respect to Korea Following an Armistice," 7 June 1953, ibid., 1344–46.

32. Rhee to Dulles, 11 July 1953, ibid., 1370–73.

33. Memo, Secretary of State, Special Korean Briefing, 1 Aug. 1953, ibid., 1460–65; Secretary of State, Statement on Signing of the Mutual Defense Treaty between the ROK and the United States, 30 Sept. 1953, Secretarial File, 1953, RG 59.

34. Eisenhower diary, entry, 24 July 1953, in Ferrell, ed., *Eisenhower Diaries*, 248; Ambrose, *Eisenhower*, 2:101–7.

35. Secretary of State, Statement on Signing of the Mutual Defense Treaty between the ROK and the United States, 30 Sept. 1953, Secretariat File, 1953, RG 59. See also John Kotch, "The Origins of the American Security Commitment to Korea," in Bruce Cumings, ed., *Child of Conflict: The Korean-American Relationship, 1943–1953* (Seattle: University of Washington Press, 1983), 239–59.

36. Ernest R. May, "The American Commitment to Germany, 1949–55," and Walter LaFeber, "NATO and the Korean War: A Contest," *Diplomatic History* 13 (Fall 1989).

37. The alliance process in described in Melvyn P. Leffler, "Strategy, Diplomacy, and the Cold War: The United States, Turkey, and NATO, 1945–1952," *Journal of American History* 71

(March 1985); Robert J. McMahon, "United States Cold War Strategy in South Asia: Making a Military Commitment to Pakistan, 1947–1954," ibid. 75 (December 1988); George C. Herring and Richard H. Immerman, "Eisenhower, Dulles, and Dienbienphu: 'The Day We Didn't Go to War' Revisited," ibid. 71 (September 1984); Leonard H. D. Gordon, "United States Opposition to Use of Force in the Taiwan Strait, 1954–1962," ibid. 71 (December 1985); and Cole C. Kingseed, *Eisenhower and the Suez Crisis of 1956* (Baton Rouge: Louisiana State University Press, 1995).

Crisis and Confrontation: Chinese-American Relations during the Eisenhower Administration

Qiang Zhai

The 1950s was a decade of crisis and confrontation between the People's Republic of China (PRC) and the United States. Considering China as a major threat to U.S. interests in East Asia and the Pacific, the Eisenhower administration adopted a policy of political isolation, economic embargo, and military containment against the PRC. Leaders in Beijing viewed the United States as a primary enemy hostile to China's revolution and its unification with Taiwan. They maintained an intense anti-American campaign throughout the decade. How did this condition of hostility come about? How did policymakers in Washington and Beijing view each other? What objectives did the Eisenhower administration plan to achieve in pursuing a policy of toughness against the Chinese Communists? And how did Mao Zedong and his associates react to American pressure and antagonism? This essay will use recently released American and Chinese documents to answer those questions.

The conclusion of the Sino-Soviet alliance treaty in February 1950 and the outbreak of the Korean War four months later represented two major developments in the globalization of the Cold War and in the further deterioration of Sino-American relations. Before these two events occurred, some officials in the Truman administration had hoped to promote a Sino-Soviet split by reaching accommodation with the newly-established PRC. The formal alignment of the Chinese and Soviet governments and the subsequent Sino-American military clash on the Korean peninsula completely dashed the hope of those American officials who had desired to drive a wedge between Beijing and Moscow through a policy of accommodation. President Harry S. Truman's decision to deploy the Seventh Fleet in the Taiwan Strait after the onset of the Korean War prevented Mao from implementing his plan to unify Taiwan.[1]

Dwight D. Eisenhower became president of the United States in January 1953. He was determined to end the war in Korea. The Korean question had been an important factor in his victory in the 1952 election. During the campaign, he had blamed the Democratic administration for the loss of China and the outbreak of the Korean War. He had pledged to travel to Korea if elected, implying that he would find a solution to terminate the fighting on the peninsula. After winning the election, Eisenhower made his journey in December 1952. The new president believed that the war represented a diversion and drain on American resources. His political credibility depended on achieving an honorable end to the war. He adopted a policy of strength, enhanced by psychological warfare, in order to end the fighting. He took several measures to pressure the Chinese Communists to make concessions at the armistice negotiations.[2]

Eisenhower's first move was his decision to launch a United Nations offensive in the spring of 1953, employing a strengthened South Korean army and American reinforcement. The second measure was the decision to "unleash" Jiang Jieshi (Chiang Kai-shek): the United States would withdraw the orders of the Seventh Fleet to neutralize the Taiwan Strait. Largely a symbolic gesture, the decision satisfied the anti-Communist China Lobby, but U.S. officials recognized that Jiang was a liability rather than an asset. The public unleashing was accompanied by private restrictions demanding restraint. U.S. advisers were instructed not to engage in precipitate action that might trigger an expanded war with the PRC. Karl Lott Rankin, the U.S. ambassador in Taipei, was instructed to re-leash Jiang's men privately.[3] At a National Security Council (NSC) meeting on 8 April 1953, Secretary of State John Foster Dulles recommended that the United States suspend delivery of jet bombers to the Chinese Nationalists until Washington could "secure very quickly a commitment from Chiang Kai-shek that he would not use these aircraft recklessly and in a fashion to embarrass United States policy."[4]

The third measure to coerce the Chinese Communists was the nuclear threat. Unlike the Truman administration, Eisenhower and Dulles had a very different conception of the potential political value of atomic weapons. The Republican administration considered the atomic bomb useful in both military and economic terms. From the military perspective, it had the advantage of regaining the initiative that had been lost in Korea: from now on, the United States would confront the enemy on terrain and with weapons of its own choice rather than theirs. From the economic point of view, dependence on nuclear deterrence could reduce the cost of conventional force spending. Accordingly, Eisenhower publicly announced that "atomic weapons have virtually achieved conventional status within our armed services."[5]

Secretary of State Dulles was also eager to talk about American nuclear superiority. He was anxious to please the Republican right and forestall the political controversy that had beset his predecessor Dean Acheson. This made it imperative to appear tough on China. He told Emmet John Hughes, Eisenhower's assistant in April 1953, "I don't think we can get much out of a Korean settlement until we have shown—before all Asia—our clear superiority by giving the Chinese one hell of a licking." On 21 May, Dulles told Indian Prime Minister Jawaharlal Nehru that "if the armistice negotiations collapsed, the United States would probably make a stronger rather than a lesser military exertion, and that this might well extend the area of conflict." According to his note of conversation, Dulles believed that Nehru would pass the message to leaders in Beijing.[6]

The Chinese Communists watched closely the 1952 presidential election in the United States. Some officials worried about the candidacy of Eisenhower because of his military background. Du Ping, director of the Political Department of the Chinese People's Volunteers (CPV), told CPV commander Peng Dehuai in 1952 that "according to a radio broadcast, Eisenhower plans to run for the presidency. If this military general becomes the president, it is likely that the Korean War will be expanded. We'd better prepare our troops for this possible development." Peng concurred with this estimate, but added that "a military commander will not necessarily be war-like because he knows better than other people the cost of war. On the surface, war is about steel and iron, but in fact, it involves such things as politics, military, finance, materials and manpower." Without complete confidence in victory, Peng continued, a commander would not make hasty decisions to start war. Therefore, he concluded, "it is hard to say if Eisenhower will escalate the war. But, of course, it is very necessary for us to be prepared. Preparedness averts peril."[7]

Leaders in Beijing were very apprehensive about Eisenhower's visit to Korea in early December. On 2 December, the CPV command received an instruction from the Central Military Command in Beijing, which mentioned that Eisenhower had just begun his journey to Korea in the company of new Secretary of Defense Charles Wilson, Chairman of the Joint Chiefs of Staff (JCS) Gen. Omar Bradley, and Commander of the Seventh Fleet Adm. Arthur Radford. The document asked the CPV to pay attention to this development.[8]

The Chinese leadership also took Eisenhower's unleashing of Jiang Jieshi seriously. The Central Military Commission sent a memorandum to the CPV command, warning them that the United States had lifted the order to neutralize the Taiwan Strait in an effort to encourage the Nationalists to attack the mainland.[9] On 7 February 1953, Mao officially responded to Eisenhower's threat by declaring at the Fourth Session of the first National Committee of the Chinese People's Political Consultative Conference: "Because American imperialism persists in holding Chinese and Korean prisoners of war and undermining the ceasefire negotiations and, moreover, is vainly attempting to expand its war of aggression against Korea, the struggle to resist America and aid Korea must continue to be intensified."[10] Despite his unyielding rhetoric, the Chinese leader was fully aware of the stress and strain the war imposed on China's economy and the postponement that the war caused on his plan to recover Taiwan. But Stalin had been urging the Chinese and the North Koreans to continue the war and not to make concessions at the armistice talks. The Soviet leader took this position because he wanted to see the United States mired in the war in Asia, and because he wanted to keep the Chinese and the Americans at loggerheads.[11]

Once Stalin died in March 1953, his successors in the Kremlin and Chinese leaders immediately agreed on the need to end the Korean War even at the price of making compromises on the POW issue. On 15 March, senior Party Secretary Georgi Malenkov said before the Supreme Soviet that "at present there is no disputed or unsettled question that could not be settled peacefully on the basis of mutual agreement between the countries concerned."[12] On 28 March, North Korean leader Kim Il Sung and Peng Dehuai responded to Gen. Mark Clark, the head of the UN Command, accepting his offer to exchange sick and wounded POWs. They also suggested that this exchange should lead to a settlement of the whole POW issue and an armistice.[13]

Two days later, Chinese Foreign Minister Zhou Enlai announced an even greater surprise. In a conciliatory statement over Beijing Radio, he declared: "Both parties to the negotiations should undertake to repatriate immediately after the cessation of hostilities all those prisoners of war (POWs) in their custody who insisted upon repatriation, and to hand over the remaining POWs to a neutral state so as to ensure a just solution to the question of their repatriation."[14] This was an important concession on the part of the Chinese because for the first time they had abandoned their insistence on strict compliance with the 1949 Geneva Convention on POW repatriation and for the first time they no longer called for automatic repatriation of POWs. On 31 March, Kim endorsed Zhou's suggestion. The next day, Soviet Foreign Minister Vyacheslav Molotov voiced support for the Chinese and North Korean position.[15]

On 8 June, the POW issue was settled and the armistice was signed on 27 July. What caused the Chinese to make concessions on the POW issue? Eisenhower and Dulles believed it had been the American nuclear threat that forced the Chinese and North Koreans to modify their positions. Eisenhower later told his special assistant, Sherman Adams, that the reason for the final conclusion of the armistice was the menace of a nuclear war. Dulles made a similar argument at the Bermuda Conference in December 1953, where he told British and French officials that "it was their [the Communists'] knowledge of the U.S. willingness to use force that brought an end to hostilities."[16]

The American leaders, however, overestimated the effect of their nuclear threats. In actuality, the major Communist concessions were made before Washington had communicated such threats. It is doubtful whether Nehru ever transmitted Dulles's 21 May message to the Chinese. The Indian leader himself denied it.[17] There is no evidence in available Chinese sources to indicate that Beijing ever received Dulles's warning through Nehru. Throughout late 1952 and early 1953, the Chinese were more concerned with an American landing operation than a U.S. nuclear strike.

Until further Chinese documents or any North Korean records are released, it will be difficult to make a precise judgment of the efficacy of the American nuclear threats against China during the conclusion of the Korean War. It seems more plausible to argue that the general cost of the war, even without the danger of nuclear escalation, was more decisive in pushing the Chinese to make concessions at the armistice negotiations.

The Korean fighting had been an enormous drain on China's economy. To finance the war, the Chinese government had resorted to such mobilization measures as high taxes, confiscation of private enterprises, withholding of wages, intensive issuing of bonds, and voluntary contribution drives. In fact, high agricultural taxes had caused complaints from people such as Liang Shuming, a leader of the Democratic League, who called for a "benevolent policy" toward the peasants. Mao criticized this kind of sentiment at a government meeting on 13 September 1953.[18] According to one estimate, in 1951, the Chinese government allocated 41.6 percent of its total expenditure to defense and 25.6 percent to economic development.[19] Furthermore, Beijing had decided to launch its First Five-Year Plan in 1953, and money and resources were needed to implement it.

The end of the Korean War did not usher in an era of relaxation of U.S. hostility toward the Chinese Communists. The Eisenhower administration continued its containment policy against the PRC and strengthened its ties with the Nationalist government on Taiwan. To contain China, the United States signed a mutual defense treaty with South Korea in August 1953. One year later, in September 1954, Washington concluded a protocol creating the Southeast Asian Treaty Organization. In South Vietnam, the United States embarked on its experiment of nation-building by committing itself to a major aid program to the Ngo Dinh Diem regime. To fortify relations with Taiwan, the Eisenhower administration began negotiations with Jiang's government on the formation of a mutual defense arrangement. American policymakers remained determined to keep Taiwan out of the clutches of the Chinese Communists. They viewed the island as an important strategic asset with multiple values. They treated Taiwan as a base for intelligence gathering and covert operations against the PRC, as a source of military manpower for possible offensive operations outside Nationalist territory, and as a location for the emergence of a liberal political alternative to attract disaffected mainland Chinese. They wanted to use Taiwan to undermine the authority of the PRC government.[20]

Despite Chinese fear of revived Japanese militarism, the Eisenhower administration pushed ahead with its plan to rebuild Japan's economy. To turn Japan into a loyal anti-Communist ally and to keep its economy within the U.S.-led capitalist orbit, the United States rebuilt the Asian country in its image and attempted to reorient Japan's trade away from its traditional partner—China—and toward new markets in Southeast Asia. To insure Japan's separation from China, U.S. officials made a special arrangement to impose harsh restrictions on any sales to the PRC. They drafted Japan into the China Subcommittee of the Paris-based Coordinating Committee on Export Control to the Soviet bloc. Apart from limitations placed on the Europeans, Tokyo had to follow a special list of some four hundred embargoed products.[21]

Under U.S. direction and insistence, trade sanctions against the PRC were much tougher than those imposed on the Soviet Union and Eastern Europe. Known as the "China differential," this trade control policy became an issue of open dispute and bickering between the United States and its allies after the conclusion of the Korean War. Britain, Japan, France, and West Germany, among others, complained about this policy. Seizing every opportunity to scrap the differential, they eventually succeeded in doing so in 1957, with the understanding that the United States would maintain its total embargo on commercial contact.[22]

On the issue of restricting China's trade with Japan and Western European countries, Eisenhower and Dulles did not always agree with each other. Dulles wanted to use trade controls to increase pressure on the PRC, and, ultimately, bringing about frictions in the Sino-Soviet alliance. Eisenhower, on the other hand, believed that trade sanctions could increase the economic problems of U.S. allies and hurt the American economy. Within limits, the president insisted, China's trade with Japan and Britain had to be allowed. In 1954, Eisenhower quietly lifted some U.S.-imposed restrictions on Sino-Japanese trade. But not even the president intended to permit the volume of trade Tokyo needed with China to correct its unfavorable trade balance, particularly with the United States. To resolve the dilemma, the United States turned to Southeast Asia as an alternative market for Japan's trade. In general, Eisenhower confined his criticism of trade restrictions against the PRC to private discussions. In public, he justified that practice. He allowed more hard-line opinions voiced by Dulles and Vice-President Richard Nixon to frame the debate.[23]

Why did the Eisenhower administration maintain its hard-line position against the PRC when the two countries were no longer fighting each other in Korea? There were two important reasons. The first had to do with Eisenhower's intention to placate domestic anti-Communist right-wingers. Jiang Jieshi had staunch supporters in the U.S. Congress and the media. In Congress, Senator William Knowland led an influential China Bloc to demand increased American aid to the Nationalist government on Taiwan and a blockade of mainland China. In 1953, Congressman Water Judd and New Jersey Governor Charles Edison launched a campaign to oppose the admission of the PRC into the United Nations. They eventually claimed that they had gathered one million signatures on their petition against the PRC's admission, and hence called themselves the Committee of One Million. On 22 October 1953, Judd wrote to Eisenhower petitioning him to take a firm stand against the admission of the PRC into the United Nations. In his reply, the president expressed his agreement with Judd on the admission issue. Outside the Congress, Henry Luce and his media spearheaded a publicity campaign to drum up support for Jiang's government.[24]

To display their sensitivity to right-wing views on China, Eisenhower and Dulles recruited prominent anti-PRC and pro-Jiang figures to handle Chinese affairs in the State Department. Taking the recommendation of Water Judd, Dulles appointed Walter S. Robertson as assistant secretary of state for Far Eastern affairs. For the position of director of the Office of Chinese Affairs, Dulles selected Walter P. McConaughy, another well-known Beijing basher. Two strong supporters of Jiang became U.S. ambassadors to Taipei, first, Karl Lott Rankin, then Everett F. Drumwright. These men helped set the tone of China policy and contributed to the making of public opinion of Mao's regime.[25]

The second reason for the Eisenhower administration's tough stand against the PRC had to do with the desire of Eisenhower and Dulles to strain and disrupt the Sino-Soviet alliance through a high pressure policy toward the Beijing government. Both the president and his secretary of state believed that the Soviet-led international Communist camp was vulnerable and long-term historical forces would contradict Moscow's ability to control its allies. On many private occasions, they talked about the independent nature of Chinese communism and indicated intentions to undermine Sino-Soviet ties. Eisenhower expressed his belief in the possibility of exploiting tensions within the Communist movement at a NSC meeting on 1 December 1954. The meeting discussed a NSC draft statement regarding current U.S. policy in East Asia. The Central Intelligence Agency (CIA) had shown reservations about one sentence with respect to China in the draft paper, which read: "While there is now no reason to anticipate any early collapse of the regime nor any means of seeing when one might occur, inherently such regimes have elements of rigidity and instability which might produce crises or break down unexpectedly." The CIA argued that the last phrase seemed inconsistent with the rest of the sentence. Eisenhower chimed in, asking Allen Dulles, the CIA Director, whether anyone in the intelligence community had foreseen Tito's break with the Soviet Union. The president continued that these favorable developments in the Soviet bloc sometimes happened unexpectedly out of thin air. Secretary of State Dulles concurred with Eisenhower's analysis concerning the unexpected quality of such developments in the Soviet camp. In conclusion, Eisenhower insisted on keeping the sentence in the paper and reaffirmed his conviction that totalitarian regimes were excessively rigid and had inherent weaknesses on which the United States should attempt to capitalize.[26]

In an important policy document, NSC 166/1, Eisenhower's strategy planners recognized that the relationship between Moscow and Beijing "is clearly distinct from the relationship between the Kremlin and other Communist states." In their estimates, the PRC was a "junior partner," not a satellite of the Soviet Union, and the Chinese Communist leaders were "Chinese as well as Communists." The Soviets handled the satellites through disciplinary control over individual Communist party members, but dealt with Communist China "as a close, but relatively independent ally." They calculated that there were both long-term and short-term potential hazards for the Sino-Soviet partnership, and recommended that the United States should employ "all feasible means, covert and overt, to impair Sino-Soviet relations."[27]

With regard to the best way to achieve the goal of detaching the PRC from the Soviet orbit, Eisenhower's advisers raised doubt about the effectiveness of a conciliatory policy toward Mao's government. They perceived no immediate prospect of bringing about a division between Beijing and Moscow for, despite latent sources of conflicts and despite China's relative independence from the Soviet Union, the present Sino-Soviet relationship was "based on powerful ties of common ideology and mutual interests." The conflicts of interest of both partners with the Western world at the moment were much more intense than conflicts of interest between the two Communist states. The potential threat to the Sino-Soviet alliance would stem primarily from the inner workings of the partnership and only secondarily from the nature of outside pressures or inducements. Whatever the possible concessions the United States could make, it appeared unlikely that Washington could through accommodation create a situation in which Chinese conflicts with the Soviet Union would surpass those with the United States. Even major compromises such as the abandonment of Taiwan would not necessarily change China's deep hostility toward the United States, not to speak of those smaller concessions like trade or recognition. American gestures of accommodation before the Korean War had produced no results. This failure indicated "the limited efficacy of appeasement as a weapon against the continuation of the alliance."[28]

Instead of softness, the Eisenhower administration considered a hard-line policy toward the PRC as more likely to generate a rift in the Sino-Soviet alliance. "The best hope for intensifying the strain and difficulties between Communist China and Russia," Secretary of State Dulles explained at the Bermuda meeting in 1953, "would be to keep the Chinese under maximum pressure rather than relieving such pressure." He contended that "pressure and strain would compel them to make more demands on the USSR which the latter would be unable to meet and the strain would consequently increase." On the other hand, efforts to separate the two partners by "a sort of competition with Russia as to who would treat China best" would simply "put China in the best of worlds." After all, Tito had not broken away from the Soviet Union because the United States had been nice to him. "On the contrary," Dulles had noted in a letter to Chester Bowles in 1952, "we were very tough with Tito."[29]

In a discussion with Jiang's Foreign Minister George Yeh in February 1955, Dulles further illuminated his calculation of "overextending" the Soviet Union by pushing the PRC hard toward Moscow. Dulles asserted:

> The Soviet Union was trying to match U.S. military power with an industrial base only one-third or one-fourth that of the U.S. Communist China was undoubtedly pressing the Soviet Union hard for more military and industrial assistance. Through the Chinese Communists, the North Koreans and Viet Minh regimes were making large demands. The military requirements on the European satellite countries were heavy. The economies of the European satellite countries had been squeezed. The satellite people were squirming under the demands made of them. They were restive. The whole Communist domain was overextended. . . . The Communist regimes are bound to crack.

Dulles concluded therefore that it was crucial "to keep the Communist regimes under economic and other pressures . . . which will lead to disintegration."[30]

After the Korean ceasefire and the settlement of the Korean and Indochina issues at the 1954 Geneva Conference, Taiwan became a focus of Chinese-American confrontation. Mao and his comrades were both ardent nationalists and shrewd political calculators. The recovery of Taiwan would both satisfy their nationalist yearnings and consolidate their authority in China. A primary motive for Mao and his generation of young radicals to participate in revolution was to end the miserable condition of China as a weak and humiliated nation at the hands of Western and Japanese imperialism. Mao and his associates wanted to eliminate imperialist presence in China and transform the country into an independent and strong state. Aware of China's glorious civilization in ancient times, they wanted to restore their motherland to the center of international affairs. To them, Taiwan served as a symbol of imperialist domination of China ever since Japan grabbed it as a colony in 1895. After coming to power in China in 1949, the Chinese Communist Party (CCP) wanted to present itself as a defender and promoter of China's national interests. The unification of Taiwan would enhance the credibility and legitimacy of the party as a ruler of China.

Fearing that the United States wanted to make the separation of Taiwan and mainland China permanent, the CCP leaders condemned the Washington-Taipei negotiations on a mutual defense treaty. In July 1954, they decided that "in order to break up the political and military collaboration between the United States and Jiang Jieshi, we must announce to our country and to the whole world the slogan of 'liberating Taiwan.' It was improper for us not to raise this slogan timely in the wake of the Korean ceasefire. We would commit a serious political mistake if we did not start this work right now."[31] On 23 July 1954, *Renmin ribao,* the official newspaper of the CCP, set forth the theme of the liberation campaign in an editorial: "The Chinese people once more declare to the whole world that Taiwan is China's territory and they are determined to liberate it. They will never stop until their aim is achieved. The great Chinese people can never tolerate any encroachment on the territorial integrity and sovereignty of their country. Anyone bent on such encroachment will reap its due deserts."[32]

To further demonstrate China's resolve to recover Taiwan and to draw international attention to the Taiwan issue, Mao in September 1954 initiated a massive bombardment of Quemoy, one of the offshore islands located in the Taiwan Strait and occupied by Jiang's troops. To Eisenhower and Dulles, the crisis was, in the words of the secretary of state, "a horrible dilemma." On the one hand, they were aware of the political and psychological value of the offshore islands, the loss of which "would have disastrous consequences" in Taiwan, Korea, Japan, and the Philippines. On the other hand, they recognized that they did not enjoy the support of their European allies as well as a "substantial part of the U.S. people" if they committed the United States to the defense of those islands at the risk of war with the PRC. Dulles indicated that "the British feared atomic war and would not consider the reasons for our action to be justified." Eisenhower stated that "his letters from the farm areas . . . constantly say don't send our boys to war. It will be a big job to explain to the American people the importance of these islands to U.S. security."[33]

To solve the dilemma, Dulles suggested presenting the offshore islands issue to the UN Security Council. The United States would seek an injunction against changing the status quo on the ground that the Communist action was a threat to world peace. In Dulles's calculation, such a move served several purposes. First, "it offered the possibility of avoiding going to war alone with the moral condemnation of the world or having the effect of the loss of the islands on the defense of Formosa." Second, it "could put a serious strain" on Sino-Soviet relations. If the Soviets vetoed the move, it would gravely undermine their "peace offensive" and then the United States "would win a measure of support from allies and world opinion now lacking." If the Soviet Union went along in the Security Council, the Chinese Communists could be expected to react adversely in defiance of the United Nations. In that case, the PRC would again become "an international outcast." Finally, the move could reap domestic benefits. Dulles pointed out that "if we act without Congress now we will not have anyone in the United States with us. On the other hand, if we act under the UN we will not have to act without Congressional authorization." Eisenhower supported Dulles's proposal.[34]

While preparing to present the offshore islands question to the United Nations, the Eisenhower administration also accelerated the mutual defense treaty negotiations with the Chinese Nationalists. In the preceding talks, Jiang Jieshi had persistently asked the United States to help him defend both Taiwan and the offshore islands. His supporters within the administration, most notably, Arthur Radford, chairman of the Joint Chiefs of Staff, and Walter Robertson, assistant secretary of state for Far Eastern affairs, strongly promoted his case. Although aware of the psychological value of the offshore islands, Eisenhower and Dulles, preferring to keep their operational flexibility, refused to commit the United States to their defense. Therefore, before the onset of the Communist shelling of Quemoy in September 1954, Dulles repeatedly found excuses to delay treaty negotiations. Instead of preventing the conclusion of the U.S.-Taiwan defense treaty, the Communist attack on Quemoy had the unintended consequence of speeding up such a result.

On 2 December, the Mutual Defense Treaty between the United States and Taiwan was signed. The treaty committed the United States to the defense of Taiwan, the Pescadores, and "such other territories as may be determined by mutual agreement." By intentionally not mentioning the offshore islands in the text, the Eisenhower administration hoped to deter the PRC from attacking Jiang's positions there and at the same time to discourage Taiwan from using the islands as a stepping-stone to invade the mainland.[35]

In the spring of 1955, the Chinese leadership took steps to deescalate tensions in the Taiwan Strait. Zhou Enlai declared at the Bandung Conference on 23 April: "The Chinese people are friendly to the American people. The Chinese people do not want to have war with the United States of America. The Chinese government is willing to sit down and enter into negotiations with the United States government to discuss the question of relaxing tensions in the War East, and especially the question of relaxing tension in the Taiwan Strait."[36]

There were several reasons behind Beijing's policy shift. First, the conflict in the Taiwan Strait had caused the anxieties and concerns of world opinion, especially Asian opinion, which worried about the specter of a Sino-American war. At the Bandung Conference, several Asian countries expressed to the Chinese delegation serious concern about the offshore island situation.[37] A conciliatory approach would calm the fears of neutral countries and at the same time serve as a vehicle for Beijing to launch a broad anti-imperialist united international front by impressing them with China's tactical flexibility and peaceful disposition.

Second, the Soviet Union played a role in pushing China toward a peaceful posture. At this time, leaders in the Kremlin were eager to improve relations with the West. The gap between Beijing's hostility toward Washington and Moscow's desire for détente grew wider as the United States and the USSR moved toward the Geneva Summit. When Chinese Defense Minister Peng Dehuai visited the Soviet Union in 1955, Soviet leader Nikita Khrushchev told him that at the moment the United States was still very powerful, and therefore, peaceful negotiations should be encouraged to settle international disputes. He hoped that China would disarm in order to operate with the Soviet Union on the political front. Accepting the Soviet leader's advice, Peng said that international tensions should be reduced and that China also needed a peaceful period to develop the economy, train and reform the armed forces, and strengthen the defense industry as well as defense projects along the Chinese coast.[38]

Third, the role of U.S. nuclear threats has to be considered. Although, given available Chinese sources, the precise effects of those threats remain unclear, it can be argued that Mao's decision to launch China's nuclear weapons program in early 1955 was a response to the Eisenhower administration's atomic blackmail.[39] Furthermore, the apprehension of the Asian states about the tensions in the Taiwan Strait stemmed from the possibility of American use of nuclear weapons in the area.

The State Department at first reacted negatively to Zhou Enlai's proposal of 23 April. It insisted that to obtain negotiations, China should take further steps (such as the prior release of detained Americans in China) to demonstrate its good intentions and that the Chinese Nationalists should participate in any discussion concerning the Taiwan issue. The Chinese government found the American terms unacceptable. The U.S. response was poorly received both at home and abroad. Senator Walter George, chairman of the Senate Committee on Foreign Relations, called for the acceptance of the Chinese offer. Other Senate Democratic leaders echoed his position. In Bandung, neutral nations believed that the United States did not want negotiations because of its nuclear superiority. On 26 April, John Foster Dulles, who had been on vacation and had not seen his department's response, reversed its initial decision by stating that Zhou's proposal was being studied. The next day President Eisenhower also blamed the State Department's initial approach as an "error in terminology" and claimed that the United States was interested in discussing a ceasefire as well as American prisoners in China.[40]

The mediation of third parties played a role in expediting the Sino-American negotiations. On 9 May, the British chargé d'affaires in China, Humphrey Trevelyan, forwarded to Zhou Enlai an oral message from British Foreign Secretary Harold Macmillan, which said that Britain viewed Zhou's Bandung speech with great interest and was willing to pass any Chinese message to the United States. On 26 May, Zhou met Trevelyan and outlined China's position on the proposed Sino-American talks: the subject should be the reduction of tensions in the Taiwan region, and the form could be either a multinational conference as suggested by the Soviet Union or a Sino-American bilateral dialogue with the support of other countries, but under no circumstances should Taiwan be included. China was prepared to hold separate direct talks with the Nationalists. These would be two different kinds of talks: one international and the other internal.[41] On 13 July, the United States responded through Britain that Sino-American talks at the ambassadorial level be held in Geneva. The negotiations began on 1 August 1955 at Geneva and continued thereafter in Warsaw.

The 1955 talk achieved some small but useful results. Agreement was reached on the return of Americans in the PRC and Chinese in the United States. Since the Korean War, dozens of American citizens, including students and missionaries, had been stranded in China. Hundreds of Chinese students who had been trained in science and technology, had, for security reasons, been kept against their will in the United States. Despite a promising beginning, the talks soon reached an impasse over such issues as the status of Taiwan and Chinese representation in the United Nations. Beijing refused to renounce the use of force in its plan to unify Taiwan. Washington insisted that the PRC explicitly renounce the use of force against Taiwan as a condition to any larger agreement. By the end of 1957, with both sides talking past each other, the ambassadorial negotiations were suspended.[42] Although the talks did not settle any substantial issue between the PRC and the United States, they served as a useful channel of communications. In the absence of formal diplomatic relations, the talks provided a helpful forum for leaders in Beijing and Washington to communicate each other's intentions during the hostile years of mutual non-recognition and non-intercourse. Furthermore, the talks enabled Chinese and American diplomats to learn about each other's negotiating styles.

Despite the moderation of Beijing's policy since 1955, Washington refused to ease up on its harsh attitude toward China. It continued to treat the PRC as a pariah in the international community, blocking its effort to obtain admission into the United Nations. To promote its two-China policy, the Eisenhower administration informed the Jiang government that the United States objected to its plans to launch military operations to recover the mainland. In the meantime, Washington reaffirmed its commitment to Taiwan by continuing its economic and military assistance programs. U.S. officials wanted to make sure that Jiang's government possessed a sufficient military capability to defend the territory under its control. They improved Taiwan's military power in 1957 by deploying on the island Matador tactical missiles capable of carrying nuclear warheads. In the meantime, Dulles ratcheted up his rhetoric against the PRC. In an address at San Francisco in June 1957, he declared that "international communism's rule of strict conformity is, in China as elsewhere, a passing and not a perpetual phase."[43]

Why did Eisenhower and Dulles continue their unremitting hostility toward the PRC? The domestic political atmosphere continued to make any revision of China policy problematic. Both political parties in 1956 included in their presidential campaign platforms statements declaring opposition to Beijing's seating in the United Nations and affirming support for Jiang Jieshi.[44] The desire to split the Sino-Soviet alliance by maintaining maximum pressure on the PRC continued to dominate the calculations of Eisenhower and Dulles. "There are some people who suggest that, if we assist the Chinese Communists to wax strong, then they will eventually break with Soviet Russia," the secretary of state asserted in his San Francisco speech. "No doubt there are basic power rivalries between Russia and China in Asia." But it was important to bear in mind that both countries adhered to an ideology antithetical to the interests of the United States. The axis powers might well have fallen into dispute among themselves if they had triumphed in World War II, "but no one suggested that we should tolerate and even assist an Axis victory because in the end they would quarrel over the booty—of which we would be part."[45]

On 23 August 1958, without notifying Khrushchev, Mao resumed shelling of the offshore islands after a lull of over three years. In renewing tensions in the Taiwan Strait, the Chinese leader intended to kill four birds with one stone. He had messages for four audiences. First, he wanted to send a message to the Nationalist government that he remained determined to seek a unification of Taiwan. Since 1955, Jiang Jieshi had constructed permanent fortifications and increased the number of troops on Quemoy and Matsu. The reinforcement of the islands continued until the troop level reached about 110,000, approximately one-third of the total Nationalist strength. Jiang completed these projects despite the earlier American advice that he should evacuate his soldiers from the offshore islands.[46]

By demonstrating the power of his forces, Mao wanted to undermine the Nationalist morale, discredit Jiang's talk of "returning to the mainland," and stop Jiang from using troops on the offshore islands to threaten mainland ports, harass coastal shipping, and carry out raids against the Communist regime. Mao calculated that if the United States should refrain from providing strong support to Jiang, he might make some Nationalists more receptive to psychological pressures and inducements, thus driving a wedge between Washington and Taipei.

It is very likely that Jiang Jieshi, a shrewd political calculator, intended to use the presence of his soldiers on Quemoy and Mastu to trap the United States into defending the islands, on the plea that their occupation by the Communists would endanger the survival of the Nationalist government on Taiwan. It appeared that Jiang's strategy worked because when the crisis in the Taiwan Strait began in August, both Eisenhower and Dulles cited this reason to explain their decision to commit the United States to the defense of Quemoy and Mastu. Jiang's manipulation of the United States into making a commitment to the defense of his positions represents a classic case of "the tail wags the dog" phenomenon in international relations. A small power could influence the behavior of a big power.

The United States was the second audience to which Mao intended to deliver a message when he ordered the bombardment of the offshore islands. Mao wanted to make clear to the Americans that he opposed the military ties between Washington and Taipei, and that he would not bow under American pressure and intimidation. He believed that the United States had its weaknesses and vulnerabilities because its power was over-committed and over-stretched around the globe. He summarized his confrontational approach to Washington as the "noose" strategy. According to Mao's analysis, the United States was inclined to intervene against revolution globally, but each tension spot in the world could become a noose on the American neck because U.S. intervention would backfire by creating more anti-American sentiments. American meddling in the world could awaken people's revolutionary consciousness and firm up their determination to oppose imperialism. The more nooses there were on the United States, the more difficult it would become for Washington to suppress national liberation movements, and the more beneficial it would be for the cause of international socialism. After the Eisenhower administration's intervention in Lebanon in July 1958, Mao contended that a new noose had been put on the United States in the Middle East. He wanted to support the revolution in the Middle East by exerting pressure on the United States in East Asia. In Mao's calculation, the tension in the Taiwan Strait constituted an additional noose on the United States.[47] Aware of Washington's intention to separate Taiwan from China, Mao wanted to arrest any drift toward a de facto "two-China" reality.

The Soviet Union was the third audience that Mao had in mind. By 1958, Mao and Khrushchev had developed divergent views regarding the international situation and prescriptions for global strategy. The post-Stalin leadership in the Kremlin no longer believed that war between the socialist and capitalist blocs was inevitable. Khrushchev argued that it was possible for the socialist countries to prevail worldwide through peaceful competition. The increased strength of the Soviet Union, the weakening of capitalism, and the advent of atomic weapons made this strategy both likely and necessary. He was convinced that the real danger to world peace was nuclear confrontation between the two superpowers. During his visit to Beijing (31 July–3 August 1958), Khrushchev warned Mao of the menace of nuclear war to the world.[48]

But Mao rejected Khrushchev's interpretation of international affairs. The Chinese leader feared that détente with the United States would compromise his plans for recovering Taiwan. Convinced that a militant policy would better serve China's interests, Mao stressed that the Communist bloc should prepare for a vigorous challenge to the Western camp headed by the United States. As for nuclear weapons, Mao tended to dismiss the danger of atomic conflicts, still referring to America's nuclear power as a "paper tiger." When the Eisenhower administration dispatched marines to Lebanon in July 1958, Mao expected Khrushchev to respond forcefully. But the Soviet leader's failure to send Soviet troops into the area to counter the American intervention alienated Mao, who decided to show his Soviet comrades how genuine Communists should deal with imperialist challenges by shelling Quemoy.[49]

The last audience whom Mao wanted to address in making his adventurous foreign policy move in August 1958 was the Chinese population. By 1958, Mao was poised to quicken the pace of socialist transformation of China by launching the Great Leap Forward. He planned to organize Chinese peasants to establish people's communes by dismantling families, abolishing money and melting household utensils in order to produce "backyard steel." By increasing tensions in the Taiwan Strait and highlighting the threat of the American-Taiwan alliance, Mao hoped to mobilize and rally the Chinese public behind his radical social-economic project and overcome any domestic opposition and reluctance.[50]

Even before the flare-up erupted on 23 August, U.S. leaders had expressed apprehension about the tensions in the Taiwan Strait. Because Jiang Jieshi had deployed so many of his troops on the offshore islands, Eisenhower and Dulles realized the adverse effect the fall of these islands would produce on Taiwan's morale as well as that of the rest of Asia. They worried about the domino effect on the region. In a meeting with JCS Chairman Gen. Nathan Twining on 11 August, the president pointed out that there were good reasons for making the argument that the offshore islands should be abandoned, but because a great number of Jiang's forces were now stationed on the islands, their withdrawal "would be a signal to all of Asia that there is no hope that can be held out against the Communists in China."[51]

During a meeting with Eisenhower on 12 August, Secretary of State Dulles mentioned that "if Quemoy and Mastu were lost, the Chinese Nationalists do not consider that they could hold Formosa. Morale would crumble and Chiang's control would be lost." Agreeing that "the key point is an evaluation of morale," the president asked Dulles to consider declaring in a press conference that "the islands have now been so tightly integrated with Formosa that there is no possibility that all-out attack could be conducted against them without bringing in the United States."[52]

When the fighting began on 23 August, Washington's reaction was swift but equivocal in terms of U.S. commitment. On that day, the Eisenhower administration issued an implied warning to China in a widely publicized message from Dulles to Thomas Morgan, acting chairman of the House Committee on Foreign Affairs. The secretary of state stated that "over the last four years the ties between these islands and Formosa have been closer and their interdependence increased." Any effort to capture the islands, Dulles warned, would be "a threat to the peace of the area." But he stopped short of explaining the precise nature of American commitment. It would be up to the president, he wrote, to decide the "value of certain coastal positions" to Taiwan if the Communists did attack.[53]

Clearly, the Eisenhower administration's strategy was ambiguity—to keep the enemy guessing. To Eisenhower and Dulles, ambiguity had several advantages. First, it would confound China's efforts to calculate the risks. Second, it would prevent Jiang Jieshi from making reckless provocations by increasing his doubts about the availability of U.S. assistance. Finally, it would help minimize domestic opposition, which would certainly arise if a clear public commitment were made.

Jiang Jieshi, however, pressed for a clear and direct American commitment to the offshore islands. In a meeting with U.S. Ambassador Everett Drumright on 24 August, Jiang urged the Eisenhower administration to make further public statement to clarify the situation. He also instructed his ambassador in Washington, Hollington Tong, to press the Americans further. Meeting Acting Assistant Secretary of State for Far Eastern Affairs J. Graham Parsons on 25 August, Tong first expressed appreciation for Dulles's letter to Congressman Morgan and then went on to emphasize that "something stronger was needed to deter the Communists from further aggressive moves against the offshore islands." What Taiwan wanted, Tong pleaded, was a statement from Washington announcing that the United States viewed any major attack on the islands as a threat to the safety of Taiwan. Promising to consult with the United States, Tong claimed that the morale of the Nationalist troops on the offshore islands "would be seriously affected" if no retaliation were taken at the moment when they were under the mainland's heavy and persistent bombardment.[54]

While agreeing to forward Taiwan's request to Dulles, Parsons mentioned the undesirability of a further American announcement on the ground that "too many statements within a short period" would lead the Communists to "discount our words" and that "it is more useful to demonstrate our intentions by action rather than by more words." But he did not inform Tong what specific action Washington contemplated against China.[55] It is clear from this conversation that U.S. officials wanted to keep maximum flexibility in coping with the crisis in the Taiwan Strait. They were trying to balance between reassuring the Nationalists and deterring China while retaining freedom of action.

In private deliberations, U.S. policymakers considered nuclear options. On 25 August, the JCS advised Eisenhower that although political calculations might demand initial retaliation against China with conventional weapons, "we will require atomic strikes" to check the mainland's action "effectively and quickly." Eisenhower approved a telegram to the Commander in Chief, Pacific, directing that initial operations would probably be only conventional but authorizing preparation "to use atomic weapons to extend deeper into Chinese Communist territory if necessary."[56] Two days later, the State Department's Far Eastern Bureau recommended to Dulles that early use of one or two low-yield nuclear weapons against airfields in southern China might be necessary and that further, more extensive attacks might also be needed.[57]

But in public, reference to nuclear options was more indirect and ambiguous than it had been during the 1954–55 crisis. When asked at a press conference on 27 August about the discretion allowed local commanders for use of nuclear weapons, Eisenhower reaffirmed that his personal permission was required. Limiting his talk to the principle of general support to Taiwan, the president insisted that his administration would not ignore the commitment it had already made. The most explicit statement that Eisenhower was willing to make was his observation that Taiwan's stationing of one-third of its troops on the offshore islands "makes a closer interlocking between the defense systems of the islands with Formosa than was the case before that."[58]

Eisenhower's caution concerning the use of atomic weapons in the Taiwan Strait indicated his sensitivity to the sentiments of international, especially Asian, opinion. He recognized that the costs of employing them in such a situation would very possibly overweigh the prospective gains.[59] His circumspection may also have reflected his awareness of the presence of Soviet nuclear strength. He later wrote in his memoirs: "In the stridency of Mao's public boasts and threats to seize Formosa by force, this new challenge resembled the earlier one of 1955. But the current situation included new dangers that seemed to make our position more difficult. . . . For one thing, the Soviets had used the intervening years to build up their nuclear striking force, which now included a more formidable arsenal of hydrogen weapons. I did not doubt our total superiority, but any large-scale conflict stimulated here was now less likely to remain limited to a conventional use of power."[60]

To reassure Taipei and to deter Beijing, the Eisenhower administration sent ships from the Sixth Fleet to reinforce the Seventh Fleet on 27 August. At the same time, however, U.S. officials feared that Jiang intended to drag the United States into the conflict while reserving his own naval forces. This was a shared sentiment at a combined meeting of State, Defense, and CIA officials at the Pentagon on 28 August. Acting Secretary of State Christian Herter suspected that Taiwan might be withholding its naval forces in order to achieve a commitment of American forces. Admiral Arleigh Burke, chief of naval operations, believed that something along this line might be happening. Acting Secretary of Defense Donald Quarles said that it was necessary for the United States "to be very cautious about increasing our involvement." Admiral Burke proposed that the first step that should be taken was for the American forces in the area to assume the defense of Taiwan so that Jiang's troops could shoulder more actively and fully the responsibility of re-supplying and defending the offshore islands. If Taiwan was then still unable to deal with the situation by itself, Burke continued, the United States should provide naval and air escort for Nationalist convoys. U.S. naval ships would first proceed halfway to the offshore islands, then all the way; U.S. aircraft would simply go all the way over the islands.[61]

As it turned out, the approach later adopted by the Eisenhower administration was exactly the scenario Admiral Burke had described. So long as Taiwan could resist the mainland's attack on its own, the United States would play an indirect role, helping to improve the defense of Taiwan without being involved in the clash over the offshore islands. When the PRC's assault escalated, Washington would increase its military supplies, including howitzers, Sabre jets, and, eventually, Sidewinder air-to-air missiles. The administration refused to consider extending the war to the Chinese mainland, or even bombing the coast of Fujian Province, as part of its effort to keep the offshore islands in Jiang's control.

As the conflict intensified, U.S. officials felt the need to allay Jiang's fears and to restrain Beijing further. Dulles remarked at a meeting of State and Defense officials on 3 September that it was crucial that leaders in Beijing did not have the impression that the United States would not intervene, stressing that such a miscommunication would produce serious effects on Taiwan's morale. He concluded that the U.S. objective was to "deter" a "massive assault" on the offshore islands.[62] After discussions with the president at the summer White House in Newport, Rhode Island, Dulles made an official speech on 4 September, warning China that Eisenhower "would not hesitate" to use armed forces "in ensuring the defense of Formosa" if he considered such action necessary. Dulles pointed out that "the securing and protecting of Quemoy and Mastu have become increasingly related to the defense of Taiwan" and that "military dispositions have been made by the United States so that a Presidential determination, if made, would be followed by action both timely and effective."[63] Like the vague threats included in his message to Congressman Morgan on 23 August, Dulles's Newport warning continued to be ambiguous. This demonstrated the Eisenhower administration's consistent attempt to deter the Chinese Communists by creating uncertainty in their minds over the risks involved if they decided to capture Quemoy and Mastu.

Dulles's subtle but resolute response must have worked in moderating Beijing's behavior. On 4 September, the mainland suspended bombardment of the offshore islands for three days. In the meantime, Beijing declared official claim to all waters and islands within twelve miles of its coast, but the Eisenhower administration announced that it would only respect a three-mile limit.[64] At the Supreme State Conference on 5 September, Mao acknowledged that in planning the shelling of the offshore islands, "I simply did not calculate that the world would become so disturbed and turbulent."[65] The next day, Zhou Enlai announced that the PRC was prepared to resume the Warsaw ambassadorial talks with the United States.[66] Beijing's willingness to reopen the negotiations revealed its intention to take the first step toward defusing the crisis.

On 7 September, U.S. vessels began to convoy Nationalist ships carrying supplies to Quemoy. The mainland's shore batteries only attacked Jiang's ships, and the American fleet did not join the battle. By concentrating on Nationalist targets only, Mao was testing how far the Eisenhower administration was ready to go in fulfilling its treaty commitment to Taiwan. After the 7 September encounter, Mao realized that there was a limit in American involvement in the Taiwan Strait and that the United States did not intend to wage war against the PRC. The Chinese leader was making a reevaluation of U.S. policy during this period. At the meetings of the Supreme State Conference on 5 and 8 September and in a conversation with provincial officials on 12 September, Mao observed that U.S. policy toward China and the Soviet Union was primarily defensive, not offensive. Washington was mainly interested in controlling the Third World, the area between the socialist and capitalist camps. Therefore, the offensive military threat to China posed by the U.S.-Taiwan security treaty, Mao concluded, was no longer as serious or as immediate as had previously been thought. The treaty was basically defensive and constrictive, intended to restrain rather than unleash Jiang. Mao reiterated China's readiness to settle the dispute with the United States through negotiations.[67]

Mao's judgment of the defensive nature of U.S. military power against China constituted an important shift in his perceptions of Washington's China policy. Ever since the establishment of the PRC in 1949, he had been obsessed with the danger of American military threats to China. On several occasions, he had indicated that the United States planned to attack his country from the three fronts of Taiwan, Korea, and Indochina. Now his sense of China's vulnerability to U.S. military invasion was no longer as keen as it had been. Mao's reassessment of U.S. policy showed that images could be modified in the face of new information and situation.

The Sino-American ambassadorial talks resumed on 15 September, while the bombardment continued. As the danger of war with China receded, U.S. officials began to urge Jiang to reduce his troop strength on the offshore islands. They believed that it was "a military liability" to station so many Nationalist soldiers on the islands because they were difficult to re-supply and were directly under the mainland's guns.[68] By pressuring Jiang to remove his garrisons on the islands, the last physical connection between the mainland and Taiwan, they hoped to eliminate a potential source of conflict between the two contending Chinese governments and promote the emergence of two Chinas.

Both Jiang and Mao opposed Washington's two-China notions. Jiang saw the offshore islands as a symbolic stepping stone to China. Mao feared that if Jiang abandoned Quemoy and Mastu and settled down solely on Taiwan, it would serve the American interest in creating two Chinas. To prevent Jiang from deserting the offshore islands, Mao made a compromise. Early in October, Beijing announced a seven-day ceasefire and expressed hope for a peaceful solution among the Chinese in order to maintain one China. After Beijing's announcement, the United States stopped convoying Nationalist supply operations. Shortly afterwards, Beijing limited bombardment to odd-numbered days, then stopped completely. By the end of October, the crisis had passed, although the fundamental dispute remained.[69]

While Mao's fears of American military threats diminished in the wake of the 1958 Taiwan Strait crisis, he began to express increasing apprehension about Washington's efforts to encourage a peaceful change of his government from inside China. In November 1959, Mao read Chinese translations of three speeches made by Secretary of State Dulles regarding the U.S. policy of stimulating a peaceful evolution within the Communist world. The three speeches included Dulles's address titled "Policy for the Far East" delivered before the California Chamber of Commerce on 4 December 1958, his testimony before the House Foreign Affairs Committee on 28 January 1959, and his speech titled "The Role of Law in Peace" made before the New York Bar Association on 31 January 1959. Mao circulated Dulles's three speeches among a small group of party leaders for discussion, hoping to draw their attention to what he perceived as a new danger from the U.S. strategy of promoting a "peaceful evolution" in China.[70]

The years 1958–59 were a crucial period in Mao's psychological development. He began to display increasing concern with the problem of succession and worried about his impending death. He feared that the political system that he had spent his entire life creating would betray his beliefs and values and slip out of his control. His apprehension about the future development of China was closely related to his analysis of the degeneration of the Soviet Union. Mao was convinced that Dulles's idea of inducing peaceful evolution within the socialist world was already taking effect in the Soviet Union, given Khrushchev's fascination with peaceful coexistence with the West. Mao was anxious to prevent that from happening in China. Here lie the roots of Beijing's subsequent exchange of polemics with Moscow and Mao's decision to restructure the Chinese state and society in order to forestall a Khrushchev-like takeover of China, culminating in the launching of the Great Cultural Revolution in 1966. Mao's frantic reaction to Dulles's speeches constituted a clear case of how international events could influence China's domestic developments.

Conclusions

The establishment of the PRC in 1949 was a major event that changed the Cold War balance of power in East Asia. The outbreak of the Korean War and the subsequent Chinese-American military clash locked the two countries in a state of bitter hostility and separation for two decades. Inheriting the Truman administration's containment policy, Eisenhower continued to view the PRC as a dangerous state bent on changing the status quo in East Asia at America's expense. He refused to recognize the Chinese Communist government or vote for its entry into the United Nations, thereby placing major roadblocks to the PRC's quest for international legitimacy. For the Eisenhower administration, a hard-nosed attitude toward Beijing could reap two benefits. First, it could satisfy anti-Communist right-wingers at home. Both Eisenhower and Dulles remembered how the controversy over "who lost China" had handicapped the Truman administration's conduct of foreign policy. Second, a hardline approach might stand a better chance in promoting a rupture within the Sino-Soviet alliance. The United States sought to separate China from the Soviet Union by adopting a "wedge" strategy that would expose Moscow's inability to satisfy Beijing's demands and needs, and create sufficient friction to break the alliance.

After the Korean fighting, the United States and the PRC almost came to blows on three occasions: in Indochina in 1954, and in the Taiwan Strait in 1954–55 and again in 1958. In each crisis, American and Chinese leaders approached "the brink," but then deescalated before direct clashes occurred. To some extent, the harsh lessons both sides drew in Korea restrained their conduct. Although Eisenhower and Dulles maintained an unyielding hostility toward the Chinese Communists, they wanted to avoid another Korean War-style confrontation with them. They did not want to be dragged into an unwanted conflict with China by Jiang Jieshi. They secretly placed limitations on how Jiang could use American aid. After Eisenhower revoked the neutralization order of the Taiwan Strait in early 1953, U.S. officials insisted that Taiwan accept new constraints on offensive operations against the mainland. Similarly, the exchange of notes that accompanied the U.S.-Taiwan Mutual Defense Treaty broadly pledged the Nationalists to refrain from offensive military activities against the continent without prior approval from Washington. Although the Eisenhower administration endorsed small-scale raids to undermine the Communist government, it had no intention of permitting major operations that carried the risk of involving the United States in a war with China. Dialogue with the Chinese Communists through the ambassadorial talks continued throughout the Eisenhower years.

During Eisenhower's tenure in the White House, Taiwan was quickly emerging as a major issue of contention between the United States and the PRC. To weaken the Chinese Communist regime, the Eisenhower administration sought to prevent it from unifying Taiwan. In the Cold War conflict in East Asia, Taiwan was a strategic asset for the United States. It had become an important part in the network of anti-Communist alliances stretching across the Asia-Pacific area that Washington had built in the 1950s. Pursuing a de facto "two-China" policy, U.S. officials wanted to make the separation of Taiwan from China a permanent reality.[71] But neither Mao nor Jiang accepted the American proposal for two Chinas. The two crises that Mao initiated in the Taiwan Strait during the decade were designed to test and challenge

Washington's "two China" policy. By shelling Quemoy and Mastu, Mao wanted to send a political message to the international community about the status of Taiwan, namely, it was part of China. Deeming Quemoy and Mastu as not crucial to the holding of Taiwan, U.S. officials tried to convince Jiang to abandon the offshore islands and to concentrate on the defense of Taiwan. But Jiang refused because he also believed that Taiwan belonged to China and that the offshore islands served as an important link between Taiwan and the Chinese mainland. Always claiming that his government represented China, Jiang had never given up his intention to reconquer the mainland. He worked hard to entrap the United States into committing itself into defending the offshore islands.

Although Washington and Taipei shared many anti-Communist interests and goals, they also differed over a number of issues, especially the Nationalist plan to recover the mainland by force. Officials in the Eisenhower administration often conducted their dealings with Jiang and his associates with a sense of wariness and suspicion. For his part, the watchful Nationalist leader always feared that his American protector would abandon him. Lacking complete confidence in the Americans, Jiang sometimes kept them in the dark about his plans for retaking the mainland. On several occasions, he convened secret military meetings with his generals in a cave to avoid detection by American advisers.[72] On the whole, Washington exercised greater influence in decision-making in the U.S.-Taiwan alliance. Partly because Jiang needed more from the Americans than vice versa and partly because the United States was a greater power, Washington was in a position to determine the basic terms and principles of its relationship with Taiwan. U.S. officials maintained effective control over Taiwan's offensive military activities, exercised supervision over the use of economic and military aid, applied pressure to force Taipei to follow their wishes, and chose not to inform Jiang when necessary of their military moves and diplomatic initiatives concerning Taiwan.[73]

Notes

1. On the Truman administration's policy toward the Sino-Soviet relationship, see Warren I. Cohen, "Acheson, His Advisers, and China, 1949–50," in Dorothy Borg and Waldo Heinrichs, eds., *Uncertain Years: Chinese-American Relations, 1947–1950* (New York: Columbia University Press, 1980), 13–53; Nancy B. Tucker, *Patterns in the Dust: Chinese-American Relations and the Recognition Controversy* (New York: Columbia University Press, 1983); David Allan Mayers, *Cracking the Monolith: U.S. Policy Against the Sino-Soviet Alliance, 1949–1955* (Baton Rouge: Louisiana State University Press, 1986); Gordon H. Chang, *Friends and Enemies: The United States, China, and the Soviet Union, 1948–1972* (Stanford, Calif.: Stanford University Press, 1990); and Qiang Zhai, *The Dragon, the Lion, and the Eagle: Chinese-British-American Relations, 1949–1958* (Kent, Ohio: Kent State University Press, 1994). On the debate about whether there was a "lost chance" in Sino-American relations in 1949–50, see "Symposium: Rethinking the Lost Chance in China," in *Diplomatic History* 21 (Winter 1997).

2. Leonard A. Kusnitz, *Public Opinion and Foreign Policy: America's China Policy, 1949–1979* (Westport, Conn.: Greenwood, 1984), 55; Burton I. Kaufman, *The Korean War: Challenges in Crisis, Credibility, and Command* (New York: Knopf, 1986), 292–93.

3. Karl Lott Rankin, *China Assignment* (Seattle: University of Washington Press, 1964), 155. See

also Kusnitz, *Public Opinion,* 55–56.

4. Memo of discussion at the 139th meeting of the NSC, 8 Apr. 1954, *Foreign Relations of the United States, 1952–1954* (hereafter *FRUS*), 14/pt. 1:181.

5. For Eisenhower's statement, see his address to the United Nations, 8 Dec. 1953, *Public Papers of the President: Dwight D. Eisenhower* (Washington, D.C.: Government Printing Office, 1960–61), 815.

6. For Dulles's remarks to Emmet John Hughes, see Emmet John Hughes, *The Ordeal of Power: A Political Memoirs of the Eisenhower Years* (New York: Atheneum, 1963), 105. For Dulles's conversation with Nehru, see Dulles memorandum of conversation, 21 May 1953, *FRUS, 1952–1954,* 15/pt. 1:1068.

7. Du Ping, *Zai zhiyuanjun zongbu* (At the headquarters of the Chinese People's Volunteers) (Beijing: Jiefangjun chubanshe, 1989), 579.

8. Yang Dezhi, *Weile heping* (For the sake of peace) (Beijing: Changzheng chubanshe, 1987), 173.

9. Ibid., 189.

10. *Renmin ribao* (People's Daily), 8 Feb. 1953.

11. Shen Zhihua, "Sino-North Korean Conflict and Its Resolution during the Korean War," *Cold War International History Project Bulletin,* Issue 14/15 (Winter 2003–Spring 2004); "Russian Documents on the Korean War, 1950–53," (introduction by James G. Hershberg and tran. Vladislav Zubok), ibid.

12. Quoted in Robert Simmons, *The Strained Alliance: Peking, Pyongyang, Moscow and the Politics of the Korean Civil War* (New York: Free Press, 1975), 233.

13. Chai Chengwen and Zhao Yongtian, *Banmendian tanpan* (Panmunjom negotiations) (Beijing: Jiefangjun chubanshe, 1989), 258.

14. Ibid., 258.

15. Ibid., 258–59.

16. Eisenhower was quoted in Rosemary Foot, *A Substitute for Victory: The Politics of Peace Making at the Korean Armistice Talks* (Ithaca, N.Y.: Cornell University Press, 1985), 177. For Dulles's remarks, see second restricted tripartite meeting of the heads of government, Bermuda, 7 Dec. 1953, *FRUS, 1952–1954,* 5:1811–13.

17. Foot, *Substitute for Victory,* 177–81; Sarvepalli Gopal, *Jawaharlal Nehru: A Biography* (Cambridge, Mass.: Harvard University Press, 1979), 2:148. Roger Dingman's investigation of nuclear diplomacy during the Korean War suggests that "nuclear weapons were not easily usable tools of statecraft that produced predictable results." Roger Dingman, "Atomic Diplomacy during the Korean War," *International Security* (Winter 1988/89), 90.

18. For Mao's criticism of Liang Shuming's thinking, see Mao, "Speech on the Victory in Resisting American and Aiding Korea Movement," 12 Sept. 1953, in *Selected Works of Mao Tse-tung* (Beijing: Foreign Languages Press, 1977), 5:115–20.

19. Chen Xiaolu, "China's Policy toward the United States, 1949–1955," in Harry Harding and Yuan Ming, eds., *Sino-American Relations, 1945–1955: A Joint Reassessment of a Critical Decade* (Wilmington, Del.: Scholarly Resources, 1989), 239.

20. On the evolution of U.S. policy toward Taiwan from the Truman to the Eisenhower administrations, see Robert Accinelli, *Crisis and Commitment: United States Policy Toward Taiwan, 1950–1955* (Chapel Hill: University of North Carolina Press, 1996); Nancy Bernkopf Tucker, *Taiwan, Hong Kong, and the United States, 1945–1992: Uncertain Friendship* (New York: Twayne, 1994).

21. On the development of the American thinking regarding Sino-Japanese trade, see Nancy B. Tucker, "American Policy toward Sino-Japanese Trade in the Postwar Years: Politics and Prosperity," *Diplomatic History* 8 (Summer 1984); Michael Schaller, *The American Occupation of Japan: The Origins of the Containment in Asia* (New York: Oxford University Press, 1985), 291, 294–95.

22. Rosemary Foot, *The Practice of Power: US Relations with China since 1949* (Oxford, England: Clarendon, 1995), 53.

23. Walter LaFeber, *The Clash: U.S.-Japanese Relations throughout History* (New York: Norton, 1997), 305–6; Victor S. Kaufman, *Confronting Communism: U.S. and British Policies toward China* (Columbia: University of Missouri Press, 2001), 106–8; Michael Schaller, *The United States and China:*

Into the Twenty-First Century, 3rd ed. (New York: Oxford University Press, 2002), 144.

24. On William Knowland's advocacy of Jiang Jieshi's cause, see Norman A. Graebner, "Eisenhower and Communism: The Public Record of the 1950s," in Richard A. Melanson and David Mayers, eds., *Reevaluating Eisenhower: American Foreign Policy in the 1950s* (Urbana: University of Illinois Press, 1987), 68. On the Committee of One Million, see Stanley Bachrack, *The Committee of One Million: "China Lobby" Politics, 1953–1971* (New York: Columbia University Press, 1976). On Henry Luce's ties with China, see Robert E. Herzstein, *Henry R. Luce: A Political Portrait of the Man Who Created the American Century* (New York: Scribner's, 1994).

25. Nancy Bernkopf Tucker, "A House Divided: The United States, the State Department, and China," in Warren I. Cohen and Akira Iriye eds., *The Great Powers in East Asia, 1953–1960* (New York: Columbia University Press, 1990), 36–37; Foot, *Practice of Power,* 89.

26. Memo of discussion at the 226th NSC meeting, 1 Dec. 1954, *FRUS, 1952–1954,* 12:1003.

27. NSC 166/1, "U.S. Policy toward Communist China," 6 Nov. 1953, *FRUS, 1952–1954,* 14:278–306.

28. Ibid.

29. Second restricted tripartite meeting of the heads of government, Bermuda, 7 Dec. 1953, *FRUS, 1952–1954,* 5:1808–9; See also John Lewis Gaddis, *Strategies of Containment: A Critical Appraisal of Postwar American National Security Policy* (New York: Oxford University Press, 1982), 143.

30. Notes of Dulles-Yeh conversation, 10 Feb. 1955, *FRUS, 1955–1957,* 2:253–58.

31. Wang Bingnan, *Zhongmei huitan jiunian huigu* (Reminiscences on the nine-year Sino-American ambassadorial talks) (Beijing: Shijie zhishi chubanshe, 1985), 41–42. Wang Bingnan was China's chief negotiator at the Sino-American ambassadorial talks in Warsaw.

32. *Renmin ribao,* 23 July 1954.

33. Memo of discussion at the 214th NSC meeting, 12 Sept. 1954, *FRUS, 1952–1954,* 14/pt. 1:619.

34. Ibid., 619–21; Dulles memo, 12 Sept. 1954, ibid., 612.

35. For the text of the treaty, see U.S. Department of State, *American Foreign Policy, 1950–1955: Basic Documents* (Washington, D.C.: Government Printing Office, 1957), 945–47.

36. Han Nianlong, chief ed., *Dangdai Zhongguo waijiao* (Contemporary Chinese diplomacy) (Beijing: Zhongguo shehui kexue chubanshe, 1987), 77–78.

37. Wang Bingnan, *Zhongmei huitan,* 44.

38. Liu Xiao, *Chushi sulian banian* (My eight years as ambassador to the Soviet Union) (Beijing: Dangshi ziliao chubanshe, 1986), 9–13.

39. John Wilson Lewis and Xue Litai, *China Builds the Bomb* (Stanford, Calif.: Stanford University Press, 1988), 35–39.

40. J. H. Kalicki, *Patterns of Sino-American Crises: Political-Military Interactions in the 1950s* (Cambridge, England: Cambridge University Press, 1975), 164; Thomas E. Stopler, *China, Taiwan, and the Offshore Islands: Together with an Implication for Outer Mongolia and Sino-Soviet Relations* (Armonk, N.Y.: Sharpe, 1985), 106; Nancy Bernkopf Tucker, "Cold War Contacts: America and China, 1952–1956," in Harding and Yuan, eds., *Sino-American Relations, 1945–1955,* 255.

41. Han Nianlong, chief ed., *Dangdai Zhongguo waijiao,* 97–99.

42. Warren I. Cohen, *America's Response to China: A History of Sino-American Relations,* 4th ed. (New York: Columbia University Press, 2000), 185; Schaller, *United States and China,* 149.

43. Dulles, "Our Policies Toward Communism in China," speech before the International convention of Lions International at San Francisco, 28 June 1957, *Department of State Bulletin* (15 July 1957), 91–95. Dulles's speech was also designed to foreclose the possibility of rapid change in public opinion over China policy and to shore up the resolve of U.S. allies, especially those around China's periphery. Kusnitz, *Public Opinion,* 78–79. See also Chang, *Friends and Enemies,* 161.

44. Mayers, *Cracking the Monolith,* 149; Chang, *Friends and Enemies,* 162–63.

45. Dulles, "Our Policies Toward Communism in China," 94. There were, however, voices within the administration at this time that questioned Dulles's attempt to hold the line on policy toward the PRC. Robert Bowie, director of the Policy Planning Staff and a member of Dulles's "inner circle," criticized the secretary of state for failing to consider either the costs of the current policy toward

Beijing or the likelihood of its success. See Bowie's comments on Dulles's San Francisco speech, 19 June 1957, *FRUS, 1955–1957,* 3:545–49. See also, Foot, *Practice of Power,* 93.

46. Appu K. Soman, *Double-Edged Sword: Nuclear Diplomacy in Unequal Conflicts: The United States and China, 1950–1958* (Westport, Conn.: Praeger, 2000), 168–69. Mao noticed the international implications of the large Nationalist military deployment on Quemoy and Matsu. He pointed out in September 1958 that "The problem lies in the 110,000 Nationalist soldiers, 95,000 on Quemoy and 15,000 on Mastu. The United States has to pay attention to them as long as these two large garrisons remain on the islands." See Mao's speech at the Fifteenth Supreme State Conference, September 1958, in *Mao Zedong waijiao wenxuan* (Selected diplomatic works of Mao Zedong), ed. PRC Foreign Ministry and the CCP Central Documentary Research Department (Beijing: Zhongyang wenxian chubanshe and Shijie zhishi chubanshe, 1994), 341–52. For an English translation of Mao's remarks, see *Cold War International History Project Bulletin,* Issues 6–7 (Winter 1995/1996):216–21.

47. Mao explained his "noose" strategy at the Fifteenth Supreme State Conference, September 1958. See *Mao Zedong waijiao wenxuan,* 341–52. See also Wu Lengxi, *Yi Maozhuxi* (Recalling Chairman Mao (Beijing: Xinhua chubanshe, 1995), 74–81.

48. On the differences between Chinese and Soviet explanations of international affairs, see Joseph L. Nogee and Robert H. Donaldson, *Soviet Foreign Policy since World War II,* 3rd ed. (Boulder, Colo.: Lynne Rienner, 1989), 120; Chang, *Friends and Enemies,* 205–6. For the transcripts of the Mao-Khrushchev conversations, 31 July–3 Aug. 1958, see *Cold War International History Project Bulletin,* Issue 12/13 (Fall/Winter 2001):244–62.

49. Wang Bingnan, *Zhongmei huitan,* 69; A. Doak Barnett, *China and the Major Powers in East Asia* (Washington, D.C.: Brookings Institution, 1977), 33–34; Chang, *Friends and Enemies,* 206.

50. On the linkage between Mao's foreign and domestic policies in 1958, see Thomas J. Christensen, *Useful Adversaries: Grand Strategy, Domestic Mobilization, and Sino-American Conflict, 1947–1958* (Princeton, N.J.: Princeton University Press, 1996).

51. Goodpaster memo of conversation with the president, 11 Aug. 1958, Whitman File, Dwight D. Eisenhower Diaries, box 33, "August 1958 staff notes (2)" folder, Eisenhower Library, Abilene, Kans.

52. Goodpaster memo of conversation with the president, 12 Aug. 1958, box 21, ibid.

53. For Dulles's remarks, see *Department of State Bulletin* (8 Sept. 1958), 379. Eisenhower later wrote in his memoirs that the message was intentionally "well-publicized." Dwight D. Eisenhower, *The White House Years: Waging Peace, 1957–1961* (Garden City, N.Y.: Doubleday, 1965), 296.

54. Tong-Parsons memo of conversation, 25 Aug. 1958, box 3924, RG 59, General Records of the Department of State, National Archives (NA), Washington D.C.

55. Ibid.

56. Richard K. Betts, *Nuclear Blackmail and Nuclear Balance* (Washington, D.C.: Brookings Institution, 1987), 68. See also Soman, *Double-Edged Sword,* 176–77.

57. Betts, *Nuclear Blackmail,* 68.

58. *New York Times,* 28 Aug. 1958.

59. John Lewis Gaddis, *The Long Peace: Inquiries into the History of the Cold War* (New York: Oxford University Press, 1987), 141–45.

60. Eisenhower, *White House Years,* 293.

61. Memo of conversation between State and Defense Departments officials, 28 Aug. 1958, box 3924, RG 59, NA.

62. Memo of conversation between State and Defense Departments officials, 3 Sept. 1958, ibid.

63. *New York Times,* 5 Sept. 1958.

64. Han Huaizhi and Tan Jingqiao, chief eds., *Dangdai Zhongguo jundui de junshi gongzuo* (Contemporary military works of the Chinese armed forces) (Beijing: Zhongguo shehui kexue chubanshe, 1989), 1:400.

65. Quoted in Allen S. Whiting, "Quemoy 1958: Mao's Miscalculations," *China Quarterly* no. 62 (June 1975), 265.

66. Kalicki, *Patterns of Sino-American Crises,* 193.

67. Han Nianlong, chief ed., *Dangdai Zhongguo waijiao,* 106; He Di, "Evolution of the People's Republic of China's Policy toward the Offshore Islands," in Cohen and Iriye, eds., *Great Powers in East Asia,* 236–37.

68. Record of State Department meeting, 8 Oct. 1958, box 3926, RG 59, NA.

69. Han and Tan, chief eds., *Dangdai Zhongguo jundui de junshi gongzuo,* 1:411–16; Schaller, *United States and China,* 151.

70. Bo Yibo, *Ruogan zhongda juece yu shijian de huigu* (Recollections of certain major decisions and events) (Beijing: Zhonggong zhongyang dangxiao chubanshe, 1993), 2:1138–46. Bo Yibo was Chinese finance minister as well as a senior member within the CCP. For an English translation of parts of his memoirs, see *Cold War International History Project Bulletin,* Issues 6–7 (Winter 1995/1996), 228–31.

71. Scholars have debated on the extent of U.S. commitment to a two-China policy. Wang Jisi argues that the two-China concept consistently influenced American policy from the outbreak of the Korean War in June 1950 to the beginning of the Geneva ambassadorial talks in 1955. Wang Jisi, "The Origins of America's 'Two China' Policy," in Harding and Yuan, eds., *Sino-American Relations,* 198–212. Robert Accinelli points out, on the other hand, that "To the extent that decision makers adopted a two-China approach after June 1950, they did so indirectly and evasively. More an unspoken than an articulated goal, the idea was never formalized as an officially sanctioned policy objective within the government." Accinelli, *Crisis and Commitment,* 259.

72. Author's interview with a former Nationalist general in Taipei, summer 1994.

73. For further discussions about the nature of the U.S.-Taiwan alliance during the 1950s, see Accinelli, *Crisis and Commitment,* 253–65.

"Not Enough Bulldozers": Eisenhower and American Nuclear Weapons Policy, 1953–1961

Gregg Herken

President Dwight D. Eisenhower would preside over the most rapid and dramatic growth of the United States nuclear arsenal in history. Eisenhower and his secretary of state, John Foster Dulles, would also set the course for an American policy on nuclear weapons that, while it borrowed from their predecessors, was uniquely their own—and established a precedent that would, for the next fifty years, influence their successors. The policy that Eisenhower and Dulles established toward nuclear weapons had its roots in the American past, yet cast a long shadow into the future.

Growth of the Arsenal

During Ike's eight years in office, from January 1953 to January 1961, the American nuclear stockpile grew by more than an order of magnitude—from 1,750 to approximately 23,000 weapons.[1] This included not only a dramatic increase in the number of the so-called nominal yield, 20-kiloton atomic bombs that were the original mainstay of the arsenal, but also the addition of multi-megaton thermonuclear weapons to the arsenal, following the successful U.S. "Mike" test in November 1952 of the world's first hydrogen bomb.[2] This expansion was not the result of decisions made by Eisenhower himself, but by his predecessor Harry S. Truman.

Indeed, Truman, like Eisenhower, almost certainly felt that this rapid growth in the number as well as the power of such weapons of mass destruction was both unnecessary and undesirable. But it was the perhaps unavoidable result of a powerful confluence of events: unrelenting technological progress, and the political necessity of responding to the unexpectedly early end of the U.S. atomic monopoly in August 1949, when the Soviet Union tested its first atomic bomb.[3]

"Agonizing Reappraisal" and the New Look

Chastened and alarmed by the awesome power of the H-bomb, Eisenhower, early in his first term, signaled by his remarks that he considered such weapons in an entirely different category than those with which he had been familiar as Allied supreme commander in World War II. In a conversation with perennial presidential candidate Harold Stassen shortly after his briefing on the results of "Mike," President-elect Eisenhower was characteristically blunt: "Just listen to the stories of the hydrogen bomb. And it doesn't do any good to run. Some day we will get those boys up to tell us some of the facts of those things. They are terrifying."[4]

Indeed, consistently throughout his time in office, Eisenhower's public and private utterances suggest that he never wavered from the view that nuclear war would be a catastrophe unprecedented in history, and that initiating such a conflict could hardly be the act of a rational statesman. As Ike once observed, even more succinctly, concerning what one should do in the event of war with the Soviet Union: "You might as well go out and shoot everyone you see and then shoot yourself."[5]

There seems little doubt but that John Foster Dulles shared Eisenhower's views on the subject. Although Dulles would later become identified in the public mind with the administration's "New Look" military strategy, Eisenhower's influential and high-minded secretary of state—described in some press accounts as "the Presbyterian elder of American foreign policy"—evidently regarded nuclear weapons with the same visceral dislike as the president, and felt no less than Eisenhower that their deliberate use would be unconscionable.

Similarly, while famous for announcing, in December 1953, at the height of a debate over troop commitments in Europe, that he and the president were engaged in an "agonizing reappraisal" of American foreign policy, there is no evidence that either Dulles or Eisenhower wished to stray from their predecessors' policy concerning weapons of mass destruction.[6] That policy, first promulgated in a Truman administration National Security Council (NSC) memorandum of August 1948, titled "U.S. Objectives with Respect to Russia," declared unequivocally that "whatever settlement we finally achieve must be a *political* settlement, *politically* negotiated [emphasis in original]."[7]

Preparing for Eventualities

Whatever his personal views on the subject of war, Eisenhower's long experience as a battlefield commander meant that he recognized the necessity of preparing for all military eventualities—even those one dislikes. This included the possibility, however remote, that the United States would one day become the target of a surprise, Pearl Harbor-style nuclear attack from the Soviet Union.

The necessity, under certain special and terrible circumstances, of allowing control over U.S. nuclear weapons to pass from civilian hands was one such eventuality. It was a contingency that Eisenhower approached warily, however, and acceded to only reluctantly and gradually.

In 1956, near the end of his first term, Ike requested that the Defense and State Departments prepare guidelines on how authorization for the use of nuclear weapons might be prepared in advance of hostilities—"predelegated" was the Pentagon's term—and used as the basis for specific instructions to senior U.S. military commanders in the event of a surprise nuclear attack.[8]

Later that same year, Ike approved instructions giving U.S. air defense commanders the authority to use nuclear weapons to shoot down attacking bombers. By mid-1957, Eisenhower had extended predelegation authority to include the commander of the U.S. Air Force's Strategic Air Command (SAC), "in circumstances where communication between the President and the Commander of SAC is impossible because of the results of enemy attack."[9]

The man who was the commander of SAC during Eisenhower's first term, and later Air Force vice chief of staff—Gen. Curtis LeMay—left little doubt, in a 1984 interview with Air Force historians, that he would have been prepared to act on Eisenhower's instructions, had the occasion arisen. "If I were on my own and half the country was destroyed and I could get no orders and so forth, I wasn't going to sit there fat, dumb, and happy and do nothing," LeMay told the interviewers.[10] Indeed, LeMay's earlier remarks suggest that he fully expected to receive presidential authorization to retaliate against the Soviet Union in *advance* of enemy bombs landing on American soil.[11]

Whereas Eisenhower's views on predelegating the authority to respond to a Soviet attack are made clear in the documentary record, Ike's attitudes toward *preempting* an imminent attack upon the United States or—an even more drastic action—removing a prospective future danger to this country by means of *preventive war,* are more difficult to discern.[12] In the case of both the president and his secretary of state, however, intentions were revealed by actions as well as words.

The Nuclear Policies of Eisenhower and Dulles

The first indication of the path that the president would follow in the matter of nuclear weapons came early in Ike's tenure, during the so-called Solarium study, which had been commissioned by the president himself as an open-ended review of past and possible future U.S. foreign policies.[13] Assembled at the White House in the summer of 1953, a coterie of foreign policy experts that included George Kennan, the architect of the Truman administration's so-called containment strategy, laid out three different and distinct possible futures: a continuation of containment; a more aggressive foreign policy stance, which included the possibility of a nuclear ultimatum to the Soviet Union; and a declared policy of "rolling back" Soviet expansionism. While not publicly identified as such at the time, the second option proposed by the Solarium group included the possibility of launching a nuclear attack upon the Soviet Union, should the Kremlin leadership not yield to U.S. demands.[14]

Eventually opting instead for a continuation of containment, Eisenhower and Dulles would attach the term "roll-back" to the policy they adopted, largely for reasons of domestic political consumption. But what the Solarium study experts had characterized as Option B—in effect, preventive war—was never considered seriously by either the president or his secretary of state. By their subsequent statements, both public and private, Eisenhower and Dulles continued to steadfastly reject the notion of preventive war, whatever the attractions or the circumstances.

As Ike observed to speech-writer and political adviser C. D. Jackson in December 1953, "atomic weapons strongly favor the side that attacks aggressively and *by surprise.* This the United States will never do; and let me point out that we never had any of this hysterical fear of *any nation* until atomic weapons appeared on the scene [emphasis in original]."[15] During a press conference the following year, Eisenhower responded similarly to a reporter's hypothetical question regarding how long the United States would allow itself to be held hostage by the Russian threat: "A preventive war, to my mind, is an impossibility today. . . . I wouldn't even listen to anyone seriously that came in and talked about such a thing."[16]

The question of preempting an imminent enemy attack or one already underway was a different matter. From the outset of the nuclear era, preemption was considered a possible, morally-defensible—and perhaps even necessary—alternative for U.S. military planners. In a seminal article in the January 1956 issue of *Foreign Affairs,* Paul Nitze, formerly one of the key architects of the Truman administration's defense policies, drew a distinction between the government's "declaratory policy" on nuclear weapons—the "statements of policy which we make for political effect"—and its actual or "action" policy.[17] As Nitze argued, whereas deterrence and retaliation were and always had been America's declaratory policy, the country's actual policy—what we built our military forces for—was preemption.

The importance of preemption in American nuclear planning was likewise clear to the man who would have carried out President Eisenhower's orders in the event of a Soviet nuclear attack: SAC Commander LeMay. As LeMay once observed, regarding the advantages of preemption over retaliation, "You don't compare going first with going second. You compare going first with not going at all."[18]

Finally, Eisenhower himself seemed to acknowledge that preemption was a likely option in the event that the United States received sufficient warning of a Soviet attack. In January 1959, when the president discussed with his National Security Council the latest top-secret NSC planning document, "U.S. Objectives in the Event of General War with the Soviet Bloc," Ike did not mince words. American policy in the event of war, he said, was simply to "hit the Russians as hard as we could. . . . The Russians 'will have started the war and we will finish it.' That is all the policy the President said that he had," according to notes taken by Ike's staff secretary, Brig. Gen. Andrew Goodpaster.[19]

The Gaither Report and Preventive War

Following the Solarium report, there would be one other occasion when the prospect of preventive war was raised in the Eisenhower administration, during Ike's second term. Ike's commissioning of a blue-ribbon panel of experts in spring 1957 to study and recommend steps that the United States might take to prepare for a possible nuclear war predated the *Sputnik* crisis that fall. But the Soviets' launch on 4 October 1957 of an Earth-orbiting satellite—as well as their successful test of an intercontinental-range ballistic missile, just a few weeks before—gave a new salience and fresh urgency to the findings of the Gaither Committee's report, "Deterrence and Survival in the Nuclear Age."[20]

Among the controversial recommendations included in the report was a proposal to spend up to $50 billion on a nationwide system of blast and fallout shelters to protect Americans from nuclear attack. Indeed, Eisenhower's prompt and wholesale rejection of such drastic measures, and of the report itself, would draw some of the most intense fire of his presidency from long-time critics of the administration.

For one of the principle authors of the Gaither report, Boston industrialist Robert Sprague, passive defensive measures were not enough. On 3 January 1958, following the briefing of the president by the Gaither Committee, Sprague laid out an alternative strategy to Secretary of State John Foster Dulles and Dulles's aides at the State Department. As one of the alternatives to continued containment of the Soviet Union, Sprague suggested that Dulles empower a secret study of the feasibility of launching a preventive war against the Soviet Union, with the aim of knocking out the Soviets' long-range bomber force in a sneak attack. As Sprague noted, "We could destroy this Soviet striking power, and if 'clean' weapons were used we could do this without killing a great many Soviet non-combatants. . . . After striking out the Russian strategic bombardment capability, we could then dictate disarmament terms."[21]

Dulles's reaction to Sprague's proposal was prompt and unambiguous, according to minutes of the meeting: "The Secretary said that he had long felt that no man should arrogate the power to decide that the future of mankind would benefit by an action entailing the killing of tens of millions of people, and he believed that the President agreed with him." Indeed, Ike did. Eisenhower's response to the White House briefing on the Gaither report was the occasion for a self-professed moment of epiphany among another of the report's authors—engineer and presidential science adviser, Jerome Wiesner.

For Wiesner, who would later serve as chairman of the President's Science Advisory Committee (PSAC) under President John F. Kennedy, Eisenhower's simple observation at the conclusion of the Gaither briefing prompted a moment of crystal clarity that the experts, because of their concern with the minutiae of defense planning, had overlooked because of its obviousness. "You can't have this kind of war," the president had declared matter-of-factly. "There just aren't enough bulldozers to scrape the bodies off the streets."[22]

To Wiesner, the president's subsequent entreaty to the Gaither Committee represented the only sensible alternative to the course of the action that the experts, himself included, had laid out. "Why don't you fellows help me with this nuclear test ban?," Eisenhower had asked the experts.[23]

Eisenhower's Legacy

There would be other, less pressing crises during the remaining years of the Eisenhower administration, when experts advising the president would recommend similarly drastic measures to deal with the threat from the Soviet Union. For the president, a particular disappointment would be the cancellation of the Paris summit, which followed the 1 May 1960 shoot-down in Russia of the U-2 spy plane piloted by Francis Gary Powers.

Since the consolidation of power in the Soviet Union by Premier Nikita Khrushchev, Eisenhower had hoped that he and Khrushchev might come to an agreement at Paris that would result in at least a slackening of the pace of the nuclear arms race—and perhaps, ultimately, an end to the sterile competition that constantly threatened ruin for both sides. One expert who had participated in the Gaither study would later claim that the celebrated warning contained in Eisenhower's farewell address—concerning the unwarranted influence of both a "military-industrial complex" and a "scientific-technological elite"—constituted a thinly-veiled criticism of those who had frustrated his efforts to put an end to nuclear testing.[24]

Instead of an end to the arms race, Eisenhower's lasting legacy would be that he kept the nation at peace—at a time when military conflict with the Soviet Union was prophesized by many to be inevitable. In the process, Ike rejected the advice of those supposedly wiser heads whose counsel had been either aggression, or despair.

Notes

1. Thomas B. Cochran, William M. Arkin, and Milton M. Hoenig, eds., *Nuclear Weapons Databook*, vol. 1, *U.S. Nuclear Forces and Capabilities* (Cambridge, Mass.: Ballinger, 1984), 14–15.

2. President-elect Eisenhower was briefed on the results of "Mike" on 18 November 1952. The 10.4-megaton blast had completely obliterated a coral atoll. Concerning Eisenhower and "Mike," see Gregg Herken, *Cardinal Choices: Presidential Science Advising from the Atomic Bomb to SDI* (New York: Oxford University Press, 1992), 69–70.

3. Concerning the political pressures for establishing "nuclear plenty" in the United States, see Gregg Herken, *Counsels of War* (New York: Oxford University Press, 1987), 39–45.

4. Stephen Ambrose, *Eisenhower: The President* (New York: Simon & Schuster, 1984), 617. A year after assuming the presidency, Eisenhower told an aide that he continued to "worry over people's seeming reluctance to recognize the threat of the hydrogen bomb." Herken, *Cardinal Choices*, 70. Another, relatively recent book documents Ike's early and evolving views on nuclear weapons. See Campbell Craig, *Destroying the Village: Eisenhower and Thermonuclear War* (New York: Columbia University Press, 1998).

5. Craig, *Destroying the Village*, frontispiece.

6. Concerning the "agonizing reappraisal," see "Strong Words," *Time*, 21 Dec. 1953.

7. NSC 20/1, 8 Aug. 1948, in Thomas H. Etzold and John Lewis Gaddis, eds., *Containment: Documents on American Policy and Strategy, 1945–1950* (New York: Columbia University Press, 1978), 193.

8. Concerning predelegation and Eisenhower, see Peter J. Roman, "Ike's Hair-Trigger: U.S. Nuclear Predelegation, 1953–60," *Security Studies* 7 (Summer 1998).

9. "Policy Regarding Use of Atomic Weapons," Robert Bowie and Gerard Smith to the secretary, 15 May 1957, Nuclear History Collection, National Security Archives, George Washington University, Washington, D.C.

10. Richard H. Kohn and Joseph P. Harahan, eds., "U.S. Strategic Air Power, 1948–1962: Excerpts from an Interview with Generals Curtis E. LeMay, Leon W. Johnson, David A. Burchinal, and Jack. J. Catton," *International Security* 12 (Spring 1988):84.

11. In a telephone conversation with the author, Curtis LeMay indicated that he was confident SAC would receive "unambiguous strategic warning" of a Soviet attack far enough in advance to preempt that attack. Telephone conversation with LeMay, 9 Feb. 1984.

12. The U.S. Defense Department's *Dictionary of Military Terms* defines *preemption* as, "An

attack initiated on the basis of incontrovertible evidence that an enemy attack is imminent." *Preventive war* is defined as, "A war initiated in the belief that military conflict, while not imminent, is inevitable and that to delay would involve greater risk." (www.dtic.mil/doctrine/jel/ doddict).

13. On the Solarium study, see John Lewis Gaddis, *Strategies of Containment: A Critical Appraisal of Postwar American National Security Policy* (New York: Oxford University Press, 1982), 145–46.

14. Herken, *Counsels of War*, 102–103.

15. Eisenhower to Jackson, 31 Dec. 1953, DDE diary, Ann Whitman file, December 1953 folder, box 4, Dwight D. Eisenhower Papers, Eisenhower Library, Abilene, Kans.

16. Gaddis, *Strategies of Containment*, 149.

17. Paul Nitze, "Atoms, Strategy, and Policy," *Foreign Affairs* (January 1956), 187–88.

18. Author's telephone conversation with LeMay, 9 Feb. 1984.

19. Craig, *Destroying the Village*, 94.

20. Concerning the Gaither report, see Herken, *Counsels of War*, 112–18; and David L. Snead, *The Gaither Committee, Eisenhower, and the Cold War* (Columbus: Ohio State University Press, 1999).

21. Memo of conversation, 3 Jan. 1958, *Foreign Relations of the United States: 1958–1960* (Washington, D.C.: Government Printing Office, 1996), 3:1–3.

22. Cited in Herken, *Counsels of War*, 118.

23. Ibid.

24. Physicist Herbert York, who also participated in the Gaither report, made this observation in an interview with the author. Cited in Herken, *Counsels of War*, 133.

The Invisible Hand of the New Look: Eisenhower and the CIA

Clayton D. Laurie

Upon his inauguration as president of the United States in January 1953, Dwight D. Eisenhower inherited a war in Korea, then well into its third year, a continuing expensive defense build-up dating from the issuance of NSC 68 in January 1950, and an increasingly ominous "Cold War" with an ever-bellicose USSR and People's Republic of China. Soviet military occupation and political control had placed much of Eastern Europe behind an "Iron Curtain," denying contact with the West, while technological advances, in particular the detonation of a Russian atomic bomb in August 1949 and ongoing efforts to develop a hydrogen bomb, threatened American security at home and that of U.S. friends and interests abroad. American allies in the West, considerably weakened by the demands and costs of World War II that had ended just eight years before, continued the long and difficult road to recovery unable in most cases to contribute much toward their own defense.[1]

A career soldier most noted for his roles as SHAEF commander, U.S. Army chief of staff, temporary JCS chairman, and lastly as supreme allied commander in Europe, Eisenhower adopted a different view toward American defense from his predecessor, Harry S. Truman, and a national security posture contrary to what many would expect from a man with a long military career dating back to 1915. The Cold War with the USSR, Eisenhower believed as he entered office, had already evolved into a full-blown ideological, diplomatic, military, *and economic* struggle likely to endure for decades, demanding pro-active American responses in each area beyond the policies of his predecessors that emphasized containment and an enormous military build-up: a build-up even beyond that demanded to wage the Korean War.[2]

To meet the challenges of this protracted struggle against Communist totalitarianism, Eisenhower asserted, the United States had to build and maintain an adequate defense and craft a national security strategy that could protect the country and its interests and allies abroad, and deter or counter threats from potential adversaries, but not at the risk of precipitating a nuclear world war, or at the expense of bankrupting the economy through excessive military expenditures, or at the risk of militarizing American society and sacrificing the civil liberties and freedoms that made the nation strong and unique.[3]

In 1953, the Eisenhower administration formulated the strategy of the New Look that rested national defense nearly exclusively on strategic air power and atomic weaponry, to, in John Foster Dulles's words, "deter aggression 'primarily upon a great capacity to retaliate, instantly, by means and places of our own choosing.'"[4] The threat of a devastating U.S. atomic attack on the USSR—the proponents of the

New Look reasoned—would prevent Communist aggression or any activities perceived as significantly threatening U.S. interests or national security. This strategy emphasizing "massive retaliation" promised immediate and sizeable reductions in defense spending, especially on modernized, yet dramatically smaller and reorganized, naval and ground forces,[5] thus obtaining lower, annually consistent defense budgets, while maintaining American economic strength—a fundamental goal of fiscal conservatives like Eisenhower and many of the businessmen who accepted administration positions.[6]

The New Look strategy proved unpopular and controversial from the outset. Democrats, many Republicans, soldiers, civilians, and academics in and outside of government claimed that a defense based on atomic deterrents or massive retaliation, in reality, precluded any response. Atomic weapons were just too devastating to use. Allowing conventional forces to wither in favor of large airborne atomic strike forces only increased risks, critics maintained, and tied American hands abroad when crises demanding a lesser response arose.[7] Further, Soviet and other Communist conventional military forces and expenditures allegedly continued to increase, as did their advances in nuclear, aviation, and missile technology. The United States, adhering to the New Look, predicated on saving money—obtaining "more bang for the buck" in Eisenhower's words—risked falling behind in numbers and in technological sophistication, actually diminishing American security. The bomber and missile "gaps" of the 1950s, which critics publicized, reflected such fears.[8]

Yet those questioning the wisdom of this strategy, and the administration's concept of contesting, if not rolling back, communism, were not privy to Eisenhower's overall program and, in particular, were unwitting of his use of, and reliance upon, the Central Intelligence Agency (CIA) as a key support to U.S. military and foreign policies.[9] Eisenhower created a sophisticated, well thought out, and complex national security policy and defense strategy that the public would have recognized as prudent, balanced, and acceptable, if not for the fact that a significant portion of it was a CIA responsibility and thus remained invisible—completely hidden from public view and discussion—as much of it still remains today. The president did reveal to select individuals the existence of an invisible force working in the nation's security interests. In 1954, the president explained to Senator William Knowland (R-Calif.): "'in the conduct of foreign affairs, we do many things that we can't explain. . . . There is a very great aggressiveness on our side that you have not known about and I guess that is on the theory of why put burdens on people that they don't need to know about.'" The president confided to the senator "that he himself 'knew so many things that I am almost afraid to speak to my wife.'"[10]

In effect, through his two terms of office, what atomic weapons and reduced conventional forces could not accomplish without risk of armed confrontation or a third world war, Eisenhower relied on the CIA to accomplish through its three major areas of expertise: intelligence collection through technical means and espionage, intelligence analysis and early warning, and covert action. Rather than functioning in just an intelligence support role, as William M. Leary has written, "the Agency emerged as an integral element in high-level United States policymaking." In addition, at the president's behest, through the National Security Council (NSC), "the CIA assumed the initiative in defining the ways covert operations could advance U.S. policy objectives and in determining what kinds of operations were suited to particular policy needs."[11] Thus during the years that Allen Welsh Dulles served as the director of central intelligence (DCI), what many have termed the CIA's "Golden Era," the Agency became the "invisible hand" of the New Look—Eisenhower's chief weapon for fighting the Cold War in the 1950s. During this period, unlike any time before or since, the CIA provided the important third leg of a national security and defense triad whose other supports rested on growing and untapped economic strength, and military power in a leaner conventional force structure with expanded strategic air capabilities for massive nuclear retaliation.[12]

Formed as a result of the National Security Act of 1947, the CIA was the largest single organization capable of providing all-source strategic intelligence to the president—the biggest entity in a fledgling, less capable Intelligence Community that functioned in an era of more focused threats and leader attitudes favoring smaller government. While President Eisenhower inherited the CIA from his predecessor, the Agency fit his needs well, and, with notable exceptions, met his expectations. During both terms, Eisenhower did not create new organizations, or significantly supplement the CIA or Intelligence Community that existed when he took office. The fact that the CIA was a civilian-dominated organization, as was the growing community that supported it, clearly meshed with what Eisenhower the career soldier wanted—civilian control of the CIA and the entire national intelligence apparatus with minimal military involvement. The Agency thus would play a major role in the 1950s—perhaps a bigger and far more exclusive role than at any other time in the nation's history—just as Eisenhower wanted. As the president once told CIA employees, "Upon the quality of your work depends *in large measure* the success of our effort to further the nation's position in the international scene."[13]

President Eisenhower's World War II experiences educated him to the value of tactical and strategic intelligence, an awareness he brought to the White House in 1953.[14] He once stated:

> In war nothing is more important to a commander than the facts concerning the strength, dispositions, and intentions of his opponent, and the proper interpretation of those facts. In peacetime the necessary facts are of a different nature. They deal with conditions, resources, requirements, and attitudes prevailing in the world. They and their correct interpretation are essential to the development of policy to further our long-term national security and best interests.[15]

The president recognized and consistently sought out current intelligence to inform his decisions. Like his immediate predecessor, Eisenhower had access on demand to the CIA daily written intelligence summaries. He could also receive regular briefings in the White House from Agency officials. Instead, he chose to rely on periodic high-level briefings and formal National Intelligence Estimates (NIEs)—actually avoiding reading daily intelligence reports from any one agency—preferring to see the finalized consensus view filtered through many analytical offices that were polished in the end at the CIA before they reached the Oval Office. On the top end, DCI Dulles personally provided the vast majority of the high-level intelligence briefings the president received at the opening of each weekly NSC meeting on broad subjects of interest to Eisenhower, cleared in advance with the NSC secretary and the president's national security advisors.[16] According to the president's staff secretary, Gen. Andrew Goodpaster:

> Eisenhower expected Dulles to provide the latest intelligence on the crisis of the moment but, more important, to concentrate primarily on providing the intelligence background to whatever larger or longer term planning issue was on the agenda. Because of this long-term focus, most of the briefing materials used by the DCI were prepared by the CIA's Office of National Estimates [ONE].[17]

The CIA thus provided the president with current intelligence, as well as a comprehensive, multiple-source, longer-term views of trends and projections that no other federal military or civilian organization then in existence could equal. Eisenhower's primary focus remained the Soviet Union and its worldwide overt and covert political, military, diplomatic, and economic activities, but increasingly, as Agency analytical capabilities increased manyfold during the 1950s, and following the mid-decade advent of the U-2 and other later technical collection assets, the Agency expanded analytical reporting to potential trouble spots in Asia, Africa, and Latin America.[18] Dulles provided most of the political and economic intelligence briefings at NSC meetings, deferring to Agency subject experts for scientific and military issues outside the DCI's purview. The NSC briefing process served both chief executive and the Agency well. DCI Dulles always enjoyed unfettered direct access to the president, and a venue where he could provide CIA-gathered and analyzed intelligence to all major participants in the policymaking process at one time and place, while at the same time receiving a good indication of the president's interests, wants, and needs.[19]

The major intelligence issue always of foremost interest to President Eisenhower, and to the vast majority of American military and civilian leaders of his generation, was the need for early warning of a possible Soviet surprise attack on the United States—a prospect made ever more dangerous by 1953 due to the advent of a new generation of nuclear weapons. "No one wants another Pearl Harbor," Eisenhower stated, "This means that we must have knowledge of military forces and preparations around the world, especially those capable of massive surprise attack."[20] DCI Dulles fully agreed with the president's assessment on the crucial nature of the early warning role of the CIA. "An intelligence service today," Dulles wrote,

> has an additional responsibility, for it cannot wait for evidence of the likelihood of hostile acts against us or until after the decision to strike has been made by another power. Our government must be both forewarned and forearmed. A close-knit, coordinated intelligence service, continually on the alert, able to report accurately and quickly on developments in almost any part of the globe, is the best insurance we can take against surprise. The fact that intelligence is alert, that there is a possibility of forewarning, could itself constitute one of the most effective deterrents to a potential enemy's appetite for attack.[21]

The CIA thus kept the president advised on Soviet capabilities and intentions relating to a potential surprise attack through weekly NSC briefings, but also in the broader long-term NIEs—an entirely new type of intelligence product the CIA first introduced through the ONE in 1950.[22] President Eisenhower used and respected the NIEs, and often requested through the NSC that the CIA analyze specific issues or decisions before the council on the nature of the Soviet threat or just to gain insight on Soviet strategic policies, capabilities, or behaviors. The Agency responded on a regular basis with estimative intelligence, continually updating the NIEs with the most recent intelligence available from all sources, human and technical, gathered worldwide. "National estimates" implied, as to the president's preference, a collaborative effort, with the input, or at least concurrence of, the National Security Agency, the military service intelligence organizations, and intelligence bureaus of the Atomic Energy Commission, Treasury and State Departments, and the Federal Bureau of Investigation—all contributing under supervision of the United States Intelligence Board (USIB).[23] As the CIA developed the estimative process, and designed its final product, they tended to dominate the process and Agency views were those President Eisenhower most frequently heard. Between 1954 and 1958, for example, several iterations of the same NIE appeared with titles and subjects such as SNIE 11-8-54 *Probable Warning of Soviet Attack on the U.S. Through Mid-1957,* NIE 11-7-55 *Soviet Gross Capabilities for Attacks on the U.S. and Key Overseas Installations and Forces Through Mid-1958,* and SNIE 11-7-58 *Strength and Composition of the Soviet Long-Range Bomber Force*—all giving the president as much of an objective and accurate assessment as possible given available intelligence sources on the size and capabilities of Soviets strategic forces. Midway through Eisenhower's second term, through their revelations, the CIA could dispel in the president's mind the existence of a "bomber gap," as critics of New Look policies had claimed existed as early as 1954.[24]

When Soviet actions indicated a course away from long-range bomber development and production—an area where superiority over the United States proved elusive—to the design and construction of intercontinental ballistic missiles, a capability demonstrated in the fall 1957 launching of Sputnik I and Sputnik II, the CIA provided further estimates on this new threat. In this case, the CIA had anticipated Soviet missile development years earlier, as well as President Eisenhower's eventual interest. In late 1955, DCI Dulles committed Agency resources to this difficult and ongoing and unanswered intelligence question, declaring "Soviet ICBMs a topic 'of the highest priority, probably of even greater ultimate importance to our national security than atomic energy intelligence.'"[25]

In the process of evaluating Soviet ballistic missile research and development, the Agency learned a great deal about the overall sophistication of Soviet science and technology relative to the West—providing scientific, engineering, and other technological information of interest to government offices outside the Intelligence Community and Department of Defense.[26] In spite of General Secretary Nikita Khrushchev's bombastic rhetoric concerning Soviet missile advances and burgeoning ICBM inventories, CIA estimates during the final years of Eisenhower's presidency were well on their way to relegating the "missile gap" to the same mythic realm as the earlier bomber gap—although definitive figures were not forthcoming until the mid-1960s when space-based overhead reconnaissance systems had sufficiently covered the Soviet Union. Yet the Agency could give reasonable analysis indicating that the Soviets, given more frugal financial resources and less sophisticated production capabilities, could not realistically hope to gain nuclear superiority over the United States. This prevented a jettisoning of the New Look, and the massive expenditures for additional and unnecessary armaments that surely would have followed.[27]

Although of lesser interest to the president than surprise nuclear attack, the CIA provided a limited number of estimates on Soviet and Communist Bloc conventional military capabilities—having previously left such tactical force analysis to the military intelligence services. The CIA emphasized that the initial Soviet focus on strategic long-range bomber development, and then strategic nuclear missile forces later on, prevented major conventional force enhancements and modernization throughout the USSR and East Bloc. Indeed, as CIA estimates revealed, what Eisenhower sought to gain in the New Look—reduced budgets, streamlined and modernized conventional forces, unfettered economic strength, and robust deterrents—the Soviets could not similarly achieve, already testing their system and stretching their limited resources increasingly thin in the late 1950s and early 1960s.[28]

The intelligence collected and analyzed by the CIA became incorporated into policymaking processes at the top, through the NSC, before filtering down to lower echelon executive branch boards and offices.[29] Although estimates were not always 100 percent accurate in their descriptions, nor in terms of the number of weapons or systems described, nor in predicting beyond any doubt Soviet intentions, capabilities, and motivations, they could provide technical data, show long-term patterns and trends, and define continuities in Soviet rhetoric and behavior to the extent necessary for President Eisenhower and his policymakers to make reasonable assumptions and more informed decisions.[30] As one CIA historian noted:

> The estimates of the 1950s portray the Soviet Union as aggressive but unwilling to take foolish risks. The assumption running through the estimates is that, while the USSR would use every opportunity to extend its influence, it would not do so in areas or ways that could escalate into general war with the United States. The essential intelligence question then became to determine what risks the Soviet Union would be willing to take in any given instance. These estimates reveal that the Office of National Estimates reassured policymakers and planners that the USSR would not deliberately go to war unless it thought that its vital interests were at stake. The Office counseled vigilance rather than panic in American responses to Soviet moves.[31]

Collectively, the NIEs provided President Eisenhower with the substantive background to decisions he was considering, or actions he was planning to take, and clearly show the degree to which intelligence became integrated into the foreign policy and defense strategy process. No president before or since has so heavily relied on the NIEs, and, as a result, Eisenhower became reasonably sure in the late 1950s that he could predict a Soviet attack in time to craft a non-military response—or, in the worst case scenario, fashion a response that would not escalate to the level of a nuclear exchange and global catastrophe.[32]

The regard the president had for Agency estimates stemmed in large measure from his equally high opinion of DCI Dulles as an intelligence professional. As Andrew Goodpaster recalled "Eisenhower had a lot of respect for Allen Dulles growing out of Dulles's work during the war. The President thought he was very skilled at top-level intelligence—collecting it and analyzing it."[33] In addition, the fact that the DCI was also the brother of Secretary of State John Foster Dulles, further cemented the CIA role in top-level policymaking circles. "Whatever the formal relationships among the State Department, the NSC, and the CIA, they were superceded by the personal and working association between the brothers. Most importantly, both enjoyed the absolute confidence of President Eisenhower."[34]

CIA espionage activities, and the acquisition of several high-level "walk-ins" from the USSR during the 1950s,[35] provided information for Eisenhower's use, but this human intelligence never equaled the quantity and importance of that originating from an increasing number of technical collection systems.[36] During his presidency, Eisenhower initiated the dawn of the era of technical collection within the CIA, and as a result had access to a growing and ever more reliable number of intelligence sources on the USSR and Communist Bloc. The CIA developed and operated these assets at Eisenhower's explicit direction. The U-2 high-altitude reconnaissance aircraft was perhaps the most famous—and later most publicized—intelligence collector that President Eisenhower selected the CIA to manage and operate over the military; emphasizing the Agency's ability to keep secrets, to operate covertly with plausible deniability, to spend from a "black budget," to undertake and complete projects with the bare minimum of bureaucracy, and to produce cost-effective, definitive results in rapid order from existing technology. Although Eisenhower authorized the continuation of U.S. Air Force peripheral and SENSINT flights near and into the USSR until late 1956, the CIA took increasing responsibility for aerial strategic intelligence collection— Eisenhower believing that CIA civilian pilots were potentially less provocative if downed over hostile territory than their uniformed counterparts.[37]

The U-2, derived from an aircraft designed by Lockheed Aircraft Corporation's Clarence R. "Kelly" Johnson as the CL-282, was built at a secret "Skunk Works" under the CIA code-name Project AQUATONE, with Dr. Richard M. Bissell, Jr. (the future Deputy Director/Plans), Dulles's special assistant for planning and coordination, as project manager.[38] The aircraft, whose existence was known to only a few hundred people, went from drawing board to operational flight stage in a mere 18 months. Described by Edwin H. Land,

> The Lockheed super glider will fly at 70,000 feet, well out of the reach of present Russian interceptors and high enough to have a good chance of avoiding detection. The plane itself is so light (15,000 pounds), so obviously unarmed and devoid of military usefulness, that it would minimize affront to the Russians even if through some remote mischance it were detected and identified.[39]

Eisenhower had significant qualms about conducting U-2 flights over the USSR, and demanded that the CIA have his personal approval for each Soviet mission. Yet he also realized the enormous potential of the aircraft in Agency hands to provide the critical intelligence the CIA, the military, especially the Strategic Air Command, and his administration needed so desperately.[40] Indeed, the twenty U-2s built for about $35 million would revolutionize intelligence collection in terms of the quality of information provided on "denied areas" in high-resolution photographs, and through the sheer quantity of images returned after each of the twenty-four overflights of the USSR between 4 July 1956 and 1 May 1960.[41]

The president's enthusiasm for technical collection and his confidence in the CIA-Lockheed/Bissell-Johnson overhead reconnaissance team prompted the additional assignment to the CIA to develop the first photo-reconnaissance satellite in early 1958. Project CORONA, again under the same CIA management as Project AQUATONE, with crucial Air Force and private industry support, returned the first of 145 buckets of images of the USSR in mid-August 1960, again revolutionizing intelligence collection and providing a treasure-trove of vital information for future CIA analysis and Intelligence Community use.[42]

The ability of the CIA to successfully manage these projects resulted in administration approval of Project OXCART in late 1958, although the president would not give the full go-ahead for development of the A-12 ultra-high altitude supersonic reconnaissance aircraft until June 1960, following the Soviet shoot down of Francis Gary Powers's U-2 the previous month. The A-12 did not become operational during Eisenhower's term of office, and would encounter a host of technological obstacles before its first successful flight in 1962 and deployment in 1966, yet it indicated the CIA's "can-do" attitude toward intelligence collection, even if Eisenhower initially expressed skepticism as to whether this new reconnaissance aircraft was necessary given costs and other advancing intelligence collection technologies.[43]

Yet, upon leaving office, President Eisenhower had launched, under CIA auspices, the development of three revolutionary intelligence collection systems in the U-2 and A-12 aircraft, and the CORONA space-based imagery satellite, while also laying the ground work for the expansion and formation of the National Photographic Interpretation Center, under CIA management, and the National Reconnaissance Office, also entailing a significant Agency presence. The intelligence windfall left to Eisenhower's successors through these reconnaissance systems more than made up for the seemingly exorbitant funds expended at the time in research and development and initial testing and operational phases. In addition, the "million dollar photography," in CIA officer Frank Wisner's words, that these overhead reconnaissance systems provided, ultimately saved the nation vast amounts of unnecessary defense expenditures.[44]

Agency accomplishments in overhead collection systems were matched through the CIA's efforts to intercept communications and general electronic data, and to gather missile telemetry during the Eisenhower years. These operations most notably included the Berlin Tunnel operation in 1955 and a similar operation in Vienna, and intelligence collected from installations on the Soviet periphery in Iran, Turkey, Alaska, and elsewhere. Indeed, the CIA pioneered many forms of what became known as SIGINT or signals intelligence during Eisenhower's terms, starting their efforts in fall 1953.[45]

Perhaps no endeavor of the CIA during the Eisenhower years, or since, has drawn so much popular and scholarly attention as the Agency's involvement in various covert endeavors implemented by the Clandestine Services. Due to the interest of DCI Dulles in such activities, as well as that of the secretary of state, President Eisenhower continued and expanded the use of paramilitary operations, espionage, and political action started under Truman—to actively combat Communist expansion and to foment unrest to ultimately roll back, or, at the very least, to prompt a diversion of Soviet attention and resources toward suppressing dissent or preventing rebellion in the East Bloc. The CIA's war in the shadows needled the Communists through Eisenhower's terms, with his direct knowledge and input, establishing precedents followed for the next thirty years. As Christopher Andrew has asserted, Eisenhower "believed there was no other way of fighting the Cold War effectively against a ruthless enemy. 'I have come to the conclusion,' he wrote privately, 'that some of our traditional ideas of international sportsmanship are scarcely applicable in the morass in which the world now founders.'"[46]

The CIA's Clandestine Services were well established prior to Eisenhower's assuming office, and Agency expertise, especially in political action and paramilitary operations, were recognized and respected. The new president accepted covert operations as a vital tool in pursuit of U.S. policy objectives.[47]

Dismayed with containment policies implemented in 1950, in summer 1953 Eisenhower initiated a study to examine alternatives. Named Project Solarium, after the room in the White House where the study was first discussed in May 1953, Eisenhower named Lt. Gen. H. A. Craig, USAF, to oversee committees comprised of soldiers and civilians to examine three possible national strategies: containment, liberation, and a moderate course somewhere between the two. Two of three options presented to the president and the NSC in July 1953 consisted of Task Force A, recommending a continuing of containment policies then in place, as outlined in NSC 153/1, and Task Force B, which recommended a course whereby the Soviets would be informed that further expansion beyond areas then in their orbit would result in general war with the United States with implied massive nuclear retaliation. Task Force C represented an even more militant and extreme option and "urged 'a positive course of action designed to seize the strategic initiative and deliberately undertake the task of eliminating the Communist threat to the free world.'" This option recommended a three-phase strategy where

> The United States would complete its military buildup, construct the necessary covert apparatus, and launch an economic, political, and diplomatic offensive against the communist bloc. Successive stages would see attempts to detach satellites from Soviet control, followed by an effort to disrupt the alliance between the Soviet Union and Communist China.[48]

Several months of debate concerning Project Solarium recommendations followed.

When President Eisenhower adopted a final policy in October 1953, designated NSC 162/2, it included recommendations from all three task force options. It also advocated

> Aggressive measures, both overt and covert, to reduce the Soviet threat. They included efforts to discredit Soviet prestige and ideology, reduce the strength of Communist and other pro-Soviet groups, and prevent Communist takeovers in other nations, as well as "selective, positive actions to eliminate Soviet-Communist control over any areas of the free world." To make trouble for the Soviets generally.[49]

The covert options were a CIA purview. Covert action thus came to dominate CIA activities during the Eisenhower years, eventually commanding 54 percent of the Agency's annual budget, and a doubling of personnel devoted to such activities.[50]

Due again to his military background and World War II experiences, President Eisenhower had first-hand knowledge of clandestine operations, "of what they could and could not accomplish, how to set them up, how to control them, how to direct these covert operations so that they reinforced policy, how to tie them into a broader program of national action."[51] Far from operating independently of executive control—as a "rogue elephant" as later congressional investigators termed it in the mid-1970s—Dulles regularly briefed President Eisenhower on CIA covert projects at NSC meetings, or privately in the Oval Office, often eliciting direct presidential inquiries, suggestions, approvals, and disapprovals of various new and ongoing projects, while also receiving input from policy-guidance and review boards the president had established for just such purposes.[52] President Eisenhower further reinforced the Agency's authority for covert action later in his administration, encouraging

> CIA to "create and exploit troublesome problems for International Communism, impair relations between the USSR and Communist China and between them and their satellites, complicate control within the USSR, Communist China, and their satellites, and retard the growth of the military and economic potential of the Soviet Bloc." In addition, the CIA should seek to "discredit the prestige and ideology of International Communism, and reduce the strength of its parties." It should also "counter any threat of a party or individuals directly or indirectly responsive to Communist control to achieve dominant power in a free-world country." "Finally, 'to the extent practicable' in the Soviet Union, China, and their satellites, the CIA should 'develop underground resistance and facilitate covert and guerilla preparations.'"[53]

One particular interest of the CIA during the Eisenhower years was the idea of rolling back communism by fomenting unrest in East Bloc satellites that would actually contest Soviet rule, and to encourage the formation of resistance groups to attack enemy supply lines and commit acts of sabotage in time of war—much as resistance groups had performed during World War II. CIA efforts to determine the level of unrest, and to exploit any fissures discovered, received more resources during Eisenhower's terms than they had under Truman or at any time thereafter. Yet the NIEs concluded that while "dissidence was widespread, the likelihood of active resistance in peacetime was negligible. In general war, as long as the outcome remained in doubt, resistance would be limited to intelligence gathering, minor sabotage, and escape and evasion operations to help Western military personnel."[54] Seeing that the encouragement of uprisings would likely not bring success, especially after the failed East German and Hungarian Revolts of 1953 and 1956, the Agency concentrated on creating long-term rifts, encouraging a heightened sense of nationalism in Eastern European countries, and passive resistance to Soviet hegemony through propaganda broadcasts via Radio Free Europe, leaflet drops, and covert support of student and labor groups and dissident organizations. Carried out in a manner less likely to spark catastrophic atomic or conventional armed confrontation, the Agency nibbled at the periphery, in one historian's words, to "keep options open and the Soviets guessing."[55] CIA paramilitary activities in Indochina, Tibet, Iran, Guatemala, Indonesia, Vietnam, the Congo, and Cuba, representing both successes and failures, are only the tip of the covert action iceberg of the Eisenhower years.[56]

Yet President Eisenhower did not always receive the quality of intelligence, nor the successful covert operations that he wanted or envisioned from either the CIA or the growing U.S. Intelligence Community—frequently showing concern that Agency analysis at times, and on certain topics, tended to overestimate numbers and capabilities, and thereby the threat, or that covert operations, if not tightly controlled, or if not well thought out, may go too far, or be exposed, risking confrontation with the USSR or other Communist nations.[57] Thus while President Eisenhower trusted and respected the CIA for what it did and could do, he also recognized that there were limits as to what the Agency could realistically obtain. Although the published record is scant, President Eisenhower certainly had the experience and background with intelligence matters to realize that 100 percent knowledge of the Soviet Union would always remain elusive. He probably also realized that no covert operation was guaranteed of absolute success or of entirely predictable results—especially the lofty goal of liberating nations from Communist control. Yet through the 1950s, Eisenhower sought to reform, consolidate, organize, and then reorganize the growing intelligence community to meet his expectations of the type, quantity and quality of intelligence necessary to meet national security needs—often harking back to World War II. Eisenhower, as one historian wrote:

> Wanted Dulles to serve him as [Major] General [Sir Kenneth] Strong had served him during the war, to be in fact as well as in name his chief intelligence officer, the man who would give him an overview, to be sure the President got the information he needed to act, while screening him from petty detail.[58]

Although many of these efforts failed, such as Eisenhower's attempt to prompt DCI Dulles to exercise more control over the entire intelligence community rather than fixating on CIA covert operations as he was wont to do,[59] the president did create a number of new intelligence boards and advisory committees that bolstered Agency performance and efforts to support defense and national security policies.[60]

Through regular briefs based on worldwide all-source intelligence collection and analysis, the CIA's efforts allowed President Eisenhower to more fully and accurately determine the true nature and significance of the Soviet threat, to obtain the best assurances of early warning to prevent surprise attack available to any president to date, and to judge with a relatively fair degree of certainty, long- and short-range Soviet goals and intentions. Eisenhower in turn, incorporated CIA intelligence into the top-level national security and defense strategy policymaking process—to perhaps a greater extent than any other president. Under CIA auspices, and at Eisenhower's direction, the Agency developed ever more sophisticated technical collection systems that in turn provided ever more accurate intelligence. Armed with such information, Eisenhower could counter Soviet programs and goals with prudent defense expenditures and policies based on hard fact rather than panicked speculation. While critics of the New Look must certainly have annoyed President Eisenhower, he was able to resist intense pressures to modify or abandon altogether the New Look strategy, based on his knowledge of the true nature of the threat. CIA covert operations, although far more controversial, were never as plentiful or as successful as the public often believed, but they did undermine, keep on the defensive, or destroy nascent Communist governments or leftist movements, real or alleged—establishing precedents during Eisenhower's terms followed for decades thereafter.

The CIA thus served as a covert and lower-cost substitute for larger conventional military forces whose use anywhere risked superpower confrontation and a third, potentially atomic, world war. Eisenhower's use of what the CIA could offer provided the administration with a practical, deniable means of combating Soviet influence and expansion, while holding down defense costs.

Of all the presidents who have occupied the Oval Office since the creation of the CIA, Dwight D. Eisenhower was arguably the most astute, knowledgeable, and prudent consumer of intelligence, and probably the president most willing to utilize the Agency to the fullest extent of its charter powers. Thus during the Eisenhower years, the CIA enjoyed what later historians termed a "golden age," when Agency influence was at its height, when funding and personnel levels expanded many fold, where covert operations were sanctioned in large numbers, and where the DCI had direct access to the president, not only as a trusted and respected intelligence advisor and co-policymaker, but as a personal friend. The New Look strategy had a supporting, yet invisible hand in the CIA and the fledgling intelligence community that allowed Eisenhower to implement a far less costly national security and defense strategy than his predecessors and successors, while contesting Communist expansion through covert action and accurate knowledge of enemy capabilities and intentions.

Notes

All statements, facts, opinions, policies, and positions expressed herein are solely those of the author and have neither been approved by nor are they reflective of the policy or positions of the U.S. government or of the Central Intelligence Agency.

1. For NSC 68, see Thomas H. Etzold and John Lewis Gaddis, eds., *Containment: Documents on American Policy and Strategy, 1945–1950* (New York: Columbia University Press, 1978), doc. 52, 385–442. For Truman-era defense budgets and national security policies, see Walter S.

Poole, *The Joint Chiefs of Staff and National Policy: History of the JCS*, vol. 4, *1950–1952* (Washington, D.C.: Office of Joint History, Office of the Chairman of the JCS, 1998), esp. chaps. 2–3.

2. Russell F. Weigley, *The American Way of War: A History of United States Military Strategy and Policy* (Bloomington: Indiana University Press, 1973), 400–401, and Dwight D. Eisenhower, *The White House Years*, vol. 1, *Mandate for Change, 1953–1956* (Garden City, N.Y.: Doubleday, 1963), 446–47, and William M. Leary, ed., *The Central Intelligence Agency: History and Documents* (Tuscaloosa: University of Alabama Press, 1984), 54.

3. Eisenhower, *Mandate for Change*, 606–7, and Weigley, *American Way of War*, 400–401.

4. Dulles quoted in Lawrence Freedman, "The First Two Generations of Nuclear Strategists," in Peter Paret, ed., *Makers of Modern Strategy From Machiavelli to the Nuclear Age* (Princeton, N.J.: Princeton University Press, 1986), 740. The "massive retaliation" policy was approved by Eisenhower in October 1953 in NSC 162/2, see U.S. Department of State, *Foreign Relations of the United States, 1952–1954*, vol. 2, pt. 1, *National Security Affairs* (Washington, D.C.: Government Printing Office, 1984), 577–97 (hereafter *FRUS*). See also Richard M. Leighton, *Strategy, Money, and the New Look, 1953–1956*, vol. 3, *History of the Office of the Secretary of Defense* (Washington, D.C.: Historical Office, OSD, 2001), 188–204, esp. chaps., 2–4, and Robert J. Watson, *The Joint Chiefs of Staff and National Policy*, vol. 5, *1953–1954, History of the JCS* (Washington, D.C.: Office of Joint History, Office of the Chairman of the JCS, 1998), 21–26.

5. Armed forces strength declined from 3.4 million in December 1953 to 2.8 million in June 1957. The U.S. Army declined from 1.4 million soldiers in 20 divisions to 1 million in 14 divisions. Navy strength declined from 765,000 personnel and 1,126 ships to 650,000 personnel and 1,030 ships, while USMC strength declined from 244,000 men and 3 divisions to 190,000 men in 3 "reduced" divisions. See Stephen E. Ambrose, *Eisenhower*, vol. 2, *The President* (New York: Simon & Schuster, 1984), 223–24. Truman's projected FY 1954 defense budget was $46.3 billion. Eisenhower received appropriations for $32.5 billion for 1955, $34.9 billion for 1956, $38.3 billion for 1957, and $41.1 billion for 1958. See Kenneth W. Condit, *The Joint Chiefs of Staff and National Policy*, vol. 6, *1955–1956, History of the JCS* (Washington, D.C.: Office of Joint History, Office of the Chairman of the JCS, 1992), 41–57; Dwight D. Eisenhower, *The White House Years*, vol. 2, *Waging Peace, 1956–1961* (Garden City, N.Y.: Doubleday, 1965), 129n3.

6. This would include Defense Secretary Charles Wilson, a former GM executive, Treasury Secretary George Humphrey, formerly of Mark A. Hanna Co., Interior Secretary Douglas McKay, Commerce Secretary Sinclair Weeks, and Budget Director Joseph Dodge, among others. Even Secretary of State John F. Dulles fit this category. Although a lawyer, his firm Sullivan and Cromwell had considerable corporate dealings. Weigley, *American Way of War*, 401–3; Richard D. Challener, "The National Security Policy from Truman to Eisenhower: Did the 'Hidden Hand' Leadership Make and Difference?" in Norman A. Graebner, ed., *The National Security: Its Theory and Practice, 1945–1960* (New York: Oxford University Press, 1986), 53–56; and Leighton, *Strategy, Money, and the New Look*, 3:41. For an examination of the New Look, see Saki Dockrill, *Eisenhower's New Look National Security Policy, 1953–1961* (New York: St. Martin's, 1996), and for budgets, see Glenn H. Snyder, "The New Look of 1953," in Warner R. Schilling, Paul Y. Hammond, and Glenn H. Snyder, eds., *Strategy, Politics, and Defense Budgets* (New York: Columbia University Press, 1962). See also "Minutes of Discussion at the 165th Meeting of the National Security Council, Wednesday, October 7, 1953," *FRUS, 1952–1954*, 2/pt. 1:514–34.

7. For New Look critics, see Ambrose, *Eisenhower*, 2:171–72, 225; Eisenhower, *Mandate for Change*, 451; and Freedman, "First Two Generations," 741–43. Critics included Charles DeGaulle, James Reston, William Kaufmann, B. H. Liddell-Hart, Robert E. Osgood, Bernard Brodie, Walt Rostow, and Henry Kissinger. Army Chiefs of Staff Matthew B. Ridgway and Maxwell D. Taylor were vocal in their opposition. See Leighton, *Strategy, Money, and the New Look*, 3:39–41, and Taylor's alternative "Flexible Response" strategy adopted during the Kennedy era, as described in Maxwell D. Taylor, *The Uncertain Trumpet* (New York: Harper, 1960), and idem, *Swords and*

Plowshares: A Memoir (New York: Norton, 1972), 164–65, 168–75, and Mark E. Clark, "General Maxwell Taylor and His Successful Campaign Against the Strategy of Massive Retaliation," *Army History* 16 (Fall 1990).

8. The Gaither Report, authored by Rowland Gaither and Paul Nitze, the latter a New Look critic and co-author of NSC-68, demanded 50 percent increases in defense spending. By the time the report appeared, the U.S. nuclear stockpiles had risen from 6,000 to 18,0000 weapons, including 14 Polaris submarines each with 16 missiles. Eisenhower dismissed the Gaither Report because the CIA had informed him of the true nature of the missile gap and the Soviet missile threat. See Christopher Andrew, *For the President's Eyes Only: Secret Intelligence and the American Presidency from Washington to Bush* (New York: Harper Perennial, 1996), 241.

9. General Maxwell D. Taylor did not attend NSC meetings and had no knowledge of the speciousness of the bomber and missile "gaps," or of the extent or success of CIA activities. See Oral History Interview, Dillon Anderson, 53–54, Eisenhower Administration Project, Oral History Research Office, Columbia University, 1972, Dwight D. Eisenhower Library (DDEL). General Lucius Clay criticized Taylor stating "when a soldier criticizes his government and superiors, after resigning, and then goes back into the service again, I think this is very bad. I think that General [Maxwell] Taylor, who resigned to criticize General Eisenhower's military policies, to help a candidate for President to defeat a Republican opponent, then to be taken back in and made Chief of Staff is about as dangerous a precedent as you can have anywhere." Oral History Interview, Lucius Clay, 16 Mar. 1967, 98, DDEL.

10. Ambrose, *Eisenhower,* 2:226

11. Quotation from Leary, *Central Intelligence Agency,* 54.

12. Andrew, *For the President's Eyes Only,* 202. Deputy Director of Intelligence Ray Cline later stated that the CIA "probably never accomplished more of value to the nation than this quiet, little remarked analytical feat" of providing accurate intelligence on the actual state of the Soviet threat which allowed Eisenhower to stick to the New Look. See Stephen E. Ambrose, *Ike's Spies: Eisenhower and the Espionage Establishment* (Garden City, N.Y.: Doubleday, 1981), 255.

13. Center for the Study of Intelligence (CSI), *Our First Line of Defense: Presidential Reflections on Intelligence* (Washington, D.C.: CSI, CIA, 1996), 19; emphasis added. DCI Dulles allegedly once referred to the CIA as "the State Department for unfriendly countries," quoted in Ambrose, *Ike's Spies,* p. 178.

14. For Eisenhower's World War II intelligence experiences, see Ambrose, *Ike's Spies,* chaps. 1–10; see also Andrew, *For the President's Eyes Only,* 199–201.

15. CSI, *Our First Line of Defense,* 19.

16. For Dulles's NSC briefings, see Oral History Interview, Dillon Anderson, 48–49, DDEL. For operations of the NSC, see Stanley L. Falk, "The National Security Council Under Truman, Eisenhower, and Kennedy," *Political Science Quarterly* 79 (September 1964), John Prados, *Keeper of the Keys: A History of the National Security Council from Truman to Bush* (New York: Morrow, 1991), and Anna K. Nelson, "The 'Top of Policy Hill': President Eisenhower and the National Security Council," *Diplomatic History* 7 (1983). Although most of the minutes of NSC meetings during Eisenhower's terms are published in the State Department's *FRUS* series, the intelligence portions remain classified and are omitted. James S. Lay served through most of this period as NSC secretary. Eisenhower's national security advisors were Robert Cutler, Dillon Anderson, William Jackson, and Gordon Gray.

17. John L. Helgerson, *Getting to Know the President: CIA Briefings of Presidential Candidates, 1952–1992* (Washington, D.C.: CSI, CIA, 1993), 38–39.

18. See Scott A. Koch, ed., *Selected Estimates on the Soviet Union, 1950–1959* (Washington, D.C.: CSI, CIA History Staff, 1993), for a sampling of the variety of 1950s topics.

19. Helgerson, *Getting to Know the President,* 38–39.

20. CSI, *Our First Line of Defense,* 20. See also Ambrose, *Ike's Spies,* 160–61.

21. Allen W. Dulles, *The Craft of Intelligence* (Westport, Conn.: Greenwood, 1963), 50–51.

22. As of 1996, the CIA had declassified 108 NIEs and SNIEs from the Eisenhower era. For specific titles and subjects, see CSI, *Declassified National Intelligence Estimates on the Soviet Union and International Communism, 1946–1984* (Washington, D.C.: CSI, CIA, 1996). See also Koch, ed., *Selected Estimates,* xiv. Koch reveals that 125 estimates were written during the 1950s.

23. The USIB, chaired by the DCI, had a membership consisting of the deputy DCI and the heads of the Intelligence Community at that time. See Donald P. Steury, ed., *Intentions and Capabilities: Estimates on Soviet Strategic Forces, 1950–1983* (Washington, D.C.: CSI, CIA History Staff, 1996), xiii–xiv.

24. For these estimates, and a summary of bomber gap issues, see Steury, *Intentions and Capabilities,* 5–7, 9–54.

25. Quotation from ibid., 55, 56–57. The first NIEs related to "an initial operational capability for a Soviet intercontinental missile, issued from October 1954 to March 1957, were fairly close to the mark." See Raymond L. Garthoff, "Estimating Soviet Military Intentions and Capabilities," in Gerald K. Haines and Robert E. Leggett, eds., *Watching the Bear: Essays on CIA's Analysis of the Soviet Union* (Washington, D.C.: CSI, CIA History Staff, 2001), 140–41.

26. NIE 11-6-59 *Soviet Science and Technology,* 21 July 1959, in Koch, ed., *Selected Estimates,* 19–41. Koch indicates the Intelligence Community believed the Soviets were strong in the theoretical aspects of the basic sciences (as opposed to practical application) such as physics, mathematics, and geophysical science. They were behind the West in chemistry, biology, agricultural sciences, and some aspects of medical research (see p. 9). See also Clarence E. Smith, "CIA's Analysis of Soviet Science and Technology," in Haines and Leggett, eds., *Watching the Bear,* 105–33.

27. See, for example, NIE 11-5-57 *Soviet Capabilities and Probable Programs in the Guided Missile Field,* SNIE 11-10-57 *The Soviet ICBM Program,* NIE 11-8-58 *Soviet Capabilities in Guided Missiles and Space Vehicles,* and NIE 11-8-60 *Soviet Capabilities for Long Range Attack Through Mid-1965,* all in Steury, ed., *Intentions and Capabilities,* 59–114. See also SNIE 11-8-57 *Evaluation of Evidence Concerning Soviet ICBM Flight Tests* and SNIE 11-10-57 *The Soviet ICBM Program.*

28. Steury, *Intentions and Capabilities,* 141–46. See specifically NIE 11-4-60 *Main Trends in Soviet Capabilities and Policies, 1960–65.* Among estimates on Soviet conventional forces, see SNIE 11-6-60 *Strength of the Armed Forces of the USSR,* NIE 90 *Soviet Bloc Capabilities Through Mid-1955,* and SNIE 11-54 *Likelihood of General War Through 1957.*

29. Jim Marchio, "Resistance Potential and Rollback: U.S. Intelligence and the Eisenhower Administration's Policies Toward Eastern Europe, 1953–1956," *Intelligence and National Security* 10 (April 1995):225–26.

30. Steury, *Intentions and Capabilities,* 501–3. Steury correctly states that more important than the actual facts revealed about Soviet strategic forces was the intelligence, analytical, and estimative thought processes that developed within the CIA and the larger Intelligence Community from producing NIEs. For errors and inaccuracies, see Garthoff, "Estimating Soviet Military Intentions," in Haines and Leggett, eds., *Watching the Bear,* 135–86, esp. 139–40.

31. Koch, ed., *Selected Estimates,* xiv.

32. A number of NIEs treated this issue, assuring Eisenhower of having ample warning of a Soviet attack. See SNIE 11-8-54 *Probable Warning of Soviet Attack on the U.S. Through Mid-1957,* NIE 11-6-55 *Probable Intelligence Warning of Soviet Attack on the U.S. Through Mid-1958,* NIE 11-3-57 *Probable Intelligence Warning of Soviet Attack on the U.S.,* and SNIE 100-2-57 *Soviet Capabilities for Deception.*

33. Goodpaster recalled, "Eisenhower would read enough of the Intelligence Community estimates to get the point and the highlights and 'felt the formal estimates and papers were the genuine [unpoliticized] view.'" See Helgerson, *Getting to Know the President,* 40.

34. Quotation from Leary, *Central Intelligence Agency,* 56. See also Memorandum of Meet-

ing, Eisenhower with Doolittle and Committee, 19 Oct. 1954, F. Doolittle Report, box 2 of 2, Reference Collection of Miscellaneous Documents, DDEL, where Eisenhower tells Doolittle that the relationship between the Dulles brothers "did not disturb him because part of [the] CIA's work is [an] extension of [the] work of [the] State Department," and that the "confidential relationship between the brothers is a good thing."

35. These walk-ins included GRU Majors Vladimir Popov and Peter Deriabin, and KGB members Vladimir Petrov, Yuri Rastvorov, and Nikolai Khokhlov. See John Ranelagh, *The Agency: The Rise and Decline of the CIA From Wild Bill Donovan to William Casey* (New York: Simon & Schuster, 1986), 255–56.

36. The CIA's inability to produce USSR HUMINT prompted calls to develop technical collection systems, specifically aerial and space-based platforms, by the Technological Capabilities Panel under James R. Killian and Edwin H. Land, which met in 1954 and reported to the president in early 1955. See James R. Killian, Jr., *Sputnik, Scientists, and Eisenhower: A Memoir of the First Special Assistant to the President for Science and Technology* (Cambridge, Mass.: MIT Press, 1977), George B. Kistiakowsky, *A Scientist in the White House: The Private Diary of President Eisenhower's Special Assistant for Science and Technology* (Cambridge, Mass.: Harvard University Press, 1976), and the Technological Capabilities Panel of the Science Advisory Committee report entitled *Meeting the Threat of Surprise Attack,* dated 14 February 1955.

37. For the military program, see R. Cargill Hall and Clayton D. Laurie, eds., *Early Cold War Overflights: Symposium Proceedings,* 2 vols. (Chantilly, Va.: Office of the Historian, National Reconnaissance Office, 2002), Robert S. Hopkins, III, "An Expanded Understanding of Eisenhower, American Policy, and Overflights," *Intelligence and National Security* 11 (April 1996), and William E. Burrows, *By Any Means Necessary: America's Heroes Flying Secret Missions in a Hostile World* (New York: Penguin, 2001).

38. Gregory W. Pedlow and Donald E. Welzenbach, *The CIA and the U-2 Program, 1954– 1974* (Washington, D.C.: CSI, CIA History Staff, 1998), 34, and Leary, *The Central Intelligence Agency,* 69–72. See also David T. Lindgren, *Trust But Verify: Imagery Analysis in the Cold War* (Annapolis, Md.: Naval Institute Press, 2000), 30–35, and Richard M. Bissell, Jr., *Reflections of a Cold Warrior: From Yalta to the Bay of Pigs* (New Haven, Conn.: Yale University Press, 1996), and Ben R. Rich and Leo Janos, *Skunk Works: A Personal Memoir of My Years at Lockheed* (Boston: Little, Brown, 1994).

39. Quotation from Pedlow and Welzenbach, *CIA and the U-2 Program,* 34.

40. On Eisenhower's thoughts on the U-2 and Dulles's assurances of its safety, reliability, and plausible deniability, see ibid., 96–99.

41. Goodpaster remarked that U-2 overflights also showed what the Soviets were not doing, such as building bombers and missiles at full capacity—"no [bomber or missile] gaps existed or were likely to exist." See Ambrose, *Ike's Spies,* 277, and Jeffrey T. Richelson, *The Wizards of Langley: Inside the CIA's Directorate of Science and Technology* (Boulder, Colo.: Westview, 2001), 13–15.

42. See Kevin C. Ruffner, ed., *CORONA: America's First Satellite Program* (Washington, D.C.: CSI, CIA History Staff, 1995), Robert A. McDonald, ed., *CORONA: Between the Sun and the Earth, The First NRO Reconnaissance Eye in Space* (Bethesda, Md.: American Society for Photogrammetry and Remote Sensing, 1997), Kenneth E. Greer, "CORONA," *Studies in Intelligence* 17 (Spring 1973), Andrew, *For the President's Eyes Only,* 220–24, and William E. Burrows, *Deep Black: Space Espionage and National Security* (New York: Random House, 1986).

43. For Agency development of the A-12, see Thomas P. McIninch, "The Oxcart Story," *Studies in Intelligence* 15 (Winter 1971), and Clarence "Kelly" Johnson, "Development of the SR-71 Blackbird: Recollections from the 'Skunk Works,'" *Studies in Intelligence* 26 (Summer 1982). Goodpaster stated Eisenhower wanted the A-12 to go forward only on a low-priority basis for potential Air Force use in time of war. See Richelson, *Wizards of Langley,* 21–22.

44. Lindgren, *Trust But Verify,* 60–61. Rather than referring to money spent to develop systems to *get* photographs, Wisner was actually referring to the money *saved* in needless defense

expenditures. See Dino Brugioni, "The Million Dollar Photograph: Allen Dulles Prices a Picture," *Studies in Intelligence* 23 (Summer 1979):33–34.

45. Garthoff, "Estimating Soviet Military Intentions," 146–47. For the Berlin and Vienna tunnel operations, see Andrew, *For the President's Eyes Only,* 214–15, and Ranelagh, *The Agency,* 288–96. See also William H. Nance, "Quality ELINT," *Studies in Intelligence* 12 (Spring 1968), Charles A. Kroeger, "ELINT: A Scientific Intelligence System," ibid. 2 (Winter 1958), David S. Brandwein, "Telemetry Analysis," ibid. 8 (Fall 1964), Stanley G. Zabetakis and John F. Peterson, "The Diyarbkir Radar: Operation of a Fixed-Beam System Blanketing Kasputin Yar," ibid., Oral History Interview, Dillon Anderson, 55, DDEL, and Richelson, *Wizards of Langley,* 21–31.

46. Quotation from Andrews, *For the President's Eyes Only,* 202.

47. Leary, *Central Intelligence Agency,* 54–55. Leary credited the Agency emphasis on covert action to DCI Dulles, who believed the CIA "could make a special contribution to the advancement of United States foreign policy goals" (p. 55). For the CIA's statutory authority, see Sec. 102 of the National Security Act of 1947 in Michael Warner, ed., *Central Intelligence: Origin and Evolution* (Washington, D.C.: CIA, CIA History Staff, 2001), 29–30, and Loch K. Johnson, *America's Secret Power: The CIA in American Democracy* (Oxford, England: Oxford University Press, 1989), 16–21.

48. For quotation, see Watson, *The Joint Chiefs of Staff and National Policy,* 5:13, see also 11–14. For Project Solarium, see *FRUS, 1952–1954,* 2/pt. 1:387–442.

49. Quotation from Leighton, *Strategy, Money, and the New Look,* 3:194–95. Dulles proposed to "detach Albania from the Soviet bloc" by just covert means and to invade Hainan Island. For NSC 162/2, see *FRUS, 1952–1954,* 2/pt. 1:577–97.

50. Quotation from Leary, *Central Intelligence Agency,* 57.

51. Quotation from Ambrose, *Ike's Spies,* 156–57.

52. Eisenhower's National Security Advisor Dillon Anderson, contradicted this view, implying that Eisenhower often did not want, or did not know, operational details, trusting those within the CIA to act according to his directives and wishes. See Oral History Interview, Dillon Anderson, 108–12, DDEL. These would include the Psychological Strategy Board, formed in 1951, and replaced in September 1953 by the Operations Coordinating Board, and the 5412 Committee, or later "Special Group," or 303 Committee, established by NSC 5412/1 and 5412/2 in 1955. See Leary, *Central Intelligence Agency,* 62–63.

53. Quotation from Ambrose, *Eisenhower,* 2:285–86. See also Leary, *Central Intelligence Agency,* 60–61, and Andrew, *For the President's Eyes Only,* 211.

54. Quotation from Koch, ed., *Selected Estimates,* 163–64. See also Marchio, "Resistance Potential and Rollback," 229, and Trevor Barnes, "The Secret Cold War: CIA and American Foreign Policy in Europe, 1947–1956," in two parts, *Historical Journal* 24 (June 1981) and 25 (September 1982). See NIE 10-58 *Anti-Communist Resistance Potential in the Sino-Soviet Bloc* in Koch, ed., *Selected Estimates,* 223–47. For CIA efforts to manipulate various groups, see Ranelagh, *The Agency,* 246–52.

55. Quotation from Ranelagh, *The Agency,* 230; see also Ambrose, *Eisenhower,* 2:226–27. Robert R. Bowie, director of the State Department Policy Planning Staff from 1953 to 1957, stated that John Foster Dulles actually believed that even if the United States could foment unrest and detach Communist regimes in China and Europe from the Soviet Union, the process would probably involve the United States in a general war, and even if successful would not deal with the problem of a still-dangerous nuclear-armed Soviet Union. See "Bowie's Commentary," in Ernest R. May, ed., *American Cold War Strategy: Interpreting NSC 68* (New York: St. Martin's, 1993), 112–14.

56. Ambrose, *Ike's Spies,* 189–234, 244–51, idem, *Eisenhower,* 2:110–12, 129–30, 192–97, 555–57, Andrew, *For the President's Eyes Only,* 202–11, Ranelagh, *The Agency,* 260–269, John Prados, *President's Secret Wars: CIA and Pentagon Covert Operations from World War II Through the Persian Gulf* (Chicago: Ivan Dee, 1996), 91–106, 114–17, 130–40, 150–217.

57. Ambrose, *Eisenhower,* 2:455–56, and idem, *Ike's Spies,* 253.

58. Quotation from Ambrose, *Ike's Spies,* 242.

59. Ibid., 242–43, and Leary, *Central Intelligence Agency,* 72–75.

60. Eisenhower once stated, "I'm not going to be able to change Allen. I have two alternatives, either get rid of him and appoint someone who will assert more authority or keep him with his limitations. I'd rather have Allen as my chief intelligence officer with his limitations than anyone else I know." See Ambrose, *Ike's Spies,* 244. See also Memorandum of Meeting, Eisenhower with Doolittle and Committee, 19 Oct. 1954, F. Doolittle Report, box 2 of 2, Reference Collection of Miscellaneous Documents, DDEL, where Doolittle expressed criticisms of Dulles and his methods of managing and operating the CIA, as well as criticisms of other Agency officials. See also Philip K. Edwards, "The President's Board, 1956–1960: Overseeing the Intelligence Community," *Studies in Intelligence* 13 (Summer 1969).

Eisenhower and the NSA: An Introductory Survey

David A. Hatch

When Dwight D. Eisenhower left the presidency in January 1961, his reputation already had begun to decline. The media and many historians characterized him as out of touch and manipulated by strong-minded subordinates.

The resurgence of Eisenhower's reputation began with Fred Greenstein's writings in the 1980s on the "hidden hand" presidency.[1] Greenstein demonstrated that Eisenhower had actually been an activist president, but preferred to work behind the scenes. Parallel with this rehabilitation was the revelation of Eisenhower as active also in the field of intelligence. Stephen Ambrose, in *Ike's Spies* in 1981,[2] first showed Eisenhower as a manager and user of intelligence from World War II through his presidency. A number of later books, such as Dino Brugioni's *Eyeball to Eyeball* in 1990[3] and Philip Taubman's *Secret Empire* in 2003,[4] emphasized Eisenhower's concern to develop a well-rounded aerial reconnaissance capability for early warning.

However, with the exception of two short pages in a long chapter in Christopher Andrews's *For the President's Eyes Only* in 1995,[5] none of the revisionist books were able to discuss Eisenhower's involvement with the National Security Agency (NSA) or communications intelligence (COMINT) as president. Virtually nothing on this subject had been declassified from the 1950s.

During World War II, starting with the campaign in North Africa, General Eisenhower learned the value of Communications Intelligence. He remained aware of this source and its value, although, as supreme commander in Europe, he required that all intelligence sources be fused into one complete report. His G-2, British Maj. Gen. Kenneth Strong, became expert at providing actionable intelligence—incorporating COMINT—in the form his commander required.

As Chief of Staff of the Army in the period immediately after the war, Eisenhower continued his interest in COMINT. His first visit to an outside post was to Arlington Hall Station, the home of the Army's cryptologic organization, in early February 1946. He met with William Friedman, Frank Rowlett, and Solomon Kullback, three of the four "founding fathers" of modern Army COMINT.[6] In fact, Eisenhower, with his considerable experience with COMINT during World War II, as president involved himself in many aspects of NSA activities.

Most of the material concerning Eisenhower's interest in the NSA is still classified. This paper therefore will be confined to just two cases in which Eisenhower played a direct role: one in which his actions added to the NSA's capabilities, one in which he took advantage of its expertise.

The World of the New Administration

When the Eisenhower administration took office in 1953, American officials had an abundance of theories but little enough solid knowledge about the sources of policy or immediate goals of the USSR. While striving to do whatever necessary to deter a Soviet "sneak attack," Eisenhower also sought moderation in defense spending. He believed that fear could lead to unchecked expenditures for national security and, eventually, economic ruin. Considering the Soviet threat, and with a new defense posture, accurate and timely intelligence would be a must. To facilitate paperwork and coordinate issues across organizational lines, Eisenhower established a strong staff secretary position for the National Security Council (NSC). In September 1954, he brought in Colonel, later General, Andrew J. Goodpaster to fill the position; Goodpaster had worked with him in the Office of Chief of Staff at NATO.[7] Eisenhower's management style was to block out wide issue areas, give policy direction, and then leave subordinates to handle details. He required his chief of staff to follow up on details and prompt him about areas needing attention. This style was manifested in Eisenhower's dealing with intelligence no less than other issues of domestic and foreign policy.

Goodpaster received daily and weekly intelligence reports from the Central Intelligence Agency (CIA) that included COMINT, and rewrote them for the president. When Goodpaster or his staff gave intelligence to the president, they sent in no more than thirty or forty items, and kept them concise, that is, around five lines. Another source of the president's intelligence was the weekly NSC meeting, usually 10:00 A.M. every Friday. The group, however, generally followed an agenda that had been set weeks in advance, and thus did not necessarily discuss *current* intelligence.[8]

Goodpaster rated the president "extremely competent" in analyzing the intelligence brought to him. Eisenhower did not ask about sources and methods, but insisted that the president receive the "best available" intelligence.[9] In one instance, a special meeting of most senior officials in the intelligence and defense community in the president's office in early 1957, Eisenhower complained that he was getting too many papers containing "scattered details," and wanted reports only when they gave "clear evidence of definite conclusions." In that meeting, the group discussed how to keep NSA costs from rising. Director of Central Intelligence (DCI) Allen Welsh Dulles gave his opinion that the government received "great value" from NSA activities, but Secretary of Defense Charles Wilson—NSA executive agent in the government—disputed that assertion. President Eisenhower came to the NSA's defense and said he agreed with the DCI.[10]

NSA and COMINT in the 1950s

National-level intelligence organizations in the United States began only after World War I and continued developing structure, process, and technique during

World War II. Immediately after the war, each of the three military services had COMINT organizations, with civilian as well as military customers. The postwar atmosphere of budget and personnel retrenchments, however, made it difficult to maintain three separate organizations. When early attempts to consolidate the three organizations and funding failed, President Harry S. Truman established the National Security Agency in 1952. Although it traced its antecedents directly to organizations of the 1930s, the NSA as the government's central cryptologic organization had been in existence as such for less than a year when Eisenhower took office. It was far from clear to that new administration that the NSA had the optimum internal structure or operated at the required level of proficiency.

The NSA, subordinate to the Department of Defense, was responsible for national-level COMINT and also for national communications security (COMSEC) doctrine and policy. The first director of NSA (DIRNSA) was Maj. Gen., later Lt. Gen., Ralph Canine, USA. Although not a career intelligence officer, Canine learned the essentials of cryptology quickly, and built an effective organization. In 1956, he retired and was replaced as DIRNSA by Lt. Gen. John Samford, USAF.

The first two civilian NSA deputy directors did not work out, for different reasons. The first, with a background in the communications business, turned out not to have the requisite experience for the position. The second, Dr. Howard Engstrom, had been tasked with managing special technical projects rather than administrative tasks, but Samford wanted a deputy who would be his *alter ego*. This led to the appointment of Dr. Louis W. Tordella in 1958. "Dr. T" had been in charge of a major Navy collection station during World War II; postwar, as a civilian, he had had an important role in developing joint-service COMSEC devices and early computers for cryptologic tasks. Tordella became the longest-serving deputy director at the NSA, holding the post until his retirement in 1974.

The Baker Panel and IDA

After an initial series of meetings and conferences in early 1954, President Eisenhower appointed a special task force to study defense, striking power, and intelligence. He asked Dr. James R. Killian, president of the Massachusetts Institute of Technology, to take charge of it. Killian's panel had a subcommittee on intelligence, chaired by Edwin Land, of Polaroid fame, and included prominent figures from universities and private industry. Killian was indoctrinated for COMINT by the CIA in August 1954.[11] Although its actual title was "Meeting the Threat of Surprise Attack," the final report was known throughout the intelligence community as the "Killian Report," "TCP [Technical Capabilities Panel] Report," or the "Surprise Attack Report."[12]

Four of the TCP Report's five sections dealt with details of continental defenses and the effect of technology on the military. The first section, however, said the United States should have the "best-informed government in the world," not only for defense, but also to help resolve the debates between "contending views and fantasies" that appear in the democratic process.[13]

In later years, recalling the Technical Capabilities Panel, Killian expressed a belief that the panel had helped restore trust between scientists and government. He also noted that Eisenhower was pleased that, unlike other panels, there were no leaks from the TCP.[14] The success of this panel put Killian in a position to make further recommendations about the intelligence community. When Killian, by then Eisenhower's science advisor, made a report to the president in early 1957, among his recommendations was one calling for a panel of about fifteen scientists to study COMINT. Eisenhower agreed, and appointed a special panel under Dr. William O. Baker of Bell Telephone Laboratories.[15]

Baker received his Ph.D. from Princeton University, and joined Bell Laboratories in 1939. He had served as a Bell vice president; and would serve as vice president of research from 1955 to 1980.[16] Recalling this period later in life, Louis Tordella, longtime NSA deputy director, commented that "I doubt that in the knowledgeable community in Washington that NSA . . . had a better friend than William O. Baker. . . . I also doubt anyone in Washington knew more sensitive material about the U.S. government defense state and CIA than Baker."[17]

Most panel members had no prior concepts of the specifics of cryptology, but over a period of months the panel studied all phases of COMINT production from the general to the specific. Baker's recommendation included a proposal to separate basic research from practical intelligence production at the NSA. As might be imagined, this proposal did not sit well with NSA leadership, and they opposed the concept.

Despite its initial reservations, the NSA eventually warmed to the Baker Panel recommendations for a cryptologic think tank. This was particularly so after the idea evolved, when it no longer meant splitting the NSA, but creating a group for long-range support in theoretical cryptanalysis to supplement the Agency's activities. Given a presidential directive that the research institute be managed by a contractor in an "academic atmosphere," NSA's director, General Samford, selected the Institute for Defense Analyses (IDA) in Princeton, New Jersey. This allowed the NSA to take advantage of an existing Department of Defense contract. The department approved the arrangement.[18]

When the IDA Board of Trustees met in October 1957, NSA Deputy Director Dr. Howard Engstrom presented them with a proposal to do directed research on behalf of the Agency. The IDA accepted in June the following year.[19] The research institute was to study basic concepts and operations of cryptology, as well as long-range applications of techniques. Another important aspect of the research would be computer assistance to cryptology. Although the desired number of employees for the research institute was established initially at thirty-six, budget limitations reduced the number to be hired immediately to twenty-four. Of these, twelve would be NSA employees released to the institute.[20] Over time, the IDA in fact did make significant contributions to cryptanalysis and computer development.

Communications

As seniors in the administration strengthened existing intelligence capabilities and fostered new ones, they realized that communications were critical to this endeavor. Improvements to intelligence were pointless if the resulting data did not reach decision-makers in time to be of use. The president, in particular, was concerned that he was not getting crisis information in a timely way.

This problem was assigned to the Department of Defense, and became known as CRITICOMM, for critical communications. The goal was to get vital information to the president within ten minutes. Louis Tordella had first learned of the CRITIC plans while on assignment to the Assistant Secretary of Defense (Special Activities), retired U.S. Marine Gen. Graves B. Erskine. When he returned from his "downtown" assignment to the NSA in August 1958, he was assigned to work on the problem with Capt. Arthur Enderlin, USN, who was in charge of NSA telecommunications. They developed the system concepts and a briefing for the NSC about it.[21]

Tordella, with NSA Director Samford and Enderlin attending, presented the draft plan at a meeting of the National Security Council on 27 August 1958. The NSC, chaired by President Eisenhower, was meeting to consider NSCID #7, which would establish the secretary of defense as executive agent for the government for critical communications.

After DCI Allen Dulles talked about the importance of the new system, Tordella addressed the meeting. He noted that Department of Defense and the Joint Chiefs of Staff had selected NSA communications as the most adaptable for the proposed network. The COMINT communications system had been operating twenty-four hours per day, seven days per week since World War II, and had demonstrated that it could move large volumes of traffic at all classifications faster than any existing system. Moreover, it was calculated that 200 of 245 potential sources of CRITICs were already COMINT sources tied into the system.

Even at that, the COMINT system would have to be expanded and made more efficient before it could be used for critical messages. The existing COMINT communications system was described as a "loosely integrated world-wide system of trunklines and tributary circuits" without a central point of control. Although it was the best existing system, it was unable in its current configuration to satisfy the presidential criterion of moving messages to senior decision-makers within ten minutes.

In order to establish the CRITICOMM system, the NSA would assume the role of system manager, and would immediately establish special procedures for handling the messages. For the future, the Defense Department and NSA would purchase advanced automatic switching centers and make circuit arrangements so that critical messages could be transmitted automatically and without delay. All CRITIC messages regardless of source would "funnel" into the NSA communications center at Fort Meade, Maryland, and then be relayed automatically to the president and appropriate senior government officials. Simultaneously, messages would be transmitted to other organizations, including overseas locations, where the information was needed.

Tordella emphasized that the goal of a ten-minute transit time to the White House could not then be achieved, and probably would not be attainable until as late as 1965.[22] Eisenhower sat doodling during Tordella's briefing. At the end, he turned to Deputy Secretary of Defense Donald Quarles and simply said, "Don, can we do it?" Quarles had once been an executive at Bell telephone, and understood communications technology. When Quarles replied, "Yes, I think so," Eisenhower said, "let's do it."[23] Tordella was impressed with the simplicity of the decision-making process on such an important matter.

In November 1959, a Defense Department communications officer briefed the president's Board of Advisors on Foreign Intelligence Activities about improvements already implemented in the CRITIC system. He noted that during the period from March through October 1959 the COMINT system had handled 105 CRITIC messages. Although one message originating in Alaska had achieved two minutes transit time, the median handling time for these messages ranged from eleven to twenty-nine minutes.[24] The desired improvements in time were not achieved until the early 1960s, during the Kennedy administration.

Observations

There are no startling revelations about President Dwight D. Eisenhower in his relationship with the NSA. Eisenhower was the consummate staff chief, one who had mastered the art of delegation for research and action. Thus, although we find few direct fingerprints from him on NSA and COMINT developments, he was no less influential. Eisenhower had greater involvement with the burgeoning reconnaissance programs because these were essentially new programs, and, moreover, programs that had the potential for causing international incidents. With the NSA and COMINT, Eisenhower was dealing with institutions, structures, and processes already in existence that needed reforming.

The primary tool for his actions toward the NSA was a chain of panels that studied intelligence issues. Eisenhower initiated the studies, considered their recommendations, and took appropriate actions based on them. He put first-rate minds from government, academia, and industry on the panels to study the intelligence community and NSA. Their involvement ensured that the NSA and its components would get the best analyses possible.

In cases such as the CRITIC communications system, the results were not apparent during his administration. Change was slow for a variety of reasons. The CRITIC system moved steadily toward implementation, but technical challenges were great and the physical challenges of emplacing the system on a global basis were daunting.

Change did come, however. The major areas in which he fostered change would not have happened naturally; they required Eisenhower's concern and intervention. The changes Eisenhower initiated, even if not fully realized during his time, had profound impact in keeping the NSA ahead of the technological curve, ensuring that its technical proficiency would be the highest. That, in turn, was an important factor in keeping the American people secure in the decades after.

Notes

All NSA documents cited are available from the library of the National Cryptologic Museum, Fort Meade, Md.

1. Fred I. Greenstein, *The Hidden-hand Presidency: Eisenhower as Leader* (New York: Basic Books, 1982).

2. Stephen E. Ambrose, *Ike's Spies: Eisenhower and the Intelligence Establishment* (New York: Doubleday, 1981).

3. Dino A. Brugioni, *Eyeball to Eyeball: The Inside Story of the Cuban Missile Crisis* (New York: Random House, 1990).

4. Philip Taubman, *Secret Empire: Eisenhower, the CIA, and the Hidden Story of America's Space Espionage* (New York: Simon & Schuster, 2003).

5. Christopher Andrew, *For the President's Eyes Only: Secret Intelligence and the American Presidency from Washington to Bush* (New York: HarperCollins, 1995).

6. "Eisenhower Visits Arlington Hall," *Hall Herald,* 21 Feb. 1946, 1. The fourth "founding father," Abraham Sinkov, was probably still overseas.

7. New York Times Oral History Program, Eisenhower Administration Project, interview of General Andrew J. Goodpaster by Ed Edwin, 25 Apr. 1967 (interview no. 1), 9, 13, 24, 31.

8. Richard Kovar, "An Interview with Richard Lehman," www.cia.gov/csi/studies/summer00/art05.html.

9. Hatch telephone interview with General Goodpaster; Goodpaster interview by Edwin, *op. cit.*

10. Memorandum, "Discussion at the Special Meeting in the President's Office on Thursday, January 17, 1957," 18 Jan. 1958, Special Assistant for National Security Affairs, 1952-61, box 6-7. Records of the White House Office, Dwight D. Eisenhower Library, Abilene, Kans.

11. LCDR P. J. Karl, USN, Memorandum for Mr. Hugh S. Erskine, "The President's Science Advisory Committee," 9 Mar. 1955. NSA ARC ACC# 20659 CBJG 16.

12. James R. Killian, Jr., *Sputnik, Scientists, and Eisenhower: A Memoir of the First Special Assistant to the President for Science and Technology* (Cambridge, Mass.: MIT Press, 1977), 64-70.

13. Ibid., 79-80.

14. Oral History Collection, pt. 4, "Killian, James P., Jr.," 29, 36, Columbia University.

15. Memorandum, "Discussion at the Special Meeting in the President's Office on Thursday, January 17, 1957."

16. "The Bell Laboratory Cronies: The William O. Baker Page," http://ourworld/compuserv.com/homepages/CarolASThompson/Baker.html.

17. Oral History Interview, OH-1990-08, Dr. Louis W. Tordella, by Charles Baker, Thomas Johnson, Guy Vanderpool, and David Hatch, 2 July 1990.

18. John A. Samford, Director, NSA, Memorandum for the Deputy Secretary of Defense, "NSA Research Institute," 21 Feb. 1958, Memorandum for General Erskine, ibid., 6 Mar. 1958, and Memorandum for the Secretary of Defense, ibid., 4 Apr. 1958.

19. H. T. Engstrom, Deputy Director, NSA, letter to Major General James McCormack, Jr., USAF (Ret), President, Institute for Defense Analyses, 17 June 1958.

20. Samford Memorandum for General Erskine, 6 Mar. 1958; H. T. Engstrom, Deputy Director, NSA, letter to Dr. Albert G. Hill, Institute for Defense Analysis, The Pentagon, 16 May 1958.

21. Tordella interview, OH-1990-08.

22. Captain Arthur Enderlin, USN, Memorandum for the Record, "NSCID #7, Action on the 'CRITICOMM' Plan," n.d., but probably close to the 27 August 1958 NSC meeting.

23. Tordella interview, OH-1990-08.

24. Admiral Dorsey, "CRITICOMM Briefing for the President's Board of Advisors on Foreign Intelligence Activities," 19 Nov. 1959.

Clandestine Victory: Eisenhower and Overhead Reconnaissance in the Cold War

R. Cargill Hall

As Supreme Commander of Allied Forces in Europe in World War II, Dwight D. Eisenhower had supervised the destruction of the continental Axis powers. He knew first-hand the social, political, and economic consequences of total war. He also knew well the value of intelligence to the success of military operations. The Japanese surprise attack on Pearl Harbor and the intelligence failings associated with it had been etched in his and other contemporary American leaders' psyches in a way that authorities today would find hard to imagine.[1] When the wartime alliance with the USSR foundered in the years immediately after 1945, military and political confrontations in Europe and Asia replaced prior collaboration in what came to be termed the "Cold War." Publicly committed to the destruction of the Western democracies, the Soviet Union blockaded the city of Berlin in June 1948, tested an atomic device in August 1949, and along the way acquired TU-4 long-range bombers that could deliver nuclear weapons against Europe and against America on one-way missions.[2] Communist forces subsequently conquered Mainland China in October 1949, and the Soviets authorized a client state, North Korea, to launch a surprise attack against the Republic of Korea in June 1950. The pace and scale of these events prompted American political and military leaders to believe that their Soviet counterparts might launch a surprise attack against Western Europe, possibly coincident with a surprise aerial attack on the United States.

International tensions had not eased when, on 20 January 1953, Dwight Eisenhower was inaugurated as the thirty-fourth president of the United States. Like his predecessor, the new president judged the Soviet Union to be the gravest threat to the country's continued survival. To meet that threat, the president needed *reliable* intelligence of Soviet economic resources and military preparations—intelligence at that time almost entirely unavailable. Reliable intelligence could reduce military uncertainty by providing advance warning of an impending atomic attack. With such intelligence, furthermore, one also could select a military or diplomatic response and do so economically without having to prepare militarily for every possible contingency. This task of acquiring intelligence that could reduce the threat of surprise attack in the Cold War is nowhere to be found in Eisenhower's first State of the Union Address in February. But, as subsequent executive action makes clear, it unquestionably numbered at or near the top of the list of national security concerns that he brought with him to the White House.

Within ten to twelve months of taking office, President Eisenhower authorized and a few trusted advisors had established a clandestine project in compartmented channels to acquire exactly this kind of strategic intelligence. It involved conducting *in peacetime* periodic, high-altitude photoreconnaissance overflights of potential foreign adversaries. The Sensitive Intelligence security control system established for these missions, or SENSINT as it came to be called, was far more than a "hidden hand"; SENSINT was entirely "off the political table." Because aerial overflights of "denied territory" in peacetime violated international conventions to which the United States was a contracting party, these efforts were so closely held that only a select few in the executive branch, congress, the intelligence community, the Joint Chiefs of Staff (JCS), and the military services even knew of their existence. Underscoring Eisenhower's concern for absolute secrecy, neither SENSINT nor its aerial and space overflight successors ever appeared on the agenda of the National Security Council (NSC). And, except for the high altitude U-2 airplanes that became public knowledge when the Soviet Union shot one down in 1960, Eisenhower and his confidants took the secrets of all these projects and their control systems with them to the grave. But if his overhead reconnaissance efforts eventually prompted an international furor and scuttled a summit conference—they also succeeded spectacularly: they would illuminate the course over which the Cold War would play for the next thirty years.

A Wartime Decision Foreshadows a Peacetime Policy

The sudden, unexpected North Korean attack on the Republic of Korea on 25 June 1950 shocked and completely surprised American leaders. The country's intelligence establishment, military and civil, not only failed to recognize the tell-tale signs of an impending invasion, it was woefully unprepared to conduct operations in Korea on the far reaches of the Pacific Rim. Military leaders at the Pentagon in Washington, D.C., schooled in World War II, had supposed that the semi-mountainous Korean peninsula was unsuited to, and would not see, armored warfare. Other American military leaders headquartered in Japan and encumbered with other conceits, believed that veiled Chinese Communist threats to intervene in the conflict were a bluff. The latter miscalculation, made just five months after the war's unexpected outbreak as United Nations forces drove North Korean troops back toward the Chinese border, resulted in a second intelligence failure of even greater magnitude. Late in November 1950, the Chinese People's Liberation Army, having moved some nine armies surreptitiously into the field, attacked. Within a few days UN forces in North Korea were in full retreat. Speaking with reporters on 30 November, an agitated President Harry S. Truman announced that the United Nations coalition "would use the atomic bomb, if necessary, to assure victory."[3]

Following that announcement, British Prime Minister Clement Attlee hurriedly flew to Washington on 4 December to confer with the president. During three days of talks, the two Western leaders agreed that there would be no concession to aggression in Asia or elsewhere, that both countries would expand the production of arms and munitions as rapidly as possible, that the defense of Western Europe would be increased and a supreme commander of allied forces appointed "soon," and, most important, that the United States leaders would "inform" the British if world conditions had reached a point where they considered seriously employing atomic weapons. In a *quid pro quo,* the available evidence suggests, Attlee also agreed to join the United States in coordinated, periodic overflights of the Soviet Union to locate its air bases and long-range bomber forces capable of conducting surprise atomic attacks on the west.[4] In the event, the British would concentrate subsequent overflight missions on European Russia and the Baltic States, while the Americans would focus on the Soviet Far East.

Meanwhile, other, related developments cascaded. Truman issued an executive order that established a Federal Civil Defense Administration. On 6 December, in a classified cable to JCS Commands (today called Specified Commands), General of the Army and Joint Chiefs of Staff Chairman Omar Bradley warned that "the current situation in Korea has greatly increased the possibility of a general war," and he directed each command "take such action as is feasible to increase readiness without creating alarm."[5] The next day, bespeaking febrile nationwide fears on the ninth anniversary of the Japanese attack on Pearl Harbor, a Gallop poll revealed that 55 percent of the American public believed that World War III had begun.[6] Other actions taken in Washington confirmed these perceptions. On 16 December 1950, President Truman issued a "Proclamation of National Emergency" that gave him special executive powers, called numerous National Guard units to active duty, and he signed another executive order creating an office of Defense Mobilization to control all executive branch mobilization activities including industrial production, procurement, manpower and transportation. And, on the 18th, he recalled General of the Army Dwight Eisenhower to active duty.[7] Eisenhower, who believed in collective security and the North Atlantic Treaty Organization (NATO), traveled to Washington, D.C. at month's end to confer with legislative and executive leaders before assuming his duties as Supreme Commander, Allied Powers in Europe (SACEUR). Afterward his son John S. D. Eisenhower recalled, "he expressed to me his disgust with the terrified atmosphere pervading all of Washington, from the president on down."[8]

However one perceived the "atmosphere" in Washington, President Truman, in keeping with the Anglo-American agreement forged early in December, authorized American overflights of the Peoples' Republic of China *and* the Soviet Far East.[9] The fourth B-47B swept-wing jet bomber was pulled from the production line and modified to carry reconnaissance cameras on a deep penetration overflight of eastern Siberia, to be staged from Alaska in the fall of 1951.[10] In South Korea, responding to instructions relayed through Far East Air Forces (FEAF), units of the 67th Tactical Reconnaissance Wing in 1951 began shallow penetration overflights of Communist China and the Soviet Maritime Provinces using specially equipped RB-26s for nighttime missions, and, in the daytime, RF-80s and, later in 1952–53, RF-86 fighter aircraft.[11] But could American and British leaders explain their overflights of the Soviet Union in the event one of the intruders was shot down? Because the USSR continued to furnish military supplies, aircraft, and combat pilots to Communist China, it became an "unannounced co-belligerent" in the Korean War. Legal experts told the president and prime minister that that status, under the terms of Chapter VI of the UN Charter, justified overflights of the Soviet Union during the hostilities.

In Britain, Prime Minister Attlee arranged with the Air Ministry for USAF reconnaissance bombers from the Strategic Air Command (SAC) to be accommodated at Sculthorpe Royal Air Force Base (RAFB) in East Anglia, and for a select group of RAF pilots to train in them in the United States. The British aircrews selected for the overflight missions, led by Squadron Leader John Crampton, formed a "Special Duty Flight." On 1 August 1951, they arrived at Barksdale Air Force Base (AFB) in Louisiana and began training in SAC's air-refuelable, long-range, jet-turbine-powered, straight-wing RB-45Cs. Returning to England with four of these aircraft in December, they flew their first mission on the night of 17–18 April 1952. Three RB-45Cs, dressed in British livery, departed Sculthorpe and flew tracks that took one over the Baltic States, a second penetrated through Byelorussia toward Moscow, and the third aircraft flew to the south through the Ukraine past Kiev, toward Stalingrad. The "targets" were Soviet air bases of its long-range air armies, missile sites, and similar targets of strategic importance. The navigators took 35mm photos of the aircraft radar displays when these sites were identified and located. All three RB-45Cs returned safely to Sculthorpe RAFB on 18 April.[12]

In the United States, events did not proceed as smoothly for the first long-range daytime overflight of eastern Siberia. Headquarters SAC selected to command this mission the primary Air Force B-47 test pilot, Col. Richard C. Neeley. With preparations completed, in late July 1951 Neeley and his crew flew the modified B-47B to Eielson AFB near Fairbanks, Alaska. On 15 August 1951, while awaiting clear weather in Siberia and authorization to proceed, the B-47B caught fire during fueling operations and burned on the tarmac. While the wreckage still smoldered, orders to conduct the overflight mission arrived at Eielson.[13] That accident set back the Siberian reconnaissance mission for a full year. President Truman approved a second attempt in August 1952. It was conducted with two reconnaissance-modified, jet-turbine-powered B-47B bombers from the 306th Bombardment Wing. Staging from Eielson AFB in Alaska on 15 October, the aircraft flew west, north of the Siberian coast, and one of them turned south and penetrated the mainland near Ambarchik, then swung east across Siberia, exiting at Provideniya on the Bering Strait. The second aircraft turned back along the Siberian coast and overflew Wrangel Island on its homeward leg into Alaska. Both returned safely. No photographic evidence of Soviet preparations for an aerial surprise attack was uncovered.[14]

All the while during the Korean War, the 67th Tactical Reconnaissance Wing, especially its 15th Tactical Reconnaissance Squadron (15th TRS), conducted periodic, secret daytime overflights of Communist China north of the Yalu River and of the Soviet Maritime Provinces, as directed.[15] Beginning in 1951, deep penetration nighttime reconnaissance missions that collected radarscope photography over the same regions also were performed by a three-airplane detachment of RB-45Cs from SACs 91st Strategic Reconnaissance Wing, that rotated on temporary duty to Yokota Air Base, Japan.[16] Imagery from all of these missions identified military installations and tracked the number, movement, location, and kinds of military aircraft and naval vessels that opposed UN forces in the Far East. When Communist Chinese and Western officials signed the Korean War Armistice that ended hostilities, if not the state of war, on 27 July 1953, members of the 15th TRS were about to receive a specially modified RF-86F-30 that mounted twin vertical 40-inch focal length K-22 cameras and a reinforced wing with four fuel drop tanks for longer range. Whatever their expectations, at that time reconnaissance overflights of the Peoples Republic of China and the Soviet Union ceased, while officials in Washington and London contemplated the international situation.

SENSINT

Dwight D. Eisenhower took the oath of office as the thirty-fourth president of the United States shortly before the July 1953 Armistice that ended hostilities on the Korean peninsula. In the weeks just before and after his January inauguration, the new president occupied himself organizing his administration. He relied in that effort, and in subsequent efforts at reordering clandestine intelligence collection, on a few close advisors. For special intelligence projects they would adopt compartmented wartime security access and control procedures; only a few Americans, those who absolutely had to know, would be "witting" of the entire enterprise. Among the principals in this select group were the Dulles brothers, John Foster and Allen F., Donald A. Quarles, Herbert C. Hoover, Jr., James H. Doolittle, Robert (NMI) Cutler, Paul T. (Pete) Carroll and his successor Andrew J. Goodpaster,[17] and, from the academic and scientific community, James R. Killian, Edwin H. (Din) Land, William O. Baker, Edward M. Purcell, and George B. Kistiakowsky. Military members included Adm. Arthur W. Radford, chairman of the Joint Chiefs of Staff, and the chief of staff and vice chief of staff of the United States Air Force, Gens. Nathan F. Twining and Thomas D. White, respectively.[18]

In the White House, Eisenhower appointed Robert Cutler to a new position as the first "special assistant to the president for national security affairs." Cutler, a 1922 graduate of Harvard Law School and prominent Boston attorney, was well prepared for this assignment. During World War II, he had acquired a solid reputation in Washington, D.C., while serving on the staffs of the Secretary of War Henry L. Stimson and Army Chief of Staff Gen. George C. Marshall. After the war in the Truman Administration, Cutler was named a special assistant to Secretary of Defense James Forrestal; he subsequently joined the NSC senior staff as the deputy director of the Psychological Strategy Board.[19] Eisenhower charged his special assistant with reorganizing the NSC and managing its operations. Cutler did so most effectively. He limited its members to eight, in addition to the president and vice president, and established a Planning Board composed of senior officials that represented each of the standing members of the NSC, but responsible to the president, not to their respective agencies. The Planning Board members evaluated and prepared options and proposed solutions to problems of national security for consideration by the NSC.[20]

While the Planning Board considered issues on their way into the NSC, Cutler also established an Operations Coordinating Board (OCB) intended to coordinate and ensure that the policies agreed upon by the NSC and approved by the president were carried out. Chartered formally by executive order on 2 September 1953, chaired by the undersecretary of state, it subsumed the functions of the old Psychological Strategy Board and consisted of the deputy secretary of defense, the deputy director for mutual security, an executive officer, the directors of Central Intelligence and the U.S. Information Agency, and Cutler himself. The OCB issued periodic "reports on the measures being taken to implement . . . policy, the results achieved, and changes in the world situation that affected the assumptions on which the policy was based, sometimes with a recommendation that its revision be considered."[21] Until the issuance of NSC 5412 the following March, an OCB group of seniors also determined the desirability and feasibility of covert operations, including overflights of "denied territory," for the president's consideration. Moreover, this group coordinated support for these operations among the departments of state and defense, and the CIA. (Previously, a senior group in the Psychological Strategy Board had performed this function under the terms of NSC 10/5, approved by President Truman on 23 October 1951.[22]) Following the Korean Armistice, the question of conducting peacetime overflights to provide advance warning of a Soviet surprise aerial attack came sharply to the fore in the fall of 1953.

Back in December 1952, shortly before leaving office, President Truman had approved a distant early warning line (DEW Line) of radar pickets across the continent above the Arctic Circle, to detect and warn of Soviet aircraft approaching North America over the pole. (President Eisenhower later authorized construction of the DEW Line, with Canada's consent.) When operational, this defensive warning system could be expected to detect an attack in progress, but it would not forewarn of any preparations for an attack. Furthermore, it would not become operational for another four or five years. Accordingly, in January 1953 Truman formed a special subcommittee of the NSC to "evaluate the net capabilities of the Soviet Union to inflict direct injury on the United States, up to July 1, 1955." On 18 May, the Net Evaluation Subcommittee reported its findings to Eisenhower's NSC. America's continental defenses were judged inadequate to neutralize or even seriously impede any aerial or covert attack that the USSR could now launch against the United States. Such an attack employing atomic weapons, even though limited to the nation's capital and a few major cities, would jeopardize the continuity of government, the continuity of production, the industrial mobilization base, and expose millions of citizens in the metropolitan centers to death or injury. The state of these defenses, Eisenhower learned, "constituted an unacceptable risk to our nation's survival."[23]

The disturbing continental defense report reached the president just a few weeks after the death of Soviet dictator Joseph Stalin in March. The appearance of an absolute successor remained clouded, with all that a Kremlin power struggle implied for stability in East-West relations. Moreover, in August, shortly after the end of hostilities in Korea, the Soviet Union "tested a 300 to 400 kiloton boosted fission weapon and publicly claimed that it had achieved thermonuclear capability." That action seems to have affected the president greatly, and, in the absence of a clear successor to Stalin, focused his attention increasingly on the ramifications of nuclear war. As he emphasized for a group of legislative leaders some time later,

> What do you think would happen if this city were hit today by an H-bomb? Do you think you would vote or ask me to send the troops at Fort Meade overseas—or would you be knocking on my door to get me to bring them in to try to pick up the pieces here in Washington? We have to do that. All our military plans are based really on two main things—One, to destroy the enemy's production and two, protect [our] own. To do that we need not just more men. We need more equipment, an expanded air force and an expanded warning system. As the President was talking, you could hear a pin drop in the room.[24]

President Eisenhower approved NSC 162/2, a new basic defense policy that drew heavily on the product of a James Doolittle-guided Project Solarium study, on 30 October. The New Look policy, as it came to be called, also reflected the findings of the Net Evaluation Committee. "The USSR," it said, "has sufficient bombs and aircraft, using one-way missions, to inflict serious damage to the United States, especially by surprise attack."[25] Seven days later, Eisenhower issued Executive Order 10501, which restricted the authority of government officials to classify records, and it set the basic classification categories for information affecting national security that still exists today: Confidential, Secret, and Top Secret.[26] At about this time, or shortly afterward in late 1953 or early 1954, the president, in consultation with his Secretary of State John Foster Dulles, Director of Central Intelligence (DCI) Allen Dulles, Chairman of the Joint Chiefs Adm. Arthur Radford—and doubtless James Doolittle—approved an unannounced, separate document control and access system for special intelligence activities. Among the first programs to employ this system for handling sensitive compartmented information (SCI), was a Top Secret military enterprise that conducted overflights of the USSR and Communist China in peacetime to acquire indications and warning of any surprise attack preparations.[27]

Known as the Sensitive Intelligence (SENSINT) security control system, its photographic products, which existed separately in a WINDFALL compartment, were shared with the CIA. For this effort, conducted between early 1954 and the end of 1956, defense department directors of SENSINT relied on available military reconnaissance aircraft or specially modified versions of them. Deep penetration overflight missions used air-refuelable reconnaissance bombers of the Strategic Air Command, particularly the RB-45C and RB-47E. High performance reconnaissance fighter aircraft, the RF-86 and supersonic RF-100 in particular, were modified to mount cameras and extra fuel tanks for shallow penetration missions. Finally, for this program, the U.S. Air Force contracted for reconnaissance versions of the British Canberra bomber, which were built in America under license. These included a featherweight version, the RB-57A-1, known as "Heart Throb," and a long-winged, air-refuelable modification, the RB-57D-0. The Air Force pilots that flew SENSINT missions and the military and CIA photo-interpreters that analyzed their WINDFALL product would know only that piece of the puzzle with which they were directly associated.

Like Executive Order 10501 that set basic security classification categories, SENSINT set a postwar compartmented security control precedent that the Central Intelligence Agency and National Security Agency (NSA) would refine in the years that followed. And, like ULTRA in which America had participated, the British would collaborate in this effort and share the intelligence acquired from it at least until April 1955 when Anthony Eden succeeded Winston Churchill as prime minister. The government of the Republic of China (ROC) on Taiwan also participated in SENSINT, although not as a partner entitled to intelligence collected by the USAF and Royal Air Force (RAF). Beginning in the Korean War, the USAF furnished reconnaissance aircraft to the ROC Air Force. The Republic of China subsequently furnished to the United States copies of the photoreconnaissance film taken on overflights of the Chinese mainland.[28]

To evaluate and recommend for or against these and other intelligence operations, on 15 March 1954 President Eisenhower approved NSC Directive 5412 "on covert operations." It defined them as "all activities conducted pursuant to this directive which are so planned and executed that any U.S. Government responsibility for them is not evident to unauthorized persons and that if uncovered the U.S. Government can plausibly disclaim any responsibility for them." And it established a committee composed of representatives of the secretaries of state and defense, and the DCI, for that purpose. The Operations Coordinating Board remained the normal channel for securing coordination of support for covert operations among the CIA and Departments of State and Defense.[29] As events transpired, the 5412 committee would consist of the DCI, the undersecretary of state and deputy secretary of defense, and be chaired by the president's special assistant for national security affairs—an arrangement made formal in 1955 with the issuance of NCS 5412/1 and 5412/2. To the few who knew of its existence, it became known as the 5412 Special Group, or simply, "the Special Group." According to Roger Rhodarmer, a USAF liaison officer for SENSINT at the Pentagon, theater commanders witting of the program and leaders of the intelligence community could request that a specific site in the Sino-Soviet Bloc be overflown and imaged, along with ample justification to support taking the risk. The request cycled for approval through Headquarters USAF, the Joint Chiefs of Staff, and thence to the special group. The president made the final decision. Notification of an approved overflight passed back down the chain in the same fashion. In SENSINT, Rhodarmer recalled, missions were sometimes approved in lots of two or three or more, although the president tightened and limited these approvals in the years that followed.[30]

A few days after Eisenhower approved NSC 5412, in the Far East on 22 March 1954, the first SENSINT missions took place conducted by three RF-86Fs of the 15th TRS. The reconnaissance aircraft departed South Korea, overflew the port city of Vladivostok and vicinity to its north, and recovered in Japan. More of these missions followed in April.[31] In Europe, British Prime Minister Winston Churchill approved the first SENSINT mission for Crampton's Special Duty Flight, which took place from Sculthorpe RAFB on the night of 28–29 April.[32] Shortly thereafter, on 8 May, the

United States attempted a daytime overflight of European Russia with an RB-47E launched from Fairford RAFB in Great Britain. After the British had stirred the air defense cauldron with their nighttime overflights just nine days before, however, the Soviets were ready and waiting. The SAC bomber was intercepted by MiG-17s and nearly shot down, but managed to return to England.[33] That ended low-altitude reconnaissance bomber daytime overflights of European Russia, though not higher altitude daylight SENSINT missions over the Eastern European satellite states with specially modified RF-100s and RB-57As, which arrived in the Europe in May and August 1955, respectively.

The most impressive, sustained SENSINT overflights occurred during April and early May 1956 in "Project Home Run." Conducted by SAC RB-47E and H reconnaissance bombers launched over the North Pole from Thule Air Base in Greenland, these missions flew behind the Ural Mountains to photograph the hidden cities of Norilsk, Igarka, and Dudinka, and essentially photo- and electronically-mapped the entire lightly-defended northern tier of the USSR. The Home Run missions did not detect any threatening concentration of long-range bombers on the few snow-covered Soviet far north air bases. In its aftermath, one can only imagine the frustration, rage, and abrupt ending of careers that beset leaders of the Soviet air defense forces. Needless to say, the SENSINT overflights provoked sharp, albeit private, Soviet protests, and the protest of Project Home Run was especially bitter. On 28 May, President Eisenhower met with Undersecretary of State Herbert Hoover, DCI Allen Dulles, JCS Chairman Admiral Radford, and USAF Chief of Staff Nathan Twining to consider the matter of "special reconnaissance flights." Twining advised that the operations protested had already ceased. Hoover read a draft of the proposed reply to the Soviets and the president suggested a passage be added about navigational errors that might have occurred during training flights in the Arctic regions.[34] Whatever formal diplomatic excuses might be offered, however, Soviet leaders knew the truth, and the American aerial intrusions became an increasing irritant in U.S.-Soviet relations during 1956.

That year began with U.S. camera-carrying balloons sailing the jet stream west-to-east across the USSR in January and early February. A number of them were shot down, and the Soviet Union publicly protested.[35] The SENSINT Home Run missions in April and early May likewise prompted a strong protest, and the first U-2 overflights of the Eastern Europe satellite states in June, and of Leningrad and Moscow on 4–5 July, resulted in more private and pointedly heated protests. Later that fall, meeting with advisors at the White House, President Eisenhower expressed grave reservations about continuing the overflights because they affected so adversely any chances for improved relations between the two countries.[36] He was, nevertheless, persuaded to authorize one more military overflight of Vladivostok and vicinity, opposite Japan, this time with three high-altitude, long-winged RB-57Ds newly arrived in the SENSINT inventory. Conducted on 11 December, the three SAC aircraft entered Soviet airspace shortly after lunchtime in weather near perfect for imaging. Although the imagery obtained of the Soviet Pacific Fleet in harbor proved valuable, the resulting protest on 15 December 1956 left no doubt about the ability of Soviet air defenses to detect and identify aircraft. More to the point, this diplomatic note concluded with a veiled threat: in the event of any repetition in future, "the United States of America will have to bear the full responsibility for the consequences of such violations."[37]

Three days later, during the morning of 18 December, Secretary of State John Foster Dulles telephoned the president to discuss this protest. "We are in trouble about these overflights," he asserted. Given the tracking and identification of all three RB-57s, Dulles continued, "I think we will have to admit this was done and say we are sorry. We cannot deny it. Relations with Russia are getting pretty tense." Eisenhower demurred, the United States would not admit to the overflights. Nevertheless, to preclude any further deterioration in relations, the president said he would order a "complete stoppage of the entire business."[38] Early that afternoon, Eisenhower instructed his staff secretary Col. Andrew Goodpaster to relay an order to Secretary of Defense Charles Wilson, USAF Chief of Staff Gen. Nathan Twining, and DCI Allen Dulles, terminating immediately all American overflights of "Iron Curtain countries."[39] The president's 18 December 1956 directive ended the SENSINT military overflights of the early Cold War. But when intelligence in 1957 brought word of Soviet preparations to test intercontinental ballistic missiles (ICBMs), Eisenhower would authorize the resumption of U-2 overflights in the TALENT security control system.

TALENT

About the time that the Soviet Union exploded a hydrogen device in the fall of 1953, an American military attaché sighted a new Russian bomber at Ramenskoye airfield southeast of Moscow. The swept-wing, jet turbine-powered machine was the Myasishchev-4 (My-4), later named "Bison" by NATO. Based on its description, the airplane was judged to be an indigenous equivalent of the Boeing B-52 intercontinental bomber then approaching serial production in the United States.[40] Coupled with the test of a potential thermonuclear weapon, the reported sighting provoked genuine concern among American civil and military leaders. Apparently at the prompting of Robert Cutler and Trevor Gardner, the "technologically evangelical assistant secretary of the air force for research and development," President Eisenhower met with the Office of Defense Mobilization's (ODM) Science Advisory Committee on 27 March 1954 to discuss this sighting and the threat it might represent. Speaking to committee members, the president addressed the subject of a surprise attack on the United States in the nuclear age, of the pressing need to forewarn of such an attack planned in secret by a "closed society," and he challenged the scientists "to tackle this problem." They did. Encouraged by committee chairman and Caltech President Lee DuBridge, on 15 April a subcommittee chaired by the president of Massachusetts Institute of Technology (MIT), James Killian, recommended forming a task force "to study ways of avoiding surprise attack" in a thorough "review of weapons and intelligence technology."[41]

Eisenhower, meanwhile, asked Allen Dulles and the CIA to identify and track warning "indicators" that would presage a surprise attack, and, shortly after meeting with the Science Advisory Committee, approved formation of an organization devoted exclusively to that subject: the National Indications Center. Chaired by the deputy director of Central Intelligence and composed of specialists drawn from U.S. intelligence agencies and the Departments of Defense and State, the center formed the interagency staff of the National Watch Committee, which consisted of presidential advisors such as the secretaries of state and defense, and the DCI. Chartered on 1 July 1954 for the express purpose of "preventing strategic surprise," the indications center drew on information furnished by all national intelligence organizations. It assessed the military, economic, and social demands involved in mounting a surprise attack and issued a weekly "watch report" to the Watch Committee members. To that end, staff members expanded a list of key indicators developed earlier under the direction of James J. Hitchcock in the CIA, created a matrix, monitored and applied to it actions that would have to be taken to mount a surprise attack in the nuclear age. The military, economic, and technical indicators in this matrix successfully predicted the Suez war in 1956 and have been monitored and reported in one form or another to national command authorities ever since. Eisenhower, Hitchcock recalled years later, was a man "bore-sighted on early warning of surprise attack."[42]

A few weeks later, on 26 July, Eisenhower authorized Killian and the ODM Science Advisory Committee to formally assay the threat of surprise attack, ways to defend against it, and methods to forewarn of it. Killian, who took a leave of absence from MIT, organized thirty-five of the nation's leading scientists into three projects and a Communications Working Group that evaluated the country's offensive, defensive, and intelligence capabilities. Killian, James B. Fisk, vice president of research at Bell Telephone Laboratories, and James Doolittle served on the steering committee of what would be named the Technological Capabilities Panel (TCP).[43] The smallest of the three groups, the intelligence Project Three led by Edwin (Din) Land, the founder and chief executive officer of the Polaroid Corporation that had produced "one-step photography," was known informally as the "Taxicab Committee." It consisted of Land, James G. Baker, a Harvard University astronomer and acclaimed aerial camera and optics designer, chemist Joseph W. Kennedy of Washington University in St. Louis who had helped isolate the element plutonium, physicist and Nobel Laureate Edward M. Purcell of Harvard, the mathematician John W. Tukey of Princeton University who had contributed the algorithm to the Cooley-Tukey fast Fourier transform, and an engineer Allen Latham of Arthur D. Little, Incorporated.[44] One solution to the intelligence problem, Baker advised his Project Three colleagues, was a reconnaissance airplane that operated at altitudes well above those of military aircraft and Soviet air defenses.

In August 1954, Allen F. Donovan of Cornell Aeronautical Laboratory, who served as an advisor and unofficial member of Project Three, brought word to its members of just such a high-altitude spy plane recommended by Lockheed's premier designer, Clarence "Kelly" Johnson. The single-engine, jet-powered aircraft featured bolt-on sail plane wings and low structural loading, which would allow it to operate at altitudes of 70,000 feet or better—far above contemporary Soviet air defenses. Johnson's unsolicited design, the CL-282, had been rejected by the Air Force some months before in favor of a Bell Aircraft-designed twin-engine reconnaissance airplane dubbed the X-16. Air Force desires notwithstanding, Project Three members thoroughly examined all aspects of the CL-282 and, by the end of October, had come to view it as an integrated intelligence-collection platform that "could find and photograph the Soviet Union's Bison bomber fleet and, thus, resolve the growing 'bomber gap' controversy." At that time Din Land discussed its potential with Trevor Gardner, Air Force assistant secretary for research and development, and he urged DCI Allen Dulles to accept and undertake the project. Gardner judged the CL-282 superior to the service-preferred X-16, and became an enthusiastic supporter. At the CIA, Dulles politely declined the honor. A graduate of the Office of Strategic Services (OSS) during World War II, he preferred classic intelligence gathering that relied on agents in the field or airdropped "behind the lines," a perspective representing the agency's institutional culture at that time.[45] Beside, Dulles doubtless mused, the CIA received the entire intelligence take from the ongoing SENSINT military overflights, while the USAF and the RAF took all of the risks.[46]

Back on 26 July, the same day that he authorized Killian to proceed with the surprise attack study, Eisenhower also had asked James Doolittle to form a small committee and evaluate the organization and covert operations of the CIA, and report back to him by the end of September.[47] Doolittle chose three others to join him in this study: William B. Franke, assistant secretary of the Navy for financial management; Morris (NMI) Hadley, a Harvard-trained lawyer and partner in the New York firm of Milbank, Tweed, Hadley and McCloy; and William D. Pawley, a business man who, in 1940, had helped organize for China the American Volunteer Group later known as the Flying Tigers. The president instructed Allen Dulles to give this team unfettered access to the CIA, and the four men completed their assessment and returned it to the president on 30 September 1954. The report, like others before it, judged the Soviet Union and its Communist allies to be intent on world domination. But it was sharply critical of the CIA's failure to establish any viable agent network in the USSR, and of its resistance to adopting anything more than a few ground-based technical collection systems that might offset this disadvantage. The CIA, the Doolittle group advised the president, had to bring in people who would embrace twentieth-century science and technology and develop it for intelligence collection—including overhead reconnaissance.[48] Doolittle and his group met with Eisenhower to discuss the findings on 19 October. Although the president defended Allen Dulles, he knew that current technology had to be employed if American intelligence collection was to reveal the state secrets held close behind the Iron Curtain. Three days later, on the 22nd, Eisenhower gave Doolittle's report to Allen Dulles with instructions that he should show it to no one else and "report back to me about [its] several conclusion and recommendations."[49] Dulles's response to the president is not recorded, but on reading the Doolittle assessment, he surely realized that the CIA could no longer defend intelligence collection practices that relied almost exclusively on a time-honored tradecraft.

Killian and Land continued to press the case for the Lockheed CL-282 in November in meetings at the CIA and the Pentagon, with the proviso that the project be managed by the Agency, not by the military. Allen Dulles, mindful of the Doolittle report, accepted the inevitable and so notified the nation's Intelligence Advisory Committee, which approved of the arrangement on 23 November. The next day, in a meeting in the oval office with the secretaries of state and defense and senior CIA and Air Force officials, Eisenhower approved the program under CIA management. Because the intelligence agency possessed no infrastructure or personnel to bring it into operation, the president ordered the Air Force to furnish all of the assistance needed to train, base, and operate the new reconnaissance aircraft.[50] In the days that followed, Dulles appointed Richard M. Bissell, Jr., a Yale-trained economist who had recently joined the agency as his special assistant, as the program manager. Bissell subsequently formed a team with USAF Col. (later Brig. Gen.) Osmond J. Ritland as his deputy, and Col. Marion C. "Hack" Mixson, who had been responsible for training the RAF Special Duty Flight, as another key person in his Washington program office. Trevor Gardner arranged for the Lockheed contract, signed in December 1954; Kelly Johnson promised delivery of the first of the spy planes in eight months.[51]

While Johnson's Lockheed team in Burbank, California, labored to create what would become known as the U-2 reconnaissance airplane in the early months of 1955, other members of Bissell's team selected a remote airstrip in Nevada and began to refurbish it for flight tests. Harvard's Jim Baker, of Din Land's Project Three, set to work designing the cameras that would be carried onboard.[52] Still others in Nevada, under the direction of Air Force Lt. Col. Philip O. "Robbie" Robertson, began selecting and, later in the year as airplanes became available, training the pilots.[53] Shrouded within its own SCI cocoon between 1955 and mid-1960, fewer than 350 people in the country knew about the U-2 and its actual use, and that included four at the White House, four or perhaps six members of Congress, the CIA and Air Force participants, and the Lockheed designers, maintenance personnel, and pilots. Known to these few as AQUATONE, when overflight operations approached in 1956, it was subsumed in the TALENT access and control system, still a Top Secret enterprise whose imagery products were separated into two other access compartments called CHESS[54] and CHURCHDOOR. Indeed, this high-altitude overflight program was so closely held that it does not appear anywhere in the final TCP report submitted to the president and the NSC in early 1955. According to James Killian in an oral history interview with a CIA historian, the proposals for the U-2 and the submarine-launched ballistic missile (later known as Polaris) were submitted in separate annexes, "eyes only," to President Eisenhower.[55]

While the U-2 neared its first test flight in Nevada, on 21 July 1955 at a Four Power Summit Conference in Geneva, Eisenhower directly addressed the subject that most concerned him. The absence of trust and the presence of "terrible weapons" among states, he advised Soviet leaders in attendance, provoked in the world "fears and dangers of surprise attack." To eliminate these fears, he urged that the Soviet Union and the United States provide "facilities for aerial photography to the other country" and conduct mutually supervised reconnaissance overflights.[56] Before the day ended, First Secretary of the Communist Party Nikita Khrushchev, who was well acquainted with the SENSINT overflights, privately rejected the president's plan as an obvious attempt to "accumulate target information."[57] "We knew the Soviets wouldn't accept it," Eisenhower later confided in an interview, "but we took a look and thought it was a good move."[58] Although Soviet leaders might object, they had received formally the *raison d'état* for continued overflights. Eleven months later, some five months after he terminated the balloon reconnaissance program, Eisenhower approved the first U-2 overflights of Eastern Europe and the USSR.

Between 20 June and 10 July 1956, U-2s launched from West Germany made eight overflights inside the Iron Curtain, five of them over the Soviet Union. Among other sites, they imaged downtown Leningrad and Moscow. Earlier, the U.S. Air Force had claimed that the USSR already possessed over 100 My-4 (Bison) long-range heavy bombers, but the CHESS photography belied it. These U-2 missions covered nine Soviet long-range bomber bases in European Russia, including the Fili airframe plant near Moscow that produced the bombers, and they failed to uncover any of them. That revelation, a CIA history asserted, permitted the White House "to deny Air Force requests for additional B-52 bombers to 'catch up' to the Soviets."[59] Nevertheless, the crescendo of Russian diplomatic protests generated by the TALENT and SENSINT overflight missions during 1956 caused President Eisenhower to terminate "the entire business" on 18 December, although he would reconsider the issue.

In a meeting at the White House on 6 May 1957, Eisenhower conferred with Deputy Secretary of Defense Donald Quarles, Air Force Chief of Staff Nathan Twining, Acting Secretary of State Christian Herter, and DCI Allen Dulles. Intelligence suggested that the Russians were preparing to test long-range ballistic missiles. All of them urged the president to reconsider TALENT overflights. He relented, though agreeing only to missions over the Soviet Far East, such as the Kamchatka Peninsula, Lake Baikal, and the atomic test site at Semipalatinsk. The missions resumed on 8 June when a U-2 launched from Eielson AFB in Alaska flew into the USSR.[60] Others followed, launched from various locations. Altogether, between July 1956 and May 1960, twenty-four overflights of the USSR were conducted under TALENT. Later U-2 missions found and photographed the Tyura Tam ballistic missile test range in Kazakhstan, and the surface-to-air (SAM) and anti-ballistic missile test range at Saryshagan, stretching westward from the shores of Lake Baikal.[61] But the first confirmed test of a Soviet ICBM from Tyura Tam in August 1957, and the orbiting of Sputnik I, the world's first artificial earth satellite from the same site in October, provoked a firestorm of political criticism in the United States, virtually all of it directed at the Eisenhower administration. Throughout the national debate in the months that followed, the president refused to reveal the TALENT secrets that could have refuted much of the nation's expressed concern.

Chief among the charges leveled at the administration after 1957: it had allowed a "missile gap" to emerge that entirely favored the Soviet Union. In fact, however,

Eisenhower had authorized the development of land-based ICBMs and sea-launched ballistic missiles with the highest of national priorities back in 1954–55, and by 1960 the missile gap actually favored the United States. Regrettably, none of the U-2 missions, which often followed railroad lines on which Soviet ICBMs moved, had found any operational ICBM bases in the southern USSR, though at the beginning of 1960 one was known to be under construction far to the north, at Yurya, with another one probable at Plesetsk. According to a retired CIA official, to find and photograph these sites and end the controversy, Eisenhower approved a flight from Pakistan to Norway, across the Soviet Union. Scheduled for late April, it did not take place until 1 May, the Communist "All Saints Day," just fifteen days before another Four Power Summit Conference. The pilot, Francis Gary Powers, flew north over Stalinabad, the Tyura Tam missile test center, and then proceeded northwest toward Yurya and Plesetsk, the submarine shipyard at Severodvinsk, the naval bases at Murmansk, with recovery scheduled in Norway late in the day. While operating at its design altitude of 70,000 feet, thirteen miles high over the city of Sverdlovsk in the USSR, Powers's plane was brought down by a SA-2 surface-to-air missile. Remarkably—and unexpectedly—the pilot survived.[62]

The resulting international furor mightily embarrassed the administration, which at first attempted a "plausible denial," until the Soviets produced the pilot and charged him with espionage. It also ended the Summit Conference almost before it began, with Khrushchev demanding a personal apology from Eisenhower, one that would not be forthcoming. But the president announced that the United States would not in future conduct clandestine aerial overflights of the Soviet Union.[63] That ended all prospects for any more overflights with an Eisenhower-approved TALENT follow-on program called OXCART, then in its development phase, which in the early 1960s would produce the high-altitude A-12 and its two-place variant, the SR-71 Mach 3 aerial reconnaissance platforms. Thus the TALENT overflights of the USSR ended publicly and rather more dramatically than their SENSINT predecessors. Fortunately for the United States, however, Eisenhower already had selected and drawn from his over-flight hand one more card that he would play, one that would change the way in which the Cold War unfolded.

TALENT-KEYHOLE

The Technological Capabilities Panel surprise attack report, submitted to President Eisenhower on 15 February 1955, resulted in a number of important alterations in U.S. defense preparedness. It recommended, and the president subsequently approved, accelerating procurement of intercontinental ballistic missiles (Atlas, and later Titan and Minuteman ICBMs), of intermediate-range ballistic missiles (Thor and Jupiter IRBMs), and speeding construction of the DEW Line in the Arctic (declared operational in August 1957). The president also approved a TCP proposal submitted separately to build a sea-launched ballistic missile, and the U.S. Navy began work on that project (later called Polaris) in 1955. Even more important, perhaps, were the recommendations of Din Land's Project Three. Part V, "Intelligence: Our First Defense

Against Surprise," proposed various methods to acquire and use strategic pre-hostilities intelligence. Beside Project AQUATONE, also approved secretly and separately back in November 1954, it urged the construction and launch of a small scientific earth satellite that would operate in outer space at altitudes above the sovereign "airspace" of the nations over which it would pass. "And although it is clear that a very small satellite cannot [now] serve as useful carrier for reconnaissance apparatus, . . . it can serve ideally to explore or establish the principle that space, outside our atmosphere, is open to all." This vehicle, Project Three members believed, might establish the principle "freedom of space" in international law and make straight the way for that time when "we probably shall conduct extensive reconnaissance by means of large and complex satellites."[64]

The TCP proposal for a scientific satellite struck a responsive chord. American scientists and engineers since 1954 had urged just such a program as part of the U.S. contribution to the International Geophysical Year (IGY) planned by the International Council of Scientific Unions to take place from 1 July 1957 through 31 December 1958. Donald A. Quarles, a Bell Telephone Laboratories' executive then serving as assistant secretary of defense for research and development, numbered among those witting of SENSINT and the nascent TALENT—and of their potentially adverse international political and legal ramifications. Convinced that securing international acceptance of the TCP report's freedom of space principle would be crucial to future American intelligence operations, Quarles in late February 1955 privately urged the U.S. National Committee for the IGY in the National Academy of Sciences to request formally a scientific satellite project, which it did. As he intended, that satellite proposal along with others landed on his desk in April. Quarles referred them for evaluation to his own Advisory Group on Special Capabilities. The next month, on 20 May, he submitted to the NSC a proposal for launching an IGY satellite and the national policy to guide this activity. Meeting on 26 May, the NSC endorsed Quarles's recommendations. The next day, "after sleeping on it," Eisenhower approved the satellite project and the proposed space policy crafted to establish the principle in international law of freedom of space and the right of unimpeded overflight that went with it.[65]

A few weeks later on 29 July 1955, shortly after returning from the Four Power Summit Conference in Geneva, Eisenhower issued a press release that announced plans for launching "small unmanned, earth-circling satellites" as part of the U.S. participation in the IGY.[66] Following by days the Soviet rejection of his Open Skies proposal in Geneva, the satellite announcement was hardly coincidental. But the statement avoided any hint at the IGY satellites underlying purpose: to establish the principle in international law of "freedom of space"—with all that that implied for strategic reconnaissance conducted at altitudes above the "airspace" to which the states beneath claimed exclusive sovereignty. Not to be outdone, Kremlin leaders on 30 July announced formally that the Soviet Union, too, intended to launch a scientific earth satellite during the IGY.[67] And just days later, in early August, Quarles's advisory group selected a U.S. Navy-sponsored scientific satellite, called Vanguard, over a U.S. Army-sponsored competitor, as the American entrant.[68]

In the event, the U.S. Air Force, which had funded reconnaissance satellite studies with The RAND Corporation since the late 1940s, already had issued General Operational Requirement No. 80 (SA-2c) in March 1955. This military requirement approved construction of and provided technical requirements for just such space vehicles that could collect imagery and signals intelligence. Although Quarles, Killian, and Land, among other authorities, did not believe that reconnaissance spacecraft could be fielded in the immediate future, the service selected three firms to compete in a one-year design study of a preferred vehicle. In June 1956, the Air Force chose Lockheed's newly formed Missile Systems Division to design and build its military reconnaissance satellites, now called Weapon System (WS) 117L. Lockheed's winning proposal featured a large, second-stage booster satellite stabilized in orbit on three axes with a high pointing accuracy. Eventually known as "Agena," this spacecraft was to be designed, constructed, and tested to meet an operational capability in the third quarter of 1963. While the diminutive Vanguard scientific satellite was projected to weigh tens of pounds and be launched by a modified sounding rocket during the IGY, the proposed WS 117L satellite would weigh thousands of pounds and be launched atop an Atlas ICBM later in the decade. But in the months that followed, the two programs proceeded slowly; neither the scientific satellite nor its military counterpart shared any national priority.[69]

That state of affairs changed dramatically in October–November 1957, after the Soviet Union launched the world's first two artificial earth satellites: Sputniks I and II. Collectively, they had a "Pearl Harbor" effect on public opinion, and introduced into space affairs the issues of national pride and international prestige. Though downplaying the importance of the accomplishment, the administration moved quickly to restore confidence at home and prestige abroad. The defense department authorized the army to launch a scientific satellite as a backup to the faltering National Science Foundation–Navy Vanguard Program, and the president established the Advanced Research Project Agency (ARPA) in early 1958, assigning to it temporary responsibility for all U.S. space projects. More funds were showered on the Air Force WS 117L reconnaissance satellite effort, shortly to be renamed Samos, which at that time consisted of an Eastman Kodak near-real-time film readout system and a film capsule recovery system. Kodak's film readout contribution featured a six-inch focal length lens in a camera mounted on the Agena that spooled a special bimat film. The exposed negative film was developed in a semi-dry chemical process, and then scanned by a flying spot line-scanner. Converted to an electrical signal whose strength varied with the density of the film's emulsion layer, the images would be radioed to earth as frequency-modulated analog signals, to be assembled much in the manner of a wire photo, each image built up in swaths. The film recovery concept, advanced earlier by Richard Raymond, Merton Davies, and Amrom Katz at The RAND Corporation, had been adopted in the WS 117L family of missions as Program IIA in August 1957. It employed a Thor IRBM launch vehicle, a small upper stage, and a spin-stabilized football shaped satellite that contained a Fairchild transverse panoramic slit camera with a 12-inch focal-length lens. Wide-angle scanning, accomplished by spinning the satellite, moved the lens across the field during the exposure time. Pictures would be taken only when the lens, mounted perpendicular to the roll axis, swung past the earth below. After a few orbits of the earth, a small solid-propellant recovery rocket would decelerate the satellite into a reentry trajectory, a parachute would deploy, and the reentry vehicle would be snatched in mid-air by a recovery airplane.[70]

Indeed, as 1957 drew to a close, others familiar with the two reconnaissance satellite systems increasingly shared reservations about film readout. Operating at a bandwidth threshold of six megahertz, without an exposed film storage capability, and in view of a ground station for only a few minutes as it passed overhead, the Kodak payload would be unable to relay to earth all of the pictures it had taken during each orbit. On 12 November, RAND's president Frank R. Collbohm sent an abbreviated version of a Davies report on the film recovery system directly to Air Force Lt. Gen. Donald L. Putt, deputy chief of staff for development and an early convert to the U-2 program. In his cover letter, Collbohm affirmed that this simplified reconnaissance satellite "will collect at least as much information in its one-day [of] operation as the 'early' 117L vehicle will in its useful life." After examining the report, Putt was won over, and on 25 November his executive assistant so notified his deputy: "General Putt has reviewed the attached report and commented as follows: 'General Swoffordd: This is one we should start immediately. Request DRD make recommendations to me as how we might proceed.'"[71]

By this time, however, the question of fielding a reconnaissance satellite quickly had moved well above and beyond the air staff at the Pentagon. In 1957, James Killian and Din Land both shared keys to the Oval Office, both had conducted assessments of the two reconnaissance space systems, and both concluded that film recovery was the way to go. Moreover, in response to the Sputnik crisis, on 15 November, the president appointed Killian to be his special assistant for science and technology and serve as chairman of a new President's Science Advisory Committee (PSAC). Other reviews of the Air Force reconnaissance satellite program in November and December, conducted by Richard E. Horner, assistant secretary of the Air Force for research and development, and Donald Quarles, now deputy secretary of defense, confirmed that the film recovery satellite would reach operational status at least one year before the WS 117L film readout satellite.[72]

Maneuvering easily among leaders of the defense and intelligence communities, on 6 February 1958 Killian and Land met with DCI Allen Dulles, Defense Secretary Neil McElroy, and Undersecretary Quarles. They agreed to separate the Air Force film recovery Program IIA from the WS 117L program and assign it to another CIA-Air Force team, again led by Bissell. The next day Killian and Land met with the president to discuss the plan. Land explained that satellites would provide a lower resolution of objects at the earth's surface in photographs taken from space, compared with what had been achieved with the U-2, but that the satellites would be nearly undetectable. The media already had identified the Air Force WS 117L as a space reconnaissance program, which deeply distressed Eisenhower who insisted on absolute secrecy in matters of intelligence. After listening to the plan, he agreed that an interim film-recovery satellite project should begin independently and covertly, separated from the Air Force reconnaissance satellite program, and managed by the CIA in a manner like the U-2, with the Air Force supplying the infrastructure and trained personnel. The president's decision bespoke his preference for civilian control of national intelligence assets and his confidence in the men who had quickly and successfully executed TALENT.[73]

Before month's end at the CIA, Richard Bissell drew personnel from his development projects staff for this effort, and he selected as his deputy director Air Force Brig. Gen. Osmond J. Ritland, at that time Lt. Gen. Bernard Schriever's vice commander at the Air Force Ballistic Missile Division, who had served him so ably as his first deputy on TALENT. Under Ritland, the Air Force would furnish everything except the camera payload and security control system. That is, it would furnish the booster and upper stage, integrate the payload, test and launch them, and command and control all of the reconnaissance satellites on orbit, in addition to providing recovery of the film capsules above and, in conjunction with the U.S. Navy, on the surface of the Pacific Ocean. To do so, however, Eisenhower officials had first to eliminate the publicly known WS 117L Program IIA, and resurrect it as a covert satellite project with a plausible "cover" (or "second story"). To that end, Donald Quarles prepared a directive that was signed by ARPA's newly named director, Roy W. Johnson, which he sent to Secretary of the Air Force James H. Douglas, Jr., on 28 February. It cancelled the Thor-boosted reconnaissance satellite recovery component of the WS 117L Program and authorized in its place the "Discoverer Project," intended to develop a biomedical capsule for the recovery of biological specimens lofted into space atop Thor-Agena launch vehicles. The new scientific biomedical project, the directive asserted, was expected to contribute to America's early achievement of manned space flight.[74]

In the aftermath of the Soviet Sputniks, no one could hide a major space project from public view. Quarles, Bissell, Killian, and Land instead had hidden the film recovery satellite effort in plain view, where it masqueraded as a biomedical research project named Discoverer. In the weeks that followed in March, the enterprise acquired a code name: Corona, the reverse side of the obverse Discoverer coin. Bissell and Ritland confirmed the choice of the Douglas Aircraft Thor booster and Lockheed second stage Agena for Corona, and they made the Lockheed Missile Systems Division the system engineer, responsible for the technical direction and integration of the entire effort. In April, they selected a novel panoramic camera proposed by a new firm, Itek, over the Fairchild spin-stabilized camera. Itek offered a reciprocating 70-degree field panoramic camera with an f/5 Tessar-type 24-inch focal length lens, which required a stable space platform provided by the Agena. It promised to achieve a resolution at the earth's surface of at least 20 feet.[75]

The subsequent Corona story is well explored in various publications.[76] In this account it will suffice that Corona's CIA-Air Force team built, tested, and launched twelve satellites between February 1959 and June 1960, all of which failed. The physics of electromechanical and film operations in the hard vacuum and extreme temperatures of outer space was little known and painfully learned. Through it all, Eisenhower, though increasingly dismayed, backed his team. The loss of a U-2 over the USSR on 1 May 1960, however, changed the American intelligence equation completely. With that loss, the imagery intelligence produced by America's overhead aerial assets went dark—and promised to stay that way until a reconnaissance satellite could be made to work. But if the covert Corona film recovery satellite project was struggling, the overt though ostensibly Secret Air Force Samos film readout satellite program thus far had generated only unwanted publicity while failing to launch a single spacecraft. With only eight months remaining in his second term in office, on 10 June the president instructed Secretary of Defense Thomas S. Gates, Jr., to form a small team and assess whether Samos could meet national intelligence requirements, and, if it were to continue, recommend improvements in its organization and operation to the National Security Council. To oversee the study, Gates selected Eisenhower's special assistant for science and technology, Harvard chemist George B. Kistiakowsky (who had succeeded James Killian in 1959).[77]

Kistiakowsky called on James Killian to chair the Samos review, assisted by two PSAC staff assistants, Harry G. Watters and George W. Rathjens, and by two individuals named by Secretary Gates: Joseph V. Charyk, undersecretary of the Air Force (formerly Air Force assistant secretary for research and development), and Herbert F. York, recently appointed Defense Department director of defense research and engineering (formerly director of the University of California's Lawrence Radiation Laboratory). Killian, assisted by these gentlemen and others that he chose, Richard Bissell, William O. Baker, Din Land, Edward Purcell, and Carl Overhage (director of MIT's Lincoln Laboratory) conducted the study during July and early August. Air Force military leaders, meanwhile, well aware that they might lose control of the Samos reconnaissance satellite project, which at that time amounted to some 90 percent of planned military space operations, mounted a vigorous rear-guard action at the Pentagon to maintain their position. But they were overtaken by Samos's technical and organizational deficiencies, and by Corona's success. Some three months after TALENT overflights over the Soviet Union ended, Eisenhower's resolve to stay the course was rewarded. On 11 August 1960, the first Corona reentry capsule was recovered in the Pacific Ocean. Although it carried only a United States flag, the recovery confirmed that the substitution of cold gas jets to spin-up the film capsule, in place of small solid-propellant rocket motors, had solved the reentry problem.[78]

On the West Coast, Bissell's Lockheed and Air Force elements mounted an Itek camera and film in the next Agena, this time with a film take-up spool in the reentry capsule. Launched from Vandenberg AFB in California on 18 August, Corona 14 performed perfectly and the reentry capsule with its precious cargo was recovered next day in mid-air, near Hawaii. While the film was flown from Hawaii to the Eastman Kodak Company in Rochester, New York, to be developed and assayed, Killian and his review panel completed their Samos report in Cambridge, Massachusetts, preparatory to its presentation at the next NSC meeting on the 24th. Panel members determined, technically, that Samos would not yield the intelligence "results of the necessary quality within a short time," and they recommended that the film readout system continue only as a research and development effort. They also recommended that the program be reoriented to emphasize high-resolution film recovery systems, which had now become feasible and demonstrated in the Corona Project, and that it be integrated with a meteorological satellite to maximize cloud-free photography. Furthermore, their report judged reconnaissance satellites to be a vital national intelligence resource, a resource best placed under the direct control of civilian, rather than military, authorities. They recommended that Samos management be removed from the regular Air Force and vested in a new civilian office. The chain of command would be simple and direct: the Air Force officers and civilians conducting the reconnaissance satellite project would report directly to a civilian office under the secretary of the Air Force, whose director, in turn, would report to the secretary of defense. Finally, the review group affirmed that the conduct of all reconnaissance operations in space, like the U-2 aerial overflights before them, had best be conducted in absolute secrecy lest Soviet leaders be provoked to interfere with or destroy these satellites. Kistiakowsky briefed these findings and recommendations to Defense Secretary Gates on 23 August, who endorsed them.[79]

The next morning at 8:15 A.M., before the NSC meeting began, James Killian, Din Land, Gordon Gray (the national security advisor who had succeeded Robert Cutler), and George Kistiakowsky met with President Eisenhower to show him the first reconnaissance satellite photographs of the Soviet Union returned by Corona 14 a few days earlier. On entering the Oval Office, Din Land unrolled a reel of developed film across the carpet to the president standing beside his desk, with the words: "Here are your pictures Mr. President!" After the viewing, and to avoid informing or provoking Soviet leaders, Eisenhower declared that no American satellite reconnaissance photographs ever should be released publicly—a policy his successors adhered to for many years. Those attending the NSC meeting had received the agenda and knew that they would consider the organization and conduct of the nation's reconnaissance satellite program. After the presentation and discussion, Eisenhower approved the Samos review panel's recommendations, as did Secretary of Defense Gates. Air Force Secretary Sharp issued the requisite organizational directives at the end of the month. The new reconnaissance satellite office, called the Office of Missile and Satellite Systems, a name later shortened to Office of Space Systems, in the office of the secretary of the Air Force, would be directed by Air Force Undersecretary Joseph Charyk, who in this capacity reported to Gates. A special projects office on the West Coast, headed by an Air Force flag officer and responsible for the Samos project, reported to Charyk and no one else.[80] This action removed the "regular" Air Force from any direct role in American reconnaissance satellites for the remainder of the twentieth century.

With Corona producing images and Samos separated from the regular Air Force, on 26 August the president sent a memorandum to the secretaries of state and defense, the attorney general, the chairman of the atomic energy commission, and the DCI that announced a new TALENT-KEYHOLE security control system that strictly limited access to reconnaissance satellite products and activities, and controlled the flow of that information. "Within your agency," Eisenhower told its recipients, "you shall be personally responsible for the selection of those personnel who will have access to the [reconnaissance satellite] information and for determining the scope of that access. Access is to be on a 'must know' basis related to major national security needs." Underscoring his concern for "must know" and the strict need to limit access to this new SCI control system, the president requested that the addressees and each member of his staff cleared for TALENT-KEYHOLE initial the memorandum, which they solemnly did.[81] Corona's photographic images, or "product," later would be separated into another compartment within TALENT-KEYHOLE, called RUFF, which would remain in effect until the Corona program itself concluded in 1972. That product, and its photo-interpretation and the delivery of imagery and intelligence findings to national command authorities, also would become an issue with which President Eisenhower would have to deal before leaving office.

One year earlier, on 24 August 1959, President Eisenhower had approved yet another unacknowledged reconnaissance satellite program eventually known as the Galactic Radiation and Background (GRAB) experiment, designed to collect electronic intelligence (ELINT) from Soviet air defense radars.[82] This satellite mounted two payloads: one of them, a scientific experiment announced publicly, measured Solar Radiation (SolRad) and served as the cover for the second, unannounced and highly classified ELINT package. Launched on 22 June 1960, GRAB operated on orbit for a number of months and thus holds the distinction of the country's first successful reconnaissance satellite. The Naval Research Laboratory managed GRAB for the director of naval intelligence and the National Security Agency (NSA), which collected, analyzed, and disseminated communications and electronic intelligence.[83] In the months that followed, this project, too, would fall under the TALENT-KEYHOLE reconnaissance satellite system control blanket, although its ELINT product would be placed into a separate control system administered by the NSA.

If the NSA served as the principal United States agency that collected, analyzed, and distributed signals intelligence products, what could be said for its counterpart that collected, analyzed, and distributed imagery products? One could say nothing about such an agency because in 1960 it did not exist. Each of the military services and the CIA possessed their own photo-processing, interpretation and distribution organizations. Realizing that a national photographic intelligence center would be needed to consolidate and process the flood of photographs projected from Corona and future imaging space projects, in the spring of 1960, at about the same time that he authorized the Samos review, President Eisenhower commissioned a second study of this very subject, with its findings and recommendations likewise to be furnished to the NSC. This review, which concluded shortly after the Samos assessment, recommended that all military and CIA photo-interpretation assets be combined in a single National Photographic Interpretation Center (NPIC), located in Washington, D.C. But should NPIC be directed by a military flag officer, as was the NSA, or by a civilian official as was the case in the newly established Office of Missile and Satellite Systems in the Department of the Air Force? The secretary of defense, Joint Chiefs of Staff, and service chiefs argued strongly for the former arrangement, while the CIA argued for the latter. Once again, Eisenhower chose civilian control of the nation's photo-interpretation center, making it a component of the CIA under the direction of the DCI. A few days before President Eisenhower left office, NPIC was established, headed by Arthur C. Lundahl, formerly chief of the CIA photographic intelligence division.[84]

In the meantime, a second successful CORONA flight in early December 1960 had added greatly to film coverage of the Soviet Union, and photographed the Plesetsk missile center. These early CORONA findings confirmed Eisenhower's assessment based on imagery taken by U-2 airplanes, one that ran counter to the views previously expressed by incoming President John F. Kennedy. In his farewell address to the country on 17 January 1961, the outgoing president emphatically declared the "missile gap," like the earlier "bomber gap," to be a fiction. Indeed, a few weeks later on the evening of 6 February, President Kennedy's secretary of defense, Robert McNamara, meeting with reporters, publicly acknowledged that a new administration study had found no evidence of a missile gap.[85] CORONA flights later that spring confirmed that the United States possessed far more operational ICBMs than did the USSR.

The clandestine signal intelligence and imaging reconnaissance satellite programs that President Eisenhower had approved and that entered operation during his last year in office made his 1955 "Open Skies" proposal a reality in the 1960s. With them, advanced technology had overtaken the secretive masters of the Kremlin. Hesitantly, they, too, would embrace inspection from space to help contain expenditures for intercontinental weapons and limit the threat of annihilation for Communist rule that these weapons posed. With the SALT I Treaty of 1972, reconnaissance satellites would be recognized formally as the "national technical means" for policing the terms of international arms control agreements. By that date, these remarkable overhead technical systems provided the strategic "transparency" that a prescient leader had sought: they helped ensure that the Cold War remained "cold." In fact, by that date American reconnaissance satellites had turned Eisenhower's "intelligence problem" of the 1950s, when virtually no reliable information about Soviet military capabilities could be obtained, upside down. Now intelligence officers faced an avalanche of satellite data, nearly all of it totally reliable. Reconnaissance satellite-generated electronic and visual information overwhelmed analysts and began to occlude the processing systems that exploited and disseminated it—and this "issue of plenty" would continue to challenge the intelligence community in the years ahead. Although many of these developments did not occur in his lifetime, on leaving office on 20 January 1961 Eisenhower surely could take satisfaction in the knowledge that he and his closest advisors had engineered a revolution in intelligence. Together, within a span of eight years, they had opened the Soviet Union and Communist China—indeed the entire world—to American scrutiny.

Epilogue

All of these actions and events involving SENSINT, TALENT, and TALENT-KEYHOLE took place in the utmost secrecy in the 1950s. They were not declassified until shortly after the Cold War abruptly ended, when the Soviet Union, like the Berlin Wall before it, was suddenly and unexpectedly pulled down. Although the overhead reconnaissance programs contained in these security control systems had contributed mightily to this outcome, they remain relatively unknown. Uninformed historians and fatuous media personalities continue to instruct their students and the American public that Dwight D. Eisenhower was a "caretaker," "do-nothing" president. Not long ago the author of a review in the *New York Times* smirked: "Harry S. Truman was followed by eight years of Dwight D. Eisenhower, who was rumored to have died early in his term without there being any visible change in his style of governing."[86] More recently, in a tribute to the musician Ray Charles, another representative of the fourth estate enthused: "I've been a Ray Charles fan since high school days—those innocent days when Ike was snoozing in the White House and all our parents had to worry about was whether we were somewhere dancing to 'What'd I Say.'"[87] Nevertheless, one of the most perceptive assessments of the thirty-fourth president came from the *New York Times* Washington D.C. bureau chief upon completing research for a book. Eisenhower, he reflected, authorized and superintended "a formidable array of . . . exotic spy planes and satellites, nuclear-powered submarines and aircraft carriers, intercontinental ballistic missiles and nuclear warheads compact enough to fit atop missiles. All in all, it was a time of landmark advances in defense, *a record unequaled by nine subsequent presidents.*"[88]

President Eisenhower and his administration did prepare the United States to counter successfully the threats and exigencies of the Cold War in the twentieth century. The collapse of the Soviet Union marked the end of that struggle and the emergence of the Unites States as the world's solitary "superpower." If that change ended fears of a thermonuclear cataclysm, it also portended international repercussions among former allies and adversaries. And after a quarter-century of sporadic attacks on American and Western interests, shortly after the turn of the Millennium on 11 September 2001, Islamic extremists seized four U.S. commercial airliners in flight. Within hours, these acolytes of the al Qaeda terrorist organization had flown two of them into the twin towers of New York City's World Trade Center, and a third into the Pentagon headquarters of the defense department across the Potomac River from Washington, D.C., in Virginia. Passengers onboard the fourth airliner, bound to strike the nation's Capitol building, engaged their captors, and in the ensuing struggle the plane crashed in Pennsylvania. This twentieth-century surprise attack killed more than 3,000 Americans—more than the number who died in the Japanese military surprise attack against Pearl Harbor on 7 December 1941. And just as 7 December marked U.S. entry into World War II, 11 September committed the country and its citizens to another world war—this time against shadowy religious zealots around the globe intent on destroying a "decadent" America and, if they could, all of Western civilization. What lessons might Eisenhower's legacy of preparing to conduct the Cold War suggest for this nation's leaders who contend today with implacable Islamists at home and abroad?

To assess and conduct the war against Islamic terrorists, which likely will last longer than the Cold War that preceded it, a president would be well advised to convene secretly another panel of the nation's best scientists and technologists, once again mandated and organized along the lines of Eisenhower's precedent-setting Technological Capabilities Panel. Although applied science itself will not solve intractable political issues, the TCP's recommendations demonstrated that applied science does furnish methods for meeting and controlling them. Acting on the TCP recommendations, Eisenhower underscored another precedent. When a president judges the nation's security to be so threatened as to be in grave jeopardy, he will authorize extra-legal activity to monitor, disrupt, or eliminate that threat. Acquiring actionable intelligence about an adversary *in peacetime* through high-altitude aerial reconnaissance is a classic example of this kind of activity. Other commanders-in-chief have so acted before: Abraham Lincoln in the Civil War to preserve the Union, and Franklin D. Roosevelt in World War II to preserve Western democracy. I would expect, or at least hope, that others in future will act in a similar fashion when faced with extraordinary threats to the nation's security.

Finally, let me consider *only* Eisenhower's revolution in overhead reconnaissance applied to the war against Islamic terrorists. National leaders today face a committed adversary that is not a nation-state; America's adversary is currently composed of diffuse bands of loosely aligned religious fanatics who move and operate frequently in single-digit numbers. Among other intelligence initiatives, the country will have to field overhead platforms that can loiter over specific regions of the earth for extended periods—*for days,* not for hours or minutes. Eisenhower's low-altitude imaging satellites in the physical grip of Newtonian mechanics, which pass by in a matter of minutes as the earth rotates beneath them, cannot meet that requirement. In rapidly changing tactical or crisis situations, they cannot provide the constant stream of intelligence that circumstances on the ground may demand. To my view, only extremely high altitude, stealthy unmanned aerial vehicles (UAVs) that can linger over areas of interest for extended periods will provide that kind of intelligence *at an affordable cost*. But it requires acting on another Eisenhower precedent, authorizing aerial overflights. When operated over another country without its permission, UAVs of the kind described are relatively unobtrusive. Countries overflown presumably will be unable to counter them and can easily ignore their presence—which may often be the most sensible political expedient. Lodging international protests might prove of limited moral or even legal suasion if the intelligence revealed that the country in question was harboring, sustaining, or training terrorists. Will another American president choose Eisenhower's approach to solve this particular intelligence problem? In the clandestine world of overhead reconnaissance, we may not know when or even if that question is answered.

Notes

I am indebted to Dr. David Haight, Senior Archivist at the Dwight D. Eisenhower Library, whose assistance proved indispensable in the preparation of this study.

1. Stephen E. Ambrose, *Eisenhower* (New York: Simon & Schuster, 1984), 2:257. Regarding his appreciation for intelligence, Eisenhower numbered among but a few Allied military leaders witting of the Ultra German radio communication intercepts and decryption. He fully appreciated its value and the value of aerial photo-reconnaissance to military success. Compartmented in a special control channel, Ultra remained for many years among the least known and darkest of wartime secrets. Indeed, information about this program and its importance to wartime success on land and at sea would not become public knowledge for another twenty years, until the 1970s.

2. Von Hardesty, "Made in the USSR," *Air & Space Smithsonian* 15 (February–March 2001). The reverse engineering of the B-29 to create the TU-4 forced the Tupolev design bureau and Soviet industry to modernize aviation electronics and aerostructure fabrication, which brought with it manifold benefits for Soviet aviation in the 1950s and 1960s.

3. *New York Times*, 1 Dec. 1950, 1.

4. The classified agreement struck between the two leaders has not yet been found at the Harry S. Truman Library or in the records of the Department of State at the National Archives. The Minutes of the Meetings of the Joint Chiefs of Staff that would contain references to it have been removed and destroyed for this period of the Cold War and no copies of them are known to exist.

5. JCS to LeMay and other JCS commanders, 6 Dec. 1950, box B-196, Papers of Curtis E. LeMay, Library of Congress.

6. R. Cargill Hall, "Early Cold War Overfights, an Introduction," in R. Cargill Hall and Clayton D. Laurie, eds., *Early Cold War Overflights, 1950–1956: Symposium Proceedings*, 2 vols. (Washington, D.C.: Office of the Historian, National Reconnaissance Office, 2003), 1:2n2.

7. R. Cargill Hall, "From Concept to National Policy: Strategic Reconnaissance in the Cold War," *Prologue* 28 (Summer 1996):112.

8. John S. D. Eisenhower, *Strictly Personal* (New York: Doubleday, 1974), 156–57.

9. John T. Mason, Jr., Interview with Gen. Nathan F. Twining, USAF (Ret), 17 Aug. 1967, Arlington, Va. Twining Taped Interview, no. 3 of 4, 1131–32, transcribed 1973; Columbia University Oral History Research Collection, Butler Library. See associated Air Force mission execution documents in *Early Cold War Overflights*, 2:app. 2, 1951 and 1952.

10. Vance O. Mitchell, interview with Brig. Gen. Richard C. Neeley, USAF (Ret), 7 Mar. 1966, Las Vegas, Nev. Transcript in NRO History Files; see also docs. 20 and 21, *Early Cold War Overflights*, 2:app. 2.

11. See memoirs in *Early Cold War Overflights*, 1:47–88. An excellent first-hand account of Korean War aerial reconnaissance and photo interpretation can be found in Ben Hardy and Duane Hall, *Photographic Aerial Reconnaissance and Interpretation, Korea, 1950–1952* (Manhattan, Kans.: Sunflower, 2004).

12. John Crampton, "RB-45C Overflight Operations in the Royal Air Force," *Early Cold War Overflights*, 1:153–64.

13. R. Cargill Hall, "The Truth About Overflights," *Military History Quarterly* 9 (Spring 1997):28.

14. See Donald E. Hillman with R. Cargill Hall, "A Daytime Overflight of Soviet Siberia," *Air Power History* 43 (Spring 1996), and Lloyd F. Fields, "Wrangel Island and Project Home Run Overflights," *Early Cold War Overflights*, 1:259–72.

15. See, for example, Mele Vojvodich, Jr., "Overflights Conducted During the Korean War," *Early Cold War Overflights*, 1:67–76.

16. Stacy D. Naftel, "RB-45C Overflights in the Far East," and Howard S. Myers, Jr., "RB-45C Overflight Operations During the Korean War," ibid., 57–66 and 99–104, respectively.

17. Brigadier General Pete Carroll, USA, who served as Eisenhower's staff secretary and

defense department liaison, was witting of all covert programs. He died in office on 17 Sept. 1954 and left virtually no written records. Were it not for his successor, Col. Andrew Goodpaster, USA, who prepared memoranda of meetings and conversations in which these subjects were discussed, posterity would be dependent almost entirely on the recollections of the few participants who survived until the overhead programs were declassified in the 1990s.

18. Until the termination of the SENSINT Program in December 1956, the Army and Navy representatives on the Joint Chiefs of Staff, specified commanders, and theater commanders overseas were briefed on and involved in the aerial overflights that affected them, but apparently did not have access to information on the entire operation worldwide. For example, Gen. Curtis E. LeMay, commander of the Strategic Air Command, was witting of the deep penetration reconnaissance bomber overflights for which he was responsible, but he would not have been aware of the tactical overflights conducted from Japan and South Korea under the auspices of the Far East Air Forces. He had "no need to know."

19. Robert R. Bowie and Richard H. Immerman, *Waging Peace* (New York: Oxford University Press, 1998), 86; Robert Cutler, *No Time for Rest* (Boston: Little, Brown, 1965), *passim*; Geoffrey Perret, *Eisenhower* (New York: Random House, 1999), 446.

20. Bowie and Immerman, *Waging Peace,* 91. When considering the workings of the Eisenhower administration, especially the NSC, this volume and Cutler's *No Time to Rest* are indispensable. On reflection, Eisenhower called Cutler "[my] right arm . . . the real mainspring responsible for many National Security Council tasks of vital importance to the nation . . . a very close friend." So tactful and circumspect was he as the president's first national security advisor that he did not grant press interviews and Cutler remains to this day all but unknown to history. In fact, he is not even listed among the worthies in Eleanora Schoenebaum's *Political Profiles: The Eisenhower Years* (New York: Facts on File, 1977)!

21. Kenneth W. Condit, *History of the Joint Chiefs of Staff,* vol. 6, *The Joint Chiefs of Staff and National Policy, 1955–1956* (Washington, D.C., Historical Office, Joint Staff, 1992), 4; Bowie and Immerman, *Waging Peace,* 93–95.

22. David Haight, Dwight D. Eisenhower Library, email to the author, "Re: Predecessors of 5412 Committee," 23 Sept. 2004; also see *Foreign Relations of the United States, 1964–1968* (hereafter *FRUS*) (Washington, D.C.: Government Printing Office, 2000), 16:xxxii–xxiii.

23. David Alan Rosenberg, "The Origins of Overkill," *International Security* 7 (Spring 1983):31–32. This net assessment report also prompted President Eisenhower to propose, and Congress to approve, the construction of three secret underground "emergency relocation centers" to ensure the continuity of government in the event of atomic attack. Completed in the late 1950s and in 1960, one of the centers housed members of the Executive Branch, a second command center housed the nation's military leaders, and the third accommodated all of the members of Congress, both House and Senate. After the collapse of the Soviet Union in 1991, a disgruntled federal employee or perhaps a member of Congress "leaked" the location of the congressional bunker to the press with the result that that installation was abandoned. It is now open to public tours in White Sulphur Springs, W. Va. See Ted Gup, "The Last Resort," *Washington Post Magazine,* 31 May 1992, and Bill Gertz, "Congress Ex-bunker a Haven for Tourists," *Washington Times,* 31 Oct. 1999, C1.

24. "Diary Entry by the President's Press Secretary (Hagerty), Washington, 1 February 1955," *FRUS, 1955–1957,* 19:40–41. The president had told Republican legislative leaders much the same thing a few weeks earlier, in December 1954, adding, however: "Now, everything points to the fact that Russia is not seeking a general war and will not for a long, long, time, if ever. Everything is shifting to economic warfare, to propaganda, and to a sort of peaceful infiltration." Robert H. Ferrell, ed., *The Diary of James C. Hagerty: Eisenhower in Mid-Course, 1954–1955* (Bloomington: Indiana University Press, 1983), 13 Dec. 1954, 133. See also a sobering net evaluation of a Soviet surprise attack presented to Eisenhower on 23 Jan. 1956, in Robert H. Ferrell, ed., *The Eisenhower Diaries* (New York: Norton, 1981), 311–12.

25. Bowie and Immerman, *Waging Peace,* 153.

26. Press release, James C. Hagerty, 6 Nov. 1953, with EO 10501 attached.

27. The records of this action are not to be found at the Eisenhower Library. If they exist, they would be held in the minutes of the special groups in the presidential intelligence files at the NSC, which are not released to presidential libraries. Whether they exist or not, the program emerged in early 1954, and it could only have been authorized by President Eisenhower, especially since discussions of the SENSINT program subsequently occurred in the oval office and were recorded by his staff secretary, Andrew Goodpaster. The last Korean War overflight conducted by the 15th TRS occurred on 27 July 1953, and the first one under the SENSINT Program took place in March 1954. Colonel Samuel Dickens, USAF (Ret.), email to the author, 15 Dec. 2004. Throughout his two terms in office, on all matters of intelligence and national security, Eisenhower consulted with and confided in James Doolittle, a Shell Oil Company executive and World War II comrade who commanded the Eighth Air Force in England. Doolittle, in effect, functioned as a minister without portfolio and other administration leaders all knew it. But Doolittle's crucial role in affairs of state, like that of Robert Cutler, has been almost entirely ignored by historians.

28. Hall, "Introduction," *Early Cold War Overflights,* 1:9–11. The best description of the SENSINT and TALENT access and security arrangements with which I am aware is contained in Allen Shumway, "Security for Overflight Imagery in the Early Cold War," ibid., 333–42.

29. NSC 5412, 15 Mar. 1954, declassified on 20 Dec. 1977; see also *FRUS, 1964–1968,* 16:xxxiii.

30. Roger K. Rhodarmer, "Recollections of an Overflight 'Legman,'" *Early Cold War Overflights,* 1:18–32.

31. Samuel T. Dickens, "RF-86 Sabre Overflights in Asia," ibid., 77–88.

32. John Crampton, "RB-45C Overflight Operations in Europe," ibid., 153–64.

33. Harold R. Austin, "A Daytime Overflight of the Soviet Union," 211–26.

34. Goodpaster, "Memorandum of Conference with the President, May 28, 1956; 11:00 AM," document 86-1, ibid., 2:app. 2, 565–66; see also idem, "Cold War Overflights, A View from the White House," 1:37–46.

35. Thomas D. Crouch, *The Eagle Aloft: Two Centuries of the Balloon in America* (Washington, D.C.: Smithsonian Institution Press, 1983), 644–49.

36. Goodpaster, "Memorandum of Conference with the President, November 15, 1956, 2:30 PM," with Secretary Hoover, Admiral Radford, Mr. Allen Dulles, Mr. Richard Bissell, and Col. Goodpaster, Eisenhower Library, documents 90-1 and 90-2, *Early Cold War Overflights,* 2:app. 2, 571–72.

37. "Soviet Note of December 15," *Department of State Bulletin,* document 91-1, ibid., 2:app. 2, 573.

38. "Phone Calls, Tuesday, December 18, 1956," DDE Diary Series, box 20, file folder "Dec '56 Phone Calls," Dwight D. Eisenhower Papers as President (Ann Whitman File), Eisenhower Library.

39. Goodpaster, "Memorandum for Record," 18 Dec. 1956. Goodpaster concluded, "each of them confirmed that he understood what the President intended," Eisenhower Library, document 93-1, *Early Cold War Overflights,* 2:app. 2, 575.

40. Gregory W. Pedlow and Donald E. Welzenbach, *The CIA and the U-2 Program, 1954–1974* (Washington, D.C.: CIA History Office), 1998, 20.

41. James R. Killian, Jr., *Sputnik, Scientists, and Eisenhower: A Memoir of the First Special Assistant to the President for Science and Technology* (Cambridge, Mass.: MIT Press, 1982), 68–69; Pedlow and Welzenbach, *CIA and the U-2 Program,* 27. Additional information can be found in James R. Killian, *The Education of a College President: A Memoir* (Cambridge, Mass.: MIT Press, 1977).

42. James J. Hitchcock, interview with the author, 23 May 1986; also see Cynthia M. Grabo, "The Watch Committee and the National Indications Center: The Evolution of U.S. Strategic

Warning, 1950–1975," *International Journal of Intelligence and CounterIntelligence* 3 (Fall 1989):369–70, and Grabo, "Warning Intelligence," *Intelligence Profession Series Number Four,* Association of Former Intelligence Officers, McLean, Va., 1987. A more complete account of this activity tied to "defense conditions" (DEFCON 5 through 1) is contained in R. Cargill Hall, "Origins of U.S. Space Policy: Eisenhower, Open Skies, and Freedom of Space," in John Logsdon et al., eds., *Exploring the Unknown, Selected Documents in the History of the U.S. Civil Space Program* (Washington, D.C., Government Printing Office, NASA SP 4407), 1:220.

43. Pedlow and Welzenbach, *CIA and the U-2 Program,* 27. Eisenhower had come to know MIT's Killian in the late 1940s when he served as President of Columbia University.

44. Technological Capabilities Panel of the Science Advisory Committee, *Meeting the Threat of Surprise Attack* (Washington, D.C.: 14 February 1955), Table of members, 2:190. See also Victor K. McElheny, *Insisting on the Impossible: The Life of Edwin Land, Inventor of Instant Photography* (Reading, Mass.: Perseus, 1998), 294, and R. Cargill Hall, "The Eisenhower Administration and the Cold War, Framing American Astronautics to Serve National Security," *Prologue* 27 (Spring 1995):62. Land believed that any committee larger than the number able to fit into a taxicab would be unable to accomplish any significant work. Nevertheless, Allen F. Donovan of Cornell University's Aeronautical Laboratory served as a seventh, ex officio member of Project Three and actively participated in its deliberations. That would have made for four in the taxicab's back seat.

45. Pedlow and Welzenbach, *CIA and the U-2 Program,* 31–32.

46. Hall, "Introduction," *Early Cold War Overflights,* 1:10.

47. Christopher Andrew, *For the President's Eyes Only: Secret Intelligence and the American Presidency from Washington to Bush* (New York: Harper Perennial, 1996), 211.

48. *Report on the Covert Activities of the Central Intelligence Agency;* the cover letter to the president, dated 30 September, is signed by all four committee members. Doolittle, then serving on the TCP steering committee, was of course familiar with the work of Din Land's Project Three and the CL-282 proposal.

49. Andrew, *For the President's Eyes Only,* 211, and Ferrell, ed., *Eisenhower Diaries,* 285.

50. Pedlow and Welzenbach, *CIA and the U-2 Program,* 36; Chris Pocock, *The U-2 Spyplane: Toward the Unknown* (Atglen, Pa.: Schiffer Military History, 2000), 17–18.

51. Colonel Marion C. ("Hack") Mixson, interview with the author, 6 Sept. 1996, transcript in Office of the Historian, NRO; see esp. 8–15.

52. James G. Baker, "The U-2 B-Camera, its creation and Technical Capabilities," *Proceedings of the U-2 Development Panel,* U-2 History Symposium, National Defense University, 17 Sept. 1998 (NRO History Office publication, including contributions by Henry G. Combs, "U-2 Design and Fabrication," Benedict J. Koziol, "The U-2 Aircraft Engine," and Ernie L. Joiner, "Testing the U-2.")

53. Colonel Philip O. ("Robbie") Robertson, interview with R. Cargill Hall and Dennis F. Casey, 29 Dec. 1997, transcript in Office of the Historian, NRO.

54. Shumway, "Security for Overflight Imagery," 333–42.

55. Neither, however, is on file in the Eisenhower Library. If any copies exist, they are held in the NSC presidential intelligence files.

56. "Statement on Disarmament, July 21," *Department of State Bulletin,* 1 Aug. 1955, 174. The term "Open Skies" was coined later by the popular press and applied to this statement on disarmament. The background of this proposal is contained in *FRUS, 1955–1957,* vol. 20, esp. items 33 through 48. By 1956–57, Eisenhower and other key administration advisors viewed aerial reconnaissance as an "inspection system" that could serve two critical functions: forewarn of surprise attack *and* supervise and verify arms-control and nuclear test ban agreements.

57. Sergei Khrushchev, interview with R. Cargill Hall and Richard S. Leghorn, 5 July 1995, NRO History Office. According to the younger Khrushchev, the fears shared by his father and other Kremlin leaders were the mirror image of those held among American leaders. Nikita had witnessed the Nazi overflights that took place before Operation BARBAROSSA in 1941 and

feared that the American overflights presaged another attack.

58. Herbert S. Parmet, *Eisenhower and the American Crusades* (New York: Macmillan, 1972), 406. See also W. W. Rostow, *Open Skies: Eisenhower's Proposal of July 21, 1955* (Austin: University of Texas Press, 1982), 7–8.

59. Pedlow and Welzenbach, *CIA and the U-2 Program*, 111.

60. Ibid., 127–28.

61. The history of the TALENT missions is well told elsewhere, and is not repeated here. The reader is encouraged to consult Pedlow and Welzenbach, *loc. cit.;* Chris Pocock, *Dragon Lady: The History of the U-2 Spyplane* (Osceola, Wisc.: Motorbooks International, 1989); Jay Miller, *Aerograph 3: Lockheed U-2* (Austin, Tex.: Aerofax, 1983), and Pocock, *The U-2 Spyplane: Toward the Unknown, loc. cit.*

62. Dino A. Brugioni, *Eyeball to Eyeball: The Inside Story of the Cuban Missile Crisis* (New York: Random House, 1990), 43–46.

63. George B. Kistiakowsky, *A Scientist at the White House: The Private Diary of President Eisenhower's Special Assistant for Science and Technology* (Cambridge, Mass.: Harvard University Press, 1976), 334; see also Pocock, *The U-2 Spyplane,* 230, 234; and Michael R. Beschloss, *Mayday: Eisenhower, Khrushchev, and the U-2 Affair* (New York: Harper & Row, 1986), 274, 287.

64. *Meeting the Threat of Surprise Attack,* 2:147–48. Robert Cutler called the TCP report's presentation to the NSC "a high point in the Council's record, for it influenced the accelerated development by the U.S. of nuclear-capable ICBM's (including the long-range Polaris missile fired from a submerged submarine)," not to mention the intelligence ramifications that he carefully avoided discussing in his public memoir. Cutler, *No Time for Rest,* 350.

65. NSC 5520, "U.S. Scientific Satellite Program," 20 May 1955, *FRUS, 1955–1957,* 11:723–33.

66. The White House, Immediate Release, "Statement by James C. Hagerty," 29 July 1955, Eisenhower Library: "I am now announcing that the President has approved plans by this country for going ahead with the launching of small unmanned earth-circling satellites as part of the United States participation in the International Geophysical Year which takes place between July 1957 and December 1958." Prior White House discussions concerning this announcement are described in Hall, "Origins of U.S. Space Policy," 223.

67. Eugene M. Emme, *Aeronautics and Astronautics: An American Chronology of Science and Technology in the Exploration of Space, 1915–1960* (Washington, D.C.: Government Printing Office, 1961), 15 Apr. and 30 July 1955, 77–78.

68. On the IGY satellite decision, see R. Cargill Hall, "Origins and Development of the Vanguard and Explorer Satellite Programs," *The Aerospace Historian* 11 (October 1964). The story of the American IGY satellite program is perhaps best told in Constance McL. Green and Milton Lomask, *Vanguard: A History* (Washington, D.C.: NASA SP-4202, 1970).

69. Hall, "Origins of U.S. Space Policy," 222–24.

70. R. Cargill Hall, *Samos to the Moon: The Clandestine Transfer of Reconnaissance Technology Between Federal Agencies* (Washington, D.C., National Reconnaissance Office, 2001), 2, and idem, "Postwar Strategic Reconnaissance and the Genesis of Corona," in Dwayne Day et al., eds. *Eye in the Sky: The Story of the Corona Spy Satellites* (Washington, D.C.: Smithsonian Institution Press, 1998), 110.

71. RAND Corporation, Project RAND, *Recommendation to the Air Staff: An Earlier Reconnaissance Satellite System,* 12 Nov. 1975, with Collbohm cover letter and attached memo for Maj. Gen. Swofford (AFDRD), 25 Nov. 1957, in NRO History Files.

72. Hall, "Postwar Strategic Reconnaissance and the Genesis of Corona," 111. Killian retained his post as chairman of the President's Board of Consultants on Foreign Intelligence Activities, a board on which Din Land also served.

73. Ibid., 112.

74. Kenneth E. Greer, "CORONA," *Studies in Intelligence,* Supplement 17 (Spring 1973), as reprinted in Kevin C. Ruffner, ed., *CORONA: America's First Satellite Program* (Washington, D.C.: Center for the Study of Intelligence, 1995), 5; and Johnson to Douglas, "Reconnaissance Satellites and Manned Space Exploration," 28 Feb. 1958.

75. Hall, "Postwar Strategic Reconnaissance and the Genesis of Corona," 117.

76. For the most authoritative accounts, see Frederic C. E. Oder, James J. Fitzpatrick, and Paul E Worthman, *The Corona Story* (National Reconnaissance Office, 1987); Curtis Peebles, *The Corona Project, America's First Spy Satellites* (Annapolis, Md.: Naval Institute Press, 1997), Day et al., eds., *Eye in the Sky,* and Philip Taubman, *Secret Empire: Eisenhower, The CIA, and the Hidden Story of America's Space Espionage* (New York: Simon & Schuster, 2003).

77. Carl Berger, "The Air Force in Space, Fiscal Year 1961," Office of Air Force History (1966), 34. Preliminary discussions leading to this decision were held on 26 May 1960. See Goodpaster, "Memorandum of Conference with the President," 31 May 1960 (Others present: Dr. Kistiakowsky, Mr. Gordon Gray, General Goodpaster), Eisenhower Library.

78. Hall, "The Eisenhower Administration and the Cold War," 67.

79. Berger, "Air Force in Space," 38–40; Kistiakowsky, *Scientist at the Whitehouse,* 387–88; and Office of the Special Assistant to the President for Science and Technology, *Report of a Special Panel on Satellite Reconnaissance,* 25 Aug. 1960, *passim.* Panel members: James R. Killian and Edwin H. Land co-chairmen, with William O. Baker, Richard M. Bissell, Jr., Carl F. J. Overhage, and Edward M. Purcell.

80. SECAF Order 115.1, "Organization and Function of the Office of Missile and Satellite Systems," 31 Aug. 1960; and SECAF Order 1116.1, "Organization of the Samos Project Office," 31 Aug. 1960. The latter directive named the Samos Project Office as a field extension of the Office of Missile and Satellite Systems (MSS), and specified that its director would be responsible and report directly to MSS.

81. Eisenhower, memo for the secretary of state, the secretary of defense, the attorney general, the chairman, Atomic Energy Commission, and the director of central intelligence, no subject, 26 Aug. 1960.

82. Eisenhower, memo for the secretary of defense, no subject, 24 Aug. 1959, NRO History Files. Said Eisenhower: "I hereby approve the project recommended in your memoranda to me of 13 July and 18 August for inclusion of an electronic intelligence device in each of two planned satellite firings." Then, he mused, "this approval highlights the need for a control organization within the Defense Department to provide effective and unified operational control and coordination of these and other [reconnaissance] satellite devices designed to serve operational purposes." One year later, he would authorize and the secretary of the Air Force would establish that organization. See note 80, *supra.*

83. R. Cargill Hall, "The NRO in the 21st Century: Ensuring Global Information Supremacy," *Quest* 11 (Summer 2004):4–5.

84. Marion W. Boggs, "Discussion at the 474th Meeting of the National Security Council, Thursday, January 12, 1961," 13 Jan. 1961, 6–9, 16, Eisenhower Papers, 1953–61, Ann Whitman File, Eisenhower Library, See also Hall, "Eisenhower Administration and the Cold War," 68.

85. Robert S. McNamara, interview with the author, 25 Mar. 1999, 6, NRO History Office files. Kennedy, it must be said, was not briefed on the U-2 and Corona programs and what they had revealed until *after* his election in November. Eisenhower had not permitted it, and the move quite possibly cost Richard Nixon the election.

86. Viki Goldberg, "The Cars Were Big and Elvis Was Young," *New York Times,* 20 Feb. 1998, B35.

87. Larry Thornberry, "God Shed His Grace on Ray," as reprinted in *Washington Times,* 16 June 2004, A2.

88. Taubman, *Secret Empire,* "Preface," emphasis added, xiii.

Eisenhower and Space:
Politics and Ideology in the Construction of the U.S. Civil Space Program

In the summer of 1957, six-months into Dwight D. Eisenhower's second term and before the Sputnik crisis winter of 1957–58, the president asked the National Security Council (NSC) to review the military space programs of the United States to ensure that the level of investment and progress being made was adequate. He intended to field the first intercontinental ballistic missiles (ICBMs) and reconnaissance satellites by the time he left office. These capabilities in the new high ground of space would ensure that the United States could compete effectively with the Soviet Union in the Cold War rivalry that gripped the world. Eisenhower learned that through fiscal year 1957 the nation had spent $11.8 billion in then year-dollars on military space activities. "The cost of continuing these programs from FY 1957 through FY 1963," the NSC reported, "would amount to approximately $36.1 billion, for a grand total of $47 billion."[1]

By any measure, this should be considered a significant investment on the part of the Eisenhower administration, and it suggests that Eisenhower had developed a strategy for ensuring U.S. technological comparability, and eventual superiority, in the global game of one-upmanship and rivalry that was the Cold War. Eisenhower was always cognizant of the need to develop space activities in an orderly fashion, and without excessively burdening the federal budget. When adjusted for inflation, only Presidents Ronald Reagan and Bill Clinton made similar investments in space technology.[2] Those assets also found use on both the military and civilian sides of the space program during subsequent years.[3] In an irony of proportions too great to ignore, Eisenhower found himself branded by the Democrats in October 1957 after the launch of Sputnik 1 as an incompetent for allowing the Soviet Union to beat the United States into orbit by launching the first satellite. With his long-term strategy, however, Eisenhower did not see a need to improvise; instead he was convinced that U.S. efforts in space during his administration had been both reasonable and considerably more forward-looking than those of his Democratic predecessor.[4]

The NSC reported an acceptable level of spending Eisenhower believed, correctly as it turned out, but if ways could be found to reduce it Eisenhower would have been receptive to hearing them. Accomplishing an appropriate pace of space technology development at a reasonable cost motivated every aspect of Eisenhower's space policy, and before Sputnik he was convinced that his administration was doing so. This belief informed his early responses to the launch of the Soviet satellite; but it also lent credence to political charges about his lackadaisical attitudes. In some respects, on the other hand, it was a tortoise and hare story. Eisenhower believed in a definition of priorities for space missions, progress in accomplishing those priorities, a steady level of funding for the efforts necessary to carry them out, and a hands-off approach toward redirecting efforts or reevaluating positions.[5]

More than perhaps any president of the Cold War era, Eisenhower had a formal strategy for defeating the Soviet Union.[6] It was based on long-term economic, military, international, and social and moral policies that would enhance the United States as the world leader. It represented a commitment to constant pressure on the Soviet Union on a broad front, but refrained from confrontation that would require nuclear war to resolve. A key ingredient of this strategy involved not responding to every situation vis-à-vis the Soviet Union as a crisis. As Eisenhower wrote in his memoirs: "Every addition to defense spending does not automatically increase military security. Because security is based upon moral and economic, as well as purely military strength, a point can be reached at which additional funds for arms, far from bolstering security, weaken it."[7] This balanced approach to waging the Cold War served the nation well In contrast to those who believe Ronald Reagan essentially won the competition by spending the Soviet Union into oblivion, Eisenhower's strategic vision did more to establish the conditions for success than any other single set of decisions during the forty-year conflict.[8]

Eisenhower's approach to activities in space reflected his long-term strategy for winning the Cold War. He would expend appropriate resources, remain on a par with Soviet capabilities, and pressure his Soviet counterpart, but not be stampeded by those who sounded an alarm about Soviet successes. Even so, he believed that he was pressured by domestic interest groups into taking actions that he believed were counterproductive to that long-term strategy.

Indeed, the farewell address of Dwight D. Eisenhower on 17 January 1961, presented just as the thirty-fourth president departed the White House, is remembered today chiefly for his warning about the potency of the military-industrial complex, which he said had the "potential for the disastrous rise of misplaced power." What has been mostly forgotten is Eisenhower's equally strong warning about the "danger that public policy could itself become the captive by a scientific-technological elite." He cautioned that this scientific-technological elite was closely tied to the power of the military-industrial complex, indeed the technological revolution made possible by this elite largely fueled the sweeping changes in the industrial-military posture during and after World War II.[9]

Although other issues certainly helped to define Eisenhower's concerns about what he considered dangers to American institutions, the Sputnik crisis of 1957–58 and the resultant creation of the National Aeronautics and Space Administration (NASA), as well as many other initiatives undertaken within the federal government, certainly affected his perspectives on this subject in a fundamental way. A specific instance of this perception in his farewell address is Eisenhower's comment about the misplaced "temptation to feel that some spectacular and costly action could become the miraculous solution to all current difficulties." With proper deference to the importance of science and technology, Eisenhower suggested that the nation must avoid a rush to judgment in a crisis situation and refrain from establishing expensive new organizations and programs "as the only way to the road we wish to travel."[10]

In reacting to Sputnik, Eisenhower was pressed by a set of political exigencies, a critical mass of interests, and a key cadre of scientific and technical officials within the federal government and their supporters in universities, corporations, and think tanks to create a powerful, large, and costly federal agency to carry out space exploration. Eisenhower was correspondingly pressured by these forces to establish a separate federal entity, something he thought unnecessarily expensive and once created almost impossible to dismantle, to carry out a visible program of space exploration that would counteract the Soviet success with its first Earth satellite. The president, in turn, did not give those advocating major growth in the nation's space effort everything they wanted. Many advocated the creation of a cabinet-level department for science and technology, of which the space mission would be a major component. To a very real extent, Eisenhower's transformation of a small existing federal agency, the National Advisory Committee for Aeronautics, into a somewhat larger but still small organization charged with space exploration represented what might be called a preemptive strike to prevent something even less wise from being done. Furthermore, in T. Keith Glennan he placed in charge of NASA a gatekeeper who ensured that it carefully defined a limited mission, moved toward the elimination of duplicate functions within the government, and carried out a balanced program that never sought, in Eisenhower's words, to "become the miraculous solution to all current difficulties," something aggressive space advocates badly wanted.[11]

NASA's creation and its initial modest space exploration agenda were thus products of the interchange between Eisenhower's vision of government mission and organization and a loosely defined set of interest groups that pressed for aggressive but perhaps ill-considered action in the immediate post-Sputnik era. In particular, this cadre of interests sought to create a powerful government bureaucracy, perhaps even a cabinet-level department, to carry out a far-reaching and exceptionally expensive agenda in space. So successful, however, were these groups in promoting their image of space exploration, that the Eisenhower administration had to compromise its limited agenda. And after John F. Kennedy entered the White House in 1961, space advocates successfully moved to increase exponentially the size, scope, and budget of NASA.

Setting the Agenda

At the beginning of the 1950s, the advocates of an aggressive effort in space began sounding a persistent drumbeat for the opening of the federal treasury to fund space initiatives both large and small. The first and most common rationale for spaceflight was human destiny, an integral part of human nature, to explore, to learn, and to absorb new knowledge and new territories into the human experience. With the Earth so well known, space exploration advocates argued that exploration and settlement of the Moon and Mars were the next logical step in human development. Humans must question and explore and discover or die, advocates for this position insisted. Space was the "final frontier," and Americans in particular have always responded well to that challenge.

These ideas of human destiny found expression in the arguments of Wernher von Braun, the single most important promoter of America's space effort in the 1950s and 1960s. Von Braun captured the essence of American idealism and used it to justify an aggressive space exploration program.[12] Although a German immigrant to the United States after World War II, or perhaps because of it, he was remarkable in his grasp of what made Americans tick. He spoke often of "The Challenge of the Century" as a continuation of American exploration and settlement. "For more than 400 years the history of this nation has been crammed with adventure and excitement and marked by expansion," he said. "Compared with Europe, Africa, and Asia, America was the New World. Its pioneer settlers were daring, energetic, and self-reliant. They were challenged by the promise of unexplored and unsettled territory, and stimulated by the urge to conquer these vast new frontiers." Americans needed the space frontier both physically and spiritually, von Braun insisted, adding that greater efforts in moving beyond the Earth would lead to a society in which "right relationships" prevailed.[13]

When speaking and writing of these possibilities, von Braun and like-minded other space advocates explicitly used the language of the "Frontier Thesis," described in Frederick Jackson Turner's famous 1893 essay. Turner took as his cue an observation in the 1890 U.S. census that the American frontier had for the first time closed. He noted, "Up to our own day American history has been in a large degree the history of the colonization of the Great West. The existence of an area of free land, its continuous recession, and the advance of American settlement westward explain American development." He insisted that the frontier made Americans American. It gave the nation its democratic character, and ensured the virtues of self-reliance, community, and the promise of justice. He noted that cheap or even free land provided a "safety valve" that protected the nation against uprisings of the poverty-stricken and malcontented. The frontier also produced a people with "coarseness and strength . . . acuteness and inquisitiveness, that practical and inventive turn of mind . . . [full of] restless and nervous energy . . . that buoyancy and exuberance which comes with freedom." It gave the people of the United States, in essence, virtually every positive quality they have ever possessed.[14]

Repeated use of the frontier analogy for spaceflight, with its accompanying vision of new worlds and better societies, gave the American public of the Eisenhower era a distinctive perspective on spacefaring. It tapped a vein of rich ideological power. It conjured up an image of self-reliant Americans moving westward in sweeping waves of discovery, exploration, conquest, and settlement of an untamed wilderness. And in the process of movement, the Europeans who settled North America became an indigenous American people.

In America, the frontier concept has historically carried with it the ideals of optimism, democracy, and meritocracy. It also summoned in the popular mind a wide range of vivid and memorable tales of heroism, each a morally justified step toward the modern democratic state. The frontier ideal reduced the complexity of history to a static morality play. It avoided matters that challenged or contradicted the myth. It viewed Americans moving westward as inherently good and their opponents as evil. It ignored the cultural context of westward migration, It also served a critical unifying purpose for spaceflight advocates. Those persuaded by the myth recognize that it summons them not only to recall past glories but also to undertake a quest.[15]

The popular conception of "westering" remains a powerful metaphor for the propriety of space exploration and has enjoyed wide usage by supporters of space exploration. It calls upon the adventurousness of the American people and offers the promise of a utopian change in society in new, untainted places where it could remake itself indefinitely.

Invoking Frederick Jackson Turner would become increasingly counterproductive for anyone who appreciates postmodern multicultural society. Historians appropriately criticize Turner's approach as excessively ethnocentric, inappropriately nationalistic, and significantly jingoistic. Yale historian Howard R. Lamar believes the frontier thesis emphasizes an inappropriate discontinuity between a mythical rural past and an urban-industrial future. Thus, it is unsuitable as a guide for understanding the present or projecting the future. Some scholars also discount its central safety-value proposition. It may have applied in antebellum America when many did "go West," they suggest, but failed to hold after the Civil War as the prospect of migration moved beyond the reach of urban slum dwellers and others because of a lack of funds for farming and transportation. In fact, later settlers, mostly the children of farmers, arrived from the fringes of existing settlements.[16]

Despite the criticism, the Frontier Thesis has had lasting appeal, in no small measure because it tells Americans how perfect they could become. Issues of human destiny, however, garnered little support from the hardheaded realists of the Eisenhower administration. Space advocates next argued for a military presence in space. Certainly, in the Cold War–dominated 1950s national security would be something that Eisenhower and his advisors would understand. Early on the U.S. military recognized that space represented the new high ground, and that they had to control it. Numerous defense officials referred to space as the high seas of the future. The nations that could exploit the potential benefits of this ultimate strategic high ground for military purposes would dominate the rest of the world.

The perception of space as the "high ground" of Cold War competition gained credibility from the atomic holocaust literature of the era.[17] In 1947, science fiction writer Robert A. Heinlein warned *Collier's* readers that "space travel can and will be the source of supreme military power over this planet."[18] The danger of surprise attacks had been burned into the national consciousness by the Japanese attack on Pearl Harbor. In October 1951, Wernher von Braun proposed in the pages of *Popular Science* the building of a space station because "the nation which first owns such a bomb-dropping space station might be in a position virtually to control the earth."[19] In 1952, a popular conception of the U.S.-occupied space station showed it as a platform from which to observe the Soviet Union and the rest of the globe in the interest of national security. As the editors of *Collier's* magazine editorialized, in the Cold War a space station would become an imperative. The editors wrote that "the U.S. must immediately embark on a long-range development program to secure for the West 'space superiority.' If we do not, somebody else will. . . . A ruthless foe established on a space station could actually subjugate the peoples of the world."[20]

In 1952, von Braun burst on the public stage with several articles in *Collier's* about the possibilities of spaceflight. The genesis of this series began innocently enough. In 1951, Willy Ley, a former member of the German Society for Space Research and himself a skilled promoter of spaceflight, organized a Space Travel Symposium that took place on Columbus Day at the Hayden Planetarium in New York City. Ley wrote to participants, "the time is now ripe to make the public realize that the problem of space travel is to be regarded as a serious branch of science and technology" and he urged them to emphasize that fact in their lectures.[21] By happenstance, two *Collier's* writers attended this meeting. They were most impressed with the ideas presented and suggested to *Collier's* managing editor, Gordon Manning, that his magazine publish several articles promoting the scientific possibility of spaceflight. Recognizing that this idea might have real appeal, Manning asked an assistant editor, Cornelius Ryan, to organize some discussions with Ley and others, among them von Braun. Out of this came a series of major articles over a two-year period, each expertly illustrated with striking images by some of the best illustrators of the era.[22]

The first issue of *Collier's* devoted to space appeared on 22 March 1952, a few months before Eisenhower's election. An editorial suggested that spaceflight was possible, not just science fiction, and that it was inevitable that humanity would venture outward. Von Braun led off the *Collier's* issue with an impressionistic article describing the overall features of an aggressive spaceflight program. He advocated the first orbital flights by humans, development of a reusable spacecraft for travel to and from Earth orbit, building a permanently inhabited space station, and finally human exploration of the Moon and planets by spacecraft launched from the space station. Willy Ley and several other writers then followed with elaborations on various aspects of spaceflight ranging from technological viability to space law to biomedicine.[23] The series concluded with a special issue of the magazine devoted to Mars, in which von Braun and others described how to get there and predicted what might be found based on recent scientific data.[24]

The *Collier's* series catapulted von Braun into the public spotlight like none of his previous scholarly and technical activities had been able to do. The magazine had one of the four highest circulations in the United States during the early 1950s, with over three million copies produced each week. If estimates of readership were indeed four or five people per copy, as the magazine claimed, something on the order of 15 million people were exposed to these spaceflight ideas. *Collier's,* seeing that it had a potential blockbuster, did its part by hyping the series with window ads of the space artwork appearing in the magazine, sending out more than 12,000 press releases, and preparing media kits. It set up interviews on radio and television for von Braun and the other space writers, but especially von Braun, whose natural charisma and enthusiasm for spaceflight translated well through that medium. Von Braun appeared on NBC's "Camel News Caravan" with John Cameron Swayze, on NBC's "Today" show with Dave Garroway, and on CBS's "Gary Moore" program. While *Collier's* was interested in selling magazines with these public appearances, von Braun was interested in selling the idea of space travel to the public.[25]

Some of these arguments persuaded Eisenhower, and he allocated a significant amount of funding to national security objectives in space, especially the development of ballistic missiles and reconnaissance satellites. More aggressive efforts in areas of less readily apparent significance, however, failed to gain his approval. Wernher von Braun's publicity campaign on behalf of space exploration, however, sometimes proved a nuisance for the White House. Although a federal employee at the Army Ballistic Missile Agency (ABMA), and apparently with the support of the Army missileers, von Braun began to make noises that the United States could undertake a much more aggressive program than it was politically willing to do. Because of this, by the spring of 1958 Eisenhower, after complaining repeatedly, commented in a meeting with senior aides that he "is getting a little weary of Von Braun's publicity seeking."[26]

Eisenhower's Measured Space Program

Left to his own devices, President Eisenhower would have been quite pleased to undertake a modest, practically oriented space program. His balanced space program was motivated by a realistic desire to invest limited funds in space systems with military applications rather than to engage in what he characterized as space stunts.[27] Eisenhower saw the U.S. effort in space as part of a larger set of concerns. It was fundamentally a national security initiative, he believed, and he always viewed any expenditures for space activities as contributing to or subtracting from that overarching concern. Additionally, Eisenhower was committed to achieving an economical government, and the development of scientific and technical capability to gain access to space and to operate in that environment had to be balanced against a wide range of other concerns.[28] As an example of his attitudes, on 4 April 1956, Eisenhower had a meeting with two senators and several members of the White House staff to discuss Air Force appropriations, of which the missile programs were a part. Eisenhower's secretary, Ann Whitman, recorded that "The idea was to give the two Republican Senators, in General Persons' language, an 'arm twist' to familiarize them a little more with the President's way of thinking—i.e., that if we attempt to match soldier for soldiers, weapon with weapons, etc., with the Russians, we will bring on ourselves at the very least economic suicide."[29]

Eisenhower's approach to space activities had stressed the development of launch vehicles for use in the ICBM program, satellite technology for reconnaissance and communications, infrastructure required to support these activities such as tracking and launch facilities, and utilitarian science that either directly supported those missions or was a natural byproduct of them. As an example of this byproduct, in the military rocket research program early on scientists won the opportunity to place on some of the test vehicles instruments that provided data about the upper atmosphere, solar and stellar ultraviolet radiation, and the aurora. Carried out with limited fanfare and funding, this became a very successful scientific program. Participating scientists used all the military's captured V-2s, persuaded the Department of Defense (DOD) to develop new sounding rockets to replace them, and continued to use the nation's rocket development program for scientific research throughout the 1940s and 1950s.[30]

Eisenhower's space program also placed considerable emphasis upon satellite technology. During the mid-1950s, the president was preoccupied with the need to conduct surveillance of the Soviet Union and its growing nuclear capability. This led to the development of both aircraft and satellites on an aggressive basis in the 1950s. As the 1960 downing of the U-2 reconnaissance airplane revealed, however, aircraft overflights had severe shortcomings. A spacecraft was much less vulnerable. Eisenhower authorized the Vanguard satellite program in part because he wanted to establish the principle of overflight (namely that a satellite did not intrude upon a nation's air space when crossing its territory and was not subject to interception), and an internationally supported scientific satellite served this purpose better than any military launch.[31]

Eisenhower's space program, however, did not include any real commitment to, or belief in, the goal of human spaceflight. Human spaceflight did not have a serious national security component, as far he or his senior advisors could see, and therefore was probably not worthy of federal effort. Although there were several people from various interest groups who argued to the contrary, notably Wernher von Braun, Eisenhower was not persuaded. Had he been in office when the editors of *Collier's* magazine asked in a special issue devoted to human space exploration on 22 March 1952, "What Are We Waiting For?" and framed it in the context of Cold War rivalries, Eisenhower would have at best been amused. In a February 1958 legislative leadership meeting, Eisenhower expressed his basic disinterest in human spaceflight by discounting the desirability of undertaking a project to land Americans on the Moon. "And in the present situation, the president mused," according to minutes from the meeting, "he would rather have a good Redstone than be able to hit the moon, for we didn't have any enemies on the moon."[32] In spite of Eisenhower's predilection against human spaceflight, this became a central point of contention in the post-Sputnik space policy debate in the United States.

Nothing summarizes this balanced, measured approach toward space activities better than a statement he made in 1959 at a meeting with top advisors. He outlined three major goals that had to be accomplished:

> The first is that we must get what Defense really needs in space; this is mandatory.
> The second is that we should make a real advance in space so that the United States

does not have to be ashamed no matter what other countries do; this is where the super-booster is needed. The third is that we should have an orderly, progressive scientific program, well balanced with other scientific endeavors.[33]

Within the context of this philosophy, Eisenhower was willing to expend resources sufficient to meet defined objectives. These efforts yielded genuine results during the Eisenhower administration, especially in the development of intercontinental ballistic missiles. In April 1946, the Army Air Forces gave Consolidated Vultee Aircraft (Convair) Division a study contract for an ICBM. This led directly to the development of the Atlas ICBM in the 1950s. At first, many engineers believed Atlas to be a high-risk proposition. To limit its weight, Convair Corp. engineers under the direction of Karel J. Bossart, a pre–World War II immigrant from Belgium, designed the booster with a very thin, internally pressurized fuselage instead of massive struts and a thick metal skin. The "steel balloon," as it was sometimes called, employed engineering techniques that ran counter to the conservative engineering approach used by Wernher von Braun and his "Rocket Team" at Huntsville, Alabama. Von Braun, according to Bossart, needlessly designed his boosters like "bridges" to withstand any possible shock. For his part, von Braun thought the Atlas was too flimsy to hold up during launch. Reservations began to melt away, however, when Bossart's team pressurized one of the boosters and dared one of von Braun's engineers to knock a hole in it with a sledge hammer. The blow left the booster unharmed, but the recoil from the hammer nearly clubbed the engineer.[34]

The Titan ICBM program emerged not long thereafter, and proved to be an enormously important ICBM and later a civil and military space launch asset. To consolidate efforts, Secretary of Defense Charles E. Wilson issued a decision 26 November 1956 that effectively took the Army out of the ICBM business and assigned responsibility for land-based systems to the Air Force and sea-launched missiles to the Navy. The Navy immediately stepped up work for the development of the submarine-launched Polaris ICBM, which first successfully operated in January 1960.

The Air Force did the same with land-based ICBMs, and its efforts were already well developed at the time of the 1956 decision. The Atlas received high priority from the White House and hard-driving management from Brig. Gen. Bernard A. Schriever, a flamboyant and intense Air Force leader. The first Atlas rocket was test fired on 11 June 1955, and a later generation rocket became operational in 1959. These systems were followed in quick succession by the Titan ICBM and the Thor intermediate-range ballistic missile. By the latter 1950s, therefore, rocket technology had developed sufficiently for the creation of a viable ballistic missile capability. This was a revolutionary development that gave humanity for the first time in its history the ability to attack one continent from another. It effectively shrank the size of the globe, and the United States—which had always before been protected from outside attack by two massive oceans—could no longer rely on natural defensive boundaries or distance from its enemies.[35] In the space of Eisenhower's two terms as president, therefore, the United States moved from a position of having essentially no space launch capability to possessing ICBMs with a significant overkill capability.

The IGY Satellite Proposal

Eisenhower was also not unreceptive to increases in funding for space activities purely to further scientific understanding. The experience of approval of the International Geophysical Year (IGY) satellite effort is instructive on this score. As early as 1950, a small group of scientists in the United States began discussing among themselves the possibility of using Earth-circling satellites to obtain scientific information about the planet.[36] In 1952, urged on by these same American scientists, the International Council of Scientific Unions (ICSU) proposed the IGY, a cooperative scientific endeavor to study solar-terrestrial relations during a period of maximum solar activity. Some sixty-seven nations agreed to conduct cooperative experiments to study solar-terrestrial relations during a period of maximum solar activity in 1957–58.

In October 1954, at the behest of essentially this same group of U.S. scientists, ICSU challenged nations to use their missiles being developed for war to launch scientific satellites to support the IGY research program. In July 1955, largely the same enclave of American scientists convinced Eisenhower that the United States should respond to the ICSU call for participation in the IGY by launching a scientific satellite. Eisenhower's decision called for existing organizations within the Department of Defense to develop and launch a small scientific satellite, "under international auspices, such as the International Geophysical Year, in order to emphasize its peaceful purposes[;] . . . considerable prestige and psychological benefits will accrue to the nation which first is successful in launching a satellite . . . especially if the USSR were to be the first to establish a satellite." The result was Project Vanguard, carried out under the supervision of the Naval Research Laboratory. Eisenhower also approved a budget of $23.5 million, modest but considered adequate for the effort by scientific and technical personnel consulted by the administration.[37]

Although he approved the IGY satellite, Eisenhower was cost-conscious about the program, especially as it seemed to grow in cost and complexity with every review. He repeatedly wondered about its voracious appetite for public funds, especially since Vanguard supposedly took a back seat to real national security space activities, most notably the accelerating program to develop ballistic missiles. From its initial cost estimates, Vanguard had mushroomed to a cost of $67.9 million by August 1956 and to $110 million by the summer of 1957.[38] While concerned about this growth, Eisenhower did not want to cancel the program although his secretary of the treasury recommended as much.[39] Instead, the president forcefully reminded his top advisors that the "costly instrumentation had not been envisaged" that scientists were now calling for, and "stressed that the element of national prestige, so strongly emphasized in NSC 5520, depended on getting a satellite into its orbit, and not on the instrumentation of the scientific satellite."[40] Eisenhower's perception of the budgetary growth of the Vanguard program as being transformed from the simple task of putting any type of satellite into orbit into a project to launch a satellite with "considerable instrumentation" reminded him of the worst type of technological inflation, as every scientist seemingly wanted to hang another piece of equipment on the vehicle.[41]

The Space Exploration Advocate's Agenda

In the crisis atmosphere following the flight of Sputnik 1, Eisenhower's balanced space program, although still expending considerable public funds but at a level inconsistent with the public's perception of what was required to keep pace with the Soviets, fell into disrepute. There had been longstanding criticisms of Eisenhower's space efforts, but mostly from advocates of an aggressive space exploration program, and before October 1957 they did not resonate particularly well among either society as a whole or the nation's governmental leaders. In October 1952, Wernher von Braun, then technical director of the Army Ordnance Guided Missile Development Group, spoke at the Hayden Planetarium's Second Symposium on Space Travel touting a plan for ambitious exploration. He opened his speech by stating, "The conquest of space represents the outstanding challenge to science and technology of the age in which we live." Space was there to be conquered, and the U.S. government should lead the way to a visionary future. If it failed to do so, another nation would— implying the Soviet Union—and the result would be subservience to the power that occupied the "New High Ground." He stopped just short of criticizing the administration for not providing the visionary leadership necessary to begin aggressive space flight activities. Also speaking was Milton W. Rosen, director of the Naval Research Laboratory's Viking Rocket Project, who took a more sober approach that recognized rocket research as difficult and expensive work and unlikely to progress rapidly. He contended that the administration was making good effort at a measured pace.[42]

Most of the people who heard the exchange in 1952 agreed with Rosen; *Time* magazine even ran a lengthy feature story on the alternative visions of space exploration offered by von Braun and Rosen. The story characterized von Braun as "the major prophet and hero (or wild propagandist, some scientists suspect) of space travel" and criticized him (or praised him, depending on perspective) as the man who had lost World War II for Germany by diverting resources from useful activities into development of the V-2.[43] Von Braun's emerging plan of aggressive space exploration advocated building Earth-orbiting, piloted spacecraft and a space station; undertaking human expeditions to the Moon, preceded by robots; and dispatching human expeditions to the nearby planets. In each case, he cast these efforts in the context of Cold War rivalry with the Soviet Union and said it was important to carry them out to meet national security needs.[44] Most people, certainly Eisenhower and leaders in the administration, were not buying his argument. These grandiose plans were repeatedly criticized as unfeasible and unnecessary, one critic noting in 1952 that von Braun "is trying to sell the U.S. a space flight project disguised as a means of dominating the world" when there was no compelling reason to accept either his argument or his plan.[45]

Prior to Sputnik, proponents of an aggressive space program such as von Braun had been stopped at virtually every turn by the Eisenhower administration's emphasis on national security, robotic spacecraft, and fiscal conservatism. Eisenhower was never particularly concerned with beating the Soviets into space, and, with no plain and readily attainable political goal, there was accordingly no consensus among U.S.

senior policymakers for carrying on wholesale competition. Eisenhower was interested in pursuing a measured space agenda, however. Writing in his memoirs,
Eisenhower commented that "Since no obvious requirement for a crash satellite program was apparent, there was no reason for interfering with the scientists and their
projected time schedule."[46] In this environment, space exploration enthusiasts could
not move official policy toward adoption of their accelerated spaceflight agenda.

The Sputnik Crisis

Few Americans considered the reception on Friday, 4 October 1957, at the Soviet
Union's embassy in Washington, D.C., to be anything out of the ordinary. It was the
appropriate culmination of a week-long set of international scientific meetings. It was
also, in the cynical Cold War world of international intrigue between the United
States and the Soviet Union, an opportunity to gather national security intelligence
and engage in petty games of one-up-man-ship between the rivals. This one would
prove far different. The one-up-man-ship continued, but it was far from petty. To a
remarkable degree, the Soviet announcement that evening changed the course of the
Cold War.[47]

Dr. John P. Hagen arrived early at the party as he wanted to talk to a few Soviet
scientists, those he considered personal friends from long years of association in
international scientific organizations, to learn their true feelings about efforts to launch
an artificial satellite as part of the IGY. Hagen, a senior scientist with the Naval Research Laboratory, headed the American effort on Project Vanguard, and it was behind schedule and over budget. Was the same true of the Soviet Union, or would it go
up in 1958 as planned?

Hagen had been through a wringer during the past week. Beginning on Monday,
30 September, the international scientific organization known as CSAGI (Comité Speciale
de l'Année Geophysique Internationale) had opened a six-day conference at the
National Academy of Sciences in Washington on rocket and satellite research for the
IGY. Scientists from the United States, the Soviet Union, and five other nations met to
discuss their individual plans and to develop protocols for sharing scientific data and
findings. Hints from the Soviets at the meeting, however, threw the conference into a
tizzy of speculation. Several Soviet officials had intimated that they could probably
launch their scientific satellite within weeks instead of months, as the public schedule
said. Hagen worried that scientist Sergei M. Poloskov's offhand remark on the
conference's first day that the Soviet Union was "on the *eve* of the first artificial earth
satellite" was more than boastful, alliterative rhetoric. What would a surprise Soviet
launch mean for his Vanguard program and for the United States, he wondered?

Hagen did not have long to wait to learn the answer to this question. The party
had gathered in the second floor ballroom at the embassy when a little before 6:00
p.m. Walter Sullivan, a reporter with the *New York Times* who was also attending the
reception, received a frantic telephone call from his Washington bureau chief. Sullivan
learned that the Soviet news agency Tass had just announced the launch of Sputnik

1, the world's first Earth-orbiting artificial satellite. When he returned to the party Sullivan sought out Richard Porter, a member of the American IGY committee, and whispered, "it's up." Porter's ruddy face flushed even more as he heard this news, although he too suspected Sputnik's imminent launch, and he glided through the gaggles of scientists, politicians, journalists, straphangers, and spies in search of Lloyd Berkner, the official American delegate to CSAGI.

When told the news, Berkner acted with the characteristic charm of his polished demeanor. Clapping his hands for attention. "I wish to make an announcement," he declared. "I've just been informed by the *New York Times* that a Russian satellite is in orbit at an elevation of 900 kilometers. I wish to congratulate our Soviet colleagues on their achievement." On the other side of the ballroom, Hagen's face turned pale. They had beaten the Vanguard satellite effort into space. Were they really the greatest nation on Earth, as their leaders boisterously reminded anyone who would listen? Were they really going to bury us, as Soviet Premier Nikita Khrushchev announced at the United Nations as he pounded his fist and then his shoe on his desk? What could the United States do to recover a measure of international respect?

The inner turmoil that Hagen felt on "Sputnik Night," as 4–5 October 1957 has come to be called, reverberated through the American public in the days that followed. Two generations after the event, words do not easily convey the American reaction to the Soviet satellite. The only appropriate characterization that begins to capture the mood on 5 October involves the use of the word "hysteria." A collective mental turmoil and soul-searching followed, as American society thrashed around for the answers to Hagen's questions. Almost immediately, two phrases entered the American lexicon to define time, "pre-Sputnik" and "post-Sputnik." The other phrase that soon replaced earlier definitions of time was "Space Age," for with the launch of Sputnik 1 the space age had been born and the world would be different ever after.

Sputnik 1, launched on 4 October 1957 from the Soviet Union's rocket testing facility in the desert near Tyuratam in the Kazakh Republic, proved a decidedly unspectacular satellite that probably should not have elicited the horrific reaction it wrought. An aluminum 22-inch sphere with four spring-loaded whip antennae trailing, it weighed only 183 pounds and traveled an elliptical orbit that took it around the Earth every 96 minutes. It carried a small radio beacon that beeped at regular intervals and could by means of telemetry verify exact locations on the Earth's surface. Some U.S. cold warriors suggested that this was a way for the Soviets to obtain targeting information for their ballistic missiles, but that does not seem to have actually been the case. The satellite itself fell from orbit three months after launch on 4 January 1958.[48]

At the IGY reception, the scientists immediately adjourned to the Soviet embassy's rooftop to view the heavens. They were not able to see the satellite with the naked eye. Indeed, Sputnik 1 twice passed within easy detection range of the United States before anyone even knew of its existence. The next morning at the IGY conference, the Soviet Union's chief delegate, Anatoli A. Blagonravov, explained details of the launch and the spacecraft. The CSAGI conference officially congratulated the Soviets for their scientific accomplishment. What was not said, but clearly thought by Hagen and many other Americans in both the scientific and political communities, however, was first that the Soviet Union had staged a tremendous propaganda coup for the Communist system, and second that it could now legitimately claim leadership in a major technological field. The international image of the Soviet Union was greatly enhanced overnight. Soviet Premier Nikita Khrushchev, surprised by this Soviet success, quickly recovered to capitalize on it and began boasting that capitalism was a relic of the past and would soon be supplanted by communism without open military conflict.[49]

While President Eisenhower and other leaders of his administration also congratulated the Soviets and tried to downplay the importance of the accomplishment, they misjudged the public reaction to the event. The launch of Sputnik 1 had a "Pearl Harbor" effect on American public opinion. It was a shock, introducing the average citizen to the space age in a crisis setting. The event created an illusion of a technological gap and provided the impetus for increased spending for aerospace endeavors, technical and scientific educational programs, and the chartering of new federal agencies to manage air and space research and development.[50] Not only had the Soviets been first in orbit, but Sputnik 1 was much larger than the intended 3.5 pounds for the first satellite to be launched in Project Vanguard. In the Cold War environment of the late 1950s, this disparity of capability portended menacing implications.

In October 1957, those who had been calling for aggressive action in space finally found an audience. Few who were present when Sputnik burst onto the national scene failed to sense that something important was taking place. The Soviet Union had demonstrated significant technological ability, and it astounded the public. The response was a rapid and sustained whir of public opinion condemning the Eisenhower administration for neglecting the American space effort. The Sputnik crisis reinforced for many people the popular conception that Eisenhower was a smiling incompetent; it was another instance of a "do-nothing," golf-playing president mismanaging events.[51] G. Mennen Williams, the Democratic governor of Michigan, even wrote a poem about it:

> Oh little Sputnik, flying high
> With made-in-Moscow beep,
> You tell the world it's a Commie sky
> and Uncle Sam's asleep.
>
> You say on fairway and on rough
> The Kremlin knows it all,
> We hope our golfer knows enough
> To get us on the ball.[52]

The event had been a shock, creating the illusion of a technological gap and providing the impetus for a variety of remedial actions.

It was not solely the result of Soviet orbiting of a satellite that the public reacted with such fervor to Sputnik 1. A long series of confrontations between the United States and the Soviet Union had affected public perceptions of American decline.

Frank Altschul wrote to the president on 8 October 1957 about these, outlining the loss of atomic supremacy, general deterioration in the position of the non-Soviet world, successful activities by the Soviet Union in the Middle East, crushing of anti-Communist uprisings in Hungary and Czechoslovakia, Communist forays into Southeast Asia, and a host of other apparent setbacks for the West. All of this created world doubt about the outcome of the Cold War concerning democratic nations in general and the United States as its leader in particular. Sputnik was the final straw in a long series of problems. Altschul suggested that "the impression of impotence created by the failure of the Western world to find practical measures to counteract overt acts of Soviet aggression" explained the crisis situation.[53]

The most serious reaction to Sputnik came from Senator Lyndon Johnson, who opened hearings by the Senate Armed Services Committee on 25 November 1957 to review the whole spectrum of American defense and space programs in the wake of the Sputnik crisis. One of Johnson's concerns, of course, was that a nation capable of orbiting satellites was also capable of developing technology supporting the arms race. His committee found serious underfunding and incomprehensible organization of U.S. space activities, and that worried Johnson all the more. He publicly blamed the president and the Republican Party.

Johnson spoke for many Americans when he remarked in two speeches in Texas that the "Soviets have beaten us at our own game—daring, scientific advances in the atomic age." Since those Cold War rivals had already established a foothold in space while the United States had showed signs of lethargy in that arena, Johnson proposed to "take a long careful look" at what had gone wrong in the nation's space and missile program, and to chart a course that would lead to U.S. parity in space.[54] The space enthusiasts had been saying these things for years with no real response from the public, now they resonated in ways unheard of before.

The Eisenhower administration did not help itself in this crisis by displaying a "tin ear" when the criticism came after the launch of Sputnik. Repeatedly administration officials minimized the sense of fear present in the general population. Indeed, the president was far more surprised by the paranoia of the public than he was the fact that the Soviets had been successful in launching a satellite.[55] He understood that Sputnik was not true proof of a Soviet advantage in technology, although many misinterpreted it to mean this. James R. Killian, who became Eisenhower's science advisor, aptly captured the flavor of public sentiment:

> As it beeped in the sky, Sputnik I created a crisis of confidence that swept the country like a windblown forest fire. Overnight there developed a widespread fear that the country lay at the mercy of the Russian military machine and that our government and its military arm had abruptly lost the power to defend the homeland itself, much less to maintain U.S. prestige and leadership in the international arena. Confidence in American science, technology, and education suddenly evaporated.[56]

Eisenhower fully believed that Sputnik did not pose a threat to the United States, and because of this he did not take immediate action to respond to it. Instead, he acknowledged the need to "take all feasible measures to accelerate missile and satellite programs."[57] At the same time, he tried to convince the American public that all was well. He may have been abetted in his apparent nonchalance by a study that suggested that crisis was local to Washington. Representatives of the International Affairs Seminars of Washington reported on 15–16 October:

> If there was any trauma following the Russian sputnik, it occurred in Washington and not among the general public. Washington, for its part, took its cue from the newspapers and other issue makers. The misevaluation by leadership of the extent of public interest, as measured by the amount of news, coverage and the words of the issue makers, led to words and actions which further confused the issue. This situation points up the general problem for a democracy of: who is the "public" to which leadership attends and who in fact do the issue makers represent?[58]

As it turned out, failure to appreciate the depth of concern from several quarters in the United States hurt the Eisenhower administration in the Sputnik crisis more than anything else.

In his first press conference after the launch of Sputnik 1, on 9 October, Eisenhower sought to calm speculation and said that it did not raise his apprehension "one iota. I see nothing at this moment, at this stage of development, that is significant in that development as far as security is concerned."[59] Others in the administration did the same.[60] Some of his minions, however, went too far. Eisenhower Chief of Staff Sherman Adams belittled the Soviet success by calling it nothing more than an "an outer space basketball game."[61] Such basely inaccurate characterizations did little but fuel the fires of speculation about the meaning of Sputnik for the future of the United States.

The furor over Sputnik 1 actually died down in the latter part of October 1957. For instance, there was little discussion of the satellite issue in the popular press during the later part of the month and it did not come up in the president's press conference of 30 October 1957.[62] Perhaps Eisenhower's statements of reassurance about the U.S. effort in space heartened the American public, at least for a short time. While advocates of more aggressive space activities and political opponents still criticized, public confidence in the Eisenhower administration did not seem to suffer appreciably until Sputnik 2 was launched on 3 November 1957; this time the Soviet Union counted coup on the United States with an impressive 1,121-pound spacecraft that included the dog, Laika.

Interest Group Politics and the Space Exploration Agenda

In this environment, a spectrum of eager interest groups interested in spaceflight made incursion and sought to shape the government response to the Soviet technological success. Eisenhower suddenly found himself besieged by political rivals who used the Soviet launching of Sputnik as a means of discrediting the Republicans and their administration. These efforts were cheered, aided, and abetted by promoters of spaceflight, who now had an opening where they might press for the adoption of goals not previously attainable. These space advocates included "true believers" motivated by an expansive view of human voyages of discovery.[63] They also included industrialists who had been involved in the development of rocket technology for the DOD, military officials involved in space as a national security issue, and a cadre of civilian advisors who provided expertise about scientific and technological matters to federal government officials.[64] This alliance of enthusiasts, futurists, advisors, and representatives of the "military-industrial complex" combined with members of Congress to provide a powerful force for change that Eisenhower could not ignore.

With the beginning of congressional hearings, this combination of interests sought to secure an outcome that furthered their individual agendas. True believers in spaceflight urged the adoption of expensive long-term, far-reaching programs that would allow humanity to get off this planet, thereby allowing the race to survive indefinitely. In their view, the human component of spaceflight must be the central one, with robotic probes and satellites a useful but decidedly less important aspect of the exploration agenda. An emphasis on adventure and discovery was a fundamental part of the proposals advanced in response to Sputnik. The representatives of what Eisenhower called the "military-industrial complex" were less dewy-eyed about spaceflight and its potential, but they were no less adamant in their recommendations that increased government funding should be devoted to the development of technology for space travel. They emphasized, however, the need to attain superiority over the Soviet Union using standard Cold War rhetoric.[65]

The congressional staffs, some members of whom were space boosters themselves, carefully chose the witnesses for hearings about the space effort; demonstrating what many people have observed in the past, that congressional hearings are theater.[66] Although there were some who gave testimonies supporting the president as having the Sputnik situation well in hand, in the aggregate the testimony urged significantly greater administration sponsorship and especially increased funding for space exploration.[67] During the Johnson subcommittee hearings in the fall of 1957, for instance, science sage Vannevar Bush warned that "We have been complacent and we have been smug" in space efforts. "We must develop a sense of urgency," added James A. Doolittle, chair of the National Advisory Committee for Aeronautics (NACA), "we must be willing to work harder and sacrifice more."[68] Emerging from this investigation was a policy to make space exploration a concerted effort both for technological development and for the national prestige it would engender in the context of the Cold War between the United States and the Soviet Union.

Congressional inquiries also assessed the nature, scope, and organization of the nation's long-term efforts in space. Advocates of increased spending for space activities were not disappointed that the Senate voted on 6 February 1958 to create a Special Committee on Space and Aeronautics whose charter was to frame legislation for a permanent space agency. The House of Representatives soon followed suit. With Congress leading the way, and fueled by the crisis atmosphere in Washington following the Sputnik episode, it was obvious that some government organization to direct American space efforts would emerge before the end of 1958.[69]

The Presidential Response

At the same time, Eisenhower considered what should be done to rectify any problems in U.S. programs that might exist. He reviewed a wide range of options and gave the appearance that everything would be fine. He conferred with his key advisors, members of the scientific and technical community, and representatives of the emergent military-industrial complex. Much of this was done quietly. All of it opened the president's door to interest groups who wanted to loosen the purse strings of government to further space activities, and those groups would each in their own ways benefit from that loosening.

The first of these groups to gain access to the president were representatives of the scientific community. During the two weeks following Sputnik 1, more scientists visited the White House than at any time during Eisenhower's administration. They also gained admittance to the National Security Council in ways not seen before the crisis. This was a very important development arising from Sputnik 1, for it gave them the ear of the president in ways unattainable before.[70] The scientists used these meetings as a means of influencing the president to enhance the priority given to scientific efforts in the federal government. They may have been interested specifically in fostering space research and development in the immediate aftermath of Sputnik, but they were also apparently working toward a broader agenda that enhanced overall efforts.[71]

At a key meeting of leading scientific entrepreneurs with the president on 15 October, for example, they broached the possibility of the creation of a permanent science advisor to the president who would provide him a scientific point of view. Eisenhower was receptive as a response to the crisis of Sputnik 1, but he was also cautious.[72] His fear of creeping government bureaucracy and the problems of setting up another office that would then have to be funded was probably a reason for his hesitancy. This was not a new idea emanating from the scientific community, and Eisenhower's beliefs had prompted an April 1956 decision not to create a special White House advisor to coordinate basic research in the federal government.[73] Now, in the aftermath of Sputnik 1, the idea was resurrected by scientific elites and Eisenhower was suddenly receptive since it would both give the appearance of action in response to the Soviet challenge and would possibly lead to positive developments.

The DOD's space community, made up of military and civilian members, also acted (or reacted). Publicly supportive of Eisenhower, new Secretary of Defense Neil McElroy knew that the ballistic missile program had been carried on as a crash program and that good progress was being made. He also was well aware of the status of such closely held secret programs as the reconnaissance satellite development effort and knew they were proceeding as expeditiously as possible. But because of Sputnik, he was able to gain the president's support to accelerate some activities that would give the public the appearance of firm response. Washington sage Bernard Baruch wrote a cryptic note to the president which summarized this philosophy: "Mr. McElroy must drive the program hard, like Jeffers 'bulled' the rubber program in World War II, demonstrating not only that everything possible is being done, but that the 'impossible' will be done if necessary."[74]

McElroy, carrying the message from the DOD's space community, also recommended to the president on 30 October that he announce the administration "is backing up the Vanguard program with the Jupiter to make sure we fire a satellite at an early date."[75] Eisenhower knew that nothing would do more to reassure the American public than an early successful launch and approved the recommendation. Using the Jupiter was, however, an initiative that had been discussed several times before Sputnik and rejected. On 9 September 1955, the Vanguard project, proposed by the Navy, won out over the very same Army Ballistic Missile Agency (ABMA) proposal to launch the IGY satellite on the Jupiter, mostly because of the fear that adding this additional non-military requirement could inhibit the administration's effort to develop ballistic missiles. In June 1956, the DOD had considered using the Jupiter again, rejecting it for the same reason.[76] Eisenhower expressed to McElroy his irritation that the DOD had not come to him for a decision during that 1956 review, but hindsight from the fallout of Sputnik 1 probably motivated him and there is no reason to believe that had the option been briefed to him beforehand that he would have been willing to spend the additional money for the ABMA effort.[77] In the aftermath of Sputnik he approved the action, and was relieved on 31 January 1958 when the Army orbited the first U.S. satellite, Explorer 1, with a modified Jupiter C ballistic missile.[78]

After Sputnik 2, Eisenhower also tried to quell public apprehensions, but with less success this time. All of the charges that had been raised before became a sustained chorus, and Eisenhower could fashion very little effective public response. Privately, however, he groused about the unfairness of it all. The third-degree administration leaders received on Capitol Hill in Johnson's hearings prompted him to comment at one time that, "You have got to have some conviction and faith in people's standards of honesty, morality and decency."[79] He was a believer in those standards himself, and he thought he and his supporters were being needlessly chastised for political benefit.

Eisenhower was far from ineffective in his response to the two Sputniks throughout November and December 1957. In addition to following through on his earlier commitments—accelerating missile programs, putting more focus on science and technology in the government, approving the Explorer satellite effort, and appointing a presidential science advisor on 9 November—he also created, at the suggestion of scientists in Washington, a President's Science Advisory Committee (PSAC) that began operation on 20 November.[80]

The Organizational Imperative

Eisenhower was seemingly prepared to stop with the actions taken thus far, but a critical mass had emerged in favor of the creation of an entirely new organization to undertake science and technology advancement for the government, one that would consolidate space projects and oversee all of them. A new organization was never on his agenda; he was mission oriented and saw no reason to pursue the creation of a new bureaucratic entity to undertake this mission. Indeed, the debate during the winter of 1957–58 seemed to turn on whether to create a formal space bureaucracy or to create a formal space program. These are different issues, and the former does not guarantee the latter. (In fact, officials are too often misled into thinking that reorganization affects programs when such is rarely the case.) Most of the attention lavished on the national space policy debate during this period, as Eisenhower understood, dealt with organization. Eisenhower, the military man, had an objective and was willing to use the structure as it was then in place to achieve it. He knew that a new organization would not solve the space exploration problem; in fact, it could make things worse.

Lyndon B. Johnson, ever the legislator, pushed to create a new special agency to accomplish the mission and thereby to diffuse public discontent. Johnson seemed to prefer to attack problems by passing laws and approving programs. Some of his staffers called Johnson's approach as "government by press release" because every new problem elicited a press release announcing the creation of a new program. There was, interestingly, very little debate over missions in space in this process. There was, however, intense debate over the organization to conduct it. How it would be structured, how it would be run, and what federal elements would make it up were debated at length.[81]

After the two successful Soviet Sputniks, and the rather spectacular failure of a televised Vanguard launch on 6 December 1957, Eisenhower was under the gun once again to take positive action. Proposals were emerging to create a major new, possibly cabinet-level, department to handle space activities and perhaps other scientific and technical areas as well. As early as 10 October, it was suggested to Eisenhower that he should consider setting up an organization to "accomplish some of the next great break-throughs first—for example, the achievement of a manned satellite, or getting to the moon."[82] In early November, his new White House science office, led by James Killian, suggested much the same.[83] The American Rocket Society offered a similar proposal, complete with recommendations for structure, budgets, and missions. The head of the society, Robert C. Truax, prefaced the proposal with the comment that his organization "opposes stop-gap measures to counter the propaganda aspects of the current Russian effort." Only a new organization with a broad charter and substantial funding could meet the Soviet challenge in a realistic way.[84]

Eisenhower was also bombarded with demands and proposals for a new organization from within the government. The least acceptable approach, from Eisenhower's perspective, was a plan to create a Department of Science and Technology, sponsored by Representative John M. McClellan (D-Ark.) and Senator Hubert Humphery.[85] Eisenhower definitely thought this organizational slant would multiply costs and create powerful constituencies; he did not want to establish a long-term bureaucracy to solve a short-term problem. As far as he was concerned, the space program of the

United States could be conducted under the operational control of the Department of Defense, with the non-military aspects of it taking direction from the National Science Foundation as had been done for many years.

Eisenhower's approach was opposed by all manner of people, some of them trusted aides in his administration. Killian took issue with his approach and lobbied for the creation of a separate organization to conduct non-military space activities.[86] The vice president, Richard Nixon, favored a separate organization because he thought the "military would be deterred from things that had no military value in sight." Although Eisenhower "did not preclude having eventually a great Department of Space," clearly it was not his first choice.[87]

Establishing NASA

The president resisted as long as possible these efforts to create a new governmental organization to manage space efforts. A turning point came on 4 February 1958 when he finally capitulated and asked Killian to convene the PSAC to come up with a plan for a new organization. Interestingly, the PSAC had been quietly considering the creation of a new civil space agency for several months and quickly came forward with a proposal that placed all non-military efforts relative to space exploration under a strengthened and renamed NACA. This was an approach that its members believed would find support from Eisenhower when a more grandiose plan probably would not. Established in 1915 to foster aviation progress in the United States, the NACA had long been a small, loosely organized, and elitist organization known for both its technological competence and its apolitical culture. It had also been moving into space-related areas of research and engineering during the 1950s, through the work of a Space Task Group under the leadership of Robert L. Gilruth. While totally a civilian agency the NACA also enjoyed a close working relationship with the military services, helping to solve research problems associated with aeronautics and also finding application for them in the civilian sector. Its civilian character; its recognized excellence in technical activities; and its quiet, research-focused image all made it an attractive choice. It could fill the requirements of the constrained job Eisenhower envisioned without exacerbating Cold War tensions with the Soviet Union.[88]

Somewhat reluctantly, and probably because it was the least bureaucracy he could get away with creating in the crisis atmosphere following Sputnik, President Eisenhower accepted the PSAC's recommendations. He had members of his administration draft legislation to expand the NACA into an agency charged with the broad mission to "plan, direct, and conduct aeronautical and space activities"; to involve the nation's scientific community in these activities; and to disseminate widely information about these activities. An administrator appointed by the president was to head NASA, and an interagency council would coordinate activities. During the summer of 1958, Congress passed the National Aeronautics and Space Act and the president signed it into law on 29 July 1958. This ended the debate over the type of organization to be created and other plans died a quiet death. The new organization started functioning on 1 October 1958, less than a year after the launch of Sputnik 1.[89] As such, the National Aeronautics and Space Act of 1958, which Eisenhower's lieutenants had drafted, represented something of a preemptive strike on those who advocated an even more far-reaching bureaucratic organization, perhaps even a cabinet-level department.

At the same time, Eisenhower directed the PSAC to formulate a coherent, inexpensive, and meritorious space policy. Brought to the president's attention in the early part of March and then sent back for revision, the administration formally released the report on 26 March 1958. This PSAC report outlined a modest space exploration program. With Eisenhower's strong endorsement, the policy statement emphasized scientific discovery but recommended a cautiously measured pace. "Since there are still so many unanswered scientific questions and problems all around us on earth, why should we start asking new questions and seeking out new problems in space? How can the results possibly justify the cost?" asked the PSAC. It broke space exploration initiatives down into three broad headings without a defined timetable for completion—"Early, Later, Still Later"—each with its own projects. Only well into the "Later" phase would humans fly in space.[90]

With these actions Eisenhower was able to placate and partially deflect the coalition of interests that advocated an aggressive space program. He had been forced by a cadre of interest groups to make NASA into something more than he had wanted. But he had thwarted some of their most cherished goals, a large, independent bureaucracy and expensive crash programs to race the Soviet Union into space and to accomplish spectacular feats that would impress the world. He saw to it that NASA did not "compete with the Russians on a shot-for-shot basis in attempts to achieve space spectaculars." His hand-picked NASA administrator, T. Keith Glennan, commented that "Our strategy must be to develop a program on our own terms which is designed to allow us to progress sensibly toward the goal of ultimate leadership in this competition."[91] Others were interested in racing the Soviets, however, and Lyndon Johnson vowed to put additional funding into any NASA budget submission so that it could do so. Glennan wrote in his diary that "Congress always wanted to give us more money. . . . Only a blundering fool could go up to the Hill and come back with a result detrimental to the agency."[92] But how well NASA could use those funds in any given year was problematic. A determined, orderly advance in space operations, therefore, motivated the management of NASA, and the Eisenhower administration viewed those who wanted to commit the nation to an all-out race with the Soviets as "spinning" so many wheels and wasting the public's resources. Eisenhower's goal, as Pulitzer Prize–winning historian Walter A. McDougall concluded, was to refrain from beginning a race against the Soviets that "might kick off an orgy of state-directed technological showmanship that would be hard to stop, might spill over into other policy arenas, and would relinquish to the Soviets the initiative in defining the fields of battle for the hearts and minds of the world."[93]

Parallels

At several levels there are intriguing parallels between the Sputnik crisis of 1957–58 that Eisenhower faced and the aftermath of the terrorist attack on the United States made on 11 September 2001. In both instances, these events signaled that the United States was not immune from serious challenge to its society and national power. One was a symbolic attack on American might, the other a literal attack. Both sparked a response that led to serious changes in the direction of the nation, and some might argue that in both instances some of the response was ill-conceived. For example, Eisenhower was forced to respond with many actions that he believed ill-considered, among them the creation of NASA. In addition, Sputnik led directly to several critical efforts aimed at "catching up" to the Soviet Union's space achievements. On the whole, however, all proved acceptable both from a political perspective and for the long-term health of the United States. These included: (1) A full-scale review of both the civil and military programs of the United States (scientific satellite efforts and ballistic missile development; (2) establishment of a Presidential Science Advisor in the White House who had responsibility for overseeing the activities of the Federal government in science and technology; (3) creation of the Advanced Research Projects Agency in the Department of Defense, and the consolidation of several space activities under centralized management; (4) establishment of the National Aeronautics and Space Administration to manage civil space operations; and (5) passage of the National Defense Education Act to provide federal funding for education in the scientific and technical disciplines.

In the aftermath of 9/11, some parallels between Sputnik and the terrorist attacks are germane. The launch of Sputnik brought to the fore concerns about U.S. invincibility, just as 9/11 did. Both were surprises and evoked a public response of shock and then a steeling of resolve not to allow the challenge to go unmet. Feelings of insecurity at home and hysteria in Washington abounded in both cases. A sense that the nation as a superpower might be at risk and the response needed to be swift and decisive. In the case of Sputnik, it was a technological challenge, and the response involved a broad reorientation of government programs aimed at rectifying the perceived weakness. Sputnik rather "inspired" politicians to fund science as never before. In the case of 9/11, it was a direct security weakness that needed to be addressed. There were hearings and finger-pointing and an opening of floodgates of government funding for all manner of presumed security-enhancing programs. The Sputnik crisis allowed the scientific-technological community into the White House as never before and opened the public treasury to funding for all manner of efforts never given serious consideration before. The 9/11 tragedy did the same for security and intelligence specialists.

Interestingly, in both instances the president took criticism for failing to anticipate and react to the challenge, and thereby mitigating it or at least minimizing its impact. Eisenhower's supposed complacency in failing to anticipate Sputnik, and his slowness to react afterward, tarred his administration and his image for a generation. Whether he deserved that criticism is questionable, but his failure to recognize the obvious concern of the public was a shortcoming of consequence. Refusing to over-react served his and the nation's long-term needs well. Similarly, George W. Bush received criticism for the 9/11 attacks and failure to prepare for such an eventuality.[94] Like Eisenhower, Bush responded with a range of changes to the federal government to enhance intelligence gathering and national security: (1) Passage of the Homeland Security Act of 2002 created the Department of Homeland Security (DHS); (2) establishment of the Terrorist Threat Integration Center (TTIC) to coordinate the analysis of all domestic counterterrorism intelligence; (3) creation of the Terrorist Screening Center (TSC) to integrate information on various terrorist watch lists; (4) consolidation of oversight of intelligence assets under a single individual; (5) passage of the Patriot Act of 2002; and (6) other reorganizations within and among various federal agencies. Unlike Eisenhower, Bush aggressively championed these changes and generally appeared to be leading in their adoption rather than opposing some of them. This perception was misleading in both instances, for Eisenhower was fully committed to many of the reforms undertaken during his administration and Bush was opposed to some of those for which he has been applauded, especially the creation of an intelligence "czar" to oversee all intelligence organizations in the government.

In an irony of the first magnitude, Eisenhower believed that the creation of NASA and the placing of so much power in its hands by the Kennedy administration during the Apollo program of the 1960s was a mistake. He remarked in a 1962 article: "Why the great hurry to get to the moon and the planets? We have already demonstrated that in everything except the power of our booster rockets we are leading the world in scientific space exploration. From here on, I think we should proceed in an orderly, scientific way, building one accomplishment on another."[95] He later cautioned that the Moon race "has diverted a disproportionate share of our brain-power and research facilities from equally significant problems, including education and automation."[96] He believed it was used to overreact to the perceived threat. President Bush, on the other hand, embraced the use of American power in the aftermath of 9/11 and engaged in actions that some believed an overreaction to the perceived threat, especially the invasion of Iraq in 2003.[97]

Conclusion

The politics of the creation of the National Aeronautics and Space Administration in 1958 and how it coalesced during the remainder of the Eisenhower administration revolved around philosophies of government, priorities of policy, and the role of individual branches of government in responding to a perceived crisis situation in Cold War international relations. Eisenhower had been forced to create an agency that he did not want to create, and he paid for that mistake with significant budget expenditures. But that Eisenhower was able to keep from being forced into an even more expansive program by advocates of an aggressive space program was in large measure the result of the establishment of NASA. In the process, the administration refused to empower the technological elite of the nation to execute a broad-based, ambitious, and expensive program.

Since the late 1950s, the debate over civil space policy has been about what type and under what time constraints space operations would be conducted, not about whether or not to have a civil space effort. Under Eisenhower, the space program was kept relatively small and NASA's budgets were limited. As a result, promoters of a large, far-reaching program were frustrated. Eisenhower recognized this, and warned of the problems this could cause in his farewell address in January 1961. Remembered mostly for his stern caution about a "military-industrial complex," Eisenhower also complained about the power of a scientific and technical elite to manipulate the system and obtain public adoption of their policy agenda.[98]

When John F. Kennedy took office in 1961, he was less committed than his predecessor to holding the line against advocates of an assertive space program. Indeed, he viewed them as allies in dealing with many other difficult political situations present in the United States. As a result, he and his chief advisors expressed a strong consensus that science and technology, coupled with proper leadership and the inspiration of a great cause, could solve almost any problem of society. It was that faith, as well as the Cold War necessity of undertaking something spectacular to overshadow the Soviet Union, that sparked the 1961 Kennedy decision to go to the Moon and to empower experts, in this case aerospace engineers, with the decision-making responsibility and wherewithal to execute the Apollo program.[99] David Halberstam shrewdly observed that "if there was anything that bound the men [of the Kennedy administration], their followers, and their subordinates together, it was the belief that sheer intelligence and rationality could answer and solve anything." This translated into an ever-increasing commitment to science and technology to resolve problems and point the direction for the future.[100] In relation to Eisenhower's reaction to the crisis brought on by the Soviet launch of Sputnik 1, the Eisenhower White House was forced by a set of political exigencies and a critical mass of interest groups to take action that he did not want to take, but that in establishing NASA he took what was for him the least distasteful course of action. In doing so, he headed off organizational initiatives that he considered more objectionable for the long-term welfare of the United States.

Notes

Some of the analysis in this essay was previously published in Roger D. Launius, "Eisenhower, Sputnik, and the Creation of NASA: Technological Elites and the Public Policy Agenda," *Prologue: Quarterly of the National Archives and Records Administration* 28 (Summer 1996).

1. S. Everett Gleason, "Discussion at the 329th Meeting of the National Security Council, Wednesday, July 3, 1957," 5 July 1957, 2, NSC Records, DDE Presidential Papers, Eisenhower Library (hereafter DDEL), Abilene, Kans.

2. Reagan spent $233.02 billion on space issues in his eight years in office. Clinton spent $230.14 billion during his eight years in office. By contrast, Eisenhower's spending was $183.69 billion. All of these are in inflation adjusted dollars. Calculated using data in Appendix E-1A, "Space Activities of the U.S. Government," *Aeronautics and Space Report of the President, Fiscal Year 2003 Activities* (Washington, D.C.: NASA NP-2004-17-389-HQ, 2004), 140.

3. Much has been made of dual-use technology over the years, and space access has been an especially important part of this capability. On space access, see Roger D. Launius and Dennis R. Jenkins, eds., *To Reach the High Frontier: A History of U.S. Launch Vehicles* (Lexington: University Press of Kentucky, 2002).

4. This was demonstrated repeatedly in the weeks following Sputnik 1. For example, in a 1960 press conference, Eisenhower was asked, "as far as man's effort to enter space, as well as the development of military missiles, do you feel any sense of urgency in catching up with the Russians?" He responded, as he had so many times before: "I am always a little bit amazed about this business of catching up. What you want is enough, a thing that is adequate. A deterrent has no added power, once it has become completely adequate, for compelling the respect of any potential opponent for your deterrent and, therefore, to make him act prudently." "The President's News Conference of February 3, 1960," *Public Papers of the Presidents of the United States: Dwight D. Eisenhower, 1960–61* (Washington, D.C.: Government Printing Office, 1964), 24.

5. On the economics of spaceflight, see Henry R. Hertzfeld, "Measuring Returns to Space Research And Development," in Joel S. Greenberg and Henry R. Hertzfeld, eds., *Space Economics* (Washington, D.C.: American Institute of Aeronautics and Astronautics, 1992), 151–69.

6. See David Callahan and Fred I. Greenstein, "The Reluctant Racer: Dwight D. Eisenhower and United States Space Policy," in Roger D Launius and Howard E. McCurdy, eds., *Spaceflight and the Myth of Presidential Leadership* (Urbana: University of Illinois Press, 1997), chap. 1; Ivan W. Morgan, *Eisenhower Versus the Spenders* (New York: St. Martin's, 1990), John W. Sloan, *Eisenhower and the Management of Prosperity* (Lawrence: University of Kansas Press, 1991); James L. Sundquist, *Politics and Policy: The Eisenhower, Kennedy, and Johnson Years* (Washington, D.C.: Brookings Institution, 1968); and Steven Rabe, "Eisenhower Revisionism: A Decade of Scholarship," *Diplomatic History* 17 (Winter 1993). For a comprehensive review of the literature on Eisenhower's presidency, including the latter-day scholarship that accounts for the remarkable improvement of his historical reputation, see the bibliographical essay in Chester J. Pach, Jr. and Elmo Richardson, *The Presidency of Dwight D. Eisenhower* (Lawrence: University of Kansas Press, 1991), 263–72. For an analysis of Eisenhower's leadership style, see Fred I. Greenstein, *The Hidden-Hand Presidency: Eisenhower as Leader* (New York: Basic Books, 1982).

7. Dwight D. Eisenhower, *The White House Years: Waging Peace* (Garden City, N.Y.: Doubleday, 1965), 217.

8. On this issue, see Jay Winik, *On the Brink: The Dramatic, Behind-the-Scenes Saga of the Reagan Era and the Men and Women who Won the Cold War* (New York: Simon & Schuster, 1996); John Lewis Gaddis, *The United States and the End of the Cold War* (New York: Oxford University Press, 1992); Michael Hogan, ed., *The End of the Cold War: Its Meaning and Implications* (New York: Cambridge University Press, 1992); Edwin Meese III, "The Man Who Won The Cold War," *Policy Review* 61 (Summer 1992); and Warren E. Norquist, "How the United States Won the Cold War," *Intelligencer* (Winter/Spring 2003).

9. "Farewell Radio and Television Address to the American People," 17 Jan. 1961, *Papers of the President, Dwight D. Eisenhower 1960–61* (Washington, D.C.: Government Printing Office, 1961), 1035–40.

10. Ibid., 1037.

11. On Glennan, see J. D. Hunley, ed., *The Birth of NASA: The Diary of T. Keith Glennan* (Washington, D.C.: NASA SP-4105, 1993).

12. It is important to understand that this effort to colonize the cosmos was not limited to von Braun. Hermann Oberth wrote: "This is the goal: To make available for life every place

where life is possible. To make inhabitable all worlds as yet uninhabitable, and all life purposeful." Hermann Oberth, *Man into Space* (New York: Harper & Brothers, 1957), 167.

13. Wernher von Braun, "The Challenge of the Century," 3 Apr. 1965, Wernher von Braun Biographical File, NASA Historical Reference Collection, NASA History Office, NASA Headquarters, Washington, D.C.

14. Frederick Jackson Turner, "The Significance of the Frontier in American History," *The Frontier in American History* (New York: Holt, Rinehart, & Winston, 1920).

15. Richard Slotkin, *Gunfighter Nation: The Myth of the Frontier in Twentieth-Century America* (New York: Atheneum, 1992).

16. See John Mack Faragher, *Rereading Frederick Jackson Turner: The Significance of the Frontier in American History, and Other Essays* (New York: Holt, 1994); Allan G. Bogue, *Frederick Jackson Turner: Strange Roads Going Down* (Norman: University of Oklahoma Press, 1998); and Ray Allen Billington, *America's Frontier Heritage* (Albuquerque: University of New Mexico Press, 1974).

17. See "The A-Bomb's Invisible Offspring," *Collier's,* 9 Aug. 1947; "Power on Glory and Wings," ibid., 27 Mar. 1948; "Fear, War and the Bomb," *New Republic,* 29 Nov. 1948; "Defense Against Atom-Bomb Blitz? None Yet," *Newsweek,* 14 Nov. 1949. One of these includes a statement that then-Congressman John F. Kennedy was one of the few public figures concerned about the dangers of atomic attack.

18. "The A-Bomb's Invisible Offspring," *Collier's,* 9 Aug. 1947.

19. "Giant Doughnut is Proposed as Space Station," *Popular Science,* October 1951, 120–21.

20. "What Are We Waiting For?" *Collier's,* 22 Mar. 1952, 23.

21. Willy Ley to Heinz Haber et al., 13 June 1951, Hayden Planetarium Library, New York.

22. On these articles, see Randy Liebermann, "The *Collier's* and Disney Series," in Frederick I. Ordway III and Randy Leibermann, eds., *Blueprint for Space: From Science Fiction to Science Fact* (Washington, D.C.: Smithsonian Institution Press, 1991), 135–44.

23. "Man Will Conquer Space *Soon*" series, *Collier's,* 22 Mar. 1952, 23–76 *passim.*

24. Wernher von Braun with Cornelius Ryan, "Can We Get to Mars?" ibid., 30 Apr. 1954, 22–28.

25. Liebermann, "*Collier's* and Disney Series," 141; Ron Miller, "Days of Future Past," *Omni,* October 1986.

26. "Pre-Press Briefing," 16 Apr. 1958, PPF, Ann Whitman, DDE Diary Series, box 32, "April 1958 Staff Notes (2)," DDEL. This was just about as serious a negative comment about an individual as one can find in Eisenhower's papers. See also Col. A. J. Goodpaster, "Memorandum for the Record," 20 Jan. 1956, White House Office of Staff Secretary, box 18, "Missiles (January 1956–January 1960(1))," ibid.; Brig. Gen. A. J. Goodpaster, "Legislative Leadership Meeting, Supplementary Notes," 18 Mar. 1958, PPF, Ann Whitman, DDE Diary Series, Box 32, "April 1958 Staff Notes (2)," ibid.

27. See Dwight D. Eisenhower, "Why I Am a Republican," *Saturday Evening Post,* 11 Apr. 1964, 19; President's Science Advisory Committee, Executive Office of the President, "A Statement by the President and the Introduction to Outer Space," 26 Mar. 1958, Eisenhower Presidential Files, NASA Historical Reference Collection, NASA History Office, NASA Headquarters, Washington, D.C.

28. For example, the Eisenhower administration repeatedly tried to find ways to conduct necessary research and development (R&D) in the most expeditious and cost-effective way. This involved streamlining functions to eliminate duplication of effort, transferring some activities to non-governmental organizations, and prioritizing projects to eliminate those of questionable value. See Joseph M. Dodge, Bureau of the Budget, "Research and Development," 9 June 1953; L. Arthur Minnich, Assistant White House Staff Secretary, Memorandum of Conference with the President, "Coordination of Basic Research," 10 May 1956, with attachments, both in White House Central Files, Official File, box 743, "Research (1)," DDEL.

29. Ann Whitman Diary, 4 Apr. 1956, 2; Wilton B. Parsons, memo for record, "Appointment of Senator Duff and Senator Saltonstal with the President, April 4, 1956 (5:45 p.m.)," both in DDE Presidential Papers, ibid.

30. The military created the V-2 Upper Atmosphere Panel in 1946 to oversee this activity. In 1948 it became the Upper Atmosphere Rocket Research Panel and in 1957 the Rocket and Satellite Research Panel. See Lyman Spitser, Jr., "Astronomical Advantages of an Extra-Terrestrial Observatory," *Astronomy Quarterly* 7 (September 1946):19–20; James A. Van Allen, *Origins of Maqnetospheric Physics* (Washington, D.C.: Smithsonian Institution Press, 1983); Homer E. Newell, *Beyond the Atmosphere: Early Years of Space Science* (Washington, D.C.: NASA SP-4211, 1980); George K. Megerian, "Minutes of V-2 Upper Atmosphere Research Panel Meeting," V-2 Report #13, 29 Dec. 1947; idem, "Minutes of Meeting of Upper Atmosphere Rocket Research Panel," Panel Report #35, 29 Apr. 1953, both in NASA Historical Reference Collection.

31. R. Cargill Hall, "The Origins of U.S. Space Policy: Eisenhower, Open Skies, and Freedom of Space," *Colloquy* 14 (December 1993); idem, "Origins of U.S. Space Policy: Eisenhower, Open Skies, And Freedom of Space," in John M. Logsdon, gen. ed., *Exploring the Unknown: Selected Documents in the History of the U.S. Civil Space Program,* vol. 1 (Washington, D.C.: NASA SP-4407, 1995), chap. 2.

32. "What Are We Waiting For?" *Collier's,* 22 Mar. 1952, 23; L. Arthur Minnich, Jr., "Legislative Meeting, Supplementary Notes," 4 Feb. 1958, PPF, Ann Whitman, DDE Diary Series, box 30, February 1958 Staff Notes, DDEL.

33. Brig. Gen. A. J. Goodpaster, "Memorandum of Conference with the President, October 12, 1959," 23 Oct. 1959, Records of the White House Office of Science and Technology, box 12, ibid.

34. Richard E. Martin, *The Atlas and Centaur "Steel Balloon" Tanks: A Legacy of Karel Bossart* (San Diego: General Dynamics, 1989); Robert L. Perry, "The Atlas, Thor, Titan, and Minuteman," in Eugene M. Emme, ed., *The History of Rocket Technology* (Detroit: Wayne State University Press, 1964); John L. Sloop, *Liquid Hydrogen as a Propulsion Fuel, 1945–1959* (Washington, D.C.: NASA, SP-4404, 1978), 173–77.

35. This story is told in Edmund Beard, *Developing the ICBM: A Study in Bureaucratic Politics* (New York: Columbia University Press, 1976); Jacob Neufeld, *Ballistic Missiles in the United States Air Force, 1945–1960* (Washington, D.C.: Office of Air Force History, 1990).

36. This group included Lloyd Berkner, Joseph Kaplan, Fred Singer, James Van Allen, and Homer Newell. The fingerprints of these core leaders are all over every decision relative to the IGY satellite program and the U.S. decision by Eisenhower to sponsor a satellite. See the discussion of this effort in Constance McL. Green and Milton Lomask, *Vanguard: A History* (Washington, D.C.: Smithsonian Institution Press, 1971), 6–39; Rip Bulkeley, *The Sputniks Crisis and Early United States Space Policy: A Critique of the Historiography of Space* (Bloomington: Indiana University Press, 1991), 89–122; R. Cargill Hall, "Origins and Early Development of the Vanguard and Explorer Satellite Programs," *Airpower Historian* 9 (October 1964).

37. National Security Council, NSC 5520 "Draft Statement of Policy on U.S. Scientific Satellite Program," 20 May 1955; United States National Committee for the International Geophysical Year 1957–1958, "Minutes of the First Meeting, Technical Panel on Earth Satellite Program, October 20, 1955," both in NASA Historical Reference Collection; Don Irwin to Mr. Rockefeller and General Parker, "Pentagon Briefing on Earth Satellite Program," 12 Oct. 1955; Richard Hirsch to Elmer B. Staats, "Pentagon Meeting on Earth Satellite Program," 13 Oct. 1955, both in White House Office of Special Assistant for National Security Affairs, NSC, OCB Central Files, box 11, "OCB 000.9 (National & Physical Sciences)," DDEL.

38. Percival Brundage to Dwight D. Eisenhower, "United States Scientific Satellite Program," 8 Oct. 1957, White House Central Files, Official File, box 744, "Outer Space Box, Earth-Circling Satellite Folder," DDEL.

39. "Memorandum of Discussion at the 283d Meeting of the National Security Council, Washington, May 3, 1956," in John P. Glennon, ed., *Foreign Relations of the United States 1955–1957* (Washington, D.C.: Government Printing Office, 1988), 11:734–42.

40. "Memorandum of Discussion at the 322nd Meeting of the NSC, May 10, 1957," ibid., 749.

41. He even commented obliquely on this in his first press conference after Sputnik 1. See *Public Papers of the Presidents of the United States: Dwight D. Eisenhower, 1957* (Washington, D.C.: Government Printing Office, 1958), 719.

42. William J. Laurence, "2 Rocket Experts Argue 'Moon' Plan," *New York Times,* 14 Oct. 1952; Robert C. Boardman, "Space Rockets With Floating Base Predicted," *New York Herald Tribune,* 14 Oct. 1952.

43. "Journey into Space," *Time,* 8 Dec. 1952, 62–73, quote from p. 62.

44. This became the major NASA effort in the latter 1950s and has been hauled out repeatedly since then as the model approach to space exploration. See "Minutes of Meeting of Research Steering Committee on Manned Space Flight," 25–26 May 1959, 2, NASA Historical Reference Collection; Dwayne A. Day, "The Von Braun Paradigm," *Space Times: Magazine of the American Astronautical Society* (November/December 1994), 12–15.

45. "Journey into Space," *Time,* 72.

46. Eisenhower, *Waging Peace,* 209.

47. This paragraph, and the ones that follow, are based on the information contained in Green and Lomask, *Vanguard.*

48. At a personal level, perhaps Sputnik's most significant result was how it served to inspire many young people to study math and science so that they could participate in this new and exciting type of exploration. For one, Homer H. Hickam, Jr., *Rocket Boys: A Memoir* (New York: Delacorte, 1998), describes how his life changed during the Sputnik winter as it inspired him to study math, gain a scholarship to college, and become a NASA engineer.

49. Murrey Marder, "Khrushchev Changed East-West Relations," *Washington Post,* 16 Oct. 1964, 6F.

50. International Affairs Seminars of Washington, "American Reactions to Crisis: Examples of Pre-Sputnik and Post-Sputnik Attitudes and of the Reaction to other Events Perceived as Threats," 15–16 Oct. 1958, U.S. President's Committee on Information Activities Abroad (Sprague Committee) Records, 1959–1961, box 5, A83-10, DDEL.

51. This proved incorrect, however, and Eisenhower worked behind the scenes while giving the appearance of inaction, and in most instances his indirect approach to leadership was highly effective. This has been demonstrated for Eisenhower's space program in R. Cargill Hall, "Eisenhower, Open Skies, and Freedom of Space," IAA-92-0184, paper delivered on 2 Sept. 1992 to the International Astronautical Federation, Washington, D.C.

52. G. Mennen Williams, quoted in William E. Burrows, *Deep Black: Space Espionage and National Security* (New York: Random House, 1987), 94–95. See also Derek W. Elliott, "Finding an Appropriate Commitment: Space Policy Under Eisenhower and Kennedy," Ph.D. Diss., George Washington University, 1992.

53. Frank Altschul to Dwight D. Eisenhower, 8 Oct. 1957, PPF, Ann Whitman, DDE Diary Series, box 27, "October 1957 Diary Staff Memos," DDEL.

54. Speeches of Lyndon B. Johnson, Tyler, Tex. 18 Oct. 1957, and Austin, Tex. 19 Oct. 1957, both in Statements file, box 22, Lyndon B. Johnson Presidential Library, Austin, Tex.

55. Eisenhower, *Waging Peace,* 206.

56. James R. Killian, *Sputnik, Scientists, and Eisenhower: A Memoir of the First Special Assistant to the President for Science and Technology* (Cambridge, Mass.: MIT Press, 1977), 7.

57. Eisenhower, *Waging Peace,* 211.

58. International Affairs Seminars of Washington, "American Reactions to Crisis," 15–16 Oct. 1958.

59. *Facts on File,* 17 (October 1957):330.

60. Ibid., 331; Richard M. Nixon, *The Memoirs of Richard Nixon* (New York: Grossett & Dunlap, 1978), 111.

61. Kenneth E. Shewmaker, "The Sherman Adams Papers," *Dartmouth College Library Bulletin* 10 (April 1969); John E. Wickman, "Partnership for Research," ibid.; *Historical Materials in the Dwight D. Eisenhower Library* (Abilene, Kans.: Dwight D. Eisenhower Library, 1989), 8, 48; *New York Times,* 28 Oct. 1986, D-28.

62. *Public Papers of the Presidents of the United States: Dwight D. Eisenhower, 1957,* 774–87; NASA clippings file, "October 1957," NASA Historical Reference Collection.

63. Indicative of this perspective is the series of planning efforts conducted on space exploration that have been developed over the years, and the commonality that they display. See Arthur C. Clarke, *The Exploration of Space* (New York: Harper & Brothers, 1951), 61–62; Harry J. Goett to Ira H. Abbot, "Interim Report on Operation of 'Research Steering Committee on Manned Space Flight,'" 17 July 1959, NASA Historical Reference Collection; *America's Next Decades in Space: A Report of the Space Task Group* (Washington, D.C.: National Aeronautics and Space Administration, September 1969); National Commission on Space (Thomas O. Paine, chair), *Pioneering the Space Frontier: The Report of the National Commission on Space* (New York: Bantam Books, 1986), esp. the Manifest Destiny statement on p. 3; Harvey Brooks, "Motivations for the Space Program: Past and Future," in Allan A. Needell, ed., *The First 25 Years in Space: A Symposium* (Washington, D.C.: Smithsonian Institution Press, 1983), 3–26.

64. U.S. Senate, Hearings before the Preparedness Investigating Subcommittee of the Committee on Armed Services, 85th Cong., 1st and 2d Sess., 25, 26, and 27 Nov., 13, 14, 16, and 17 Dec. 1957, 10, 13, 15, 16, 17, 20, 21, and 23 Jan. 1958 (Washington, D.C.: Government Printing Office, 1958), list of witnesses.

65. Ibid., *passim;* U.S. House of Representatives, Hearings before the Select Committee on Astronautics and Space Exploration, 85th Cong., 2d sess. on H.R. 11881, 15, 16, 17, 18, 21, 22, 23, 24, 25, 28, 29, and 30 Apr., 1, 5, 7, 8, and 12 May 1958 (Washington, D.C.: Government Printing Office, 1958), *passim.*

66. For the Senate, these included Eilene Galloway from the research staff of the Library of Congress; Glen P. Wilson, an aeronautical engineer; and Homer Joe Stewart, who had been intimately involved in the IGY satellite project, to handle scientific matters. For the House investigation S. Fred Singer, an astrophysicist at the University of Maryland, served as the scientific consultant and played a key role in the committee's hearings. See Alison Griffith, *The National Aeronautics and Space Act: A Study of the Development of Public Policy* (Washington, D.C.: Public Affairs Press, 1962), 27–43; Glen P. Wilson, "Lyndon Johnson and the Legislative Origins of NASA," *Prologue* 25 (Winter 1993).

67. This is not surprising, given that the list of witnesses at these hearings reads like a who's who of the scientific and technological/military-industrial complex elite.

68. *Senate Hearings,* 21, 28, 60, 63–65, 113.

69. Griffith, *National Aeronautics and Space Act,* 19–24; Enid Curtis Bok Schoettle, "The Establishment of NASA," in Sanford A. Lakoff, ed., *Knowledge and Power* (New York: Free Press, 1966), 162–270.

70. *New York Times,* 11 and 28 Oct. 1957; Schoettle, "Establishment of NASA," 178.

71. Killian, *Sputnik, Scientists, and Eisenhower,* 12–16; Brig. Gen. A. J. Goodpaster, "Memorandum of Conference with the President, October 8, 1957, 8:30 AM," 9 Oct. 1957, "Memorandum of Conference with the President, October 8, 1957, 5 PM," 9 Oct. 1957, and "Memorandum of Conference with the President, October 15, 1957, 11 AM," 16 Oct. 1957; all in PPF, Ann Whitman, DDE Diary Series, box 27, "October 1957 Staff Notes (2)," DDEL; "Discussion of the 339th Meeting of the National Security Council, Thursday, October 10, 1957," 11 Oct. 1957, PPF, Ann Whitman, National Security Council, ibid.

72. Goodpaster, "Memorandum of Conference with the President, October 15, 1957, 11 AM," 16 Oct. 1957.

73. L. Arthur Minnich, "Memorandum for the Record," 25 Apr. 1956, attachment to L. Arthur Minnich, "Memorandum of Conference with the President, March 10, 1956—9:00 AM," 10 May 1956, White House Central Files, Official File, box 743, "Research (1)," DDEL.

74. Bernard M. Baruch to President, 23 Oct. 1957, PPF, Ann Whitman, DDE Diary Series, box 27, "Oct 1957 Diary Staff Memos," ibid.

75. Brig. Gen. A. J. Goodpaster, "Memorandum of Conference with the President, October 30, 1957," 31 Oct. 1957, PPF, Ann Whitman, DDE Diary Series, box 27, "October 1957 Staff Notes (2)," ibid.

76. Homer J. Stewart to Assistant Secretary of Defense (R&D), "Vanguard and Redstone," 22 June 1956; E. V. Murphree, DOD Special Assistant for Guided Missiles, to Deputy Secretary of Defense, "Use of the Jupiter Re-entry Test Vehicle as a Satellite," 5 July 1956; C. C. Furnas, Assistant Secretary of Defense, to Deputy Secretary of Defense, 10 July 1956, all in White House Office, Office of the Staff Secretary: Records, 1952–1961, box 6, "Missiles and Satellites," ibid; Dwayne A. Day, "Early Space Policy: New Revelations about the American Satellite Program Before Sputnik," *Spaceflight* 36 (November 1994):372–73.

77. Goodpaster, "Memorandum of Conference with the President, October 30, 1957," 31 Oct. 1957, 4.

78. Robert A. Divine, *The Sputnik Challenge: Eisenhower's Response to the Soviet Satellite* (New York: Oxford University Press, 1993), 93–96; Roger D. Launius, *NASA: History of the U.S. Civil Space Program* (Malabar, Fla.: Kriege, 1994), 26–27.

79. "Pre-Press Conference Notes," 15 Jan. 1958, PPF, Ann Whitman, DDE Diary Series, box 30, "January 1958 Staff Notes," DDEL.

80. *Public Papers of the Presidents of the United States: Dwight D. Eisenhower, 1957,* 789–99; Dwight D. Eisenhower to James R. Killian, 22 Nov. 1957, NASA Historical Reference Collection.

81. The classic study of this subject is Harold Seidman and Robert Gilmour, *Politics, Position and Power: From the Positive to the Regulatory State* (New York: Oxford University Press, 1986), esp. 329–41; Howard E. McCurdy to author, 10 Mar. 1995.

82. "Discussion at the 339th Meeting of the National Security Council, Thursday, October 10, 1957," 11 Oct. 1957, DDE Papers, Ann Whitman File, National Security Council, DDEL.

83. David Z. Beckler to Brig. Gen. Andrew Goodpaster, "Proposals by the Science Advisory Committee," 6 Nov. 1957, White House Office of Staff Secretary, box 23, "Scientific Advisory Board (1956) (3)," ibid.

84. Robert C. Truax to I. I. Rabi, 6 Nov. 1957, ibid.

85. "Who Should Control Space?" *Time,* 17 Feb. 1958, 20; "Who'll Map Space Conquest?" *Electronic Week,* 3 Feb. 1958, 5–6.

86. L. Arthur Minnich, Jr., to Percival F. Brundage, 4 Feb. 1958; Minnich, "Legislative Leadership Meeting, Supplementary Notes," 4 Feb. 1958; Brig. Gen. A. J. Goodpaster, "Memorandum of Conference with the President, February 4, 1958 (following Legislative Leaders meeting)," 6 Feb. 1958, all in PPF, Ann Whitman Files, DDE Diary Series, February 1958 Staff Notes, box 30, DDEL.

87. Minnich, "Legislative Meeting, Supplementary Notes," 4 Feb. 1958.

88. Divine, *Sputnik Challenge,* 100–105; Alex Roland, *Model Research: A History of the National Advisory Committee for Aeronautics, 1915–1958* (Washington, D.C.: NASA SP-4405, 1985), 290–300.

89. Lyndon B. Johnson, *The Vantage Point: Perspectives of the Presidency, 1963–1969* (New York: Holt, Rinehart & Winston, 1971), 277; Killian, *Sputnik, Scientists, and Eisenhower,* 137–38; Robert L. Rosholt, *An Administrative History of NASA, 1958–1963* (Washington, D.C.: NASA SP-4101, 1966), 12–17.

90. President's Science Advisory Committee, Executive Office of the President, "A Statement by the President and the Introduction to Outer Space," 26 Mar. 1958, NASA Historical Reference Collection.

91. Hunley, ed., *Birth of NASA,* 31.

92. Ibid., 17.

93. T. Keith Glennan to James R. Killian, Jr., 27 May 1959, NASA Historical Reference

Collection; Walter A. McDougall, . . . *the Heavens and the Earth: A Political History of the Space Age* (New York: Basic Books, 1986), 202.

94. This includes everything from such polemics as Gore Vidal, "The Enemy Within," *The Observer* (London), 27 Oct. 2002, to more the reasoned analysis of The National Commission on Terrorist Attacks Upon the United States, *The 9/11 Commission Report* (Washington, D.C.: Government Printing Office, 22 July 2004).

95. Dwight D. Eisenhower, "Are We Headed in the Wrong Direction?" *Saturday Evening Post,* 11–18 Aug. 1962, 24.

96. Dwight D. Eisenhower, "Why I Am a Republican," ibid., 11 Apr. 1964, 19.

97. Ronald Brownstein, "Using and Abusing 9/11 Fears to Set National Security Policy," *Los Angeles Times,* 21 June 2004.

98. *Public Papers of the Presidents of the United States: Dwight D. Eisenhower, 1960–61,* 1035–40.

99. This deference to the authority of expertise was also seen in other technical arenas. See Bruce E. Seely, *Building the American Highway System: Engineers as Policy Makers* (Philadelphia, Pa.: Temple University Press, 1987); Samuel P. Hays, with Barbara D. Hays, *Beauty, Health, and Permanence: Environmental Politics in the United States, 1955–1985* (Cambridge, England: Cambridge University Press, 1987); Thomas L. Haskell, ed., *The Authority of Experts: Studies in History and Theory* (Bloomington: Indiana University Press, 1984); John G. Gunnell, "The Technocratic Image and the Theory of Technocracy," *Technology and Culture* 23 (July 1982); Mark H. Rose and Bruce E. Seely, "Getting the Interstate System Built: Road Engineers and the Implementation of Public Policy, 1955–1985," *Journal of Public Policy* 2 (1990).

100. David Halberstam, *The Best and Brightest* (New York: Viking, 1973), 57, 153; Peter Kihss, "Killian Critical of Space Spending," *New York Times,* 14 Dec. 1960.

Eisenhower and Joint Professional Military Education

John W. Yaeger

Dwight D. Eisenhower had a significant influence on the development of joint professional military education. He had a close association with the oldest joint professional military education institution, the Industrial College of the Armed Forces (ICAF). Later, Eisenhower ensured the resources were available to establish two other colleges, the National War College (NWC) and Joint Forces Staff College (JFSC). Today, these three institutions are key components of the National Defense University (NDU) where they are devoted to educating military and civilian leaders in complex political, information, military, and economic issues. This paper will provide an overview of professional military education, define joint professional military education, and describe Eisenhower's influence on the joint professional military education system that exists today.

Overview of Professional Military Education

The armed services have recognized the value of an education and they have placed special emphasis on the importance of professional military education. An officer's responsibilities and challenges change with each promotion. The education system developed by the military is reflective of this increasing scope of an officer's responsibilities. The Services initially demand competencies from the ensigns and lieutenants in service specific weapons. This broadens to requirements for strategic-level thinking from the generals and admirals. There is somewhat of a blurring of the lines between the military education system and the training system that has evolved over the years. Generally, the training programs are highly utilitarian while the educational system, particularly at the senior level, is similar to that of a traditional liberal arts education.

The reason for having a system of higher education in the military is fundamentally the same reason civilian higher education institutions exist. The professional military education system fulfills an array of purposes and this large spectrum is not unique to military colleges; both the military and civilian sectors of American society need educated leaders. The nature of the type of education has been debated for quite some time. In 1828, the faculty at Yale debated and reported on the purposes of higher education. Some faculty firmly believed students should acquire content applicable to the professions they would be joining. Others thought an education should be more liberal, teaching students how to think.[1] The professional military has deliberated the same question. Today's professional military education system includes the spectrum of possibilities. The goal of the senior service college's education is comparable to that described in the 1828 Yale Report and that is to exercise the students' minds to teach them how to think. Other institutions in the system, such as the primary-level schools, provide very content-specific educations.

The Framework for Professional Military Education of Officers in the United States Armed Forces

The educational framework corresponds to the progressive nature of an officer's career (see Table 1). There are five levels: precommissioning, primary, intermediate, senior, and general/flag officer. The curriculum of each level is designed to build upon the knowledge attained at a previous level.[2] Progression through the professional military education system is a responsibility of the respective Service. The Service needs to weigh the individual's professional development with other needs of the Service and decide whether or not an officer should participate in an education program at that point in his or her career.[3]

The highest level of professional military education is CAPSTONE and only occurs at National Defense University. Every newly selected flag and general officer is required by Congress to attend this course at NDU. The six-week curriculum concentrates on national security strategy and joint matters. There is a provision to waive the congressional requirement if operationally necessary.[4]

Joint Professional Military Education

Within the professional military education system is a program of joint professional military education. This program contains curriculum components designed to

Table 1. *Progression in U.S. Military Education*

Commissioned Service (Years)	Officer's Rank	Eligible Level of Education
24–30	BG/RADM	CAPSTONE (6 weeks)
16–23	LTC-COL/CDR-CAPT	Senior Service or NDU College (10 months)
7–15	MAJ/LCDR	Intermediate Service College (10 months)
2–7	CPT/LT	Officer Advanced or Specialist Courses (3–9 months)
0–2	2LT/ENS	Officer Basic or Specialist Courses (3–6 months)
0		Cadet/Midshipman Service Academy or ROTC (4 years)

educate students in preparation for working with officers and civilians from other Services, agencies, and countries. The schools at NDU are specifically designated joint professional military education schools.

The educational philosophy of a joint education is to foster intellectual growth and development through an understanding of multiple perspectives. This is accomplished through curriculum and having a faculty and student body that represent multiple viewpoints. President Eisenhower was a great believer and supporter of joint professional military education.

Eisenhower's Influence

At the end of any major conflict, the United States military has gone through a period of assessment and instituted change based on lessons learned. Following the Vietnam War, in the mid-1970s, political and economic considerations evolved to a point to induce the merger of two joint professional military education colleges. The Industrial College of the Armed Forces[5] and the National War College joined together to create the National Defense University. The Armed Forces Staff College (AFSC)[6] joined the University in 1981. Dwight D. Eisenhower attended and taught at the Industrial College and had great influence on establishing NWC and AFSC.

The Industrial College of the Armed Forces

The oldest component of NDU is ICAF, situated at Fort Lesley J. McNair in Washington, D.C. This institution was created as a result of America's inability to efficiently support war efforts in a time of need. This section will describe the circumstances leading to the establishment of ICAF and a synopsis of its early history.

World War I was the conflict that brought to light the need for ICAF. American industries and the military had a difficult time coordinating the war effort.[7] For example, the War Department ordered approximately 50,000 pieces of 75mm field artillery for use during World War I, yet only 143 American-made units were available to U.S. forces on 11 November 1918. The statistics for U.S. wartime production were similarly dismal for critical war items such as tanks, aircraft, and food.

During the postwar assessment, American industries and businessmen were strongly criticized, not only by the U.S. government but by U.S. allies as well. David Lloyd George, Britain's prime minister during the war, later reflected:

> No field guns of American pattern or manufacture fired a shot in the War. The same thing applies to tanks. Here one would have thought that the nation who were the greatest manufacturers of automobiles in the world could have turned out tanks with the greatest facility and in the largest numbers, but not a single tank of American manufacture ever rolled into action in the War.
>
> Transport was so defective that ships sometimes took a couple of months to turn round at the ports, and on land it was so badly organised that, in spite of help which was forthcoming from other armies, a large number of the American troops who fought so gallantly in the Argonne in the autumn of 1918 were without sufficient food to sustain them in their heroic struggle in a difficult terrain. The American soldiers were superb. That is a fact which is acknowledged, not only by their friends and British comrades, but by their enemies as well.

There were no braver or more fearless men in any Army, but the organisation at home and behind the lines was not worthy of the reputation which American business men have deservedly won for smartness, promptitude and efficiency.[8]

The War Department's supply bureaus and supply programs were sharply condemned in a series of congressional hearings held in 1918 and 1919.[9] Tension between Congress and manufacturers led directly to the War Department's review of America's industrial preparedness. Political pressure forced the War Department to come up with a solution to preclude the mistakes of World War I from ever being repeated.

One of the initial steps taken to solve the problems was the National Defense Act of 1920, which reorganized the structure of the War Department. As a result of the new legislation, a new position was created, the assistant secretary of war. This individual was charged with the responsibility that the department would be prepared for future wartime mobilization efforts.[10] Additionally, this new assistant secretary was empowered to plan for the entire wartime economy, a daunting task[11] President Warren G. Harding appointed John M. Wainwright to this post in the spring of 1921. One of the first individuals with whom Wainwright consulted was the chairman of the War Industries Board, Bernard Baruch. Wainwright's staff constantly asked Baruch to review their plans for industrial mobilization. Proposals of how to train and educate individuals in the arena of industrial support for a war were discussed frequently by the staff and reviewed by Baruch over the next several years.[12] Wainwright was unable to procure funding to establish an educational institution for such training that he regarded as necessary.[13] Before Wainwright left his assignment, he kept the possibility of a school alive by assigning eight officers to plan for a curriculum, so if a college were approved, plans would be in place to begin classes.

President Harding replaced Wainwright with a new assistant secretary of war on 21 March 1923. Dwight F. Davis, a former colonel in the American Expeditionary Force in France, became the new assistant secretary. Davis had a strong interest in educating more officers in procurement and industrial mobilization planning. Four months after taking office, two of Davis's staff members presented him with a proposal to establish a school specializing in the education of industrial mobilization. Initially, Davis was skeptical.[14] He carefully examined the preparations his staff officers had made for such a school. Davis is considered one of the founding fathers of the Industrial College.[15]

Originally chartered as the Army Industrial College, the institution was established by the War Department's General Orders, Number Seven, on 25 February 1924. The orders read:

> Establishment of The Army Industrial College. 1. A college, to be known as the Army Industrial College, is hereby established for the purpose of training Army officers in the useful knowledge pertaining to the supervision of procurement of all military supplies in time of war and to the assurance of adequate provision for the mobilization of material and industrial organization essential to war-time needs.[16]

A major voice in the creation of the college was Bernard Baruch, a well-known industrialist and personal advisor to Presidents Woodrow Wilson and Warren G.

Harding. Baruch and fellow industrialist R. S. Brookings[17] comprised the new college's advisory board. Baruch was a frequent lecturer and friend at the Army Industrial College and urged the students to question him "mercilessly and pitilessly."[18] He considered each invitation to lecture as a great event. Baruch had great appreciation for the complexities and challenges of mobilization and for industries' ability to support national defense. During a lecture to students at the Army War College on 12 February 1924, a student asked Baruch his opinion on how the United States should be organized in time of peace so it would be ready to mobilize in time of war. Baruch[19] stressed the importance of establishing:

> [A] little school or something of the kind . . . where those of us who did serve . . . could give the benefit of our experience to these possible industrial leaders. . . . Let it be a living thing. . . . The military-minded man who has to devise the machines of destruction should keep in touch with the man of industry who can go out and get those things and who knows how he can turn a factory that is making one thing into another thing. They should keep in touch all the time so that if war has to come, we shall be ready for it.[20]

Simply put, it was Baruch's vision for the college to stay in touch with industry. This would serve society's best interest by ensuring that the military knew the capabilities of industry to support a national security strategy and thereby avoid the problems encountered in World War I. Today, the purpose of ICAF is the same as the vision that Bernard Baruch had for the institution in 1924.

Baruch became an advisor to several U.S. presidents. Most notably, during World War II Baruch advised President Franklin D. Roosevelt on economic mobilization. Also, during World War II Baruch had some influence on other eventual components of NDU. After the war, Baruch played a prominent role in formulating policy at the United Nations regarding international control of atomic energy.

Two other individuals, both Army officers, had early associations with the Army Industrial College and would later become instrumental in establishing institutions which would eventually become a part of NDU. Major H. H. (Hap) Arnold, who would become one of the pioneers of military aviation, was a member of one of the first classes to graduate from the Army Industrial College.[21] The other was Maj. Dwight David Eisenhower who began lecturing to the Army Industrial College in 1931 shortly after his graduation from the Army War College. Earning a degree while teaching, Eisenhower graduated with the Army Industrial College class of 1933 and continued to teach at the institution during the interwar years.[22] During this time, he established a close relationship with Bernard Baruch. According to Eisenhower, few people understood the importance of the Army Industrial College as well as Baruch.[23]

Eisenhower had great appreciation for the purpose of the Industrial College and its joint education. He told the students during the fourth lecture of the year for the Class of 1932 of the importance of those planning for war working with those that resource the war. Eisenhower described a "cleavage" that had developed between those that plan for operations and those that would supply the efforts.[24] Those responsible for planning had direct access to the secretary of war and secretary of the navy, while those responsible for mobilizing and resourcing the war were further down in the chain of command. Eisenhower's concern is the point of the ICAF curriculum in 2005; that is, the planning of a national security strategy must be accomplished with those responsible for resourcing the strategy. In the development of joint professional military education, Eisenhower would ensure the plan for the education system was resourced.

Almost from the beginning, the Army Industrial College included students from other Services and stressed the importance of understanding each Service's capabilities. The first Navy students arrived in February 1925. When Eisenhower was a student, 25 percent of the Class of 1933 was composed of Navy and Marine Corps officers.[25] The positive aspects of a "joint" student body were something that Eisenhower would frequently refer to later in his career.

As the U.S. strategy to win World War II found success, extensive recognition and publicity was given to the Army Industrial College for helping the United States to prepare for war.[26] The first joint professional military education college validated the importance of students from different Services learning together. The institution also helped the nation avoid the problems of mobilization encountered during World War I.

The National War College

The Army Industrial College was the first joint professional military education institution but it had a very specific mission: mobilizing and resourcing a nation for war. Other educational needs were identified, requiring new schools. To help define the exact requirements, several studies were undertaken. The organization of the Armed Forces and the education system to support the Services needed to be examined so an informed decision could be made on any new institutions. This section will describe the evolution of events leading to the establishment of NWC. The progression begins with the creation of the Joint Army-Navy Staff College, followed by a decision on the organization of the postwar military, and then a decision on the post–World War II joint education system.

The Creation of the Joint Army-Navy Staff College

Early on during World War II, it was apparent to the key leaders within the Services that there was a need for officers educated in joint operations. A new means of education was desired to alleviate the conflicts surrounding respective roles and capabilities of the Army and Navy.[27] This section will address a school created in minimum time to fulfill an immediate requirement.

A graduate of the Army Industrial College, Lt. Gen. H. H. Arnold, Commanding General of the Army Air Forces, submitted a proposal to his fellow members of the Joint Chiefs of Staff (JCS): Gen. George C. Marshall, Army Chief of Staff, and Fleet Adm. Ernest J. King, Commander in Chief of the U.S. Fleet and Chief of Naval Operations. These three were the original members of the newly created JCS.[28] Arnold proposed that a study be undertaken by the JCS to determine the feasibility of the establishment of a United States War College. Arnold's recommendations established the initial groundwork for two colleges that today are a part of NDU. The two institutions are AFSC and NWC. Arnold's 26 December 1942 memorandum stated that the purpose of the War College would be twofold:

> 1. To train selected officers of the Army and Navy for command and staff duties with unified (Army-Navy) commands.
>
> 2. To develop methods and ideas for the most effective unified employment of all arms and services and to translate lessons learned in the field into appropriate doctrines. Conclusions reached should be spread through the services both by service publications and by the influence of the graduates of the College in planning and conducting operations.[29]

Arnold proposed that the college be located in the vicinity of Washington, D.C. to maintain contact with the "high command" and take advantage of existing facilities.[30]

The JCS resolved a few issues with the proposal and on 10 April 1943, Marshall signed a memorandum titled: "Establishment of a United States War (Staff) College." This memorandum documented the requirement for a special course of instruction to train Army, Navy, and Marine Corps officers for staff and command duties with unified commands. The course of instruction would fall under the jurisdiction of the JCS.[31] The Army-Navy Staff College was established in Washington, D.C. on 23 April 1943 with a mission to train selected officers for command and staff duty in unified or coordinated commands. The students in the initial class were told to meet in Washington, D.C. on 5 August 1943 in the new War Department Building at 21st Street and Virginia Avenue, N.W.[32] In a display of the nature of the unity of effort envisioned for the college, General Marshall and Admiral King each spoke at the opening ceremony and the individual responsible for proposing the college, Lieutenant General Arnold, provided the concluding remarks.[33] Admiral King's remarks may have summed up the spirit behind the college the best. Referring to the purpose of the college, he stated:

> Certainly it is to promote better teamwork, to enable unified or coordinated commands to work more effectively, but to my mind what may be called a by-product is the most important of all, and that is to indicate that there is basically but one uniform in the armed services—that of the United States.[34]

The composition of the student body reflected the desire for an increased understanding of each other's Service. Classes for the four months of instruction were composed of officers from each Service, and at times included officers from the United Kingdom and Canada. An Australian officer participated in one class. To help fulfill the goal of producing students who understood the relationship between the diplomatic corps and the military, the eighth, and all subsequent classes of students, included one to three foreign service officers from the State Department.[35] The backgrounds of the students created a joint learning environment.

What became of the new Army-Navy Staff College following the war was a function of the postwar educational requirements. The military leadership believed that joint professional military education was beneficial, and they demonstrated this conviction by evolving the Army-Navy Staff College into two institutions: NWC and AFSC.

Deciding on the Organization of the Post–World War II Military

Planning for the organization of the postwar military began prior to the end of World War II. At the heart of the issue was whether or not the Services should operate independently, as they had been, or fall under an umbrella organization such as a new Department of Defense. Once the structure of the Services was established, plans could be made for the professional military education system necessary to support the organization. The sequence of establishing the organization first, then determining the education required to support the system, was important. Separate Services implied that a system of independent Service colleges was necessary; whereas, if the new organization stressed a more unified approach, then new "joint" colleges might be necessary. The purpose of this section is to frame the debate about the organization of the military and portray the final decision.

Determining the nature of the postwar military required that several broad issues be addressed. Among the concerns were: Should there continue to be separate Services? What should become of the Army Air Corps? How "joint" should the military be? To answer those questions, the Joint Chiefs of Staff formed the Special Committee for Reorganization of the National Defense in late 1944.[36] The committee was frequently referred to as the Richardson Committee after its chairman, retired Adm. James O. Richardson.

To answer the questions posed above, the Richardson Committee interviewed senior military officers worldwide in over eighty meetings. Ultimately, the Richardson Committee was in favor of a "single department system of organization" for the military. A two-department arrangement had a War Department and Navy Department whereas this proposal would have a single department of defense and the Navy and Army would operate within that structure. The committee's report pointed out that a new Department of the Air Force, if established at a later date, could fall under either a unified defense department or three-department system. One member of the committee was very much opposed to changing from the current system and cast a dissenting opinion. That member was the chairman of the committee, Admiral Richardson. Richardson thought the two-department system under the Joint Chiefs of Staff would be adequate if a joint secretaryship were added.[37] The premise behind the joint secretaryship was that the civilian secretaries would form a committee to take joint action on areas of mutual interest. The majority of the committee members felt this would never work because any decision would require unanimous agreement.[38] Important decisions would be unduly delayed trying to reach agreements among different Services. The committee's final recommendation in April 1945 included Richardson's objections, but made it clear the rest of the members favored a single department of defense. The debate on the organization and relationship of the Army and Navy escalated to Congress shortly after World War II. While the different options were being considered in congressional hearings, the Senate Military Affairs Committee prematurely provided Richardson's report and recommendations to the press on 3

November 1945. To add to the commotion, Secretary of the Navy James V. Forrestal let the press know that Admiral King was in disagreement with Generals Marshall and Arnold regarding the recommendations in the report.[39] The effect of these dissentions was to prolong a final decision about the organization of the Services, causing the loss of precious time to plan for a military education system.

General Eisenhower and Fleet Admiral Nimitz returned to Washington, D.C. following the war and each became the officer in charge of his respective Service. They participated in the congressional hearings, each voicing opposite opinions of how the Armed Forces should be structured. Eisenhower supported consolidation of the administration of the War and Navy Departments into a single department. Nimitz adamantly opposed the change, particularly since a major world war had just been won with the existing organization. On 16 November 1945, the Senate Committee on Military Affairs questioned General Eisenhower on his views on unification of the Armed Forces. General Eisenhower stated at the hearings:

> Competition is like some of the habits we have. In small amounts, they are very, very desirable. Carried too far, they are ruinous. When we have such competition in industry to produce such things as that, I do not think that competition produces the best. I believe that coordinated, scientific development and research is what we need to produce the best. Certainly it is more economical.
>
> If we do not integrate the executive management of the three members of our fighting team [Navy, Army and the proposed Air Force], our postwar security establishment will become the patchwork improvisation that is inevitable where independent departments, at different times compete before separate congressional committees. With integration we can buy more security for less money. Without it we will spend more money and obtain less security. . . . Finally, there is no such thing as a separate land, sea, or air war; therefore we must now recognize this fact by establishing a single department of the armed forces to govern us all.[40]

This testimony was only one side of the debate. General Eisenhower and Admiral Nimitz led U.S. forces to victory in opposite theaters of combat during the war, and similarly were in opposite theaters in considering how the defense establishment should be structured. Each had a different wartime experience, and each was successful, but their views on how the military should be organized and educated were radically different. This was not an Army versus Navy argument as plenty of individuals from each Service differed in their views. Some feared that in the joint environment Service identity would be lost. They also believed that competition was healthy for an organization. Nimitz was a strong supporter of maintaining separate departments. In his congressional testimony he stated:

> But it is open to serious question that a merger of the War and Navy Departments would actually produce greater teamwork between the Army and Navy. If either service felt that the merger threatened its ability to discharge its peculiar functions, the result would not be teamwork, but discord within the new Department. Competition between the services—for example in the development of aircraft engines—has been healthy and will continue to be as long as it is in the open. To stifle it might well have unhealthy effects. . . . A single Department of National Defense will have one of two consequences for the naval component. Either the Navy will retain all the autonomy, integrity, and prestige necessary to carry out its functions, in which case

it might as well remain a separate department; or it will lose these advantages, either gradually or at once, and become a secondary service.[41]

With the military leaders of the Navy and Army so polarized, it was necessary for the commander in chief to go public with a unifying position. President Harry S. Truman wanted Congress to make a timely decision on the organization of the Armed Forces. On 19 December 1945, Truman forwarded a special message to Congress recommending the establishment of a Department of National Defense. His message contained many indirect references to the need for joint education:

> I recommend that the Congress adopt legislation combining the War and Navy Departments into one single Department of National Defense. Such unification is another essential step—along with universal training—in the development of a comprehensive and continuous program for our future safety and for the peace and security of the world.
>
> True preparedness now means preparedness not alone in armaments and numbers of men, but preparedness in organization also. It means establishing in peacetime the kind of military organization which will be able to meet the test of sudden attack quickly and without having to improvise radical readjustment in structure and habits.
>
> A total security program has still other major aspects. A military program, standing alone, is useless. It must be supported in peacetime by planning for industrial mobilization and for development of industrial and raw material resources where these are insufficient.[42]

This message from the president helped the military leaders put to rest the controversy of what should be done with the two-department system under which they had been operating. They could focus on planning for the training and education necessary to support a Department of Defense. Proceeding with the planning turned out to be a wise decision because Truman did not approve the National Security Act of 1947 until 26 July of that year. The act provided for a secretary of defense and for a National Military Establishment comprising Departments of the Army, the Navy, and the Air Force, and related staff agencies.[43]

Deciding on the Organization of the Post–World War II Education System

President Truman's message clarified for the military that the commander in chief was in favor of a single department. The Services could stop any internal debates and devote their energy to finalizing the plans for developing a professional military education system to support a Department of Defense. This section will describe the progression of those efforts.

While the debate on how the Services should be organized was ongoing, the Services began to examine the possibilities for improving professional military education. In January 1944, the commandant of the Army-Navy Staff College, Lt. Gen. John Dewitt, was tasked with examining the future of joint education. One of the two civilians named to assist the commandant in this study was Bernard Baruch. Dewitt's study recommended that a national military university be established and that it should be composed of three colleges: a Joint Industrial College, a Joint War College, and a State Department College.[44] These recommendations were set aside in 1944 until the organization of the Services was understood. The Richardson Committee provided recommendations for the structure of the national defense system, which included professional military education in the United States. In fact, the committee report included recommendations for the institutions that would later become a part of NDU. The report stated:

> There are three basic requirements of the Armed Forces for the program of joint education and training. First there must be an exchange of duties and joint training on appropriate levels particularly designed to enable juniors to work together in the execution of joint plans drawn by their seniors. Second, joint education must be provided at intermediate levels to develop officers capable of planning and participating in joint operations. Third, joint education must be provided at high levels to develop officers capable of formulating strategic concepts and conducting, in command positions, large-scale operations employing all components.[45]

The third level of education referred to in the Richardson Committee's report was directly applicable to NWC and ICAF. Intermediate-level education would be attained at AFSC, which today is a part of NDU. (The early history of this college is presented later in this paper.) The committee recognized that the Army Industrial College already functioned as a joint institution, since its faculty and student body were composed of both Army and Naval officers. The Army oversaw the Army Industrial College since its creation in 1924. The committee's intent was to place responsibility of the Army Industrial College with the Joint Chiefs of Staff instead of the Army, and to have the name of the college reflect the inclusion of all Services.[46]

The Richardson Committee recommendations pertaining to the eventual creation of NDU were:

> That a joint college be maintained in Washington, D.C. to complete the formal joint education, at about the 25-year level of commissioned service, of senior officers of the armed forces in military strategy and war planning.

> That the Army Industrial College be reconstituted as a joint institution to provide joint education of senior officers of the armed forces in the field of industrial mobilization for war and related subjects.

> That the joint college of the armed forces, the proposed joint industrial college, and the State Department college (if established) conduct high-level education in all matters related to war and national policy, each within its own field, but with integrated effort in common fields. In the absence of the establishment of a State Department college, the continuation of the policy of accepting foreign service officers as students in the joint college of the armed forces is recommended.[47]

These recommendations would eventually result in three actions that shaped the nature of NDU. In response to the first recommendation came NWC. In response to the second recommendation the Army Industrial College would become the Industrial College of the Armed Forces (ICAF) and the Joint Chiefs of Staff would oversee its operations.[48] The third recommendation loosely described a function of a university when it referred to an integrated effort in common fields. However, without some entity fulfilling the function of a university, this goal was not achieved until NDU was actually established years later. Instead of a State Department College being established as stated in the third recommendation, foreign service officers were included in the student body of NWC from the beginning and later added to the student population at the Army Industrial College/ICAF.[49] Establishing NWC, renaming the Industrial College, and adding foreign service officers to both schools did not occur immediately because Congress and the president had not made a decision on how the Services would be organized.

Every war fighter testified of the need to fight together as a team, but unified peacetime training and education was another matter.[50] One of the fundamental questions was how professional military education should be structured: Is it more constructive to educate forces in a joint environment, like the Army Industrial College with students from both Services, or in a separate environment, like the Army War College? Admiral Nimitz subscribed to the philosophy of separate organizations and education:

> There is need for improvement in the systems of interservice education and training in order to insure maximum efficiency of all arms under unified command in the field. Such a system can be inaugurated without impairing technical proficiency in each service and at the same time preserving the morale and esprit de corps of the individual services. It seems unnecessary to enforce a merger upon the services to accomplish the needed improvements in this field.[51]

Eisenhower participated in the same congressional hearings as Nimitz, expressing an opposite point of view. Eisenhower's congressional testimony, in response to questioning, highlighted the importance of determining the overall structure of the military first, then deciding the education requirements. Eisenhower's words clearly reflected his belief that officers should be educated together, a theme he would return to when he became commander in chief:

> Senator Austin: I am curious to know whether you regard it important for us to determine upon this general organization before we undertake to determine such details as education, military education?
>
> General Eisenhower: I am absolutely certain of it. For example for one thing, I think there should be one grand over-all war college for all three of them. But we cannot have that if we do not know how we stand. And if we do not know that we are going to have such a combined war college, soon we will have an army war college, a navy war college, and an air war college. I am talking now about the very highest level of military intelligence, not the special services.
>
> There are a number of things involved there. Suppose I come up and ask you gentlemen for a special, separate amount of money for research and development. If I do that, then the Navy and the Air Force will be trying to get as much money as the War Department, they will be coming up and asking for money for their services.
>
> Senator Austin: Yes. Then, may we judge from what you have said, General, that the idea of postponing the consideration of this very vital subject in order to give a special commission appointed by the President time to restudy and go over it again, would not strike you as in the interest of the services or according to the public good.
>
> General Eisenhower: Senator, I adhere to one simple principle—there may be exceptions to this generalization, as there are, certainly, to all generalizations—but I

believe in people studying and deciding and bearing responsibility. This committee bears the responsibility to the Senate and through them to the people of the United States; the War Department heads bear responsibility to the Government and to the Army. And it is the same with the Navy; they have a responsibility to this Congress and to the people. The Congress bears the responsibility to the people, because they are the people.[52]

This debate on whether or not a single war college or separate war colleges are desirable was not resolved in 1945 and, to a certain extent, remains with the military today. Eisenhower, in his last response to Senator Austin, recognized that the discussions could go on but that it was the responsibility of Congress to make a decision. Congress was not yet ready to decide if joint professional military education was preferable to the Services providing each branch a separate education. The Joint Chiefs of Staff[53] continued to develop a postwar joint education plan while Congress was considering the reorganization of the Armed Forces.[54] Soon after Truman's special message to Congress, the War Department commissioned another major study of officer education. The commandant of the Army's Command and General Staff School, Lt. Gen. Leonard T. Gerow, was placed in charge of the study board, and the board report became known by his name. The Joint Chiefs of Staff, in emphasizing the need for joint education, heavily influenced the group's report. Gerow updated them frequently and the Joint Chiefs of Staff in turn provided him with feedback.[55] The board met in Washington, D.C. 3–12 January 1946, and interviewed individuals knowledgeable about joint professional military education. Among those interviewed was Lieutenant General Dewitt, who was by now retired. Dewitt had been the commandant of the Army-Navy Staff College and had previously conducted a study proposing improvements to the military education system. Gerow's report had many similarities to Dewitt's proposals from two years earlier. In February 1946, Gerow submitted his board's recommendations to General Eisenhower who was now chief of staff of the army. The "Gerow Board" proposed five joint colleges, which would collectively form a National Security University located in Washington, D.C. and fall under the direction of the JCS. In addition to ICAF and NWC, Gerow's Board proposed a Joint Administrative College, a Joint Intelligence College, and a Department of State College. The function of the university was to provide guidance, determine overarching policy, and supervise instruction for the five colleges. Specifically, the report went on to state:

> Close and definite coordination is required on the highest military educational level. This should be accomplished by the establishment of a *National Security University* under the jurisdiction and control of the Joint Chiefs of Staff and the Under Secretary of War (because of his legal responsibility for industrial mobilization). The National Security University will be interested in all problems concerning the military, social and economic resources and foreign policies of the nation that are related to national security.[56]

The board's report clarified that the recommendations should be implemented regardless of the pending decision on the reorganization of the Armed Forces.[57] Ultimately, the fate of the proposed university and the five colleges came down to a matter of resources. The Gerow report recommended that the Army War College, which suspended operations during World War II, remain closed; that the new NWC occupy the facilities; and that the Army War College funding be used for the new college. The proposals for a National Security University, Joint Administrative College, Joint Intelligence College, and Department of State College were ultimately rejected as a result of limited resources.[58]

The Establishment of the National War College

As the Gerow Board was meeting and developing an overall education plan in 1946, there was a desire by the Joint Chiefs of Staff to simultaneously work on the specific details for a NWC. To do the actual planning for the curriculum, student composition, and other essential specifics for NWC, the chief of naval operations, Admiral King, selected Vice Adm. Harry Wilbur Hill.[59] Hill replaced DeWitt as the commandant of the Army-Navy Staff College and was responsible for creating an implementation plan for NWC. Hill took over the Army-Navy Staff College in August 1945. When the twelfth and last class graduated on 7 December 1945, Hill was able to devote his full attention to plans for a new college. Intent on keeping the JCS fully informed of the progress, Hill forwarded his proposed curriculum to General Eisenhower and Admiral Nimitz, who had assumed responsibilities of army chief of staff and chief of naval operations, respectively.[60]

Nimitz and Eisenhower were satisfied with the curriculum, but the location and funding needed to be resolved before the doors could open. Admiral Hill brought up the subject of the location for the college and submitted the identical proposal contained in the Gerow report for using the building in Washington, D.C. that had been occupied by the Army War College. General Eisenhower not only donated the Army War College building, he ensured the Army would provide the funding to maintain and operate the institution.[61] The Army's funding included the hiring of civilian faculty members.[62] The Joint Chiefs of Staff authorized NWC on 23 April 1946.

The first class started on 3 September 1946 and had a joint student body and faculty. The class was made up of thirty Army ground force and service officers, thirty Army Air Force officers, thirty Navy and Marine officers, and ten foreign service officers. This student composition established a balance that would remain for at least the next fifty years. The military students were divided into thirds: one-third Army, one-third Air Force (Army Air Corp at that time), and one-third Sea Service (Navy, Marine Corps, and later Coast Guard).

The faculty selected to serve at NWC provided a mixture of backgrounds. Similar to the students, a blend of military and civilian faculty members was desired so that as courses were developed, military and civilian perspectives could be incorporated.[63] To demonstrate the State Department's full support of the new college, a well-regarded State Department representative was hand-selected to join the faculty. Secretary of State Byrnes assigned George F. Kennan to the faculty to act as Hill's deputy for foreign affairs. Kennan was a career diplomat and recognized as one of the State Department's outstanding experts on Russia.[64] The selection of such a prestigious individual for assignment to NWC was an indication of the tremendous support the State Department offered to the institution. Other civilian faculty members were well-known names in educational circles. They included Professors Hardy Dillard, University of Virginia; Bernard Brodie and Sherman Kent, Yale University; and Walter L. Wright, Jr., Princeton University.[65] The civilian faculty had the credentials and backgrounds to add instant prestige to NWC.

The second joint professional military institution that would eventually become a part of NDU had now been established, thanks to Eisenhower's support. The purpose of the new college was to prepare military graduates for the highest echelons of leadership in the armed forces and State Department. Additionally, its purpose was to develop an understanding among the students of capabilities of State Department and other agencies. It was located near the heart of the U.S. government, at the Army War College in Washington, D.C.[66]

The Armed Forces Staff College

ICAF and NWC educated military officers at a senior level. There was still a recognized need to educate mid-grade officers, something accomplished by the Army and Navy Staff College. This section will depict events which led to the establishment of AFSC, an institution designed for mid-grade officers.

NWC was not the only college that evolved from the Army and Navy Staff College. The Richardson Committee's report recommended an intermediate-level school to develop officers capable of preparing and participating in joint operations. However, no detailed planning had been conducted to arrange for a joint college to fulfill that requirement. Recognizing this, General Eisenhower sent the following memorandum to Admiral Nimitz on 17 April 1946:

> As I indicated over the telephone Monday [15 April] there is a need for a school which will conduct short courses of approximately five months duration in joint staff technique and procedures in theatres and joint overseas operations. These courses will be similar to those conducted at ANSOL [Army and Navy Staff College] during the war. I visualize that this school will be operated on a co-equal basis by the Army, Navy and Air. There is a distinct joint necessity for a school of this type for officers of our services prior to attendance at the National War College, thus permitting the scope of this college to embrace national planning and strategy. Since the National War College and the Industrial College are located at an Army installation, I presume you would like to have this new school located at a Naval installation.[67]

This initiative set into motion a working group that would develop a plan for establishing such a college.

Eisenhower's presumption that Nimitz would like to have the new school located at a Naval installation turned out to be correct. Upon receiving the memorandum, Nimitz assigned two admirals to work out the details with their Army counterparts. The committee was directed to identify a wartime facility that would no longer be of use to the Navy. The chosen site was the Receiving Station of the Norfolk Naval Operating Base.[68]

Soon after the working group drafted a plan for the school, a disagreement surfaced between General Eisenhower and Admiral Nimitz concerning the curriculum. Nimitz sent a memorandum to Eisenhower indicating he was unhappy with the scope of the courses as described in a draft of the curriculum. He thought there should be a clear distinction between NWC and the proposed staff college. The War College should teach joint command and stress the development of commanders and doctrines associated with joint operations; these disciplines should not be taught at the new staff college.[69]

The draft directive Nimitz was referring to contained the following objectives:

> To produce officers of all armed services qualified to function effectively as commanders and key staff officers in joint and overseas operations.
>
> To develop commanders and key staff officers of all armed services, qualified to establish theaters of operation and coordinate and direct strategic, tactical, and logistical operations therein.
>
> To foster mutual confidence and understanding among officers of the Army, Navy, and Air Force.
>
> To develop and recommend improvements in standard practice, instruction, and doctrine for joint overseas operations.[70]

Nimitz initially disagreed with all but the third proposed objective. He felt that the other objectives were either accomplished elsewhere or unnecessary.

Eisenhower responded a few days later and stated:

> While I agree that the college must primarily teach joint staff procedure, I believe that the functions of command and staff are inseparable and that the former cannot be ignored in the instruction given the school. Since this is the only college in the school system where the basic mission will be to give instruction on the theater and major joint task force level, it is the only one in which the functions of command and staff on that level can be logically and efficiently taught. I feel that this college should be a prerequisite for entrance into the National War College where selected ground, air and naval officers will be trained for meeting responsibilities in the highest echelons of the armed forces.[71]

Nimitz ended up assenting to Eisenhower's argument and concurred with the proposed objectives.

An appropriate name for the new institution was also negotiated between Nimitz and Eisenhower. Nimitz wanted to ensure that the distinction of its mission was clear by including the word "Staff" in the name for the college. Eisenhower, conveying his belief that there would soon be an additional branch of the armed services, countered Nimitz's proposal of "Army-Navy Staff College" with "Armed Forces College"[72] The special committee of flag and general officers selected by Eisenhower and Nimitz drafted a directive for the new college and submitted it for approval to the Joint Chiefs of Staff. The proposed name, "Armed Forces Staff College," addressed both of the leaders' concerns. The planned scope of instruction did include "study of the organization, composition, and functions of theaters and major joint task forces and responsibilities of the commanders" as Eisenhower had suggested.[73] The Joint Chiefs of Staff accepted the proposal and approved the Armed Forces Staff College on 28 June 1946, a mere two months after Eisenhower's original memorandum. The stated mission of the college was "to train selected officers of the armed forces in joint operations."[74] Similar to the students selected at NWC, the students and faculty selected to attend and teach at the AFSC had equal representation in land, sea, and air forces. The student body and instructors were entirely military because the curriculum was focused on joint military operations. The first class of students arrived in late January 1947 for their five-month course of instruction, which ran from 3 February until 28 June 1947. The students all lived on the 55-acre site that had been used during the war for processing and reassignment of Navy personnel. The U-shaped barracks housed the students and their families and each building was named after a World War II joint land, sea, and air operation such as Sicily, Iwo Jima, and Okinawa.[75] The superintendent of the Naval Academy, Rear Adm. James L. Holloway, spoke to the students during opening ceremonies for the first class. His remarks captured the idea of improving relationships through acculturation. Holloway said: "You officers of the Navy, Army and Marine Corps will work together and play together; your wives and children will live within the same compound and will come out of it as friends, with a mutual understanding and mutual customs."[76] The theme of attaining mutual understanding of different perspectives as part of an educational experience, in and out of the classroom, is the underpinning of "joint" in joint professional military education. The goal of attaining an enhanced appreciation for each other is the major difference between a Service school, such as the Army's Command and General Staff College and a joint school.

A third joint professional military education institution had now been established, again as a result of Eisenhower's support. The Joint Chiefs of Staff had oversight of all three. They were funded independently and operated independently. It was Eisenhower's vision that students would attain one level of knowledge at the AFSC then build upon that knowledge later in their careers when they attended NWC. To build on knowledge would imply close coordination of curriculum development. Operating independently made coordination challenging. This would change once the schools became parts of one university. Although the AFSC was initially not a part of NDU, it joined the institution in 1981.

Summary

Joint professional military education fosters intellectual growth through exposure and understanding of multiple perspectives. Eisenhower understood the importance of this type of education. Today the Joint Forces Staff College (previously the Armed Forces Staff College), National War College, and Industrial College of the Armed Forces educate leaders for the twenty-first century. They are able to accomplish, thanks to the support of Dwight D. Eisenhower.

Improving the education system has been a solution to problems facing the nation and the military. The U.S. military been encouraged to reorganize, reform, and transform—in other words, *change*. Change begins in the mind and that is why education has been the key. To achieve this, joint professional military education contains curriculum components designed to educate students in preparation for working with officers and civilians from other services, agencies, and countries. The birth of the Industrial College may be credited to Davis, Baruch, and others, but the birth of the system should be credited to its graduates. Eisenhower appreciated the joint education he received at the Industrial College. He appreciated it when he was Supreme Allied Commander, Europe, and later when he was commander in chief. A few weeks before he passed away, President Eisenhower wrote a note to the ICAF commandant. He closed the note by stating: "It is my conviction that the educational programs conducted by the [Industrial] College are of the greatest importance in developing the kind of enlightened military and civilian leadership our Nation must have if its purposes and security are to endure."[77] These words are as true today as when Eisenhower penned them from Walter Reed Hospital in 1969, and they are also applicable to the system of joint professional military education.

Notes

1. "The Yale Report of 1828," in L. F. Goodchild and H. S. Wechsler, eds., *ASHE Reader on the History of Higher Education,* 2d ed. (Boston, Mass.: Pearson Custom, 1997), 191-99.

2. Henry H. Shelton, "Chairman of the Joint Chiefs of Staff Instruction on Officer Military Education Policy" (2000), Special Collections, National Defense University Library, Washington, D.C.

3. Ibid.; Richard Cheney, *Professional Military Education: An Asset for Peace and Progress* (Washington, D.C.: Government Printing Office, 1997).

4. Ike Skelton, *Panel on Military Education of the One Hundredth Congress; Report of the House of Representatives Committee on Armed Services,* 21 Apr. 1989 (Washington, D.C.: Government Printing Office, 1989).

5. ICAF was originally established as the Army Industrial College and its name change is addressed later in this paper.

6. Congress changed the name of AFSC to Joint Forces Staff College (JFSC) in 2000.

7. James L. Abrahamson, *The American Home Front: Revolutionary War, Civil War, World War I, World War II* (Washington, D.C.: Government Printing Office, 1983); Alan Gropman, *The Big L.* (Washington, D.C.: Government Printing Office, 1997); Paul Koistinen, *Planning War, Pursuing Peace: The Political Economy of American Warfare, 1920-1939* (Lawrence: University Press of Kansas, 1998).

8. David Lloyd George, *War Memoirs of David Lloyd George 1917-1918* (Boston: Little, Brown, 1936), 452-53.

9. "Annual Report of the Assistant Chief of Staff, Director of Purchase, Storage and Traffic; F.Y. ending June 30, 1919" (1919), Special Collections, NDU Library.

10. Eisenhower, "Lecture to the Army Industrial College by Major D. D. Eisenhower on the History of Planning for Procurement and Industrial Mobilization since the World War" (1931), Special Collections, NDU Library.

11. Francis W. A'Hearn, "The Industrial College of the Armed Forces: Contextual Analysis of an Evolving Mission, 1924-1994, in Education" (Ph.D. diss., Virginia Polytechnic and State University, 1997), 172.

12. Harold W. Thatcher, *Planning for Industrial Mobilization: 1920-1940* (Washington, D.C.: Government Printing Office, 1943).

13. Theodore W. Bauer, *History of the Industrial College of the Armed Forces* (Washington, D.C.: Government Printing Office, 1983).

14. Davis, an outstanding tennis player during his undergraduate days at Harvard, is better known today for the sports-celebrated trophy he donated (the Davis Cup) than he is for being one of the founding fathers of the Industrial College.

15. Terrence Gough, "Origins of the Army Industrial College," *Armed Forces and Society* 17 (1991).

16. "War Department General Orders No. 7," 25 Feb. 1924, 1, Special Collections, NDU Library.

17. Brookings founded a graduate school, later to become a part of the Brookings Institute, the same year the Army Industrial College was established.

18. H. B. Yoshpe, "Bernard M. Baruch: Civilian Godfather of the Military M-Day Plan," *Military Affairs* 29 (1965), 15.

19. Bernard Baruch, The War Industries Board, in "Lecture at the Army War College, 12 February 1924" (1924), Special Collections, NDU Library.

20. Yoshpe, "Bernard M. Baruch," 15.

21. A'Hearn, *Industrial College of the Armed Forces.*

22. Eisenhower, "Remarks by President Dwight D. Eisenhower at Dedication of New ICAF Building Sept. 6, 1960-10:30 a.m." (1960), Special Collections, NDU Library; and Letter to Lieutenant General John Hardy, 14 Feb. 1969, ibid.

23. Eisenhower, "Remarks by President Dwight D. Eisenhower at Dedication of New ICAF Building."

24. Eisenhower, "Lecture to the Army Industrial College" (1931).

25. A'Hearn, *Industrial College of the Armed Forces.*

26. Bauer, *History of the Industrial College of the Armed Forces.*

27. F. R. Sweeney, "The Army and Navy Staff College," *Command and General Staff School Military Review* 23 (1943):9-10.

28. John W. Chambers II, ed., *The Oxford Companion to American Military History* (Oxford, England: Oxford University Press, 1999); William J. Lucas, *Joint Chiefs of Staff Special Historical Study: Role and Functions of the Joint Chiefs of Staff a Chronology* (Washington, D.C.: Historical Division, Joint Secretariat, Joint Chiefs of Staff, 1987).

29. H. H. Arnold, "Memorandum Proposing United States War College" (1942), 2, Joint Chiefs of Staff Library, Pentagon, Arlington, Va.

30. Ibid.

31. George C. Marshall, "Memorandum for the Joint Chiefs of Staff: Establishment of a United States War (Staff) College, JCS Document" (1943), Special Collections, NDU Library.

32. O. R. Kinworthy, "Minutes of Meeting Held in Room 113, the Combined Chiefs of Staff Building, on Wednesday, May 12, 1943 at 0930" (1943), ibid.

33. H. H. Arnold, "Address to the First Class of the Army and Navy Staff College" (1943), ibid.

34. Ernest J. King, *Address to the First Class of the Army and Navy Staff College* (5 Aug. 1943), 7, ibid.

35. Paul Reading, "History of the Army and Navy Staff College" (1972), unpublished manuscript, ibid.

36. "JCS 962/2: Joint Chiefs of Staff General Plan for Postwar Joint Education of the Armed Forces," 22 June 1945, ibid.

37. "Report of the Joint Chiefs of Staff Special Committee for Reorganization of National Defense," in *Committee on Military Affairs, United States Senate* (Washington, D.C.: Government Printing Office, 1945), 786.

38. Ibid., 416

39. A. Leviero, "Merger Row Heads for White House," *New York Times,* 5 Nov. 1945, 11.

40. "Statement of the General of the Army Dwight D. Eisenhower before the Committee on Military Affairs on November 16," in *Hearings before the Committee on Military Affairs, United States Senate, Seventy-ninth Congress, First Session* (Washington, D.C.: Government Printing Office, 1945), 359-82.

41. "Statement of the Fleet Admiral Chester W. Nimitz before the Committee on Military Affairs on November 17," ibid., 392.

42. *Public Papers of the Presidents of the United States: Harry S. Truman* (Washington, D.C.: Government Printing Office, 1961). Quotations from 547, 550, 554.

43. Ibid.

44. A'Hearn, *Industrial College of the Armed Forces.*

45. "Report of the Joint Chiefs of Staff Special Committee," 433.

46. "JCS 962/2" (1945), 32.

47. Ibid., 19.

48. Ibid., 32.

49. Harry W. Hill, "Memorandum on the Outline of the Curriculum and Mission of the Postwar Army and Navy Staff College, JCS Document," 22 Jan. 1946, Special Collections, NDU Library.

50. "Report of the Joint Chiefs of Staff Special Committee for Reorganization of National Defense" (1945).

51. "Statement of the Fleet Admiral Chester W. Nimitz before the Committee on Military Affairs on November 17" (1945), 393.

52. "Statement of the General of the Army Dwight D. Eisenhower before the Committee on Military Affairs on November 16" (1945), 370-71.

53. The Joint Chiefs of Staff worked throughout the war without legislative sanction or even formal presidential definition. They were officially sanctioned in the National Security Act of 1947.

54. "JCS 962/2."

55. John W. Masland and Laurence I. Radway, *Soldiers and Scholars: Military Education and National Policy* (Princeton, N.J.: Princeton University Press, 1957).

56. Leonard T. Gerow, "Report of War Department Military Education Board on Educational System for Officers of the Army," in *War Department: 99* (1946), 27, Special Collections, NDU Library.

57. Ibid., 7.

58. Masland and Radway, *Soldiers and Scholars.*

59. Harry W. Hill, "Memorandum: Postwar Joint Education of the Armed Forces," 4 Dec. 1945, Special Collections, NDU Library.

60. Hill, "Memorandum on the Outline of the Curriculum."

61. "War Department: General Orders No. 51 (GO 51) [AGO 3857B—June 696323—46]," 10 June 1946, Special Collections, NDU Library.

62. "Annual Report of the National War College 1946-1947" (1947), Special Collections, NDU Library.

63. Harry W. Hill, Letter to the Honorable James F. Byrnes, 26 Jan. 1946, and Memorandum, State Department Participation in Postwar ANSCOL, 25 Jan. 1946, ibid.; War Department, Letter to the Honorable James F. Byrnes. 26 Jan. 1946, ibid.

64. G. D. Horner, "State and War Teamplay May Bolster U.S. Policy," *Washington Star,* 7 Sept. 1946, 1.

65. Ibid.

66. The name of the Army post did not change until 1948. Until then, the National War College was located at the Army War College. This frequently caused confusion until the post was renamed in honor of Lt. Gen. Lesley J. McNair, U.S. Army, who was killed in action on 25 July 1944.

67. Eisenhower, "Memorandum for Admiral Nimitz: Establishment of the Armed Forces Staff College," 17 Apr. 1946, 1, JFSC Library, Norfolk, Va.

68. Alvin D. Whitley, *Armed Forces Staff College: Command History 1946-1981* (Norfolk, Va.: National Defense University Press, 1981).

69. Chester W. Nimitz, "Memorandum for General Eisenhower on the Project for the Armed Forces College," 3 June 1946, JFSC Library, Norfolk, Va.

70. Whitley, *Armed Forces Staff College.*

71. Eisenhower, "Memorandum for Admiral Nimitz on establishment of the Armed Forces College," 12 June 1946, 1, JFSC Library, Norfolk, Va.

72. Nimitz, "Memorandum for General Eisenhower on the Project for the Armed Forces College," 3 June 1946; Eisenhower, "Memorandum for Admiral Nimitz on Establishment of the Armed Forces College," 12 June 1946.

73. "Joint Chiefs of Staff Meeting on the Proposed Directive for the Armed Forces Staff College, JCS meeting 962/21" (1946), Special Collections, NDU Library.

74. Ibid.

75. Whitley, *Armed Forces Staff College.*

76. James L. Holloway, "Remarks at Armed Forces Staff College Opening Exercises," 3 Feb. 1947, JFSC Library, Norfolk, Va.

77. Eisenhower, Letter to Lieutenant General John Hardy, 14 Feb. 1969.

Appendix A

Eisenhower and National Security for the 21st Century: Roundtable and Discussion

This discussion was conducted on 28 January 2005 as part of the symposium hosted at the National Defense University's Industrial College of the Armed Forces. The panel members were former staff secretary and defense liaison officer to the president (1954–61) Gen. Andrew J. Goodpaster, United States Army (Ret.); Dr. Louis Galambos, Johns Hopkins University, co-editor of *The Papers of Dwight David Eisenhower;* and Gen. Montgomery C. Meigs, United States Army (Ret.), The panel was chaired by former national security advisor to the president (1973–75) Lt. Gen. Brent Scowcroft, United States Air Force (Ret.), with closing remarks made by Lt. Gen. Michael Dunn, United States Air Force, President, National Defense University.

As general and president, Eisenhower took great interest in the intellectual development of the officer corps, asserting the importance of both professional military education and advanced education at the best civilian institutions. That legacy endures and flourishes. Generals Goodpaster, Scowcroft, and Meigs graduated from West Point in 1939, 1947, and 1967; and during their military careers earned doctorates at Princeton, Columbia, and the University of Wisconsin, respectively.

General Scowcroft: It is a particular honor for me to participate in the symposium and especially to chair such a distinguished panel. I have had two role models as I have worked my way from being a West Point cadet to a long involvement in public affairs. The first role model was President Eisenhower. He gave me my college diploma and my commission as a second lieutenant. I went from that to reading *Crusade in Europe,* and I became a devotee of him. The second is General Andy Goodpaster, who was my commandant at the National War College and whom I revere as the epitome of brilliant, selfless service to his country at the cutting edge of many of the more vexing problems our great country has faced. So I am truly honored to be here.

As I thumb through this impressive document on Eisenhower's legacy supplied by the Eisenhower Memorial Commission [*Eisenhower's Legacy: The General, The President, The Public Servant,* ed. Louis Galambos, 2003], I was struck again, as I have been so many times in the past, by the prodigious breadth of Eisenhower's interests, his impact, and of course his legacy. As we grapple with our own challenging problems in a very different era, there is scarcely one issue that we confront which does not contain Eisenhower's fingerprints—either in substance, in structure, or in conceptualization. We have had two-and-a-half days and five sessions: Eisenhower and the Changing National Security Environment; Eisenhower, Science and the National Security Environment; Eisenhower's Organization of the Intelligence Community; and Eisenhower—International Perspectives. Our panel will bring all this together for you.

Briefly, Dr. Galambos will give you the whole Eisenhower: a wrap-up of the specific sessions into a picture of Eisenhower as a decision-maker. General Goodpaster is going to personalize the legacy as only he can do. General Meigs will project that legacy into the world that we face today.

Dr. Galambos: I'm very glad to be here. I have taken eight pages of notes, and I've been writing furiously. As that indicates, I have learned a lot myself. And it seems to me as I look back over our program that there were three points of major importance to General and President Eisenhower. One was to be informed: to have the knowledge needed to take a course of action. That was incredibly important to Eisenhower given his staff experiences and his experience with information as a military commander. The second point was to be prepared, to be ready: to have the resources you needed and the organization you needed in order to take action. Finally, good choices depended upon judgment and experience, and Eisenhower was prepared to trust himself on both counts. The papers that dealt with methodology, with space exploration, with the intelligence community, with overhead spy satellites, with the National Security Administration—all of them reflected Eisenhower's interest in having good information, in being informed, in ensuring that the people that advised him had a full understanding of the issue and making that understanding known to Eisenhower. Going through the JCS papers and reading his hand-written notes on the side of them makes obvious how important it was to him to have complete information.

A lot of what Eisenhower did, it seems to me, reflected a distinction that economists and insurers make between uncertainty and risk. Uncertainty can't be predicted. You can't make odds on it; you can't make book on it; you can't make an investment based on it. Because you don't know when it is going to happen, why it's going to happen, or what is going to happen. With risk you can make a calculation of the probability. You can understand what is likely to happen and make an informed decision about when it might happen. Much of what Eisenhower did was to convert uncertainty into risk, so that a reasoned decision could be made on the basis of the available information. It was never perfect. Eisenhower knew it would never be perfect. He knew what terrible forces were available, and if he made mistakes he knew what the price could be.

Reflected in Eisenhower's whole approach to the presidency was an interest in being prepared: prepared in the right way to deal with the real world that was there then at that time—not the world that existed in the First World War or even in the Second, but the world that existed in the 1950s. Eisenhower wanted to be prepared for that, and he wanted to be prepared with an asterisk on it. He was thinking of the long term. Being prepared meant being prepared without destroying the American economy. The economy ultimately was our base and our strength. The economy was particularly important to Eisenhower because of the pressure to seek total security. Eisenhower had a good strong sense from the beginning that total security was impossible. Always, he wanted to be prepared, but he wanted to be prepared for the long term— and he was thinking of one hundred years, I believe; he was thinking that we might be in the Cold War for a hundred years. I don't think that Eisenhower foresaw the end of it coming as soon as it did.

So he wanted to be really prepared for the long term. But even when he had the information and had the force, he had to decide when and where to use it. And that Eisenhower knew was a judgment and a decision. He could get all the staff reports, he could hold all the discussions. The cabinet could come together and make all its opinions known,but in the end one person had to decide, and Eisenhower knew who that one person was. He never had any doubt about that. As president, he made those decisions. He took the responsibility for them and he was prepared intellectually and morally to do that.

In dealing with the Soviet Union, Eisenhower believed he had to be firm and at the same time had to keep talking. He didn't want to go to a bogus conference; he didn't want to get everybody wound up because a meeting was scheduled. The British pressed him to have a lot of conferences; they always wanted to talk at the top level. A lot of politics goes into summitry, and Eisenhower was always very restrained. He said, "You've got to really be prepared to make progress. I want to know ahead of time what we are going to do and what we are going to talk about and what we are likely to achieve so we just don't go and get headlines." A long time ago, John Kenneth Galbraith described the "no business conference"—when the only business is to hold a conference. They just take pictures of important people going into the White House and it reassures the public that somebody is doing something. But summits set expectations very high and Eisenhower resisted that.

With China, Eisenhower again recognized that he should be firm, and there he was firm to the point where it caused problems with America's allies. They were understandably very worried about the offshore islands in particular. Again, Eisenhower was making a very precise judgment call. He decided that the issue of the islands was where he had to draw that line. At the same time, there was never any doubt in his mind about the importance of Europe to the United States in holding the alliance together. But he saw that process as reciprocal. It was very important to him to keep talking. One of the things that was so insulting to him about Suez was that there wasn't consultation ahead of time. Force was exercised without talking first in the context of maintaining the alliance.

In part we are judging Eisenhower the man. In part we are judging choices he made in situations that are a little more obvious some fifty years later than they were at the time. These were all questions of risk, all questions based on a certain amount of limited information, and finally in the end questions of whether to use force and how to use it.

General Scowcroft: Thank you very much Dr. Galambos. General Goodpaster?

General Goodpaster: First, let me applaud the coverage, the keen insights, and the depth which this symposium has afforded. It is extremely important. The Germans have a saying that the devil is always in the details—no problem is solved until the particulars have been dealt with. I am going to discuss how we went about dealing with the breadth of Eisenhower's opportunities—why specific decisions were made, and with what results.

Four key points, in my view, provide a framework useful for understanding Eisenhower's approach that can be of lasting value. These were first, the goals or objectives that his administration should and would serve; second, the *modus operandi*, or operating machinery that he would use; third, the key policies, programs, and actions by which he sought to serve his objectives and fulfill his responsibilities; and fourth, a very brief assessment of principles, successes, and failures and with a comment, in some cases, on the reason for failure.

Let us begin with the guiding objective of Eisenhower's administration. This emerges more and more clearly, and explicitly, as a phrase in his own words: "Now wait a minute boys. Let's ask what is best for America." It may sound like a banality, but it was far from it. Eisenhower welcomed, insisted upon, full and open discussion with no non-concurrence through silence. But he would not be driven by "second order" or "parochial," terms he sometimes used almost as epithets, objects of lesser standing and lesser rank—not by those of the military-industrial complex or the scientific elite; not even by a military-industrial-congressional iron triangle when it departed from the country's well thought out ends. Eisenhower took his lead from Lincoln: his presidential powers should serve a government of the people, by the people, and for the people—not lesser convictions, special interests, political parties, or even personal reelection except as these might serve a broader, truer national purpose.

Second, Eisenhower set up and made use of carefully thought out *modus operandi*, or operating organizations, drawn out of his experience in Britain during World War II, in North Africa in the Mediterranean, the complex and massive cross-channel operation, and the attack through Western Europe. He made use as well of his observation of the U.S. government under Franklin Roosevelt, when he himself served with General MacArthur, the Army Chief of Staff. He shaped many of the *modus operandi's* main lines on his way back from Korea where he had gone immediately following his election. He was accompanied aboard the cruiser U.S.S. *Helena* by many of his future administration leaders, who took part in this work.

Four weekly meetings were the backbone of Eisenhower's organizational process. Tuesday featured a meeting with congressional leaders, as many as ten to a dozen as I recall, most often just of his own party but bipartisan whenever foreign matters were involved. On Wednesday morning he held a full-blown press conference, following a discussion in depth with senior staff, many of whom had carefully canvassed principal departments and agencies, especially their heads, for their views on topics of priority and importance. On Thursday came the NSC meeting, reflecting especially the preparatory work of the planning group and the actions of the operations coordination board. The papers considered, meticulously developed by the planning groups, customarily contained financial annexes to ensure that ends and means were closely and realistically joined. Finally, on Friday, came the cabinet meeting, normally devoted to issues of a domestic nature. Often focused, in Lincoln's terms, on the things people could not do by themselves or should well do by themselves, these meetings took up grave social issues as well, bearing on the well-being of America's people and notably its minorities. In and around these set-piece events, all disciplined by prepared agendas, carefully developed policy analyses and recommendations, were clusters of individual meetings, extending from my daily intelligence update and operations report to discussions in depth, quite typically, with the secretary of state or the president's economic advisors. In all of this there was to be no non-concurrence through silence. This president was entitled to, and expected to hear, the full range of his responsible associates' views before making his decisions.

The third key point was the substantive product or output: the payoff at the level of action. Such actions included major policy-setting directions, of which the Solarium Project and Atoms for Peace were typical initiatives. Eisenhower's response to the surprise British-French-Israeli seizure of Egypt's Suez Canal in 1956 was another example. There were in addition a myriad of initiatives, many bilateral, that sought to implement the broad purposes and principles that Eisenhower staked out. On occasion, notably on the domestic side, it was necessary for him to meet privately with Sam Rayburn, leader of the Democrat-controlled house, and Lyndon Johnson, leader of the Democratically controlled Senate, to dislodge jammed-up issues. Often, it helped give to Johnson the public credit—neither Rayburn nor Eisenhower felt the need for it.

Under Eisenhower's steady hand, the dangerous intensity of the nuclear-armed Cold War confrontation was reduced, notably at the Geneva summit in 1955. Tensions and differences continued, in particular over Germany, but avenues of communications improved and expanded. A sense that with restraint and wisdom, nuclear holocaust could be avoided increasingly took root. The idea of a date of maximum danger dropped from sight, as did proposals for forcing a showdown. Controversies and disputes continued, over Germany most particularly, in China and outlying areas such as Cuba, Indonesia, and the like. In these situations, Eisenhower's own injunction—to "be slow to pick up the sword," reserving that for great and direct threat or attack—had a telling effect. In fact, he was anticipating the argument of his successor Ronald Reagan, that nuclear war could not be won and should never be fought. To accomplish that result by safeguarding the security of America and his allies stood foremost among his goals.

But assessment of the aggregate of successes and failures shows a more mixed picture, and this is the fourth key point deserving to be taken into account. Eastern Europe still lay under the Soviet boot. Germany continued divided. A hostile China lay across the Taiwan Straits. Cuba had turned against us and was trying to foment the spread of communism into Central and South America. The breakup of the Paris summit in mid-1960 over the U-2 affair, clumsily handled by the United States—a clumsiness in which I myself had a part—was a particularly grievous setback to Eisenhower's hopes and goals. His invitation to visit Russia, to which he looked forward eagerly for personal and foreign policy reasons, was quickly withdrawn. In the 1960 presidential election, the candidate he hoped would succeed him was defeated. But on a higher plane, there was much in which Eisenhower could and did take pride and satisfaction. He had answered his country's call when he well knew that it needed him. He felt that he had met his responsibilities as our people's president—responsibilities always uppermost in his mind. The nuclear threat that could destroy the world was held in containment. During the last morning of his presidency, when he and I talked alone, he spoke of the great pride he felt that in the eight years of his service, our security was maintained; no territory was lost by us or our allies; and above all, that this was done without the loss of American troops in combat.

General Scowcroft: Thank you very much. General Meigs?

General Meigs: Well, as someone who is new to the study of Dwight D. Eisenhower, it is a real challenge to follow all of you, and certainly my old boss at West Point, General Goodpaster. But as someone who has run one or two fairly large organizations and is a student of decision theory, it is also good to think back on what has been talked about during this symposium, what is coming out in the new, historical treatments of President Eisenhower, and what this research means for how executive decisions should be made.

In that context, some things truly stand out about President Eisenhower. For instance, as a manager and trainer of his executive team—and General Goodpaster alluded to this—on the *Helena,* joined by those figures in Hawaii that didn't go to Korea, President-elect Eisenhower was in fact training his new team. Prior to that, he had had a meeting of his new cabinet and his key advisors and introduced the fact that he was going to read his inaugural speech to them. And he did, and they clapped, and he said, "no, you don't understand. I appreciate your applause but I want you to get out your blue pencils because I want you to tear this thing apart!" And that was the verb that he used. Now think about that for a minute. You are a newly appointed cabinet member, successful, ambitious, confident. And here is someone of the stature of Dwight D. Eisenhower, and he hands you *his* paper and says I want *you* to tear this apart for *me.* And this is his opening act with his new team.

I'm drawn to the phrase "no non-concurrence by silence." And reading through the primary materials of, for example, the discussions of Indochina conveys a wonderful sense of Eisenhower as a person who used raucous, cacophonous debate among his subordinates to help do what Dr. Galambos is talking about: to try to reduce the uncertainties of decision. There is that defining meeting where Admiral Radford—one can almost see him pounding on the table about the need to intervene, to go help Dien Bien Phu, and President Eisenhower says, "This is a decision for statesmen." Now, those of you that are wearing, or have worn, a uniform will know, that when a senior political official makes a statement like that, that you have been told, "thank you very much, that's enough." And it was done in a very deft, impersonal way. When General Eisenhower took a few statesmen into the other room to work out the final elements of the decision, he took Radford with him which meant, "I asked you to stop, but you are still on the team"—a very subtle, powerful signal not lost on the rest.

The next lesson to emerge is Eisenhower's tremendous self-discipline and self-lessness. To send the kind of subtle signals that he sent to Admiral Radford at such a difficult time took—for a man with something of a temper—a fair amount of self-control and discipline. Also, Eisenhower was a man who never said anything negative about colleagues, associates, and other officials in public, or at least tried not to. In his professional, most intimate circle, yes, but always warning them that, "This stays here. We cannot have destruction of goodwill because it takes too long to earn it back." And Eisenhower never asked for credit. General Goodpaster gave us the wonderful example of Sam Rayburn and President Eisenhower making sure that the absolutely least secure person in that triangle—Lyndon Johnson—got the credit for problem-solving. And consider service to nation—again General Goodpaster reflected that to us: General Eisenhower not really wanting to be president; yet being called, served.

Finally, there remains this tantalizing idea of the hidden hand. Again we go to the decision about not intervening in Indochina. As the debate rumbled on, President Eisenhower said to Radford and Dulles, "I want you to go brief the key senators and congressmen." I have to believe in the back of his mind he sensed what was probably going to happen, because when Dulles and Radford come back, they say, "Boy, this is going to be a hard sell." There was no political capital required to make that decision. With some presidents, with Eisenhower as with Kennedy and Johnson, if you watch their decisions there is always a right limit and a left limit, and they seek the middle way in order to buy the time required to convert some of the uncertainties into risks. Critics of the Clinton administration frequently describe non-participation of the president while decisions are being kicked around. For example, for months and months and months as frustrations grow over America's Bosnia policy, the president is not involved in the debate. That was never the case with Eisenhower. Even when he seemed quiescent in public he would be fostering within his circle the debate as a way of generating better courses of action. And as Dr. Galambos points out, Eisenhower was never reluctant to make the decision when the time had come.

As a soldier, to me Eisenhower is at his best when General Strong comes in at the beginning of the Battle of the Bulge and says, "We're seeing this unit, and this unit, this unit, this is starting to happen." And immediately Eisenhower says, "this is a big attack. Get the 101st Airborne back, get the 7th Armored Division moving." That shows a command of operational art and a capacity for decision of a very high order. And then he has to do something which is extremely difficult. He has to change the subordination of his armies, and he gives Montgomery control of the whole northern flank—Montgomery who is someone with whom Eisenhower did not have, shall we say, a comfortable relationship, someone he is very close to firing later on. And he does this over the strong objection of his subordinate, good friend, and classmate General Omar Bradley, knowing the pain that this is causing. Why does he do it? Because Montgomery is an excellent operational commander and it is the right thing, operationally, to do.

Now to me, these behaviors speak of being informed, being prepared, and never being afraid to make the decision when it is time. This is a kind of theory and practice of leadership that we might well do to distill, to ensure that it leavens the discussion of decision theory and executive decision as we go forward.

General Scowcroft: Thank you General Meigs. We are now ready to take your questions.

Audience Member: In view of the fact that this whole symposium has been, in a sense, a reevaluation of Dwight Eisenhower's presidency, I wonder whether any of the members of the panel would care to suggest why there has been for so long a feeling that he was a slumbering president, a do-nothing president, and that he was spending his time on the golf fairways, whereas, in point of fact, we found out today that he was quite different.

General Scowcroft: At the end of the Eisenhower administration, I had some tinges about that, too, thinking that I had expected more than I got. And then as events evolved, and as one started to look back, I think the reason was the way he managed; that is, the sort of hidden-hand approach; not out in front, not chest-pounding, but getting things done, maneuvering people around so that the decision came naturally. And he took a country that, in the early 1950s, was alarmed by the emergences of the Soviet threat and nuclear weapons and so on—we were talking about "date-certains" for maximum peril and preemptive strikes—and he calmed it down. And he calmed America down through the way that he operated. He put us in shape for the long run. The Cold War was not an acute crisis that had to be solved today; it was something we had to learn to live with. As people like Dr. Galambos get into the record and it comes out, I think it fortifies that view. Here was a man who was focused on results.

Dr. Galambos: There is a great deal of political energy at work casting an image. Newspaper writers have to have a hook for every article, and golf and the president was a good hook. It worked pretty well because it stuck in all of our minds. But America had experienced a long period of Democratic control of Congress and the presidency. and I think that set the stage. A Republican administration was a sharp change. Eisenhower recognized that he had to deal with a Democratic congress; he recognized that he had to hold his party together and that was a major problem (you remember the Bricker amendment). And he was having a hard time holding the Republican coalition together. If he got out front too far, he was going to break down the relationships he needed for support. I think that helps explain the manner in which Eisenhower approached some of those domestic political controversies. That hidden-hand kind of operation didn't always work very well. Although there is disagreement about this, I don't think it worked very well with Senator McCarthy, for example. I think there a different kind of leadership was needed.

General Goodpaster: Maybe I could add a word to this. I'll give you some Eisenhower quotes. When things were moving a little too fast and loose, he'd say, "Now boys, let's not make our mistakes in a hurry." I once saw an article by one of the two Alsop brothers, who often wrote rather sharply. This time they started from a mistaken premise and proceeded by taking into account much less than the full breadth that Eisenhower had in mind. I remarked that I found something ought to be said about this, and the president said, "Forget it, Andy. We are not going to dance at the end of their string." Now these are aphorisms, but when you put them together as a complex, you have a man who was prepared to step up to his responsibilities. He stressed that word repeatedly to me, and especially to me. He'd say, "Look at that man. How does he take responsibility? Willingly? And then having taken it, can he handle it?" We came back to that over and over and over again. And it was his sense of responsibility that brought Eisenhower into the White House. He knew that his country needed him, and it sure enough did.

General Meigs: If you go back and read Richard Neustadt's *Presidential Power*— the original 1960 edition, not the later revisions, it's very critical of Eisenhower. A whole generation of historians was influenced by this view of the president as a weak executive. Remember Neustadt was an advisor to President Kennedy during the transition. One of the people in the room when the advice was being given was Arthur Schlesinger, Jr. At the same time, as General Goodpaster has pointed out, President Eisenhower had a very deep understanding of the "Pig Rule." The Pig Rule is never wrestle with a pig because he has a ball and you wind up washing a heck of a lot of manure out of your hair.

General Goodpaster: Let me make, if I may, one comment about Dick Neustadt. When President Kennedy came in, his administration developed the idea that the thing to do was to scrap the structure that Eisenhower had. That lasted until the Bay of Pigs. Then Kennedy talked to Eisenhower, and essentially Eisenhower's message was that he was operating blindly, without the kind of analysis that was very much needed. And Neustadt had the grace to say, "We aimed at Eisenhower but we hit Kennedy when we did that." Gradually the base structure redeveloped. But Eisenhower had anticipated the need for it, and was the first to put it together. It wasn't perfect and there were things that were left over at the end of his administration, particularly the U-2 affair, where the importance of asking the "what if?" questions was brought out with tremendous clarity. But it was in place and functioning.

Dr. Galambos: Add one thing. When this image was taking shape, remember, Eisenhower truly, truly believed in democracy. And he believed, and he had good reason to believe from the elections, that he had the people with him. And that was extremely important. Whatever his public image, Eisenhower knew that the people were with him. And the other thing he knew was that what he had to do was make big decisions on really big issues, like not destroying the world. And he knew that if he did those right, then the history would come out right. And finally, the historians have come around. It has taken some years, but the more information that comes out and the more presidents we have, the better Eisenhower looks.

Audience Member: General Goodpaster mentioned that, one of General Eisenhower's last words to you at the end of his term was that he was proud that we had never been involved in a war on his watch. And as we know, he did draw back from any intervention in Indochina. But during his terms in office, we were very close to conflict over the offshore islands: Taiwan, Matsu. It has been often said that the administration considered tactical nuclear weapons as just another bullet in the arsenal. Some have said as well that our conventional forces were drawn down in that period. Had we gotten into a conflict, as much as we tried to avoid it, was not the risk greater of it getting out of hand because we didn't have the conventional robust forces that we had later?

General Goodpaster: Eisenhower thought that the nature of war had changed forever, but his great aim was to reach beyond that. He knew the suffering, the losses, war brought. It had tremendous impact on him when he thought about what the Russians had been through. And he really had a deep conviction that with wisdom and restraint we could work our way through the confrontations peacefully.

Audience Member: What about the vice president in this situation in terms of national security? Can the panel offer perspective on the role that the vice president played in the discussions involving national security and other topics covered by this conference?

General Goodpaster: Vice President Nixon participated in several of those sessions that I described. Eisenhower himself always tried to stay at arms-length from much of that, but he had respect for the judgment of the vice president and I have to say that he found no inclination on the part of the vice president to leap into conflict.

Dr. Galambos: At the time there was a general picture of Secretary Dulles out front and Eisenhower playing golf. But after reading the presidential papers day by day, you realize just how firmly President Eisenhower had control over every decision that was made about national security. From the papers, the vice president's role was limited to two areas in particular. One was to give political advice where it was needed, particularly in dealing with Congress, and with interest groups in particular. The military-industrial complex was an interest group to Eisenhower, and he hated it, because they put their own interest ahead of the public interest. His whole life was dedicated to serving the public interest. That was what he thought should be the first order of importance, and so he left a lot of the secondary work to Nixon.

Audience Member: It seems to me that on practically ever issue that we've had papers—whether it's intelligence, or operations, or running the White House, or foreign policy—the current administration suffers by comparison with the Eisenhower administration. And to keep it non-partisan, so does practically every other administration in between. Was the Eisenhower administration a model for the conduct of national security and foreign affairs? Have we not seen its like since, or are we exaggerating these issues?

General Meigs: First of all, we have not had a president elected since President Eisenhower who had the tough schooling in executive leadership that did he and the very extensive knowledge of his counterparts all over the world. He knew Churchill, he knew de Gaulle, he knew Adenauer; he had a sense of the Russians. By comparison Jack Kennedy, a very talented, young, bright senator, had nothing near the case-hardening that President Eisenhower had. President Johnson with his amazing emotional intelligence and total insecurity, was surrounded by very bright and sur- prisingly syncophatic people whom it seems he was always leading to the decision he had already made. Jimmy Carter had one term as governor. Ronald Reagan, interest- ingly, was perhaps akin to Eisenhower in his confidence in what he was doing, but had not nearly the experience in running large, complex organizations. Nor had Reagan sustained the kind of pressures that Eisenhower had to sustain in North Africa, in Sicily, in managing the shift from the priority in the Mediterranean Theatre to the European Theatre, in telling Churchill "no" on Churchill's desire to cancel the inva- sion of southern France, Operation Dragoon [Anvil]; or in dealing with Montgomery and his other troublesome British subordinates.

Very few of the people we have elected to the presidency since and very few of the people they have selected as their key advisors have had the seasoning of Presi- dent Eisenhower and a number of his advisors. Robert McNamara had been president of Ford for about three months before he was picked to be secretary of defense. We are not going to have another national experience like World War II which would generate that type of a cauldron for the development and tempering of leadership. In the current administration, a number of officials do have fairly extensive experience in government in times of crisis. Yet the surprising thing is that they don't develop a process. They have an extremely intuitive style of leadership and decision—arguably as well a very narrow decision perspective; a very narrow decision horizon, and a very ideologically centered decision process. And that is troubling for a country that is as dynamic, talented, and broad-based as this one is.

General Scowcroft: Let me add just a small point there. I think that most of our administrations are reflections of the president and of the president's experience in the way he uses people. And I don't think we have had a president with greater experience than Eisenhower. I would say that the one that comes closest was George Bush, Sr., who was ambassador to the UN, ambassador to China, ran the CIA, and was vice president. Even more important is the way a president uses the people around him. It matters, of course, whether those people are smart, experienced, and so on. But it also matters how the president processes advice.

Audience Member: In writing my book on the Eisenhower national security policy in the early 1990s [Saki Dockrill, *Eisenhower's New Look National Security Policy,* 1996], my impression was that many Army officers felt betrayed by the way Eisenhower set up his national security policy. Although historians—including myself—praise Eisenhower as a very efficient, very pragmatic leader, does the United States Army have any kind of reappraisal of Eisenhower or does it still feel that Eisenhower as a president was not quite as good as Eisenhower as a general?

General Meigs: I think there is great respect for him. The way he is taught in the military school system is as a great captain. Now to perhaps underwrite the parochialism of military education, not much time is spent on Eisenhower as a president. And General Goodpaster is certainly a lot better versed in this to talk about the feelings of senior Army officers having to cut back so far and depend so much on technologies in which they weren't all that comfortable.

General Goodpaster: When I was a staff officer in the Pentagon I got the assignment—when Eisenhower came in as the chief of staff—of setting up a small group of not very senior officers who would begin to think through the range of implications of the new weapons, including the nuclear weapons, that had come on the scene. This was constantly in his mind. Eisenhower had great respect, great knowledge, of the weight of past thought and experience. He had respect for it. But he also had a strong view that there were changes that had by no means been thought through. Part of his education under General Marshall was a favorite questions of General Marshall's, "Now are you confident that you have thought this through?" Well, Eisenhower was a thinker-through.

Dr. Galambos: I want to say that as chief of staff of the United States Army he received a memorandum from a person with a distinguished record, proposing that we should not allow the cavalry to be dismounted because the Soviets might invade through Mexico and we'd need the horses.

Audience Member: A question about the Bay of Pigs. If the CIA and the Cuban émigrés had accelerated their planning and they were ready to go during the Eisenhower administration, would the invasion have taken place and what would the outcome have been?

General Goodpaster: Well, I'll take a little refuge in saying that is pretty theoretical. Eisenhower had a couple of experiences early where people had gotten into some clandestine operations that had not been thought through, and then finally came to him and said we should use our regular forces. He had pretty good control over his temper most of the time, but on one occasion he said, "The time to have thought about that was long ago. We are in it, now we have to deal with what we got. But let's not get into these things again."

Audience Member: The relationship of Dwight D. Eisenhower and his military advisors and his CIA director was fundamentally different than that between President Kennedy, and Dulles, and his joint chiefs of staff. Dwight D. Eisenhower would never have countenanced the military advice on the Bay of Pigs operation that was given to President Kennedy. I mean the idea of landing the force seventy miles from the mountains and saying, blithely, "Well, if they get defeated they can always slip away and go be guerillas in the mountains," as an operational planning concept. I think the relationship between the military advisors and the president was such that the advice would have been better and less contemptuous on the part of the JCS. And secondly, he would have sniffed out all of the goofy things that the CIA was doing and if he didn't have one of those classic explosions of temper he certainly would have asked them to go away and come back with something better or to not come back at all.

Audience Member: It's important to understand that the Chiefs that Kennedy had at the time of the Bay of Pigs were Eisenhower's Chiefs. And the problem was not in the Chiefs; the problem was in the way the Kennedy administration used the Chiefs at that time. The Chiefs were not cut into the CIA planning, they were never given the complete CIA plan. Essentially, the Chiefs were told, "Look at this little bit, give us your opinion; look at that little bit, give us your opinion." Kennedy canceled the plan to go up into the mountains in case of defeat because it would be too public as far as Dean Rusk, the secretary of state, was concerned. The Chiefs were told, "Okay, the good plan is off the table, look at these other possible landing sites and tell us which is the best." They picked the Bay of Pigs and they said, "It is the best of the ones we've seen, but it is not nearly as good as the plan you have just canceled." So I think it is important to realize not to make superficial statements about the Chiefs without really knowing what the process was at that time.

General Meigs: Go read the transcripts. There is this wonderful point at which the Chiefs—not the Army Chief of Staff and not the Chairman—but the Commandant, the Air Force Chief of Staff, and the CNO are in the Situation Room having a conversation they think is off the record, and the tape is still running. Are you familiar with that? And they basically condemn the president. "Boy, you really got him." And it shows a certain attitude. Now the question of the frustration about not being kept into all aspects of the plan is a valid one. One of my training mentors is sitting to my right and taught me that if I was in a situation in which I was seeing a plan develop which was dysfunctional, it would be my duty to senior civilian authority to say, "Sir, this in my view, this is not going to work." And that did not happen.

Audience Member: General, the tape you are talking about was during the Cuban Missile Crisis, not the Bay of Pigs. I know what you are talking about—it's the Chiefs after they have talked to President Kennedy the one time they had a chance to talk to him before the decision was made. It was not in the Bay of Pigs; this was a year-and-a-half later and with different Chiefs. But to support the point that you are making, when I asked General Lemnitzer, "Why, sir, as Chairman, did the Chiefs not assert themselves?" General Lemnitzer said, "We were told all the time, starting with President Eisenhower's administration, 'This is not your operation. This is a CIA operation. We will tell you what you want to hear, then if we ask your opinion, you'll give it.'"

Under President Eisenhower, I think the Chiefs would have been given the proper hearing. President Kennedy did not operate that way and that's why the Chiefs found themselves in a situation where they were looking in from the outside, being asked to make comments from time to time, but never having the full idea of what was going on. Admiral Burke said to me, at one point, "We never really knew when the president had made a decision because we were not in on the day-to-day planning." But during the crisis itself, during the Bay of Pigs crisis itself, General Lemnitzer and Admiral Burke were constantly saying, "What can we do to help the situation if we're called upon?" Admiral Burke, for example, had a Marine amphibious unit offshore. It could have gone ashore if necessary. The Navy had carrier planes; they said, "Okay, if you want us to provide cover for the bombers that are going in, fine, we'll do that." But his view was "I'll be ready in case the president asks for it, otherwise, that's the most I could do."

Dr. Galambos: I want to say that this discussion illustrates two things. First, why it is good to do historical research, and second, why it is good to have the documents you need to do research. And in that spirit, General Eisenhower wanted all his documents published by a university, not by something the family would control. He said, "History would judge him." And now, in that spirit, the Eisenhower Memorial Commission has made the entire Eisenhower presidency—eight volumes—available to the whole world, free, searchable, on the Internet at <www.eisenhowermemorial.org>. And I think that will greatly assist research and I just look forward to the time that other administrations make information available in that same way and we will be able to decide some of these issues.

General Scowcroft: I think that is a great way to bring this to a close. Thank you very much for your patience and now I will call on General Dunn.

General Dunn: President Eisenhower left us with many lessons and is widely quoted today, as we've talked about. Most people point to his historic "military-industrial complex" warning as his most famous quote. But for me personally, for most of my career, I have carried two quotes of his in my mind to guide my thinking and they continue to be, I think, most relevant for us today. The first one is, "A people that values its privileges above its principles soon loses both." And the second one is, "History does not long entrust the care of freedom to the weak or the timid." And as I look at the world today, these words are as relevant today as when he said them over fifty years ago. I might add that I now, thanks to General Goodpaster, have a third one: "Let's not make our mistakes in a hurry."

Epilogue

Ernest R. May

The essays in this volume illustrate splendidly the special strengths that Dwight Eisenhower brought to the presidency. Since Dennis Showalter begins with a penetrating overview; since each author offers a summation; and since Generals Goodpaster, Scowcroft, and Meigs and Louis Galambos review the evidence from four quite different angles, there would not seem to be much left for the writer of an epilogue.

What an epilogue can do, perhaps, is not so much to try to add to what other contributors have written as to take a slightly more distant perspective, commenting briefly on a few of the characteristics, highlighted in the essays here, which separate Eisenhower from most earlier or later presidents.

First, the hallmark of Eisenhower's presidency was *prudence*. This is not a way of saying that he lacked vision. On the contrary, as is evident not only here but in a number of other works, Eisenhower had a grand conception of what America could be—a land of equality as well as opportunity; a nation physically united by a transportation system that allowed most if not all citizens to go anywhere they wished; and above all, a place where shared resources went to making life better for individuals, and where no life was unnecessarily lost and no penny unnecessarily spent for national security.

But Eisenhower had more experience than any other president—bar none—teaching him how much could go wrong when visions had to be translated into action by large bureaucracies. Eisenhower also had, as compared with any of his predecessors or successors, not even excepting Washington, deep knowledge of the uncertainties and perils of international politics. He had, after all, been one of the organizers of victory over Hitler and one of the creators of the shield that protected Europe against Stalin.

Eisenhower's prudence, a product of interaction between vision on the one hand and lessons of experience on the other, generated the policies so well documented in this volume. While he described his hope for a world free of armaments and conflict and while he reined in spending by the Pentagon, he presided over the most thorough-going military modernization in history, and he left his successor with a nuclear arsenal that he himself found appalling.

The key to this seeming contradiction was Eisenhower's commitment to defense. He had seen presidents from Harding through FDR (in his first two terms) spend so little on military forces as to make the United States seem weak in the eyes of potential antagonists. He had seen Harry S. Truman appoint Louis Johnson secretary of defense with the explicit mission of getting U.S. defense spending back down to the levels of the 1930s; and he had then seen Truman, shocked by the Korean conflict, reverse himself entirely, order the implementation of NSC 68, and start transforming the United States so that it would be in every dimension the most awesome military power on the planet.

Eisenhower did not want to go back to the posture of the 1930s. At the same time, he thought that NSC 68 was taking the United States in the wrong direction. He believed that, if Americans did not take careful, empathetic account of how U.S. military power might be perceived by peoples elsewhere, the United States could become an object of dread and, as a result, create new dangers for itself. The only other president, before or after, with a comparable sense of the need for military forces that were strong but strictly defensive—not threatening to any other nation—was Theodore Roosevelt. TR's naval-building program had demonstrated to other powers that the United States could protect its spheres of vital interest, but he deliberately stopped short of creating a fleet that could threaten Britain or Germany, or even Japan, in their own home waters. Just so, Eisenhower's military posture demonstrated to the Soviets and Chinese that the United States could retaliate against an attack with devastating effect yet at the same time pose no threat whatsoever to the Soviet or Chinese empires.

The same prudence drove the efforts by Eisenhower, so well documented in these essays, to acquire as much knowledge as possible about potential adversaries and other nations abroad. Eisenhower's experience as a military planner and commander had drilled into him an understanding that action choices were based in part on known facts, but in even larger part on presumptions as to what might be facts. He knew that the higher the proportion of fact and the stronger the evidentiary base for presumptions, the better the plan or the operation. Hence, Eisenhower's relentless emphasis on new and improved means of gathering intelligence. Hence, too, his insistence on planning processes that forced face-to-face debate among officials whose preoccupations or policy preferences led to differing presumptions.

A word more deserves to be said about these processes. They were often characterized as cumbersome and overly bureaucratic. Participants, including Eisenhower himself, sometimes grumbled at the number of long papers circulated within the cabinet and the NSC and the amount of time eaten up by discussion of these papers. But the effects were, first, to educate all the president's high-level advisers and aides and, second, to ensure that no important dimension of a problem was lost to sight. Secretaries of state and defense had to learn about and contribute to the formulation of economic policy while secretaries of the treasury and commerce had to learn about and contribute to choices among alternative diplomatic strategies and military postures. Eisenhower was one of the few presidents—and the only one in recent decades—to follow the example developed by Washington, insisting on knowing the judgments of every constitutional officer before he, and he alone, took responsibility for a decision and its consequences.

One final point here, highlighting something more implicit than explicit in most of these essays, concerns Eisenhower's prudence in his relationship at home with the

Congress. In the army, Eisenhower had learned at first hand the truth that, while the presidency had necessarily become more powerful than the founding fathers could have imagined, Article II remained the heart of the Constitution. Ultimately, power resided on Capitol Hill, not in the White House or executive agencies. In all the presidential decisions described in these essays, one sees a respect for the authority of Congress not often evident in other presidencies, including those of men who actually served in the House or Senate.

The polls that rank presidents as "great," "near great," and so on, rely on vague criteria. Readers of this volume, if asked to vote in such polls, should surely feel themselves nudged toward giving Eisenhower a high rating. I myself think, however, that the interesting question is not how one would grade Eisenhower alongside Jefferson or Lincoln or FDR or Kennedy or Reagan but rather how one would answer if asked: Which past president would you most like to have alive now and in the White House? To that question, my own answer is unhesitatingly—Dwight Eisenhower.

Contributors

Saki R. Dockrill received her Ph.D. in History/War Studies from the University of London and holds a chair of Contemporary History and International Security at the Department of War Studies, King's College, University of London, where she has been teaching since 1990. Professor Dockrill has written extensively on defense and security relations in Europe, the United States, and Asia in the twentieth century. Her main publications include *Britain's Policy for West German Rearmament* (1991); *Eisenhower's New Look National Security Policy* (1996); *Controversy and Compromise: Alliance Politics between Britain, the Federal Republic of Germany and the United States* (ed., 1998); *Cold War Respite: The Geneva Summit of July 1955* (ed. with Guenter Bishof, 2000); *Britain's Retreat from East of Suez: The Choice between Europe and the World?* (2002); *L'Europe de l'Est et de l'Ouest dans la Guerre Froide* (ed. with Georges-Henri Soutou et al., 2002); and *The End of the Cold War Era: The Transformation of the Global Security Order* (Hodder Arnold, 2005). She is currently preparing *Advances in Cold War History* for Palgrave Macmillan.

R. Cargill Hall is Emeritus Chief Historian of the National Reconnaissance Office, an intelligence arm of the Department of Defense. He previously held a variety of posts in the U.S. Air Force History Program including tours as Contract Histories Manager at the Air Force History Support Office (1989–98) and as Chief of the Research Division and (concurrently) Deputy Director of the USAF Historical Research Agency (1981–89). Earlier, Hall served as a NASA historian at Caltech's Jet Propulsion Laboratory. He is the author of *Lunar Impact: A History of Project Ranger* (now online at http://history.nasa.gov/SP-4210/pages/Cover.htm), and is the editor of *Case Studies in Strategic Bombardment; The U.S. Air Force in Space; Early Cold War Overflights, 1950-1956;* and *Lightening Over Bougainville: The Yamamoto Mission Reconsidered.* A contributing editor to *Air & Space Smithsonian,* Hall has written numerous articles and chapters on the history of aeronautics and astronautics in various journals, anthologies, and encyclopedias. His most recent work in the open literature is a chapter on the genesis of American overhead strategic reconnaissance in *Eye in the Sky: The Story of the CORONA Satellites* (Smithsonian Institution Press, 1998).

David A. Hatch received his B.A. and M.A. from Indiana University at Bloomington, and his Ph.D. from American University in the District of Columbia. After service with the U.S. Army, he joined the National Security Agency in 1973, and had a variety of operational, staff, and supervisory positions. In 1987, he received a Congressional Fellowship from the American Political Science Association, and served a year as a Legislative Assistant in the House of Representatives. In 1990, Dr. Hatch transferred to the newly-formed Center for Cryptologic History at NSA. Thanks to a series of reorganizations and retirements, he became the NSA Historian in 1993. In addition to this position, he is also Technical Director at the CCH. Dr. Hatch is author of a number of monographs and articles about U.S. cryptologic history and NSA.

Gregg Herken is Professor of History at the University of California, Merced. He received a Ph.D. in modern American diplomatic history from Princeton University in 1974, and thereafter taught at California State University, San Luis Obispo. In 1978, he was the Fulbright-Hays senior research scholar at Lund University, Sweden. From 1979 to 1988, he taught at Oberlin,

Yale, and Caltech, and between 1988 and 2003, he was senior Historian and the Curator of Military Space at the Smithsonian Institution's National Air and Space Museum in Washington, D.C. Herken is the author of four books, *The Winning Weapon: The Atomic Bomb in the Cold War* (1981), *Counsels of War* (1985), *Cardinal Choices: Presidential Science Advising from the Atomic Bomb to SDI* (1992), *and Brotherhood of the Bomb: The Tangled Lives and Loyalties of Robert Oppenheimer, Ernest Lawrence, and Edward Teller* (2002), which was a finalist for the 2003 *Los Angeles Times* Book Prize.

Sergei N. Khrushchev is a Senior Fellow at the Thomas J. Watson Jr. Institute for International Studies, Brown University, where he focuses his research on the former Soviet Union's transition from a centralized to a decentralized society, from a central to a market economy, and its international security during this transition. He is also interested in the history of the Cold War, the turning points in U.S.-Soviet relations, and the history of Soviet missiles and space development, in which he played an active role. Dr. Khrushchev received his Soviet doctoral degree from the Ukrainian Academy of Science and a Ph.D. from the Moscow Technical University. He is the author of numerous publications, including *Khrushchev on Khrushchev* (1990), *Nikita Khrushchev: Crisis and Missiles* (1994), *The Political Economy of Russian Fragmentation* (1993), *Three Circles of Russian Market Reforms* (1995), and *Nikita Khrushchev and the Creation of a Super Power* (2000). He is currently working on a new book, *Nikita Khrushchev's Reforms.*

Roger D. Launius is Chair of the Division of Space History at the Smithsonian Institution's National Air and Space Museum in Washington, D.C. He received his Ph.D. from Louisiana State University, Baton Rouge, in 1982. From 1990 to 2002 he served as chief historian of the National Aeronautics and Space Administration. Dr. Launius has written or edited more than twenty books on aerospace history, including *Space: A Journey to Our Future* (2004); *Space Stations: Base Camps to the Stars* (2003), which received the AIAA's history manuscript prize; *Flight: A Celebration of 100 Years in Art and Literature* (2003); *Reconsidering a Century of Flight* (2003); *To Reach the High Frontier: A History of U.S. Launch Vehicles* (2002); *Imagining Space: Achievements, Predictions, Possibilities: 1950-2050* (2001); *Reconsidering Sputnik: Forty Years Since the Soviet Satellite* (2000); *Innovation and the Development of Flight* (1999); *Frontiers of Space Exploration* (1998, rev. ed. 2004); *Spaceflight and the Myth of Presidential Leadership* (1997); and *NASA: A History of the U.S. Civil Space Program* (1994, rev. ed. 2001). He is frequently consulted by the electronic and print media for his views on space issues. His research interests encompass all areas of U.S. and space history and policy history, especially cultural aspects of the subject and the role of executive decision-makers and their efforts to define space exploration.

Clayton D. Laurie is a historian with the History Staff, Center for the Study of Intelligence, Central Intelligence Agency. He began his career as a federal historian in 1986 as a staff historian with the Histories Division of the U.S. Army Center of Military History in Washington, D.C., before serving as the deputy historian at the National Reconnaissance Office. In addition to his government service, he has taught military history courses as an adjunct associate professor with the Department of History at the University of Maryland, Baltimore County, since 1991. He received his Ph.D. in history at the American University in 1990, and is the author of numerous books and articles on nineteenth- and twentieth-century American and European military and intelligence history.

Ernest R. May is Charles Warren Professor of History, Harvard University.

Allan R. Millett is the Maj. Gen. Raymond E. Mason, Jr. Professor of Military History, The Ohio State University. He was Fulbright Distinguished Professor at the Korean National Defense University in 1991 and for ten years served as an adjunct faculty member at the Marine Corps Command and Staff College. He is a retired colonel from the U.S. Marine Corps Reserve, a four-term trustee and former two-term president of the Society of Military History, former chairman, International Security Studies Section of the International Studies Association, and former president, U.S. Commission of Military History. Dr. Millett is the author of five books: *The Politics of Intervention: The Military Occupation of Cuba, 1906-1909* (1968); *The General: Robert L. Bullard and Officership in the United States 1881-1925* (1975); *Semper Fidelis: The History of the United States Marine Corps* (1980; rev. ed., 1991); *In Many a Strife: General Gerald C. Thomas and the U.S. Marine Corps, 1917-1956* (1993); and *Their War for Korea* (2002). In addition, he is co-author and co-editor of numerous volumes, the most recent of which is *Commandants of the Marine Corps* (2004). He is at work on *A House Burning*, vol. 1 of a two-volume history of the Korean War (forthcoming 2005, University Press of Kansas).

Alex Roland is Professor of History at Duke University, where he teaches Military History and the History of Technology. A 1966 graduate of the Naval Academy, Professor Roland served in the Marine Corps before receiving his Ph.D. in History at Duke in 1974. From 1973 to 1981 he was a historian with the National Aeronautics and Space Administration. Since returning to Duke in 1981, he has chaired the Department of History (1995-2000) and held the Harold K. Johnson Chair of Military History at the Military History Institute, U.S. Army War College, and the Dr. Leo Shifrin Chair of Naval-Military History at the U.S. Naval Academy. His books include *Underwater Warfare in the Age of Sail* (1978), *Model Research: The National Advisory Committee for Aeronautics* (1985), *The Military-Industrial Complex* (2001), With Richard Preston and Sidney Wise, *Men in Arms: A History of Warfare and Its Interrelationships with Western Society* (5th ed., 1991), and with Philip Shiman, *Strategic Computing: DARPA and the Quest for Machine Intelligence, 1983-1993* (2002). He has edited *A Spacefaring People* (1985) and, with Peter Galison, *Atmospheric Flight in the Twentieth Century* (2000).

Dennis E. Showalter is Professor of History at Colorado College. He has served as visiting professor at the U.S. Military Academy and the U.S. Air Force Academy. He is Past President of the Society for Military History and joint editor of *War in History*. His most recent books include *The Wars of German Unification* (2004) and *Patton and Rommel: Men of War in the Twentieth Century* (2005).

Captain John W. Yaeger, USN (Ret.) is the Director, Institutional Research at the Industrial College of the Armed Forces. He graduated from the U.S. Naval Academy in 1974. From June 1974 through July 1993 he had various assignments with U.S. Navy Aviation Squadrons and ships. Captain Yaeger was assigned to the U.S. Naval Academy from July 1993 until July 1996 as the Commandant's Operations Officer. He instructed courses in leadership and character development. Reporting to ICAF in 1996, Captain Yaeger has been a student, Professor of Grand Strategy, Associate Dean of Faculty and Academic Programs and in June of 2000 was appointed Dean of Faculty and Academic Programs, serving in that capacity until he retired from active service in June 2004. He earned a Master's Degree at the Naval Postgraduate School and a Doctor of Education at George Washington University. His dissertation, "Congressional Influence on NDU," is on the history of National Defense University.

Qiang Zhai is Professor of History at Auburn University Montgomery. He is the author of *The Dragon, the Lion and the Eagle: Chinese-British-American Relations, 1949-1958* (1994) and *China and the Vietnam Wars, 1950-1970* (2000), as well as numerous articles on U.S.-Chinese relations during the Cold War.

Index

Acheson, Dean C., 41, 43, 48, 60
Adams, Sherman, 62, 166
Adenauer, Konrad, 34, 215
Advanced Research Projects Agency, 135, 173
Aerial reconnaissance, 119–43; assessment of, 141–43; A-12 aircraft, 100; authorized by Truman, 121–23; Corona project, 137–41; events leading to, 120–23; intelligence review, 129–32; Operations Coordinating Board, 124, 126; Planning Strategy Board, 123–24; Project Home Run, 127; by satellite, 134–35; SENSINT; system, 123–28, 142; TALENT-KEYHOLE system, 140–43, 142; TALENT system, 129–33, 142; U-2 spy planes, 10, 11, 89, 99–100, 120, 131–33
Agena spacecraft, 135
Altschul, Frank, 165
Ambrose, Stephen, 3, 27, 111
American Society of Newspaper Editors speech, 20–21, 50–51
Anderson, Dillon, 23
Andrews, Christopher, 101, 111
Anglo-Egyptian treaty of 1936, 29
AQUATONE project, 99, 134
Armed forces: post–World War II, 109–92; unification of, 191–92
Armed Forces Staff College, 197–99
Armistice Agreement of 1953, Korea, 41–42
Army Industrial College, 187–88, 193–94
Army-Navy Staff College, 189–90
Arnold, H. H. "Hap," 187, 188–89, 191
Aswan High Dam, Egypt, 30
At Ease: Stories I Tell My Friends (Eisenhower), 2
Atomic Energy Commission, 97
Atoms for Peace proposal, 16
Attlee, Clement, 120–21, 122
A-12 reconnaissance aircraft, 100
Baghdad Pact, 54
Baker, James G., 129, 131
Baker, William O., 114, 123, 138
Baker Panel, 114–16
Balance principle, 26–27
Bandung Conference of 1955, 68, 69
Baruch, Bernard, 168–69, 186–87, 192
"Basic National Security Policy," 47, 53
Bay of Pigs, 213, 216–17

Berkner, Lloyd, 163
Berlin crisis of 1958–59, 34–35
Bissell, Richard M., Jr., 99, 131, 136–37, 138
Blagonravov, Anatoli A., 163
Board of Advisers on Foreign Intelligence Activities, 116
Boeing B-52 bomber, 128
Bolté, Charles L., 44
Bomber gap, 94, 141
Bossart, Karel J., 159
Bowles, Chester, 66
Bradley, Omar N., 43, 44, 46, 47, 49, 50, 51, 61, 121, 211
Brodie, Bernard, 197
Brookings, R. S., 187
Brownell, Herbert, 49
Brugioni, Dino, 111
Bulganin, Nikolai A., 9, 11
Burke, Arleigh, 74–75, 218
Bush, George H. W., 215
Bush, George W., 2, 24, 174
Bush, Vanevar, 13, 15, 16, 20, 167
Byrnes, James, 196
Camp David summit, 35
Canine, Ralph, 113
CAPSTONE, 184
Carroll, Paul T., 123
Carter, Jimmy, 2
Case-by-case approach, 27–28
Central Intelligence Agency, 29, 43, 64–65, 112
Clandestine Services, 101–3; communications interception, 100–101; covert operations, 101–3; early warning role, 96–97; Eisenhower's use of, 93–104; espionage activities, 99–100; evaluation of, 130–31; evaluation of Soviet ICBMs, 97–98; limitations of, 103; National Intelligence Estimates, 95–99; paramilitary activities, 103; policymaking role, 94–95; Project AQUATONE, 99–100; Project Corona, 100; Project OXCART, 100; report on Soviet conventional forces, 98; secrecy of operations, 99; SENSINT, 125; SIGNET, 101
Charles, Ray, 142
Charyk, Joseph V., 138, 139
Chiang Kai-shek; *see* Jiang Jieshi
China: aerial reconnaissance over, 121–23; areas of conflict with U.S., 78; and Eisenhower

administration, 59–79; and ending of Korean War, 59–63; fear of Japanese militarism, 63; hard-line policy toward, 64–66; and Korean War, 51–52; noose strategy toward U.S., 71; offshore island bombing, 67–68, 70–77; reaction to election of 1952, 60–61; and Taiwan, 66–67; and Taiwan offshore crisis, 33–34; trade with Japan, 63–64; treaty with Soviets, 59; and UN membership, 64; and U.S. trade sanctions, 63–64

"China differential" trade policy, 63

China Lobby, 60

Chinese Communist Party, 66–67

Chinese People's Liberation Army, 120

Chinese People's Volunteer Force, 51, 60–61

Chinese Revolution, 77–78

Churchill, Winston, 20, 42, 126, 215

CL-282 aircraft design, 130–31

Clandestine Services of CIA, 101–3

Clark, Mark W., 48, 49, 61

Classification of documents, 125

Clausewitz, Carl von, 25

Clinton, Bill, 151

Clinton administration, 211

Cold War; *see also* China; Korean War; National security: balance strategy, 26; case-by-case approach, 27–28; cases for U.S. intervention, 32–35; cases for U.S. nonintervention, 28–32; compared to terrorist attack, 35–36; containment policy, 16–17; early Eisenhower administration, 93; early tensions, 119; effect of Chinese Revolution, 77–78; effects of Eisenhower presidency, 142–43; Eisenhower-Khrushchev era, 7–12; Eisenhower's grand strategy, 23–26; Eisenhower's strategy, 152; Eisenhower's view of, 15–17, 23; Hungarian uprising, 31–32; initiative strategy, 26; and Korean War, 120–23; lack of symmetry, 24; need for intelligence, 119–20; and New Look doctrine, 93–104; offshore island crisis, 67–68; strategy assessment, 35–37; and Suez crisis, 29–31; threat posed by, 3–4

Collbohm, Frank R., 136

Colliers magazine, 155–57

Collins, J. Lawton, 44

COMINT, 112, 115; and Baker Panel report, 114; founding of, 111; during 1950s, 112–13

Command economy, 18

Committee of One Million, 64

Communications Intelligence; *see* COMINT

Communications interception, 100–101

Communications security (COMSEC), 113

Communism, roll-back policy, 87, 102–3

Consolidated Vultee Aircraft (Convair), 159

Containment strategy, 16–17, 87

Coordinating Committee on Export Control, 63

Corona Project, 100, 137–41

Covert operations, 101–3, 126

Craig, H. A., 101

Crampton, John, 122

CRITICOMM, 115–16

Crusade in Europe (Eisenhower), 205

Cryptologic think tank, 114

Cutler, Robert, 20, 123, 124, 128

Davies, Marion, 135

Davis, Dwight F., 186

Declaratory policy on nuclear weapons, 88

Defense Department, 28, 190; CRITICOMM, 115–16; and space program, 168–69

Defense economy, 26–27

Defense Mobilization Office, 121

De Gaulle, Charles, 42, 215

Department of Homeland security, 174

D'Este, Carlo, 3

"Deterrence and Survival in the Nuclear Age," 88–89

Dewitt, John, 192, 195, 196

Diem, Ngo Dinh, 63

Dien Bien Phu crisis, 28–29, 32

Dillard, Hardy, 197

Distant early warning line, 124

Dockrill, Saki, 4, 215

Dodge, Joseph M., 48

Domino theory, 29

Donovan, Allen F., 129

Doolittle, James H., 123, 125, 129, 130–31, 167

Douglas, James H, 137

Douglas Aircraft, 137

Drumright, Everett M., 64, 73

DuBridge, Lee, 128

Dulles, Allen W., 75, 95, 96, 99, 102, 103, 112, 115, 123, 125, 127, 128, 129, 131, 132, 136, 216; on early warning system, 96; on intelligence gathering, 130; on Soviet ICBMs, 97

Dulles, John Foster, 11, 19, 35, 46, 48, 49, 211, 214; on aerial reconnaissance, 128; China policy goals, 78–79; and China trade sanctions, 63; on deterrence, 93–94; foreign policy reappraisal, 86; hard-line China policy, 65–66, 70; and intelligence gathering, 125; and Korean War, 50, 51, 52, 60, 62; nuclear policies, 87–88; on nuclear weapons, 86; and offshore islands crisis, 67–68, 73, 99, 123; policy for Far East, 77; on preemptive war, 89; response statement, 26; and Soviet threat, 25; and Suez crisis, 30; and Taiwan Strait crisis, 69, 75

Dunn, Michael, 205; on Eisenhower legacy, 218

Du Ping, 60

Early warning system, 96–97

East Asia, effect of Chinese Revolution, 77–78

East Germany, 34–35; uprising of 1953, 31

Eastman Kodak, 135, 138

Eden, Anthony, 9, 126; and Suez crisis, 29, 30

Edison, Charles, 64

Egypt, Suez crisis, 29–31

Eisenhower: A Soldier's Life (D'Este), 3

Eisenhower, David, 10

Eisenhower, Dwight D.: American Society of Newspaper Editors speech, 20–21, 50–51; on Armed Forces Staff College, 197, 198; at Army Industrial College, 187; assessment of presidency, 141–43, 206–18, 219–21; aversion to lobbies, 17; campaign of 1952, 46–47; Cold War strategy, 152; compared to George W. Bush, 174; and Congress, 209, 220–21; critique of liberalism, 19; defense role 1947–50, 42–44; domino theory, 29; early intelligence advisers, 123; effect of Korean War on policy, 41–42; election victories, 1–2; and end of Korean War, 59–63; farewell address, 13–21, 152; foreign policy experience, 42, 215, 219; foreign policy legacy, 89–90; on garrison state, 19–20; head of NATO, 121; influence on military education, 183, 185–88; and intellectuals, 1–2; and Korea 1945–50, 42–44; and Korean War 1950–52, 44–47; and Korean War in 1953, 50–53; leadership qualities, 2–4; liberation policy, 32; on military spending, 19–20; and National Security Agency, 111–17; national security legacy, 205–18; as NATO commander, 45; Naval War College speech, 14; and need for Cold War intelligence, 119–20; nuclear policies, 87–88; on nuclear weapons, 85–86; Open Skies proposal, 8; opposition to small wars, 28; and Paris Summit failure, 11; personal dealings with Khrushchev, 8–12; on preemptive war, 87; as president-elect, 47–50; presidential candidacy, 45–47; promise to visit Korea, 47; reaction to Sputnik, 153; relations with Truman, 48; resurgence of reputation, 111; on Soviet Union, 24; and Sputnik crisis, 162–66; on strategic intelligence, 95–96; on structure of military, 194–95; and Suez crisis, 9; use of CIA, 94–104; on Vietnam War, 36–37; view of Cold War, 15–17; visit to Korea, 49, 61; in World War II, 1

Eisenhower, John S. D., 49, 121

Eisenhower: Soldier and President (Ambrose), 3

Eisenhower administration: aerial reconnaissance, 119–43; and Berlin crisis, 34–35; and China-Japan trade, 63–64; China policy goals, 78–79; Cold War strategy options, 26–28; and Cold War threat, 3–4; dealing with Jiang Jieshi, 79; and Dien Bien Phu crisis, 28–29; disrupting China-Soviet alliance, 64–66; dominant images, 1; and Eastern Europe, 103; foreign policy options, 87; hard-line China policy, 64–66; and Hungarian uprising, 31–32; intelligence sources in 1953, 112; and Korean War, 41; and Lebanon, 32–33; Mao's view of, 76; and military eventualities, 86–87; New Look doctrine, 24–25, 27, 41, 53–54, 93–104; recent reevaluation of, 2–3; relations with China, 59–79; roll-back policy, 102–3; space program, 151–75; strategy assessment, 35–37; and Suez crisis, 29–31; surprise attack study, 128–32; and Taiwan, 77–78; and Taiwan Strait crisis, 33–34; two-China policy, 70, 76

Eisenhower Doctrine, 32–33

Eisenhower Memorial Commission, 3, 205

Eisenhower (Perrett), 3

Eisenhower's Legacy: The General, The President, The Public Servant (Galambos), 205

Eisenhower's New Look National Security Policy (Dockrill), 215

Election of 1952, 1–2; China's reaction to, 60–61; Soviet reaction to, 7–8

Electronic intelligence interception, 140

Enderlin, Arthur, 115

Engstrom, Howard, 113, 114

Erskine, Graves B., 115

Executive Order 10501, 125

Eyeball to Eyeball (Brigioni), 111

Farewell address, 13–21, 152
Federal Bureau of Investigation, 97
Federal Civil Defense Administration, 121
15th Tactical Reconnaissance Squadron, 122–23
Fisk, James B., 129
Foreign Affairs, 88
Foreign Policy, 16
Forrestal, James V., 123, 191
For the President's Eyes Only (Andrews), 111
France: Dien Bien Phu crisis, 28–29; Suez crisis, 29–31
Franke, William B., 130
Friedberg, Aaron, 18
Friedman, William, 111
Frontier Thesis, 154–55
Gaither Report, 88–89
Galactic Radiation and Background program, 140
Galambos, Louis, 205, 219; on Eisenhower legacy, 206–7, 212, 213, 214, 215, 218
Galbraith, John Kenneth, 207
Gardner, Trevor, 128, 130, 131
Garrison state, 19–20
Garroway, Dave, 157
Gates, Thomas S., Jr., 138, 139
Geneva Conference of 1954, 66
Geneva Convention of 1959, 62
Geneva Four-Power Conference, 35
Geneva summit, 11, 131–32, 134
George, Walter, 69
German rearmament, 54
Gerow, Leonard T., 195
Gerow Board, 195–96
Gilruth, Robert L., 171
Glennan, T. Keith, 153, 172
Goodpaster, Andrew J., 88, 123, 128, 205, 219; on Eisenhower legacy, 207–10, 212–13, 214, 216; NSC staff secretary, 112; on intelligence briefings, 96
Gorbachev, Mikhail, 24
Grand strategy, 25
Grant, Ulysses S., 1
Great Britain; *see* United Kingdom
Great Leap Forward, China, 33
Greenstein, Fred, 2, 111
Gromyko, Andrei, 32
Gruenther, Alfred M., 25, 27, 44
Guatemala intervention, 54
Hadley, Morris, 130
Hagen, John P., 162–64
Hagerty, James, 49

Haislip, Wade, 44
Halberstam, David, 175
HALFMOON/FLEETWOOD, 42
Hall, Cargill, 4
Hallstein doctrine, 34
Harding, Warren G., 186, 219
Harriman, W. Averell, 45
Harrison, William K., 49
Hatch, David A., 4
Hazlett, Swede, 45
Heinlein, Robert A., 155
Herken, Gregg, 4
Herter, Christian, 74, 132
Hidden-Hand Presidency: Eisenhower as Leader (Greenstein), 2
Hill, Harry Wilbur, 196
Hitchcock, James, 129
Hitler, Adolf, 7, 219
Holloway, James L., 199
Homeland Security Act of 2002, 174
Hoover, Herbert C., Jr., 123, 127
Horner, Richard E., 136
Hughes, Emmett John, 60
Humphrey, Hubert H., 170
Hungarian uprising of 1956, 31–32
Huntington, Samuel P., 17, 20
Hydrogen bomb, 85
Ike's Spies (Ambrose), 111
Indo-China, 28–29
Industrial College of the Armed Forces, 3, 183, 185–88, 193–94; Eisenhower symposium, 205–18
Initiative principle, 26
Institute for Defense Analysis, 114
Intelligence; *see also* Aerial reconnaissance; Central Intelligence Agency: advisers on, 123; Cold War need for, 119–20; collection and analysis of, 140–41; Korean War and failure of, 120–21; Project Three review, 129–30
Intelligence Advisory Committee, 131
Intercontinental ballistic missiles, 97–98, 132–33, 151, 159
Interest group politics, 166–67
International Council of Scientific Unions, 134, 160
International Geophysical Year, 134, 160, 162–63
Iran: hostage crisis, 23; intervention in, 29, 54
Iran-Contra affair, 23
Itek Corporation, 137
Jackson, C. D., 46, 47, 87–88

Japan, 41; China's fear of, 63; trade with China, 63–64
Jefferson, Thomas, 221
Jiang Jieshi, 33–34, 60, 61, 64, 66–67, 67–68, 70, 71, 72, 73, 75, 76, 78, 79
Johnson, Clarence R. "Kelly," 99, 129–32
Johnson, Louis A., 43, 219
Johnson, Lyndon B., 165, 170, 172, 209, 211; and space program, 169
Joint Army-Navy Staff College, 188–89
Joint Chiefs of Staff, 42, 43, 48, 195–96
Joint Emergency War Plan No. 1, 42–43
Joint Forces Staff College, 183
Judd, Walter, 64
Kadar, Janos, 31–32
Katz, Amrom, 135
Kennan, George F., 20, 87, 196; long telegram, 16–17
Kennedy, John F., 12, 89, 141, 153, 211, 215; Bay of Pigs, 213, 216–17; compared to Eisenhower, 213, 215, 221; and space exploration, 175
Kennedy, Joseph W., 129
Kennedy administration, 174
Kent, Sherman, 197
Khrushchev, Nikita, 4, 30, 97, 163, 164; on aerial reconnaissance, 131–32; and Berlin crisis; of 1958–59, 34–35; on China-U.S. relations, 68; dealings with Eisenhower, 8–12; economic priorities, 8–9; and Hungarian uprising, 31–32; and Paris summit failure, 11, 90; reaction to U-2 flights, 11; speech on Stalinism, 31; and Suez crisis, 9, 29; and Taiwan Strait crisis, 34, 71–72; visit to U.S., 9–10
Khrushchev, Sergei N., 4, 12
Killian, James R., 113–14, 123, 128, 129, 130–31, 135, 136, 137, 138, 165, 170, 171
Kim Il Sung, 42, 50–51, 61
King, Ernest J., 188, 189, 191, 196
Kistiakovsky, George B., 123, 138
Knowland, William, 64, 94
Korean War, 25, 41–54, 93; armistice, 41–42, 52–53; China and ending of, 59–63; effect on New Look doctrine, 53–54; and Eisenhower in 1950–53, 44–47; and Eisenhower in 1953, 50–53; as intelligence failure, 120–21; Panmunjom negotiations, 51–52; prisoner of war repatriation, 61–62; start of, 44; start of aerial reconnaissance, 121–23; summary of, 42; and Taiwan, 59–

60; and Truman, 220
Kullback, Solomon, 111
Kuznetsov, Nikolai G., 9
Lamar, Howard R., 155
Land, Edwin (Din) H., 99, 113, 123, 129, 130, 133, 135, 136, 137, 138
Lasswell, Harold, 18–19, 20
Latham, Allen, 129
Launius, Roger, 4
Laurie, Clayton, 4
Leary, William M., 94
Lebanon: intervention of 1958, 32–33, 72; intervention of 1982–83, 36
LeMay, Curtis, 15–16; on preemption, 88; on use of nuclear weapons, 87
Lemnitzer, Lyman, 217–18
Ley, Willie, 156
Liang Shuming, 62
Lincoln, Abraham, 2, 143, 208, 221
Lisbon Agreement on force structure, 54
Lloyd George, David, 185–86
Lockheed Aircraft Corporation, 99, 129–30, 131, 135, 137
Lodge, Henry Cabot, 48
"Long telegram" (Kennan), 16–17
Lovett, Robert A., 45, 47
Luce, Henry, 64
Lundahl, Arthur C., 141
MacArthur, Douglas, 15, 42, 44, 45, 46
Macmillan, Harold, 35, 69
Malenkov, Georgi, 61
Mandate for Change (Eisenhower), 2
Manning, Gordon, 156
Mao Zedong, 59, 61, 62, 66, 67, 69, 73: divergence from Khrushchev, 71–72; Great Leap Forward, 33; and Korean War, 50–51; reaction to Dulles's speeches, 77; and Taiwan Strait crisis, 33–34, 70–77; and two-China policy, 78; view of U.S. policy, 76
Marshall, George C., 19, 42, 45, 123, 188, 189, 191
Massive retaliation strategy, 94
Matsu, 34, 70–71, 72–73, 78
McCarthy, Joseph R., 16, 212
McClellan, John M., 170
McConaughy, Walter P., 64
McDougall, Walter A., 172
McElroy, Neil, 136, 168–69
McNamara, Robert S., 141, 215
Meigs, Montgomery C., 205, 219; on Eisenhower legacy, 210–12, 213, 214–15, 216, 217

Melman, Seymour, 13, 18
Memories (Gromyko), 32
Middle East, 29–31
"Mike" H-bomb test, 85
Military education; *see* Professional military education
Military-industrial complex theme, 13–21, 152
Military spending, 13, 19–20; and massive retaliation strategy, 94; prior to Korean War, 43
Mills, C. Wright, 17, 18, 19, 20
Missile gap, 94, 98, 132–33, 141
Mitchell, Allan, 4
Mixson, Marion C. "Hack," 131
Molotov, Vyacheslav, 62
Montgomery, Bernard Law, 1, 8, 42, 211
Moon exploration, 161, 175
Moore, Gary, 157
Morgan, Thomas, 73
Mussadeq, Mohammed, 29
Myasischev-4 bomber, 128
NACA; *see* National Advisory Committee for Aeronautics
Nagy, Imre, 31–32
Nasser, Hamal Abdel, 29–30
National Advisory Committee for Aeronautics, 153, 167, 171
National Aeronautics and Space Act of 1958, 171–72
National Aeronautics and Space Administration, 173; creation of, 152–53, 171–74; politics of, 174–75
National Defense Act of 1920, 186
National Defense Education Act, 173
National Defense University, 3, 183, 184, 185
National Indications Center, 129
National Intelligence Estimates, 95–96; examples, 97; value of, 98–99
Nationalist China, 33–34; *see also* Republic of China
National Photographic Interpretation Center, 100, 140–41
National Reconnaissance Office, 100
National security; *see also* Cold War; New Look doctrine; Nuclear weapons: containment policy, 16–17; distant early warning line, 124; effect of Korean War, 41–42; Eisenhower's legacy, 205–18; Joint Emergency War Plan No. 1, 42–43; massive retaliation strategy, 33; policy statement, 47, 53; preparing for eventualities, 86–87; re-

quirements, 26–28; review of weapons technology, 128; surprise attack study, 128–32; task force study of 1954, 113–14
National Security Act of 1947, 192
National Security Agency, 97, 111–17; communications, 115–16; establishment of, 113; under Goodpaster, 112; during 1950s, 112–13
National Security Council, 20, 28, 96; Directive 5412, 126; Korean solution of 1953, 52; Memorandum 8, 43–44; memorandum on Russia in 1948, 86; review of space program, 151–52
National Security Council 68, 220
National Security Council 162/2, 47, 53, 102, 125
National Security Council 188/1, 65
National War College, 183, 188–97 establishment of, 196–97; National Watch Committee, 129
Naval Research Laboratory, 140
Naval War College speech, 14
Nehru, Jawaharlal, 60, 62
Net Evaluation Subcommittee, 125, 126
Neustadt, Richard, 213
New Look doctrine, 24–25, 27, 41, 125, 215; and CIA, 93–104; effect of Korean War on, 53–54; nuclear weapons in, 85–86; unpopularity of, 94
Nimitz, Chester, 191, 194, 196, 197–98
Nitze, Paul, 88
Nixon, Richard M., 2, 46, 64, 171, 214
North Atlantic Treaty Organization, 27, 28, 34–35, 45, 54, 121
Nuclear test ban negotiations, 10
Nuclear warfare, 27
Nuclear weapons: declaratory policy on, 88; Eisenhower/Dulles policies, 87–88; Eisenhower legacy, 89–90; end of U.S. monopoly, 85; growth of arsenal, 85; guidelines for using, 86–87; and Korean War, 48, 52; in New Look doctrine, 85–86; Soviet test of 1953, 124–25; and Taiwan Strait crisis, 73–74; as threat in Korea, 60
Nutting, Anthony, 30
Office of Defense Mobilization's Science Advisory Committee, 128–29
Office of Missile and Satellite Systems, 140–41
Offshore island crisis, 67–68
Open Skies proposal, 8, 16, 134
Operations Coordinating Board, 126

Operations Plan 8-52, 49, 50
Overhage, Carl, 138
OXCART Project, 100
Pakistan, 54
Panmunjom negotiations, 51–52
Paris summit failure, 11
Parsons, J. Graham, 73
Patriot Act of 2002, 174
Patton, George, 1
Pawley, William D., 130
Pearl Harbor, 142
Peng Dehuai, 60–61, 61, 68
Pentagon Capitalism (Melman), 18
People's Republic of China; *see* China
Permanent war economy, 13, 18
Perrett, Geoffrey, 3
Persons, Wilton B., 49, 157
Pescadores, 33
Photo-reconnaissance satellite, 100
Planning Strategy Board, 123–24
Polish uprising of 1956, 31
Poloskov, Sergei M., 162
Porter, Richard, 163
"Position of the United States with Respect to
  Korea," 43–44
Powell, Colin, 36
Power Elite (Mills), 17, 18
Powers, Francis Gary, 11, 89, 100, 133
Preemptive war, 88–89
Presidential Power (Neustadt), 213
President's Science Advisory Committee, 136,
  169, 171–72
Prisoner of war repatriation, 61–62
Professional military education: Armed Forces
  Staff College, 197–99; assessment of, 199–
  200; CAPSTONE level, 184; Eisenhower's
  influence, 183, 184–88; framework for, 184;
  Industrial College of the Armed Forces, 185–
  88; joint education, 184–95; National De-
  fense University, 183, 184, 185; National
  War College, 188–97; overview, 183–84;
  post-Vietnam, 185; post–World War II or-
  ganization, 192–96; post–World War I re-
  view, 185–86; progression in, 184
Project Home Run, 127
Project Three intelligence review, 129–30
Proxy wars, 24
Psychological Strategy Board, 124
Purcell, Edward M., 123, 129, 138
Putt, Donald L., 136
Quarles, Donald A., 74–75, 116, 123, 132, 134,

135, 136, 137
Quemoy, 33–34, 67–68, 70–71, 72–73, 75–76,
  78
Radford, Arthur W., 49, 61, 67–68, 123, 125,
  127, 210–11
Radford, William, 16
Radio Free Europe, 103
RAND Corporation, 135
Rankin, Karl Lott, 60, 64
Rathjens, George W., 138
Rayburn, Sam, 209, 211
Raymond, Richard, 135
Reagan, Ronald W., 2, 151, 152; compared to
  Eisenhower, 215, 221; evil empire statement,
  23–24
Republic of China, 41
Republican Party, and Hungarian uprising of
  1956, 31
Research and development threat, 15
Rhee, Syngman, 41–42, 46, 47–48, 49, 51–53,
  54
Rhodarmer, Roger, 127
Richardson, James O., 190
Richardson Committee, 190–91, 193, 197
Ridgway, Matthew, 44, 45, 48
Ritland, Osmond J., 131, 137
Robertson, Philip O. "Robbie," 131
Robertson, Walter S., 52, 64, 67–68
Roland, Alex, 4
Roll-back policy, 87, 102–3
Roosevelt, Franklin D., 42, 143, 187, 219, 221
Roosevelt, Theodore, 220
Rosen, Milton W., 161
Rowlett, Frank, 111
Royal Air Force: and aerial reconnaissance, 126–
  27; in Korean War, 122
Samford, John, 113, 114
Satellite reconnaissance, 134–35
Satellites: IGY proposal, 160; technology, 158
Schlesinger, Arthur M., Jr., 18, 213
Schriever, Bernard A., 137, 169
Science Advisory Committee, 128, 129
Scientific research, 15
Scowcroft, Brent, 205, 219; on Eisenhower
  legacy, 205–6, 212, 215
Sculthorpe Royal Air Force Base (UK), 122
Secret Air Force Samos satellite program, 138
Secret Empire (Taubman), 111
Senate Committee on Military Affairs, 190, 191
SENSINT: development and function, 125–28;
  ending of, 128; establishment of, 119–20

Sensitive Intelligence Security Control System; *see* SENSINT

Sherry, Michael, 13

Showalter, Dennis E., 219

Sino-Soviet alliance, 64–66

Sino-Soviet Treaty of 1950, 59

Smith, Walter Bedell, 46

Solarium Project, 87, 101–2, 125

Soldier and the State, The (Huntington), 17

Somalia, 36

Southeast Asia Treaty Organization, 54, 63

South Korea, 46; *see also* Korean War: continued U.S. presence, 53–54; Eisenhower's visit to, 49; withdrawal of U.S. combat troops, 43

South Korean Army, 52

South Vietnam, U.S. nation-building, 63

Soviet Union: aerial reconnaissance over, 121–23; alliance with China, 64–65; and Berlin crisis of 1958–59, 34–35; and CIA espionage, 99–100; and China-Taiwan issue, 68; compared to United States, 24; and containment policy, 16–17; conventional forces, 98; and death of Stalin, 8; downing of U-2 plane, 133; and East German uprising of 1853, 31; economic weaknesses, 8–9; Eisenhower policy options, 87; and end of Korean War, 51; first satellite, 27; at Geneva summit, 131–32; and Hungarian uprising of 1956, 31–32; ICBM program, 97–98; under Khrushchev, 8–12; and Korea 1945–50, 42; launch of Sputnik, 88, 162–66; Myasischev-4 bomber, 128; and New Look doctrine, 93–104; NSC memorandum 1948, 86; nuclear test of 1953, 124–25; post-1945 military buildup, 7; and preemptive war, 88–89; proxy wars, 24; reaction to aerial reconnaissance, 127–28; strategy to defeat, 152; and Suez crisis, 30–31; and U-2 spy planes, 99–100

Space program, 151–75; advocates' agenda, 161–62; agenda for, 153–57; balanced measured approach to, 157–59; Congressional hearings, 167; Eisenhower response to Congress, 168–69; IGY proposal, 160; and interest group politics, 166–67; under Kennedy, 175; and NASA, 171–74; NSC review of, 151–52; organizing for, 169–71; parallels with war on terrorism, 173–74; politics of, 174–75; satellite technology, 158; and Sputnik crisis, 162–66; Von Braun's role, 154, 155–57, 161

Space station proposal, 155–56

Space Travel Symposium, 156

Special Committee for the Reorganization of National Defense, 190

Special Committee on Space and Aeronautics, 167

Special Group, 126

Sprague, Robert, 89

Sputnik, 88, 97; Eisenhower's reaction to, 153

Sputnik crisis, 135, 151, 162–66, 170; parallels with terrorist attack, 173–74

Stalin, Joseph, 7–8, 31, 42, 50, 61, 124–25, 219

State Department, 97; and Paris Summit failure, 11

Statism, 18

Stevenson, Adlai, 1, 46

Stimson, Henry L., 123

Strategic Air Command, 86–87, 100, 122; aerial reconnaissance, 125–28

Strategy, 25

Strong, Kenneth, 103

Suez crisis of 1956, 9, 29–31, 209

Sullivan, Walter, 162–63

Surprise attack: indicators, 128–29; report, 113–14, 133–34; study, 128–32

Swayze, John Cameron, 157

Tactics, 25

Taiwan: and China, 66–67; defense treaty with U.S., 63, 68; Eisenhower policy, 77–78; and Korean War, 59–60

Taiwan Strait crisis, 33–34, 70–77

TALENT-KEYHOLE system, 140–43

TALENT security system, 129–33

Taubman, Philip, 111

Taxicab Committee, 129

Taylor, Maxwell, 51

Technological Capabilities Panel, 129, 143; report, 113–14, 133–34

Terrorist attack of 2001, 35–36, 142, 173–74

Terrorist Screening Center, 174

Terrorist Threat Integration Center, 174

Third World proxy wars, 24

Thompson, Llewellyn E., 11

Titan ICBM, 159

Tito, Josip Broz, 65, 66

Tong, Hollington, 73

Tordella, Louis W., 113, 114

Treasury Department, 97

Trevelyan, Humphrey, 69

Truax, Robert C, 170

Truman, Harry S., 17, 26, 43, 59, 93, 142, 195;

authorizes aerial reconnaissance, 121–23; containment policy, 16–17; distant early warning line, 124; establishment of NSA, 113; and Korean War, 44–45, 46–47, 120–22; and Louis Johnson, 219–220; and nuclear weapons, 85; relations with Eisenhower, 48; and unification of armed forces, 192

Truman administration, 54, 60, 77, 86

Tukey, John W., 129

Turkey, 54

Turner, Frederick Jackson, 154–55

Twining, Nathan W., 72, 123, 127, 128, 132

Two-China policy, 76, 78

"U.S. Objectives with Respect to Korea Following an Armistice," 52

United Kingdom; *see also* Royal Air Force: and Korean War, 120–21, 122; Suez crisis, 9, 29–31

United Nations: China membership issue, 64; in Korean War, 48; support for Taiwan, 64; Taiwan Resolution, 33; and Taiwan Strait crisis, 67–68

United States: areas of conflict with China, 78; compared to Soviet Union, 24; containment policy, 16–17; economic superiority, 8–9; end of atomic monopoly, 85; frontier thesis, 154–55; ICBM program, 132–33; intervention in Guatemala, 54; intervention in Iran, 29; intervention in Lebanon, 32–33; nation-building, 63; permanent war economy, 13, 18; reaction to Sputnik, 135, 151, 162–66; trade sanctions on China, 63–64

United States Air Force: and aerial reconnaissance, 125–28; General Operational Requirement No. 80, 135

United States Eighth Army, 42, 51–52, 53

United States Fifth Air Force, 53

United States 5th Regimental Combat Team, 43

United States Intelligence Board, 97

United States military; *see* Armed forces

United States–Republic of Korea Mutual Security Treaty, 53

United States–South Korea mutual defense treaty, 63

United States–Taiwan Mutual Defense Treaty, 63, 68, 78

United States 31st Infantry Regiment, 43

United States XXIV Corps, 42

U-2 spy planes, 10, 89, 99–100, 120, 158; development of, 131; flights over Russia, 132–33; launching of, 132; Soviet downing of, 11, 133; testing of, 131–32

Van Fleet, James, 45, 49

Vanguard satellite program, 135, 158, 160, 162–64, 169

Vietnam, 28–29

Vietnam War, 23; Eisenhower on, 36–37

Von Braun, Werner, 154, 155–57, 158, 159, 161

Waging Peace (Eisenhower), 2

Wainwright, John M., 186

Walters, Harry G., 138

War against terrorism, 143

War Department, 185–86

Warsaw Pact, 54

Washington, George, 219, 220

Weinberger, Casper, 36

West Germany, 34

White, Thomas D., 123

Whitman, Ann, 157

Wiesner, Jerome, 89

Williams, G. Mennen, 164

Wilson, Charles E., 18, 49, 61, 128, 169

Wilson, Woodrow, 186–87

Wisner, Frank, 100

World War I, and military education, 185–86

World War II, 15; armed forces after, 190–92; Eisenhower's role, 1; and military education, 192–96

Wright, Walter L., Jr., 197

Yaeger, John, 4

Yale Report of 1828, 183–84

Yeh, George, 66

York, Herbert F., 138

Zhai, Qiang, 4

Zhou Enlai, 61–62, 68, 69, 75

Zhukov, Georgi K., 7, 8

"National security requires far more than military power. Economic and moral factors play indispensable roles."

Dwight D. Eisenhower

President of the United States of America
State of the Union Message
January 10, 1957

Forging the Shield

Eisenhower and National Security for the 21st Century

Edited by Dennis E. Showalter

Approx. 256 pages with index; Forthcoming July 2005
ISBN 1-879176-44-0 (Paper)

The benefits of President Eisenhower's principled and pragmatic leadership continue in the twenty-first century. His strength, intelligence, and mastery in defining and addressing America's fundamental security issues during the Cold War are demonstrated in the contributions to this volume, based on a January 2005 symposium co-sponsored by the Dwight D. Eisenhower Memorial Commission and the Industrial College of the Armed Forces of the National Defense University.

Contents:

Introduction / Dennis E. Showalter · Reflections on Eisenhower, the Cold War, and My Father / Sergei N. Khrushchev · The Grim Paraphernalia: Eisenhower and the Garrison State / Alex Roland · Eisenhower's Methodology for Intervention and Its Legacy in Contemporary World Politics / Saki R. Dockrill · Eisenhower and the Korean War: Cautionary Tale and Hopeful Precedent / Allan R. Millett · Crisis and Confrontation: Chinese-American Relations during the Eisenhower Administration / Qiang Zhai · "Not Enough Bulldozers": Eisenhower and American Nuclear Weapons Policy, 1953–1961 / Gregg Herken · The Invisible Hand of the New Look: Eisenhower and the CIA / Clayton D. Laurie · Eisenhower and the NSA: An Introductory Survey / David A. Hatch · Clandestine Victory: Eisenhower and Overhead Reconnaissance in the Cold War / R. Cargill Hall · Eisenhower and Space: Politics and Ideology in the Construction of the U.S. Civil Space Program / Roger D. Launius · Eisenhower and Joint Professional Military Education / John W. Yaeger · Appendix A: Eisenhower and National Security for the 21st Century: Roundtable and Discussion · Epilogue / Ernest R. May

PLEASE ACCEPT MY ORDER FOR:

Quantity: _____ @ $24.95 per copy

Sub-total _____

Shipping/handling*(see below) _____

TOTAL amount to be remitted $ _____

* (Within the U.S.: $5 for the first copy; $2 for ea. add. copy / shipped Priority or UPS)
Outside the U.S.: $10 for the first copy; $5 for ea. add. copy / shipped Global Priority)

PAYMENT:

_____ Check enclosed (payable to "Imprint Publications")

_____ Charge to my: _____ Visa _____ MasterCard _____ American Express _____ Discover

Card No. _____ Exp. _____

Card holder's signature _____

(Please Note: Credit card payment to Imprint will be processed by the "Foundation for Pacific Quest")

Daytime phone: _____ Email: _____

SHIP TO:

Name _____

Address _____

_____

_____

Return Order Form to:

Imprint Publications
207 E. Ohio St., #377
Chicago, IL 60611
(773) 288-0782 / Fax (773) 288-0792
email: imppub@aol.com
www.imprint-chicago.com